Forensic Psychology

W0232314

Forensic Psychology

2nd Edition

by Professor David Canter

FOREWORD BY Donna Youngs, PhD

A Wiley Brand

Forensic Psychology For Dummies®, 2nd Edition

Published by: **John Wiley & Sons, Inc.**, 111 River Street, Hoboken, NJ 07030-5774, www.wiley.com

For general information on our other products and services, please contact our Customer Care Department within the U.S. at 877-762-2974, outside the U.S. at 317-572-3993, or fax 317-572-4002. For technical support, please visit https://hub.wiley.com/community/support/dummies.

Wiley publishes in a variety of print and electronic formats and by print-on-demand. Some material included with standard print versions of this book may not be included in e-books or in print-on-demand. If this book refers to media that is not included in the version you purchased, you may download this material at http://booksupport.wiley.com. For more information about Wiley products, visit www.wiley.com.

Library of Congress Control Number is available from the publisher.

ISBN 978-1-394-35474-0 (pbk); ISBN 978-1-394-35475-7 (ebk); ISBN 978-1-394-35476-4 (ebk)

Printed and bound by CPI Group (UK) Ltd, Croydon, CR0 4YY

C9781394354740_250226

Contents at a Glance

Table of Contents

Foreword

Forensic psychology occupies a uniquely challenging space at the intersection of human behavior, criminal justice, and scientific inquiry. It demands both intellectual precision and deep compassion, a field where the stakes are high and the consequences of misunderstanding can be profound. In this landscape, accessible, accurate, and ethically grounded guidance is invaluable. That is precisely what this book offers. Few people globally are as qualified to provide this as David Canter.

The structure of this work reflects the breadth and complexity of forensic psychology as it is practiced today. Canter harnesses his distaste for the sensational and begins by dispelling the myths that have long clouded public understanding — myths shaped by television dramas, media, and popular fascination with the criminal mind. The opening chapters clarify what forensic psychology *is* and, just as importantly, what it is *not*. It is not detective work, nor is it simply a branch of criminology. Instead, as Canter argues from his rigorous academic grounding, it is a scientific discipline rooted in psychological theory, empirical research, and the careful application of evidence to legal questions. This foundation is essential, because without it, the field risks being misunderstood or misused.

From there, the book moves into the heart of what most readers are eager to explore: the criminal mind. Renowned for his intolerance of any glamorization of criminal behaviour, Canter does so with nuance, resisting simplistic explanations or moralistic labels. The chapters on why people offend — examining biological, social, developmental, and situational influences — remind us that criminal behaviour rarely emerges from a single cause. Instead, it is the product of complex interactions between vulnerabilities, opportunities, and life trajectories. The discussion of protective factors and the reasons *not* everyone becomes a criminal is equally important, offering a balanced view that avoids pathologizing entire groups or communities. As one of the leading psychologists of the modern era, Dr. Canter's particular interpretation of this body of research is especially valuable.

The sections on assessment and diagnosis are particularly beneficial for those operating at the hands-on level or aspiring to do so, for students and practitioners alike. They highlight the tools, tests, and protocols that forensic psychologists rely on, while also acknowledging their limitations. Concepts such as reliability, validity, malingering, cognitive distortions, and psychopathy are explained in a way that is both rigorous and accessible. These chapters underscore a central truth of forensic work: Assessment is never merely a technical exercise. It is a responsibility that requires humility, critical thinking, and awareness of the profound impact such evaluations can have on people's lives.

In David Canter's hands, one of the strengths of this book is its attention to the practical realities of working with law enforcement. As the one who first established the scientific input of psychology to police investigations (in the UK), he speaks here with unparalleled insight. The chapters on interviewing witnesses, victims, and suspects illuminate the psychological principles that underpin effective — and ethical — questioning. They also confront the fallibility of human memory, the dangers of bias, and the challenges of detecting deception. In doing so, they provide a corrective to the popular belief that truth can be easily extracted or that lies can be reliably spotted through intuition alone.

Equally compelling is the exploration of victims' experiences. Too often, forensic psychology is associated solely with offenders, but this book gives victims the attention they deserve. It examines trauma, uncertainty, repeat victimization, and the psychological consequences of crimes ranging from burglary to sexual assault. The inclusion of restorative justice reflects a broader shift in the field toward healing, accountability, and community-based solutions.

The chapters on legal proceedings offer a clear and thoughtful guide to the courtroom, where forensic psychologists must translate complex psychological concepts into language that judges and juries can understand. These are issues that Canter understands from direct experience giving evidence as an expert in court.

Finally, the book turns toward rehabilitation and treatment. It asks difficult but necessary questions: Can offenders change? Does prison help or harm? How should we address violence, sexual offending, and juvenile delinquency? The answers are grounded in evidence rather than ideology, acknowledging both the promise and the limitations of current interventions. The emphasis on cognitive-behavioral approaches, narrative reconstruction, and risk assessment reflects contemporary best practice while encouraging ongoing critical evaluation.

Taken together, these sections form a comprehensive, thoughtful, and engaging introduction to forensic psychology. They invite readers not only to understand the field, but to appreciate its complexity, its ethical demands, and its profound societal importance. Whether you are a student, a practitioner, or simply someone curious about the psychology behind crime and justice, this book offers clarity, insight, and Canter's steady hand.

Dr. Donna Youngs, Professor of Investigative Psychology, University of Northumbria, UK

Introduction

I n 1985, a senior police officer at Scotland Yard asked me to attend a meeting where the police were planning a major investigation into a series of rapes and murders committed around London. Until that point during my work as a psychologist, I'd had precious little contact with the police or criminals. I was therefore rather taken aback when asked whether I could "help catch this man before he kills again." Out of curiosity about how my experiences as an applied psychologist could assist such an important task, I agreed to help with the investigation. Its eventual success in identifying and convicting the criminal changed my life. As a result, I was drawn ever more intensively into a wide range of police investigations, and then into commenting on psychological evidence presented in court. I began considering rehabilitation programs for offenders and examining processes for assessing the possible risk they posed if they were released. I talked to killers and burglars and many other criminals and their victims.

I became part of the burgeoning field of forensic psychology, reading its journals, giving keynote addresses at conferences, and debating with colleagues and students how many aspects of behavioral science (particularly psychology) were informed by, and carried consequences for, the full range of legal issues. I became increasingly enthusiastic about the evolving ways in which psychology is influencing all aspects of the legal process.

Since that fateful day, I discovered that many people, in all walks of life, have questions about what makes criminals tick and how psychology can be used throughout the investigation, prosecution, treatment, and rehabilitation of criminals and to help their victims. This book aims to answer those questions.

About This Book

Forensic Psychology For Dummies, 2nd Edition, covers the psychological aspects of what happens from when a crime is first reported through to dealing with convicted offenders and, where possible, helping them desist from future criminality. I include many examples of forensic psychology in action to bring to life the excitement of this professional activity.

Here are a few topics, however, that you *won't* read about in this book: the motives that so delight crime fiction writers (greed, jealousy, revenge — in fact, I avoid even using the vague term *motive*); whether criminals did (or did not) get along with their mothers; or whether something is wrong with their biology. Instead, *Forensic Psychology For Dummies* gives you a much wider and more interesting landscape to explore. I go beyond the myths of such popular ideas as offender profiling and deeper than whether criminals are born or made. In this book, I show you what forensic psychologists actually do, and why they do it in the ways they do.

Although psychologists tend to drift into jargon, writing about most of what they do without technical terms is perfectly possible. On the few occasions when specialist words are needed, I make sure their meaning is clear. So if you know absolutely nothing of psychology, this book is for you. Even if you've read or studied any psychology, many aspects are presented here in a new light. If you've already had some contact with forensic psychology or you're considering it as a career path, the breadth of coverage provides a map to help you find your way.

Forensic psychology is a professional area of activity. I do describe some of the requirements and challenges that professionalism creates. But even if you're only curious what all the fuss is about, knowing the underlying principles and processes may come in handy if ever you come into contact with a real-life forensic psychologist (they aren't usually scary — honest).

I think of books in a library as being in conversation with each other, drawing on what they're about and offering connections for others to pick up. *Forensic Psychology For Dummies* is part of a gaggle of books chatting to each other. Where you can get more detail elsewhere, I make that clear, but bear in mind that I'm using my own point of view to cover what's written about in other books, and, as in any conversation, not everyone agrees with each other. If you want to check out what others have to say, by all means, take a look at *Criminology For Dummies,* 2nd Edition, by Stephen Briggs (Wiley) and *Forensics For Dummies,* 2nd Edition, by Douglas P. Lyle (Wiley). Because forensic psychology has such close contacts with the law, I mention the legal issues whenever I absolutely have to, but I'm a psychologist, not a lawyer. If you want to get to grips with all that stuff, do what I do and read *Law For Dummies,* by John Ventura (Wiley), although be warned that it's about the law in the US, and every country has its own way of doing legal things. Although the views of criminologists, political scientists, historians, and anthropologists — to name just a few — are extremely valuable, I don't engage with these disciplines. This book is about forensic psychology. Psychologists focus on individuals and their relationships with others.

Conventions Used in This Book

I use a few conventions to help you find your way around this book easily:

- >> *Italic* text highlights new, often specialist, terms that I always define nearby. *Italics* are also sometimes used for emphasis.

- >> **Boldfaced** text indicates the action part of numbered steps.

Although I keep the number of technical terms and jargon to an absolute minimum, all professional activities include words that have precise meanings for people within that profession. Mastery of these italicized terms enables you to bluff your way in any discussion of crime and criminals.

I'd love for this book to be a laugh-a-minute, but squeezing humor out of rape and murder, or even the more mundane crimes of burglary and robbery, is difficult and often inappropriate. Criminals themselves aren't comic (although some of them are clowns). As an expert in court, I have managed to coax a smile out of the jury from time to time, and so whenever I can, I do the same here. But please don't see these attempts to enliven the topic as implying that anything is other than serious.

What You're Not to Read

One problem with most books is that they start at Page 1 and carry on in a straight line until they end on the last page. But ideas don't always sit along a line so neatly, and often you don't want to find out about topics in the sequence that the writer wants to tell you.

This book is written to take account of such human foibles. In general, each chapter is self-contained, and you can read the chapters in any order you like, although the book makes greater sense if you do read them in the numbered order. If the information in one chapter is elaborated in more detail in another chapter, I refer to that other chapter. To help out, I also make any information that you can safely skip easy to recognize. The shaded text boxes throughout this book (known as *sidebars*) contain historical examples or more detailed theory that may otherwise break the flow of the text. You can avoid them, or just scan them quickly to get the feel of what's going on.

Foolish Assumptions

I've lectured on psychology to many different audiences for nearly 50 years, which helped me keep a vision of you in my mind while writing this book. The word *Dummies* in the title means only that I assume you're not an expert in forensic psychology, but that you're intelligent enough to use this book in the way that works best for you. I assume that you have some combination of the following interests:

>> You're fascinated by crime and criminals but want to know more than you can gather from fictional accounts or glib documentaries.

>> You think that you may want to be a forensic psychologist, but are curious to know what it's all about.

>> You know a little about the criminal justice system and wonder how the scientific study of people can contribute to it being more effective.

>> You're studying psychology and you're fed up with artificial laboratory experiments and details of which area of the brain lights up when people do odd things, so you want to know what psychologists do in the real world.

>> You're studying crime or the law, writing an article or a book, or making a documentary, and you want to know more about psychology and how it connects with the law.

How This Book Is Organized

Except for the first and last parts, each part of this book deals with a different facet of forensic psychology. You can choose the aspect you're most curious about and start there.

Part 1: Keeping Up with Forensic Psychology

Forensic psychology is a rapidly expanding area and takes on different forms in different places. This part, therefore, gives you an overview of what forensic psychology covers to help you recognize it when you stumble across it. Chapter 1 examines what forensic psychologists do (and don't do) and who they deal with. It also outlines the crucial information about forensic psychology research that is carried out. Chapter 2 reviews the psychological contributions from the crime to its being reported, investigated, taken to court, securing a conviction, and dealing with criminals. Chapter 3 shows how forensic psychology relates to the legal process.

Part 2: Examining the Criminal Mind

Like every science, forensic psychology relies on precise and reliable measurement. But people, especially criminals, aren't static lumps of material that can be plonked on a laboratory bench to have refined measuring tools applied to them. Therefore, various assessment procedures have been developed to weigh important characteristics of offenders, such as determining their mental state and its relevance to the legal process, a subject I describe in Chapter 5. A small, but crucial, subset of criminals have no obvious mental problems and are often characterized by commentators as evil. Chapter 6 looks directly at what this description can mean and offers a less sensational account.

Part 3: Assisting Law Enforcement

Many fictional accounts of crime investigations use some sort of psychological intervention to help solve the case. In truth, this aspect is a minutely small part of what forensic psychologists do, but it does get the juices flowing and is an intriguing start on your journey into the world of forensic psychology.

Getting good information from victims and witnesses during interviews (which I discuss in Chapter 7) isn't as easy as the movies may have you believe. Not everyone the police talk to tells the truth, so detecting deception — or, indeed, barefaced lying — is a challenging topic, to which I devote Chapter 8. Making use of the information the police do collect opens up the topic often referred to as offender profiling (see Chapter 9). Chapter 10 covers the important but often neglected subject of helping the victims of crime, and Chapter 11 discusses crime prevention and reduction.

Part 4: Psychology in Court and Beyond

Forensic psychology started life as guidance to legal proceedings and is now a common feature of many court hearings. I describe how this process works in

Chapter 12. The new developments, especially in the US, of guiding lawyers to be as effective and understandable as possible are covered in Chapter 13.

Part 5: Helping and Treating Offenders

Many forensic psychologists end up in prison — to help prisoners, of course, and sometimes prison management. Chapter 14 looks at the various forms of psychological help and treatment that are now available for offenders. Two particularly important areas are violence and sex offending, so they have their own chapters (15 and 16, respectively). Youngsters who become involved in crime pose a particular challenge, so I devote Chapter 17 to them.

Part 6: The Part of Tens

If you want to know more about the professional aspects of forensic psychology, I describe ten vital aspects in Chapter 18. Chapter 19 lists ten stages in the career of many people who become professionals in this area. In Chapter 20, I describe ten fascinating examples of cases in which forensic psychology successfully made a significant contribution.

Icons Used in This Book

This book uses various icons to highlight important information. Here's what they mean:

REMEMBER

This icon indicates info that's truly worth bearing in mind.

MYTH BUSTER

This icon indicates where I set the record straight on common misconceptions.

ANECDOTE

I use this icon to show you where I draw on my own experience to bring you real-life stories.

REGIONAL TIP-OFF

This icon tips you off to where I describe differences across the globe or where I focus on one country or jurisdiction.

STRANGE BUT TRUE

This icon reveals unusual nuggets from the realms of criminal investigation and behavior.

Where to Go from Here

You can read the chapters in this book in any order you like, because I wrote them so that the text makes sense wherever you start. But if you're new to the subject it is probably best to read with the Chapter 1 first. Then you'll have a mental map of what forensic psychology covers. Most importantly, though, enjoy!

1

Keeping Up with Forensic Psychology

The work done by forensic psychologists covers an increasingly wide range of topics; everything from exploring how to detect deception and malingering all the way through to helping families who have juvenile delinquents in their midst. Other examples are helping witnesses remember and assessing how dangerous a person really is. These professional contributions occur in many different institutions: law courts, prisons, special secure hospitals for people sent there by the courts, and in the community at large. On rare occasions, they're even a part of police investigations. Forensic psychologists concern themselves with all sorts of criminals, from arsonists to terrorists and crimes starting with every letter of the alphabet in between.

At the heart of what forensic psychologists do is to develop an understanding of criminals, their actions, and the causes of their behavior. This links to many other people who are interested in criminals, such as criminologists, lawyers, geographers, and even doctors. The difference is that psychologists focus on the person rather than on patterns of crime, with that person's thoughts, emotions, and actions rather than physical or sociological processes. To get started, I have lots of ground to clear about what forensic psychology is and the basis of what forensic psychologists do. In this part, I map out the fundamentals to get you ready for the more detailed info later.

Chapter **1**

What Is Forensic Psychology?

I f you think you know what forensic psychology is, this chapter may well have a few surprises in store. The abundance of police movies, TV series, and crime novels helps you form a mental picture of what forensic psychologists do — sometimes wrongly. Yes, police movies and TV series are truly criminal in content, but often only in terms of their inaccuracies and simplifications. Forensic psychology is an ambitious and diverse discipline that overlaps with many other related disciplines. In this chapter, I take a look at some specifics of the profession to sort out the reality from the fiction.

REMEMBER

Whatever activity forensic psychologists are involved in, they're arriving at logical conclusions using systematic, scientific procedures wherever possible. The forensic psychologist's work is founded to a large extent on objective research, which isn't always easy to do, for reasons I discuss in this chapter.

THE FORENSIC ASPECT

A little Latin is a useful thing. The word *forensic* comes from the Latin *forens*, meaning the Forum, which was the meeting place for sorting out your differences in ancient Rome. The Forum is the origin of the modern court. Now, anything that provides help or a service to a court of law is known as *forensic.* That's why you have forensic scientists, forensic pathologists, and even forensic archaeologists. They draw on their own experience and knowledge to provide evidence that helps the judge and jury make decisions, or may even help the attorneys to create their arguments. Originally, only psychologists who gave expert evidence in court were called forensic psychologists. Nowadays, the term *forensic* has become so widespread that it's now attached to any psychologist who has anything to do with crime, criminals, or their victims in a way that's relevant to detection, trials, treatment or imprisonment, or the impact of crime. The term *forensic* has gone as far as including those psychologists who help in selecting people to become police officers, although their work has nothing to do with legal proceedings. *Forensic* now includes the crime psychologist (I prefer that term over criminal psychologist because that one sounds as though a dodgy psychologist is being mentioned!), police psychologist, investigative psychologist, and prison psychologist — all terms that overlap with forensic psychologist. To add to this confusion, the label takes on different meanings in various countries because different legal systems allow a variety of expert intervention. So, forensic psychology is like many terms in common use — difficult to define precisely, but you recognize it when you see it.

Don't get too worked up about defining the term forensic psychology; instead, look at what forensic psychologists do and where they do it. Some experts may think that I cast the net too wide in this book, and others may think that I leave out important areas. But I'm sure they all would agree that forensic psychology is a fascinating and vibrant part of modern psychology.

NOT ALL LEGAL ACTIVITY CONCERNS CRIMINAL ACTS

In my overview of the areas of forensic psychology, I talk about *crime* and *offending.* But that isn't the only legal process in which psychology is relevant.

Courts consider a host of other events, usually referred to as *civil proceedings,* in which no one is charged with a crime but there's a disagreement that requires a court of some sort to intercede. One example is a coroner's court in which the cause of death is to be determined. Family courts in which custody of children may be the central issue are places where you often find psychologists assessing the parents or the children, their relationships, or other related matters.

I think of some proceedings as *quasilegal*. They're rather like courts of law but don't carry the same weight or formality. Examples include employment tribunals, where a person is perhaps claiming wrongful dismissal, reviews of a person's disability in relation to an accident claim, or a claim for disability benefits from the state. As well as possible medical aspects, these examples may also feature significant psychological issues.

I also use the terms *police* and *investigation* in a rather loose way. Many of the people carrying out investigations aren't police officers, but may be insurance or arson investigators, customs and excise, tax collectors, or other government agencies involved in aspects of law enforcement. All these areas are increasingly drawing on forensic psychology.

The Origins of Forensic Psychology

Although professional forensic psychologists have only been operating in many numbers over the past half-century, activity that can be recognized as forensic psychology is as old as modern psychology, going back to the latter half of the 19th century. Indeed, just about any development in scientific psychology quickly finds an application in some aspect of the legal process. Many well-known psychological studies started in the university and found their way into court as evidence. (I describe some landmark cases in Chapter 21.)

As early as 1908, the Harvard professor of psychology Hugo Münsterberg published a book with the modern-sounding title *On the Witness Stand*, in which he described the various ways in which the discoveries of the newly emerging discipline of psychology were of relevance to expert evidence in court. Many of the topics discussed are still relevant today, such as the fallibility of witnesses' memories, false confessions, and how the court process itself can influence what people admit to. (Check out Chapter 7 for much more on memory and witnesses.) In Germany in 1909, where psychological research was also quite active, Clara and William Stern published a book that considered children's ability to remember and give effective testimony and examined the various psychological processes that may give rise to false testimonies.

Another founder of modern, scientific psychology was J. McKeen Cattell, who worked at Columbia University in the 1890s. He was interested in how people remember and how accurately they could recall events that had happened. He thus set in motion the study of the psychology of testimony that has grown ever since and thrives today.

A recurring interest in the psychology of lying and deception, and the possibility that physiological changes in the person can reveal such deception, was an early application of laboratory-derived ideas to forensic considerations. In 1915, William Marston, a student of Münsterberg, introduced the first lie detector of sorts that measured a person's blood pressure when answering questions about a past event. Within a few years, similar procedures were being used in criminal investigations. This laid the groundwork for many procedures that are in use today. I talk much more about deception in Chapter 8.

Following on from the work of the early pioneers in psychological research, an increasing number of psychological studies of relevance to legal procedures were carried out. Examining psychological issues relating to testimony and deception has become the cornerstone of this work. But broader issues, such as beliefs about rape or the social psychological aspects of jury decision-making, have now taken this far beyond those explorations of over a century ago.

ANECDOTE

The assessment of an individual for the courts is usually traced back to a famous case in 1843 when Daniel McNaughton shot Edward Drummond. Apparently, McNaughton thought he was shooting Sir Robert Peel, who was the leader of the Tory party at the time. McNaughton said that the reason for the shooting was this:

The Tories in my native city have compelled me to do this. They follow and persecute me wherever I go and have entirely destroyed my peace of mind.

This claim was taken to indicate that McNaughton was mentally disturbed, causing a furor in the British legal system at the time.

To understand this case, I need to introduce a couple of legal Latin terms.

For a person to be convicted in most places in the world, certain conditions need to be satisfied:

>> **Actus reus:** The act did actually occur (or some crime was committed because an action did not occur).

>> **Mens rea:** The individual knew what they were doing, knew that it was wrong, and did it intentionally.

In their wisdom, lawyers think of mental disturbances as (simplistically) implying that people are not guilty if their minds are not guilty. (They have a neat Latin phrase for this, but I think you've had enough Latin for now.) When lawyers start talking about the mind, though, they open the door to psychologists and psychiatrists, who are more than ready to comment on other people's minds and how in contact with reality they are.

Now, back to the McNaughton case. At the time, convicting someone who didn't appreciate the significance of their own actions, or whose actions weren't under rational voluntary control, was considered uncivilized. The confusion in the existing law that required only the second condition of *mens rea* — that their action was under voluntary control — to be met, but didn't detail how that can relate to mental disturbance, led to a clarification of the law in what became called the McNaughton rules. The rules recognized that a "disease of the mind" can exist in which the person couldn't have voluntary and conscious control over their actions or truly be aware of their significance. Therefore, on the basis of *mens rea*, McNaughton was found not guilty of murder.

The idea that the mind (rather than the brain) is an organ that can be diseased, like the liver or heart, shows how subtle (or, possibly, ignorant) lawyers can be. Plenty of illnesses of the brain don't affect a person's ability to voluntarily and consciously commit a crime. Similarly, many disturbed mental states can't be linked directly to brain disease. This means that a seemingly straightforward legal requirement opened the doors to professionals who worked with mentally ill patients to give guidance to the court on whether the defendant was in a psychologically sound state at the time of the crime to be legally responsible for his actions. This situation is still a central issue on which psychologists and psychiatrists give guidance to courts.

ANECDOTE

Another case, this time from the US, helps to illustrate this situation of clinical psychology helping the legal system. When Christopher Simmons was a few months shy of his 18th birthday, he carefully planned and carried out the murder of Shirley Crook. Simmons was given a death sentence when convicted. However, the American Psychological Association supported his appeal against the death sentence by reviewing studies of teenagers. They stated that juveniles under the age of 18 lacked the mental ability to take full moral responsibility for their actions and therefore couldn't be regarded as having *mens rea.* The US Supreme Court accepted this advice and overturned the death penalty. (Turn to Chapter 17 for more on crime and juveniles.)

The consideration of the mental state of the defendant has produced many other issues on which the court welcomes guidance, including these:

» Deciding whether, due to intellectual ability or mental state, the defendant can understand the court procedures well enough to be fit to plead

» Determining the ability of children to be witnesses and the most effective procedures for involving them in court cases (see Chapter 7)

» Predicting the likely risk that an offender may pose in the future and hence implications for sentencing

- » Deciding whether an offender's mental condition is likely to be responsive to treatment

- » Helping with the support and assistance to victims (a topic I look at in Chapter 7)

The Two Strands That Produce Forensic Psychology

Many of the earliest psychologists contributing to legal considerations were academics contributing from their scholarly studies. But clinical practitioners working directly with patients involved in legal proceedings have also contributed to developments in forensic psychology. These two parallel disciplines are summarized in this main section.

The academic strand

All the applications of psychology to crime and law that I discuss in this section have their origins in the research laboratories of universities. New procedures have come from the products of careful study, independently of the cut and thrust of legal debate or the challenges of a particular case. Later on, these procedures were applied directly to actual cases, as illustrated in the later sidebar "Defending a mayor from a charge of obscene behavior."

The law deals with all aspects of people in all the situations they find themselves. No surprise, therefore, that every major area of psychology and every significant psychologist has found relevance in some consideration of crime, criminality, investigation, and prosecution. As a result, the links of psychology to the law are most notable in those countries where psychologists have been most numerous and active. Sigmund Freud, for example, told judges in Vienna in 1906 that they needed to be aware of how witnesses can inadvertently distort information because of unconscious processes.

The clinical strand

Alongside the academic explorations of human behavior and experience that I describe in the preceding section, people working directly with patients in a clinical context have, from early in the 20th century, contributed to various aspects of legal proceedings.

Lionel Haward was a clinical psychologist carrying out therapy with patients. Some of his patients came to him through the courts, for assessment or treatment, and out of that contact, he was called on to give expert evidence. He drew on psychological procedures as illustrated in the later sidebar "Defending a mayor from a charge of obscene behavior," but as with most clinical psychologists, his main contribution to court procedure was from the point of view of a clinician offering an informed, objective opinion about a patient.

REGIONAL
TIP-OFF

In the US, issues around proceedings are more open. The delightful film *The Runaway Jury*, based on the John Grisham novel, pushes to the extreme the ways in which some knowledge of individual personality processes and social dynamics can influence juries. The attorney used this advice in the film to try to choose a jury that would give him the verdict he wanted and then to manipulate the way he presented arguments to them so that they would take his side. I won't tell you how it all pans out in case you want to watch the film or read the book, but you can be sure it wasn't as you might expect.

Some professional psychologists in the US, while not going as far as the characters in the film, do endeavor to help attorneys in selecting who should be eliminated from a jury and how to present the case to take account of how and what a jury understands about a case.

That role of forensic psychologists influencing how a jury may be selected would not be countenanced in British law courts. For starters, there's a much more limited legal allowance of who can be deselected from a jury. In the US, potential jurors can be asked about their beliefs and attitudes. That doesn't happen in UK courts. You should also be aware that in many Western democracies, usually not English-speaking ones, juries play quite a limited role in courts — or none at all. These are known as *inquisitorial* legal systems, compared with the Anglo-Saxon *adversarial* system (discussed in a little more detail in Chapter 12). As a consequence of the differences in legal systems forensic psychologists operate rather differently in adversarial systems to inquisitorial ones.

Distinguishing Forensic Psychology from Its Neighbors

You know the typical crime movie plot, which goes something along the following lines: The detectives in the film are stumped (you'd have no plot if they found the criminal sitting and crying at the crime scene). The serial killer has killed again

(Why are most killers in films the serial type?), and the pressure is on to find him (or, more rarely, her). Enter the forensic psychologist, usually grudgingly, just when he's having enough problems, with drink or his girlfriend or both. Increasingly, I'm happy to say the psychologist is a woman, but that doesn't stop her from having her own problems to deal with. The psychologist learns about the crimes and almost magically knows what the murderer was thinking, why he killed, and how the police can catch him. But the killer refuses to talk, and so the heroic forensic psychologist settles down for an intellectual battle of wits, leading to the criminal revealing all. (Along the way, of course, the forensic psychologist loses custody of their darling daughter, their partner walks out on them again, and they return to the bottle.) It's fun to mention, also, that increasingly the psychologist "profiler" gets it all wrong and is a bit of a laughingstock. That's a healthy awareness of how wrong the profiling trope is, as I discuss in Chapter 9.

I'm no scriptwriter, but I'm sure the scene is familiar to you. Well, as this book and this chapter show, the typical crime storyline has more to do with Conan Doyle's fictional detective Sherlock Holmes, and all the well-known fictional sleuths following in his footsteps, than with the work of the present-day forensic psychologist.

Often, the best way to understand the details of a professional activity is to clear the area around the profession and so establish what it's *not*. This approach is particularly important for forensic psychology, which shares friendly, neighborly relationships with many other areas and professions.

Forensic psychology is not criminology

You'd certainly be forgiven for thinking, for example, that forensic psychology is the same as criminology, although they do overlap.

ANECDOTE

Journalists often mistakenly refer to me as a criminologist, even though I'm no expert on changes in the pattern of crime over the centuries or between different countries, and I know little about the effects of different forms of punishment on the prevalence of crimes or the effectiveness of various crime prevention strategies.

I know only a little about crime as a general area but have spent my entire career as a forensic psychologist taking an interest in criminals. And yet, as a forensic psychologist, I may criticize general considerations of how to cut crime or treat offenders, but journalists generally have little understanding of what I know about how criminals act and think.

Forensic psychologists don't:

>> Study broad trends in criminality

>> Examine how the legal system works

>> Solve crimes

Forensic psychology isn't forensics

Forensic psychology isn't *forensics*, which is the application of science in legal investigations, such as the chemistry of poisons or the physics of bullets, or determining the time of death or how a person was killed. In other words, I'm talking about all the aspects of the crime scene investigation featured in many TV crime series.

The examination of the scene of a crime and the exploration of the forensic evidence that can be drawn from the crime are sometimes useful to a forensic psychologist — for example, in challenging an offender's claim in therapy.

Although in some crime fiction the forensic scientist may offer opinions about the mental state of the offender or similar speculations to keep the storyline moving, this activity is quite different from forensic psychology.

Forensic psychologists are not detectives

It's worth repeating that no psychologists, especially forensic psychologists, solve crimes. That is the job of detectives and other agents of law enforcement. As described in Chapter 9, the role of profiler is a rare one and, in reality, is not like fictional accounts. Individuals offering such services to the police may not even be psychologists.

As is clear throughout this book, there are many ways in which psychology is relevant to law enforcement. But entering into the active process of investigating crimes and trying to solve them isn't a task for professional psychologists.

Forensic psychology is not criminal law

The other confusion that's important to clear up is that there's an important and substantial difference between being a lawyer and a psychologist. Although forensic psychologists need to understand relevant aspects of the legal processes in which they are engaged, they are not experts on those processes.

Distinguishing forensic psychology from forensic psychiatry

Psychologists start out studying general psychology, focusing on such aspects as memory, learning, personality, and social interaction. Psychology students examine which bits of the brain light up when various activities are engaged in and the biological and genetic basis of human experience. Indeed, these days, many don't call themselves psychologists — they claim the much more impressive title of *cognitive* neuroscientist. But they still explore memory and thought processes and even learning and personality. They just add a neuroscience twist to their explanations. Therefore, psychology students do study some of the areas that medical students explore, but in far, far less detail.

After finishing general undergraduate training, psychologists can specialize in a number of different areas of psychology, including occupational, educational, health, or even environmental psychology. Psychologists complete further training if they want to secure a professional post in one of these areas. (In Chapter 20, I list the stages in becoming a professional forensic psychologist, although that process varies considerably from country to country.)

Psychologists working at providing assessment and therapy for mentally ill people are called *clinical psychologists*, and their activities overlap with those of psychiatrists. In the past, there was quite a turf war between clinical psychologists and psychiatrists, but in recent years, both professions have come to respect each other and recognize the value of working together.

Some psychiatrists specialize even further and work mainly with patients brought to them via the legal system. They're known as *forensic psychiatrists*. The medical profession is held in such high regard by the courts that, at one time, only psychiatrists were allowed to give evidence on the mental state of defendants. That has changed since the last century, and now psychologists often provide expert evidence in court.

Psychologists aren't *psychiatrists* — doctors treating mental illness and related matters, which some legal systems call diseases of the mind. Psychiatrists are allowed to prescribe drugs and other forms of medical treatment. They specialize in working with people who have problems in relating to, or their ability to deal effectively with, others and the world around them.

To help their patients, psychiatrists may use talking therapies as well as medical interventions. Treatment can include the type of intensive psychotherapy initiated by Sigmund Freud, called *psychoanalysis*. When they aren't prescribing pills, electric shock therapy, or (as they used to) brain surgery and are treating their mentally ill patients by non invasive means, psychiatrists are drawing on psychological research.

DEFENDING A MAYOR FROM A CHARGE OF OBSCENE BEHAVIOR

Professor Lionel Haward (1920–98), the father of forensic psychology in the UK, gave evidence in many cases, often using procedures derived from experimental psychology as the basis for his evidence.

One particularly interesting (not to say amusing) case was when Haward acted for the defense of a local mayor who was accused of indecent exposure in a public toilet. This charge resulted from two police officers following up complaints of indecent activities by hiding themselves in a cubicle in the public conveniences, peering through a grill in the door.

The defendant claimed that he'd been wearing a pink scarf at the time and that the enthusiastic police officers, keen to make an arrest, were so primed to expect indecency that they misinterpreted this innocent apparel for a part of his anatomy!

Haward set up an experiment in which naïve subjects were shown photographs under limited lighting conditions of the mayor wearing his scarf. The subjects were given the expectation that something untoward was illustrated in the pictures and asked to indicate when they saw it and what it was.

Haward found that one picture in every eight was believed to represent an indecent act. Haward offered these results together with an explanation of the psychological processes involved and citation of other studies illustrating the power of expectancies on the interpretation of ambiguous images. The attorney used this report as the basis for invalidating the police evidence. The mayor was acquitted.

MYTH
BUSTER

Although some overlap exists between forensic psychology and forensic psychiatry, most of the topics in this book — such as testimony, measuring aspects of personality and mental state, giving guidance on court procedures, and many facets of the psychological treatment of offenders — are carried out by forensic psychologists. When psychiatrists are involved in assessment and treatment, I believe that they're practicing forensic psychology. They may not agree, however.

The Building Blocks of Forensic Psychology

Academic and clinical approaches to psychology may differ. For example, academics research more general aspects of human psychology, such as perception, personality, or memory, whereas clinicians are concerned with examining the thoughts, feelings, and actions of their patients in the clinic. However, for the forensic psychologist, the academic and clinical strands have never been totally distinct. Nowadays, the two strands overlap in many different ways. This raises the interesting question of how forensic psychologists know what they know.

The chief difference between the layperson and the professional is that the professional can draw on the body of objective knowledge and findings that come from established scientific procedures. Therefore, in this section, I look at the basis on which forensic psychologists form an opinion. Having some knowledge of how this process works helps to give you a clear picture of the nature of forensic psychology.

The challenges of studying criminality

Developing an understanding of criminals, the experiences of victims, and the others who come into contact with the law isn't as easy as showing people pictures and studying their reactions, which is the traditional basis of much psychological research. Even questionnaire surveys and interviews are fraught with challenges when dealing with the sorts of traumatic situations or untrustworthy respondents that are the day-to-day aspects of forensic psychology.

Some relevant areas, such as memory or perception (see the earlier sidebar "Defending a mayor from a charge of obscene behavior"), are open to criticism for using somewhat artificial laboratory studies. But most research has to be carried out by studying real crimes and interacting with actual criminals. There are legal as well as security constraints on this strategy. There are also practical aspects and heightened concerns over confidentiality and privacy.

Gaining access to offenders usually requires cooperation with organizations within the legal sphere. They may not be as accepting of the requirements of neutral, objective research as a trained psychologist. It is thus some measure of the determination — and in some cases, courage — of researchers (see the nearby sidebar "When is a terrorist not one?") that the scientific basis of forensic psychology continues to develop so rapidly.

Experimenting

Imagine that you want to show that a particular procedure, such as detecting lying, really works. The most reliable way of doing this is by using the long-established scientific procedure of the carefully controlled experiment. This experiment needs to demonstrate that the procedure detects when people are lying better than the chance probability of, say, throwing dice, and also that the scientific procedure can detect the truth better than chance.

WHEN IS A TERRORIST NOT ONE?

A brave student of mine, who was well-connected with law enforcement agencies, managed to secure permission to interview people convicted of terrorist offenses. (This was not in any English-speaking country, where such research is almost impossible unless you're a member of one of the intelligence services.) My student gained access to a man who had been released from prison for acts of terrorism on the basis that he had renounced his former commitment to such violent crimes. However, during the close psychological interview, it became clear to my student that this man was still a terrorist and was in contact with his former associates. As soon as the student realized this, he politely and carefully withdrew from the interview and immediately left the city where the interview had taken place.

The challenge in setting up these types of experiments is that ethical limits often exist on what the subjects in an experiment can be asked to do. For example, you can't ask people to commit a real crime, mix them in with others who didn't, and then see whether you can spot the liars. You have to set up some sort of artificial situation, which means that, no matter how realistic you make it, the same emotional pressures don't exist as, for example, in a real murder case where the murderer is desperately trying to avoid being found out.

Other difficulties stem from getting a reliable comparison between the conditions that are of interest and some neutral comparable circumstances. An important example lies in experiments that are trying to improve interview procedures. What do you compare any new interview procedure with? How do you measure the differences between new and comparison procedures? As in the example of lying, interviewing people about a serious event you know is fictitious can be fruitless, but if you interview people about actual events, there may be something special about those events and how they're remembered that means they aren't typical of other situations. Does it make any difference whether you're interviewing people who have experienced a burglary in contrast to a violent assault?

These questions show how complicated setting up carefully controlled experiments in the area of forensic psychology can be.

Overall, many experiments are rather artificial. They use students who are pretending in various ways, or people are shown videos rather than experiencing actual events directly. Attempts to repeat the results in real-life situations aren't always successful.

Nonetheless, some of the basic issues, especially in the area of testimony, have been opened up by using carefully controlled academic experiments.

Studying in the field

Studies carried out in real-life situations are generally regarded as producing results that can be applied more readily to other real circumstances. The most common form of study is in evaluating the impact of a particular intervention, such as a treatment program for alcoholics or a screening procedure for selecting prison staff. Ideally, such studies also require careful comparisons, at least with what happened before the intervention, but preferably with other established procedures.

These studies can explore many related processes in large-scale analyses, such as, for example, when considering the impact on future criminality of different ways of dealing with criminals. The results from this specific research merge with more general areas of criminality. Psychologists expect to pay particular attention to making sure that like is compared with like and carrying out detailed analysis of who was being dealt with in each of the forms of treatment or punishment. Often, the impact of any intervention with an offender depends more on the nature of the offender — age or how deep they are in a criminal culture — rather than exactly the punishment or treatment instituted.

Assessing and measuring

The focus on individuals and understanding their particular psychology is such a central aspect of forensic psychology that a great deal of research and practice revolves around assessing the characteristics of individuals. In Chapter 5, I walk you through some of the processes that are used to develop assessment instruments. For now, you just need to know that this measuring is far from a casual activity.

When forensic psychologists decide that measuring an aspect of a person is useful, they take care to define the aspect precisely. It may be sexual fantasies, psychopathy, malingering, suggestibility, general levels of deviance, or a whole host of other crucial aspects that may be relevant to some area of how the judicial system deals with such people.

Having decided on what to examine, the psychologist then forms and tries out careful statements, possibly in a questionnaire, to be answered, or guidance of what's to be observed in an interview or information gathered from records about the person.

After the procedure is developed, it's tested in several ways with different samples of people so that the procedure can be effectively calibrated. Eventually, after a number of studies of the procedure actually being used, a court of law may accept it as providing a measure that can guide the court's deliberations or as the basis for determining treatment regimens or parole.

The two key aspects of reliability and validity are required before the measurement instrument can be trusted; psychological assessment measurements can't be taken at face value and have to be demonstrated through research:

>> **Reliability:** How consistently the procedure measures what it measures. For example, a measuring tape made out of elastic isn't reliable because it gives a different length for the same object every time it's used.

>> **Validity:** How well the procedure measures what it claims to measure. A measure of sexual fantasies that was in fact assessing how much pornography a person watched can be misleading, although asking the person about what they liked to watch may indicate sexual preferences.

REMEMBER

Validity is more difficult to establish than reliability because validity requires a careful definition of what the measurement is supposed to be measuring.

There are lots of other features of psychological measurements that are important before they can be used with confidence, but two are enough for now. You can find out about other psychological measurements in Chapter 5.

Studying individual cases

Many breakthroughs in medicine come from the study of an individual person. Working from a single case is much easier for doctors because usually the majority of human bodies are more or less physically the same: two arms, two eyes, the same sort of kidneys, and liver (give or take a few beers).

In contrast, one individual's psychological makeup is distinctly different from the next person's, and even if many similarities exist, everybody *thinks* that they're unique. For this reason, psychologists frown on a single study as a way of making discoveries and then applying the discovery to numberless people. However, single cases are quite useful in illustrating results drawn from other scientific procedures, which is how I use case studies throughout this book.

Getting theoretical

I don't want you to think that forensic psychology is all numbers and observation and prisoners filling in questionnaires. None of these ways of collecting information about people makes much sense unless accompanied by an explanation and understanding of what the respondents are doing. In science, such insights come from what is broadly known as *theory.*

REMEMBER

Psychological theories aren't idle speculations or impossible suggestions in the way that the word *theory* is often used in daily life. In the study of psychology, *theories* consist of carefully defined ideas that are related to each other in an argument, which is then tested by obtaining some information (usually called *data*) from actual situations.

MYTH
BUSTER

When you ask whether criminals are born or created by their experiences, called the *nature-or-nurture* question, you're really asking which of the two broad theories about the origins of crime is most plausible. Is it the theory that genetic makeup determines most of what humans do? Or is it the theory that upbringing and experience are what cause us to feel and act in the ways we do?

As I show throughout this book, when you start to define more clearly what key concepts mean and you look for the evidence, the theories usually become more subtle and more complicated. But that's what makes forensic psychology *fascinating.*

Professional ethics

All the activities that forensic psychologists are engaged in carry serious consequences, both legally and professionally: A person's life or freedom can even hinge on what the psychologist says. There are therefore many constraints and guidelines for what forensic psychologists do. I explore ten of these in Chapter 19.

Working with Others: People and Places

Forensic psychologists don't spend their time locked in prison cells while chatting with serial killers. They find themselves interacting with a great range of people in various ways:

>> **Patients:** Some people are assigned to forensic psychologists through the legal process and offered therapy or given help in other ways to cope with any psychological problems.

>> **Clients:** People, without personal problems, getting help on matters such as setting up selection procedures — say, for police or prison officers who work on sexual assault cases — or giving advice on interviewing procedures.

>> **Witnesses:** In some cases, witnesses may need special help to cope with the legal process or even to remember more clearly what happened. Young children can pose special problems to the courts. Forensic psychologists may be brought in to help with these matters.

>> **Other professionals:** Fellow professionals can turn to the forensic psychologist to assist in throwing light on the circumstances of a case or for help in understanding the actions of an individual. Assessing future risk is a particularly important service in this regard, as I describe in Chapter 14.

The following sections list some of the settings and groups of people where forensic psychology makes an important contribution.

In the courts

Forensic psychologists carry out the following tasks, for example, in relation to criminal cases:

>> Giving help in selecting jury members or giving lawyers guidance on how to present a case, especially in the US.

>> Evaluating the competence of a defendant to stand trial.

>> Providing risk and other assessments that can influence the sentencing of a convicted person.

REGIONAL TIP-OFF

>> Assessing whether a convicted person is mentally sound enough to face the death penalty (in the US).

>> They can act for the prosecution or the defense. I've done both, although not in the same trial, of course.

In civil cases and in quasilegal settings, including industrial and employment tribunals or internal reviews of employees, forensic psychologists carry out the following tasks, for instance:

>> Evaluating child custody cases

>> Assessing whether child abuse occurred

>> Appraising the competency of key individuals

>> Gauging psychological effects of trauma, personal injury, product liability, harassment, and professional negligence

>> Reviewing judgments made about behavioral material, such as offensive communications

Depending on the jurisdiction, forensic psychologists can also offer the same sort of help and expertise in criminal cases.

With victims

Forensic psychologists provide help to victims by

>> Educating and assisting those who are responsible for notifying relatives of a victim's death

>> Treating victims or witnesses of crime

>> Training people who supply services to victims

In prisons and other correctional institutions

The sorts of tasks that forensic psychologists carry out in institutions include

>> Helping to select personnel for employment as prison officers

>> Providing support, especially in stress management, for those working in institutions

>> Evaluating programs in use or proposed programs for helping offenders from reoffending, such as the anger management and sexual awareness programs I describe in Part 5

>> Contributing to decisions about how prisoners are classified and suitable placements in appropriate institutions or on the different sorts of programs I discuss in Chapters 13–16

With the police

Forensic psychologists sometimes do the following in criminal investigations:

>> Give guidance on the search for an unknown offender

>> Train and assist in interviews of victims, witnesses, and suspects

>> Advise on dealing with mentally ill people

>> Offer guidance on handling domestic violence

Forensic psychologists may also

>> Supply counseling services for police officers involved in shootings or other traumatic incidents

>> Give support in hostage negotiations

In commercial settings

There are many areas that forensic psychologists contribute to that are not directly related to law enforcement or legal procedures. These can include

>> Guidance on how to deal with threatening or extortion demands

>> Evaluating the people involved in an organization that is being bought (which I've called *probity profiling*)

>> Assisting in limiting fraudulent activity by employees or customers

The involvement of psychologists in these commercial settings is probably still quite rare. It's difficult to know how prevalent it is because any such involvement is likely to be extremely confidential.

Chapter **2**

Psychology and the Criminal Process

One way to get a grip on the innumerable contributions psychologists can make to the management, investigation, and bringing to justice of criminals is to be aware of the various stages that cover the process of criminality. These move from the initial criminal act to the treatment of offenders after they're convicted. Along this pathway are many different types of psychological contributions.

REMEMBER

Criminals come in many different varieties. They are, after all, human like the rest of us. The differences between them are more important than any similarity they may have in the type of crime they're convicted of.

Phase 1: The Crime Starts with a Criminal

A crime occurs or is created by a criminal. The crime may involve the victim suffering direct personal violence or indirectly, as in a burglary of their home when they aren't present. (The *experience* isn't indirect — I just mean that no direct personal confrontation is involved.)

A number of psychological issues are relevant at this stage — notably, the characteristics of the criminal and how they see or create the opportunities for crime. The consequences for victims of crime (an increasingly important area of forensic psychology) are important, too, although they're often forgotten about in crime fiction and sometimes in real life. (Flip to Chapter 10 for more about helping victims.)

As a forensic psychologist, I'm interested in the implications of various kinds and styles of crime. Do certain crimes require more intelligence, or are some likely to be a product of anger or a lack of self-control? The recurring debate about whether criminals are born or made (known as the *nature-versus-nurture* debate) is central to these considerations.

Not all criminals are the same

People often wonder, "What makes a criminal?" The question assumes that there's a single answer that applies to any criminal you come across. Even a brief pause for thought reveals that this cannot be the case. A scheming Bitcoin fraudster cannot be created by the same processes as a teenager who snatches a handbag from a vulnerable person. A young man who hits out at a friend who insults his girlfriend isn't driven by the same forces as a woman who slowly schemes over many years to kill her husband so that she can inherit his wealth.

Varieties of crimes

You should be aware of three major differences in types of crimes:

>> **Crimes against the person:** These are all those crimes of violence that involve direct contact between an offender and a victim. Psychologically, it's the form of interaction that is at the heart of these offenses. The victim has some sort of significance in the life of the attacker. Even if the victim is chosen apparently at random they will reflect some aspect of importance to the offender. It may just be, for example, people who use MacDonalds. This has been described as the "role" the victim plays in the personal narrative that the offenders tell themselves.

The victim may just be an *object* to their attacker, of no particular importance other than the opportunity they provide, perhaps as a source of money in a robbery or of sexual gratification in a rape. This type of criminal shows little interest in their victims other than how they can satisfy them. They have no empathy for, understanding of, or interest in the victim.

The victim may represent something or someone of relevance to the offender. The victim is a *vehicle* on which to exhibit the violence. In some sexual assaults, for instance, the offender is acting out anger and frustration that is felt to come from other women. In extreme cases, the offender wants to experience the suffering of the victim.

In other violent situations, the particular victim is significant to the attacker. They are a particular *person* with whom the offender has had, or believes they've had, a relationship. The violence comes from anger directed at that individual.

REMEMBER

The law makes a clear distinction between crimes involving violence and those that do not. Crucially, *burglary* does not involve *direct* violence against a person. However, for a crime to be regarded as *robbery,* it must involve violence or the threat of violence. Perhaps surprisingly, in many jurisdictions, property crimes are awarded more severe sentences than violent crimes.

>> **Acquisitive crime:** This is the general term for all crimes that have as their focus obtaining objects or money — everything from stealing money from a piggy bank to defrauding large sums of money via complex business dealings. They may involve direct contact with victims or, typically these days, be carried out online at a great distance from victims.

An important difference with this type of crime is whether only a single perpetrator is involved or few perpetrators are involved, compared with when the thefts are part of a network of criminals. You must remember, though, that most crimes involving theft are inevitably part of some sort of criminal network. The stolen object or money usually has to be exchanged for something else, such as narcotics. That involves another person who also has to have had contact with others to obtain the illegal drugs. When this criminal activity is part of a criminal organization, there are many others involved in supporting, and benefiting from, every particular criminal act.

>> **Victimless crimes:** This one is a misnomer because others always suffer in addition to the offender. But the term is used to characterize offenses such as possessing or using illegal substances. The point of this designation is that it helps to point to what might be regarded as anomalies in the law. The idea is to question who is being hurt by the recreational use of illegal substances. Actions between consenting individuals in private may be against the law in many places, but why should the participants suffer punishment?

Vagrancy, sex work, gambling, begging, and assisting in suicide are all criminal acts in many countries. Some acts may be thought of as only causing a nuisance, others may offend public sensibilities rather than hurting or distressing anyone. This shows that many behaviors are against the law because they are regarded as morally reprehensible or are considered religiously unacceptable. You must understand this concept because the psychological implications of breaking these laws are somewhat different from crimes in which the offense clearly hurts someone other than the offender.

Varieties of criminal actions

Within any type of crime — whether it's burglary, rape, fraud, murder, or whatever else — there are also variations. They need to be acknowledged and understood in order to make sense of the psychological processes involved. Crimes vary in many different ways, but some key psychological differences can be found in the evidence for key inherited differences between people.

Two characteristics of how people differ from each other have been shown to be partly influenced by a person's genes. One is general *intelligence,* which is the ability to understand and solve complex problems, plan ahead, and, broadly, make sense of the world. If people who have this capability are involved in crime, they likely choose offenses that take advantage of their intellectual skills. In fact, most people in prisons around the world are not bright and often have limited education. Many are illiterate — unless, of course, they're political prisoners being held under draconian laws.

Intelligent offenders are likely to be leaders of criminal groups, often involved in fraud. If they do commit more mundane crimes or are involved in violence, they are quite likely to have planned them carefully or are using the violence to achieve particular goals.

The other important difference between people is *impulsiveness*, such as people known as having a short fuse or taking risks without considering the consequences. Their crimes tend to be opportunistic and thoughtless, revealing a lack of control.

Other differences relate to the presence of mental illnesses of various kinds, including what are known as personality disorders, especially psychopathy, all considered in more detail in Part 5.

Phase 2: The Crime Is Reported

Most reports consist of a person giving a verbal account of the crime, and, if an investigation follows, the crime scene is examined (the job of trained crime scene investigators). A victim or witness in a police interview gives an account of the crime, with the interviewer attempting to coax the interviewee to remember as clearly as possible what happened. (I discuss witnesses and interviews in more detail in Chapter 7.) Psychologists have been studying memory for well over 150 years, and nowadays, much is known about how memory works, which is relevant to improving police interviews.

When a suspect is interviewed (or some witnesses), issues of lying and other forms of deception may come into play. (I describe these issues in detail in Chapter 8.) The possibility of detecting lying and deception is likely to be a great help, and plenty of psychologists have had a go at this tricky problem. Establishing whether you're being told the truth is especially important where a person may be making a false allegation that a crime occurred or in the unexpected, but not uncommon, false admission to a crime.

How awareness arises that a crime has been committed

In crime fiction, no one usually rarely questions whether a crime has occurred. Sadly, the cliché of young women being killed by a serial killer is all too common in crime fiction. Little doubt exists in those situations about a serious crime having occurred. But in many instances, people may question what has actually happened. Perhaps people heard a scream. Social psychological processes may make them reluctant to report or act on it as indicating a crime.

In some communities, any contact with the authorities is frowned on, making people hesitant about reporting crimes. This can even go so far, in high-crime areas, as to cause people to dismiss behavior as not criminal — even though it's clearly against the law.

All these considerations are relevant to how victims or witnesses may be interviewed. They may also influence how offenders interpret their actions and find ways to minimize or exonerate themselves.

STRANGE BUT TRUE

Although it was more than 60 years ago that 28-year-old Kitty Genovese was murdered outside her apartment in the Kew Gardens area of the borough of Queens in New York City, the event has become of major importance in understanding the reporting, or lack of reporting a crime. The assault on the young woman lasted more than half an hour, during which she cried out for help multiple times.

Reports at the time indicated that although many people heard her cries, few intervened to help. This became known as the phenomenon of *bystander apathy*, which means that everyone in the situation hopes someone else will help, and they fear being at risk themselves if they intervene. However, you can find many contrary examples of people stepping in to help despite the risks to themselves.

How crimes are recorded

People generally don't join the police force with the intention of spending their time at a desk filling in forms. Yet that can easily be their experience, which can lead to casualness in how crimes are recorded and information collected about criminals. Details may have gaps in them as well as inaccurate information, and offenders, victims, and witnesses may inadvertently or deliberately provide misleading information, so check carefully any account of what actually happened in a crime. That can influence all assumptions relevant to a forensic psychologist's interactions with those involved.

There's also the matter of what crimes are recorded. The same criminal actions may be recorded under different headings by different police officers. They may even have a tendency to deliberately bias the recording process to help with operational procedures. Public concern — say, over the prevalence of asylum seekers in an area or antisocial behavior — can lead to some acts being recorded in one place and not in others.

ANECDOTE

In one investigation, I had contact with the detectives, who were convinced that a particular individual was the culprit and had committed the crime in February of that year. But when they checked the possibility in police records, they found that the person had not been let out of prison until June. Determined to make sure, they returned to check the original prison records and then discovered that the person entering the information into the police records had typed *Jun* rather than *Jan!*

Phase 3: The Investigation Gets Underway

A few forensic psychologists may help with many aspects of police procedures, most famously by *offender profiling*. I put this term in italics because, as discussed in Chapter 9, the technique isn't what sensational fiction suggests. Sure, from time to time, someone crops up on TV or in the newspapers, putting themselves forward as a profiler and suggesting that they're a modern Sherlock Holmes. But if profilers are doing the job properly, they aren't basing their proposals on instinct and intuition, or even the brilliant insights that made Holmes so admired; instead, they're using established scientific procedures, which are far less exciting or even unexpected.

The complexity of major investigations

One inaccurate aspect of investigations into serious crimes portrayed in most crime fiction is the carrying out of an investigation into a murder when there is no obvious connection between the victim and the culprit. The fiction describes the investigation being carried out by a small team of, at most, four people. That may have been possible many years ago or in some small towns in the US, but in the UK, such investigations harness large teams of police officers.

When no obvious link exists between the victim and the perpetrator, the search for the culprit can be challenging. It requires many different lines of inquiry, an unfolding process that initially opens up possibilities. Eventually, the number of possible criminals is narrowed down until enough evidence exists to take a person to court. Consequently, any help that can be offered to limit effectively the search for the criminal can be of enormous value. This is where detectives' awareness of the variety and styles of criminality can be helpful.

Detectives as decision-makers

Another psychological aspect of criminal investigations relates to the challenges law enforcement personnel face in dealing with these complex endeavors. Only in the past few years have these issues been carefully examined. That's because, until recently, research psychologists have had no access to what actually goes on in a major crime investigation.

What's becoming clear is that the distortions in thinking and biases that we humans are all prone to are also present in investigative decision-making. This list summarizes the eight cognitive distortions in how investigators may carry out their decision-making:

>> **Jumping to conclusions (confirmation bias):** When they think they've found a convincing suspect, they look only for evidence that backs them up, acting on their hunch rather than on the facts.

>> **Getting stuck on first impressions (anchoring):** Finding something early that seems relevant, such as a suspect's criminal record or a confident witness's description, can influence the whole investigation.

- **Letting recent cases skew judgment (availability bias):** If a similar crime happened recently, it can affect how officers see the current case.

- **Stereotyping (representativeness heuristic):** Relying on mental shortcuts, such as "It has to be a close relative," can lead to missed leads.

- **Overconfidence:** Trusting their instincts too much can lead to errors, especially under pressure.

- **Unconscious bias:** Race, gender, age, and class can affect how victims, suspects, and witnesses are treated.

- **Sticking to the usual way (status quo bias):** Even when procedures obviously aren't working, investigators have a tendency to stick with them.

- **Chasing easy wins (resource bias):** Cases that seem easier to solve or that raise lots of public concern are likely to have more time and people available for finding the culprit.

MYTH BUSTER

A great deal of forensic psychology is concerned with helping people who've become criminals find a way out of their life of crime — or at least to cope with their imprisonment in a way that's less personally destructive.

Phase 4: An Offender Is Apprehended

The forensic psychologist gets down to work at this stage. That person assesses the individual's ability to understand the legal process, or whether any aspects of their mental state made them unable to be aware of the nature or consequence of their actions. Assessments help the court decide whether the person is fit to stand trial and whether aspects of mental capacity need to be considered during the trial. An assessment can also influence what the court decides is to happen to the defendant if convicted.

Part 3 of this book deals with many aspects of interviewing and determining the truth, especially when interviewing suspects. Part 4 looks at the psychological issues relating to aspects of the court proceedings.

Preparing the case for the court

Many of the reports I have written for cases haven't been presented directly in court. The judge may be reluctant to allow me to offer an opinion, because it may be regarded as too influential (see Chapter 12). Another reason my report may not be dealt with directly in a trial is that I created the report mainly to challenge the expert opinion being brought by the opposing side. In all the cases I've experienced, my arguments were found to be so strong that the opposition withdrew their experts' opinions from the court and my report was withdrawn from official proceedings. My report nonetheless influenced how my attorney presented arguments to the judge and jury.

Court proceedings

Considering the court process raises many intriguing psychological and social psychological questions. These questions have no simple answers, though, because what happens in a court is greatly influenced by the differences in various legal systems. For example, many courts throughout the world have no juries; legally trained professionals, magistrates, or judges make all the decisions. Where juries do exist, important differences arise in how psychological issues are dealt with and, crucially from the point of doing research, how possible it is or isn't to examine how the court operates.

Phase 5: Conviction for a Crime

Convicted individuals may receive various sentences. Psychologists may influence the actual punishment by providing an assessment of the convicted person, perhaps to indicate the level of risk that the person will commit crimes in the future. This is particularly important when a person has been convicted of a violent crime. Evaluation of a person's mental state, especially if they have a serious mental illness, may also influence the sort of sentence a person is given. This can even include requiring some sort of program of treatment.

Phase 6: After the Trial

Psychological assessments of criminals go on long after the trial is over, in prisons and in other places dealing with offenders. These assessments are the bread and butter of the day-to-day work of the majority of forensic psychologists. Assessments are made up of a variety of different, standard procedures that have been developed over the years to measure aspects of an offender's personality, intellect, experience, attitudes, and actions. (See Chapter 5 to find out more about measuring instruments.)

Another contribution made by psychologists with offenders, in some prisons, is to help them cope with their incarceration. This can be in the form of counseling as well as dealing with the problems that led them to commit crimes.

Most commonly, help is given if the person has some obvious psychological problems. Alcoholism and other forms of substance abuse are typical examples of the problem a person may be struggling with that leads to crime. Violence between people who are intimates, often called *domestic violence*, is another area where an offender can be helped to deal with personality and interpersonal issues. Sexual offending (which I discuss in Chapter 16) is a further activity that may stem from the offender's misunderstanding of the impact or significance of actions, for which psychotherapeutic interventions can help.

Treatment and other interventions with offenders are some of the fastest-growing areas of forensic psychology. I talk about treatment and interventions for offenders in Part 5.

A particularly difficult aspect of assessment and attempts at rehabilitation relates to individuals who have no obvious mental illness or other intellectual problems but who clearly have trouble relating effectively to others. At the extreme, these people may be considered evil. They pose a challenge to psychological assessment. Various approaches to this issue have been explored, but the dominant one is to think of the person as having a *personality disorder;* the main example is *psychopathy*. (I cover these issues a little more in Chapter 6.)

What Sherlock Holmes (and His Disciples) Got Wrong

As I make clear in this chapter, most criminal investigations are much more complex than Sherlock Holmes, Miss Marple, Philip Marlowe, or their descendants would have us believe. Of course the stories about these fictional detectives can be delightfully absorbing. The twists and turns of these plots and the psychological insights into the workings of the criminal mind are fascinating. However, if these stories were to be modeled closely on what actually happens in an investigation, they might become *tedious.*

I have to admit, though, that more recent crime fiction does follow more closely what actually happens in major investigations, partly because of what's known as the *long-form* television series. In six episodes, some of the reality of an investigation, with all its cognitive biases and false leads, can be explored. That's much more difficult to deal with in a short novel or a one-hour show that needs to be divided up with advertising.

Be aware of the difference between fiction and reality (see Table 2-1) because the role of all those involved, including forensic psychologists, derives from what actually happens.

TABLE 2-1   **A Comparison of Fiction and Reality in Investigations**

Topic	Fiction	Reality
Speed of investigation	Cases are solved quickly — often within a single episode or chapter.	Investigations take weeks, months, or even years; delays are common.
Use of forensics	Forensics delivers instant, conclusive results (for example, DNA or fingerprints).	Forensic analysis is slow, often inconclusive, and subject to lab backlogs.
Detective role	One brilliant detective solves the case using intuition and flair.	Investigations are team-based, involving multiple professionals across departments.
Crime scene protocol	Detectives touch everything; scenes are chaotic and dramatic.	Scenes are tightly controlled; contamination risks are high and chain of custody is crucial.
Evidence expectations	Jurors expect high-tech, irrefutable evidence in every case.	Many cases rely on circumstantial evidence and witness testimony; the "CSI effect" skews juries.
Interviewing suspects	Suspects confess dramatically under pressure or guilt.	Coercive tactics can lead to false confessions; ethical interviewing is essential (as described in Chapter 7).
Daily police work	Action-packed chases, shootouts, and dramatic confrontations take place.	Most work involves paperwork, routine interviews, and procedural steps.
Cognitive insight	Detectives divulge uncanny psychological insight into motives.	Behavioral analysis is complex, often speculative, and rarely definitive.

Chapter **3**

Forensic Psychology and the Law

orensic psychology hooks inevitably into the legal process, not least when practitioners are called to give expert testimony in court cases. Therefore, to understand how the discipline works, you must understand the legal process and how expert evidence fits into it. In this chapter, I provide a basic summary of how the law works and specify some general differences in how it operates in various countries, which in turn affect how forensic psychology expert witnesses fulfill different roles in various courts. I also demonstrate what being an expert witness entails and the ways in which the forensic psychologist can contribute in and around the courts.

In some countries, especially in Eastern Europe and non-English-speaking places, people with medical training still dominate the process of giving psychological evidence. They may be psychiatrists or even general medical practitioners. The preference for people with medical training over psychologists as experts on psychological matters, such as fitness to plead, used to apply in the UK and US. Forensic psychologists have certainly found their way into the legal limelight in the US, however, ever since the early 1960s, and they're ever more present these days in the UK, Australia, and Canada.

Understanding That Legal Systems Vary Worldwide

The central message of this section is that each country (or sometimes part of a country) has a different way of "doing" the law. Well, you wouldn't expect things to be otherwise, would you? After all, human beings invented legal systems, and because their histories and cultures vary, inevitably their institutions vary, too. These variations make different assumptions about human beings and incorporate different sorts of protections to ensure that justice is done.

REMEMBER

Throughout this chapter (and book), I refer to *jurisdiction*. By this term, I mean an area in which a particular set of laws holds sway. The word can also mean the sorts of laws that an authority has the power to enforce.

To illustrate, the Federal Bureau of Investigation (FBI) in the US has jurisdiction only over crimes that occur on government property or across state lines, or nationwide crimes such as serial killing, unless other state or city jurisdictions call them in for advice. In the UK, the Scottish legal system is quite distinct from that in the rest of the UK. Scotland is a different jurisdiction.

The adversarial system: Facing up to an opponent

If you love Hollywood and TV court case movies, you're familiar with the idea of a courtroom. A judge sits in a distinct position in the middle of one end of the room, often elevated above the rest of those present. In the UK the accused sits or stands on a boxed-in platform (called the dock) nearby, one that's typically lower than the judge. In the US the accused typically sits with their defense attorney across from the judge. And witnesses stand or sit on the other side of the judge. Across the room are two rows of people and the *jury*, who listen to the trial as it progresses and eventually present their verdict.

This arrangement is typical of Crown Courts in England and Wales and in federal and state courts in the US. In fact, the great majority of court cases in many countries take place without a jury in front of magistrates, typically composed of three people who act as judges but aren't trained lawyers, assisted by a legal advisor. A number of other types of courts occur in different places, but I'll stick with the topic of what happens in the Crown Courts with a jury because that's where the role of the psychological expert is crystal clear.

The legal process used in most courts in the UK, the US, and most Anglo-Saxon countries is known as the *adversarial system* because at its heart is the adversarial nature of the defense and prosecution sides, played out before a judge or magistrates, and sometimes a jury that watches as a series of witnesses are questioned.

Initially, the *prosecution* brings forward its witnesses. The prosecution officially represents the state or country — in the UK, this is the King — so much so that the most experienced and senior prosecutors are known as King's Counsel. This prosecuting barrister (known as the prosecution attorney in the US) first questions the witnesses called by the prosecution, during a process known in the UK and Australia as providing *evidence in chief.* The US tends to use more informal terminology. This questioning is to reveal the facts of the case as the prosecution wishes the court to see them.

Next, in the *cross-examination*, the defense barrister (defense attorney, in the US) challenges the prosecution witnesses' accounts. They may try to challenge the reliability of the witness or the clarity of what they have said, as you can see in Chapter 7. Sometimes, subsequently, a barrister asks a witness a few more questions for clarification in the light of what the person said during cross-examination. Then the defense witnesses are brought in, with the defense first questioning the witnesses to provide the facts as the defense would like the court to know them. The prosecution attorney follows with a cross-examination that again has the objective of undermining the defense witnesses' account of the facts. After all the witnesses have been dealt with, the prosecution and defense summarize the evidence as they see it. Then the judge provides an overall summary, emphasizing the legal issues the jury needs to take into account. The jury is then hidden away to make a decision about innocence or guilt, and in some jurisdictions, also to determine the sentence a person receives when convicted.

MYTH BUSTER

Don't assume that the cut and thrust in the courtroom, so beloved by filmmakers, is typical of most court cases. In my experience, court proceedings are remarkably tedious, conducted in an extremely polite manner, going over minute detail interminably. Also, a lot happens outside the courtroom, or out of hearing of the jury. The judge, or magistrate, is always in charge and may stop the attorney from being overly dramatic.

Considerable debate may take place before the jury is allowed into the court about what evidence can be presented, with the defense and prosecution bargaining over which witnesses can be called and which aspects of their evidence can be put before the jury.

In addition, reports are prepared for both the prosecution and the defense that provide background information. This typically includes reports from forensic scientists and other experts who may be called on to give evidence. In some cases, reports from forensic psychologists about the defendant may be available, as discussed in Chapter 12. Many aspects of these reports may not find their way into court, but attorneys can draw on them to influence the case they make and how they make it.

In the adversarial system, the only information that counts as evidence is what's revealed in court. Mounds of documents and reports may have been prepared in support of the case, but only what is said in court in front of the jury can be taken into account.

Many times I've written lengthy reports for court cases, but have not been allowed to present the information to the court as, for example, I would when lecturing to students. Instead, I can only answer the questions the barristers ask. Sure, these questions are based on my report, but if the barrister doesn't ask about aspects that I regard as crucial because of, for example, a lack of understanding of the psychology, the court may never hear that information in order to take it into account.

In the adversarial system, when the case is presented in front of a jury, it's the jury that makes the final decision, guided by the principles of law by the judge. Generally speaking, the judge determines the sentence when a person is found guilty, but various expert reports may guide the judge on what sentence to give.

In the UK, the police carry out the investigation into a crime and the initial preparation of the evidence. The Crown Prosecution Service (CPS) then brings (or decides not to bring) prosecutions in criminal cases.

The CPS has some similarities to the district attorney's office in the US. Some details of the US legal system are given later in this chapter.

The main point is that under most adversarial systems, the police carry out the investigations and then pass the evidence over to lawyers to conduct the prosecution. The police are in contact with the lawyers as the investigation proceeds, but in the vast majority of cases, people with formal legal qualifications have no active role in the initial investigation. This system is quite different from most inquisitorial systems, as I describe in the next section.

The inquisitorial system: Keeping things brief in court

When I mentioned to some Dutch colleagues how long I've had to sit around UK courts, waiting to hear whether a judge would allow my evidence to be presented before the jury — the days and weeks that even the simplest court case can take — they laughed and said they knew that from watching accounts of many murder trials on television and in crime fiction films.

They assured me that nothing like that could happen in courts in the Netherlands. Under the country's *inquisitorial system*, the whole process is conducted in front of one or more judges — generally known as *magistrates* — with no jury. The great majority of the legal process is carried out by way of written documents, with the court case usually being a relatively brief discussion of what the documents contain. The prosecution leads the case with some representation from defense lawyers, but the back-and-forth battle that's central to the UK and US adversarial legal process (as I describe in the preceding section) isn't common under this system.

Furthermore, an attorney officially leads criminal investigations, and the police are answerable to this person in providing evidence for a prosecution. This attorney often acts as the prosecutor in any subsequent court case, which means that a much closer link exists between the prosecution and the investigators than in the adversarial system.

The distinction between the adversarial and inquisitorial systems that I sketch in this and the preceding sections is hugely simplified. For example, some UK and US courts have no juries, such as appeal courts where cases are brought to challenge an earlier conviction, or most coroners' courts that consider the cause of death. Also, in many inquisitorial jurisdictions, versions of the jury system operate. In the French system, for instance, the judge can sit in the jury room with the jurors while they're making their decisions, to ensure that they do so legally and sensibly. In Japan concern that juries should be effective is taken a stage further than in France. For the trial of very serious crimes, such as homicide, three judges sit together with six ordinary people taken from the electoral roll to make a joint decision.

Examining the US system: Constitution, federal, and state laws

The US has a greatly elaborated legal system, with some laws that apply across all states (*federal* laws) and other laws that are state-specific, although they may be modeled on some general framework on which all states draw. In fact, some parallels exist in the UK, where Scotland has its own distinct legal system, and some aspects of the legal process have been modified from time to time in Northern Ireland.

Unlike the UK, where the law is embedded in many centuries of case examples that have shaped what's acceptable, the US has the formidable Constitution and Bill of Rights that specify in admirable detail the basic principles on which the legal system is founded (although the legal precedents of cases are certainly still relevant). The Constitution provides a framework of 7 articles and 27 amendments that lay out how the country is to be run and provide benchmarks against which any laws can be measured.

With the variety of jurisdictions comes some important flexibility in the US legal system. For example, certain states have courts specifically set up to deal with offenders who have mental illnesses. Variations in sentencing and what may be allowed as evidence, as well as issues relating to jury selection and other aspects of the legal process, can all have a significant impact on the roles that experts, especially forensic psychologists, can play. For example, virtually all the advice on jury selection that I describe in Chapter 13 is offered by psychologists in the US. There is much more room for choosing a jury than in the UK and other countries with a jury system.

To take another example that I consider in more detail in Chapter 12, the evaluation of whether a person understands the legal proceedings enough to be given the death penalty can be a challenge for forensic psychologists in countries where the death penalty still exists. This difficulty doesn't occur in the UK, which no longer has the death penalty.

Against this background of variation, the detailed US Constitution provides a firm reference point that allows many challenges to legal outcomes, which can have implications for how forensic psychologists contribute.

Considering the implications for forensic expertise

The brief outline of variations in legal systems in this section makes clear that the nature of the testimony forensic psychologists can provide as expert witnesses in court is shaped by the nature of the particular legal system to which they're contributing. Of particular importance is whether the evidence is presented in front of a jury, made up of people who are assumed to be non-experts with no particular understanding of the issues at hand (as is usual under the adversarial system) or is presented to one or more magistrates (often the case in the inquisitorial system).

Judges and magistrates are assumed to be professionals who can make up their own minds and can accept or dismiss evidence in an objective way. (Whether they authentically can is, of course, a fascinating topic that some researchers have studied with rather less rosy results than the judiciary may like to hear, as I consider in Chapter 13.) This means that expert evidence that may be allowed when no jury is present may not be allowed if a case is being held in front of a jury. This precaution is to ensure that the jury, rather than the expert, makes the decision, an issue I discuss in more detail in the later section "Detailing the Dangers: Ensuring Trial by Jury and not Trial by Expert."

COURTS DIFFER ON WHAT EXPERT EVIDENCE THEY ACCEPT

In one case in England, a man was charged with the murder of his wife, even though a suicide note was found. The court didn't allow any psychological evidence to be presented about the mental state of the deceased wife. As a result, no discussion was allowed in court about whether she may have been depressed and likely to take her own life, which weakened the case of the accused considerably. In a case in Northern Ireland, a man charged with the murder of his son, wife, and daughter claimed that his son had gone berserk and killed his mother and sister (the defendant's wife and daughter) before killing himself. In this case, psychological evidence was allowed that suggested the deaths were the result of a carefully planned execution by the father. In both cases, the men were convicted of the murders.

In inquisitorial systems, experts are often given freer rein than in the adversarial system in front of a jury, including civil and quasilegal processes where judgments aren't so much about guilt and sentencing but are aimed more toward determining solutions in disputes. These variations between courts and legal systems also help explain why expert forensic psychology evidence can play a significant role in one place but never allowed in court somewhere else — say, in a different state or country. The matter is complicated further (as it so often seems to be with legal matters) by what any particular court regards as expertise, a topic I explore in the next section.

Benefitting from the Experience and Knowledge of an Expert Witness

When experts (such as forensic psychologists) appear in court proceedings, they are, in essence, witnesses like any others. They take an oath to tell the truth and are bound to honor the court and its procedures. One crucial exception, however, distinguishes experts from other witnesses. Experts are allowed to give opinions, whereas other witnesses can only provide an account of the facts as they know them. Experts must defend their opinions and explain the basis on which they reach them. They're closely examined on whether they, genuinely have the expertise to offer the opinions they present in court.

Experts, however, cannot offer an opinion on just anything they happen to know about. What they comment on has to be an aspect that the judge or jury can't know themselves.

ANECDOTE

This reality was brought home to me in a case concerning the likelihood that a victim committed suicide. The implication was, of course, that if she didn't, she was murdered. The victim had given no overt indication that she intended to kill herself, but I knew of a number of cases of irrefutable suicide in which the person gave no hints of wanting to end their life. I thought that this knowledge was relevant to the court, but the judge ruled that a jury of ordinary people would have enough experience in their daily lives to make up their own minds from what witnesses said in court about the character of the deceased regarding whether she'd intended to kill herself. So I wasn't allowed to provide evidence on this aspect.

Being called as an expert in criminal proceedings

Here's a summary of some criteria to be met for expert testimony to be admissible in court:

>> The subject matter must be a topic a typical juror (or judge) would not usually know about or understand.

>> The expert must have the qualifications and experience to be able to give the court assistance.

>> The expertise must be objectively established and generally accepted by other experts within that area of knowledge.

>> The value in helping to form an opinion about the evidence must be greater than the likely negative influence on the decision about the defendant.

Although the defense and prosecution lawyers argue about the expert evidence when presented, the judge decides whether the court accepts the expert opinion. The judge decides whether it provides information distinct from what the jury already knows and is of sufficient reliability and relevance to the case.

A particularly tricky decision for the judge is to weigh the value of the offered expert evidence (known as its *probative value*) against how damaging it may be to the defendant (known as its *prejudicial value*). For example, if the evidence is of only marginal probative value but may be detrimental, a judge won't allow it. How valuable expert testimony is also depends on how well-founded it is.

A key pointer in determining the acceptability of expert evidence is the notion of *reliability.* In other words, is what the expert offers expertise or just opinion? Various legal guidelines on this aspect have emerged over the years, as I discuss in the following sections.

US rulings

The US legal profession features rather more formal guidelines for what is acceptable as expertise than other countries. Those guidelines emerge from previous court decisions. Significant as regards expert witnesses is a 1923 case (*Frye* v. *United States*) in which a man accused of murder wanted to bring evidence from a *polygraph* (lie detector) test (which I discuss in Chapter 8) to show he was telling the truth. But the court didn't allow that evidence to be presented. The ruling in that case on the inadmissibility of the polygraph evidence became the formal statement of what constitutes expert evidence:

The rule is that the opinions of experts or skilled witnesses are admissible in evidence in those cases in which the matter of inquiry is such that inexperienced persons are unlikely to prove capable of forming a correct judgment upon it, for the reason that the subject matter so far partakes of a science, art, or trade as to require a previous habit or experience or study in it, in order to acquire a knowledge of it. When the question involved does not lie within the range of common experience or common knowledge, but requires special experience or special knowledge, then the opinions of witnesses skilled in that particular science, art, or trade to which the question relates are admissible in evidence.

One curious aspect of this clarification is that the expert under this ruling needs no special qualifications to offer an opinion, just experience or knowledge not normally available to other people. This means, for example, that in the US a police officer who has arrested many people for the possession of drugs can offer an opinion on whether the quantity of drugs found on a particular person is likely to be only for personal use or to be offered for sale, making the person likely to be a supplier rather than just a user.

In some countries, the requirement for being an expert for the court is much stricter. In France and the Netherlands, for instance, experts are usually on a registered list.

But how is the new expertise that comes along to be evaluated, such as the polygraph in the Frye case in 1923? Well, the judge in that case was clear about the need to determine the soundness of the expertise. He said:

Just when a scientific principle or discovery crosses the line between the experimental and demonstrable stages is difficult to define. Somewhere in this twilight zone, the evidential force of the principle must be recognized, and while courts will go a long way in admitting expert testimony deduced from a well-recognized scientific principle or discovery, the thing from which the deduction is made must be sufficiently established to have gained general acceptance in the particular field in which it belongs.

In other words, no newfangled idea is to be allowed as evidence just because someone claims it works. Only when the scientific community, from which that sort of evidence comes, generally accepts the statements being claimed does the court allow it. The polygraph has never reached that acceptable standard. In general it isn't allowed as evidence in court. In rare cases in the US, both parties may agree beforehand to admit polygraph results, though judges can still reject them. In rare cases in the UK, it has been allowed to support other evidence.

This *Frye Standard* still holds in some US states, but overall, it was regarded as too restrictive, and so a different standard for judging whether expert evidence was acceptable was introduced following the case of *Daubert v. Merrill Dow Pharmaceuticals Inc.*

In 1993, Jason Daubert claimed that the birth defects he was born with had been caused by the chemical Bendectin, sold by Merrell Dow. He brought evidence from laboratory and animal studies to support his claim. His evidence was challenged as not being generally accepted by the relevant scientific community, but in the course of a complicated legal process, the US Supreme Court determined that the original Frye Standard was no longer the law and that the crucial issue was this:

If scientific, technical, or other specialized knowledge will assist the trier of fact to understand the evidence or to determine a fact in issue, a witness qualified as an expert by knowledge, skill, experience, training, or education, may testify thereto in the form of an opinion or otherwise.

This statement changed the rules and led to Daubert's evidence being admissible. Now what mattered was whether the person giving evidence was expert enough, not the general acceptance in the scientific community of the procedure being drawn on. In the curious way of the law, the effect was to make the judge the person who determines whether evidence is sound enough to be acceptable, instead of the scientific community from which the expert comes.

The Daubert ruling seems less stringent than the Frye Standard, and you'd expect courts to be more open to developments in science that aren't yet established enough to gain general acceptance by the scientific community. In many court cases, the judge reviews the proposed expert evidence and decides whether to admit it. Rather than open the floodgates to all sorts of novel scientific discoveries, however, the indications are that judges have become more conservative since Daubert. Few judges want to be the first to allow a new form of evidence that may later be shown to be rubbish! But some judges are willing to accept new evidence, which is why expertise may be accepted in some courts but not in others.

UK approaches

In contrast to the US system of an overarching set of guidelines, the UK courts rely much more on what happened in previous cases, often known as *precedent* (although, of course, rules of evidence and other frameworks can be drawn on). In general, UK courts are much more cautious about what's allowed as expert evidence than in the US, which is why many forms of evidence (notably, the syndrome evidence I discuss in Chapter 12) are much more likely to emerge in a US court first, long before it sees the light of day in the UK.

In Britain, a judge determines whether any expert is allowed to give evidence and draws on their personal understanding of the expertise involved. As far as psychology is concerned, this tends toward acceptance of views that appear to have strong medical roots. So a psychiatrist claiming that psychopathy (examined in Chapter 4) is a medical condition over which the defendant has no control, and therefore the person needs to be regarded as a patient rather than a criminal, probably gets a hearing from the judge. A psychologist proposing that a person can plan suicide without indicating this intention to anyone is far less likely to be listened to, because there is no medical basis to the opinion.

Appearing as an expert in civil proceedings

Many courts don't operate in as formal a way as criminal courts and other legal settings that deal with crimes from burglary to murder. Civil courts often operate as if they're informal courts and not bound by the same legal constraints. They can deal with a great mix of matters, including the following types of cases:

» Child custody

» Contract challenges

» Divorce

» Personal injury compensation

>> Professional negligence

>> Sexual harassment

>> Unfair dismissal

**REGIONAL
TIP-OFF**

In some US states — notably, Oregon — a need exists to determine whether a person has the mental competence to request assistance in hastening their own death. Increasingly, psychologists are active in providing guidance to such proceedings, although recent legislation in the UK only allows medical doctors to provide such guidance. In this section, I mention some of the issues that distinguish this sort of expert evidence.

REMEMBER

One crucial point is that, whereas in most criminal cases the defendant has to be found guilty *beyond all reasonable doubt*, in civil proceedings the burden of proof is much weaker, often phrased as *on the balance of probabilities*. Therefore, a much wider range of expertise is allowed into these legal deliberations.

Another important aspect of noncriminal proceedings is that the people to whom the psychologist's evidence relates are likely to be rather different from the run-of-the-mill criminals seen in most criminal courts. Youngsters, or *juveniles*, as they're known in legal parlance, are often dealt with in a much more informal context, as are children who are at the heart of child custody hearings. The psychologist, therefore, has to guide the court on such sensitive and complex matters as relationships between parents and children or how amenable a youngster is to rehabilitation.

These varied forms of consultation to civil courts make special demands on forensic psychologists that aren't nearly so apparent in criminal proceedings:

>> Care must be taken in how an individual is labeled, because this can become part of their file and can shape their life as well as how the justice system deals with them. Labeling someone with conditions such as autism and Asperger's syndrome (I consider the assessment of young offenders in Chapter 5), for instance, can give all the wrong signals and blight what a person can do for many years to come.

>> The expert has to be willing and knowledgeable not only about the problem a person has that led them to the court but also what can be done about it. Informing those present of the approaches and treatments available can be more important than assigning any diagnostic label.

>> Relationships between people, such as children and their parents or youngsters and their lawyers, are often an important part of the psychologist's

assessment. This is much more difficult to evaluate than the mental state of an individual. It requires skills in relating to people and enabling them to be honest with you that aren't so crucial in many criminal cases.

>> Often, much more heated emotion is associated with the proceedings, especially in child custody litigation. The psychologist may be vulnerable to challenges about ethics or expertise arising from the intense passions involved.

Keeping Your Lips Sealed: What an Expert Can't Comment On

As I explain in the preceding sections (possibly at more length than you expect), much legal debate exists about who's an expert and what can be allowed as expert evidence. Of course, the expertise must be relevant to the case in question, but additional constraints surround this issue that you need to understand if you're to appreciate how some psychological expertise gets into court and some doesn't.

Staying within your level of competence

Although some people may like to present themselves as all-knowing authorities on many matters (you see them on TV, and hear them in podcasts often enough), professional humility is crucial for a forensic psychology expert witness to be effective in court and avoid committing perjury or even contempt of court. Experts have to stay within their area of expertise.

This fact may seem obvious, but remember that the person deciding who a court accepts as an expert (and what that expertise is to cover) isn't a professional in the area in question but in the law — that is, a judge or magistrate. The court therefore often relies on experts themselves to indicate when they're being asked to comment on a topic outside their competence level.

For example, an expert on the use of language (whom I mention in Chapter 8) was asked to offer an opinion on the probability of a particular form of words being used. But although the expert knew about language, he didn't know much about statistics and how to calculate probabilities.

A CASE OF GETTING HIS NUMBERS WRONG

ANECDOTE

When standing in the witness box, experts can be tempted to offer an opinion on something outside their area of expertise, such as providing a statistical calculation.

In 1999, Sally Clark was convicted of the murder of her two children. The expert testimony from Sir Roy Meadows was crucial in her conviction. Sir Roy was a highly respected British pediatrician who had testified in more than 300 cases relating to children's illness and death. The defense claimed that the children died from "cot death," or *sudden infant death syndrome* (SIDS). But Sir Roy gave evidence that the chances of two children dying from SIDS in one family were 75 million to 1.

To come to this figure, he'd multiplied the probability of one child dying from SIDS by the chances of another child dying. This calculation, however, contained a basic error of which the court was unaware, but which the Royal Statistical Society demonstrated for Sally Clark's later appeal. The statistical experts looked at a variety of cases in which more than one cot death had been experienced by a family and showed that, sadly, Sir Roy's assumption when calculating the probability that the two cases were totally unrelated wasn't valid.

It's illogical to just multiply the probabilities of the combination of two events occurring when some potential link exists between them. For example, you may see a bald man in a red sports car and, from knowing the probability of bald men and the probability of red sports cars, simply multiply these probabilities to find out how rare the combination is. But if bald men like to buy red sports cars, the combination will be far more frequent.

The statisticians calculated that the chances of two such terrible deaths happening in one family were closer to 100 to 1, probably because of some genetic aspect to the deaths. The appeals court concluded that if the jury had received that information, they may not have found Sally guilty. She won her appeal.

Avoiding the ultimate question

Psychology experts in court must avoid answering what lawyers call *the ultimate question*: whether the defendant is innocent or guilty. The expert is likely to have formed an opinion on this point but get their knuckles rapped by the judge if they drift into offering such an opinion. In some cases, expert testimony may not be allowed into the court simply because it's seen as veering too close to offering a decision that is the court's prerogative.

Sometimes, the expert opinion may not seem to do the court's work for it, but in reality it does. The most obvious example is when the expert offers an opinion on whether a key witness may be lying or may not have the memories claimed. Although the opinion isn't directly commenting on guilt or innocence, the implication of the opinion is so clear that it would sway the court too much.

REMEMBER

Judges generally prefer to form their own opinions about whether a person is telling the truth and encourage the jury to do the same rather than rely on an expert opinion.

Remaining unprejudiced

As mentioned in the earlier section "Being called as an expert in criminal proceedings," judges are always concerned that expert evidence may prejudice the jury to assume the defendant is guilty, even though that evidence doesn't deal directly with the facts of the case. This is particularly problematic for many aspects of psychological evidence.

ANECDOTE

I once gave evidence for a defendant who was accused of rape and murder. He made clear to me that he was "a stud." He claimed he regularly picked up women from a local nightclub and had consenting sex with them, so he had no reason to rape anyone. This admission seemed important evidence to present to a jury, but his lawyers believed (correctly, I'm sure) that the account of such a promiscuous existence would lead the jury to see the defendant as an unsavory character and assume that if he could behave like that, he was capable of rape as well. As it happens, the jury would've been right. He eventually confessed to the rape.

Detailing the Dangers: Ensuring Trial by Jury and Not Trial by Expert

When considering the legal context of giving expert evidence, forensic psychologist witnesses need to remember that they're unprejudiced advisers to the court. Crucially, it isn't their job to support the case for the defense or the prosecution, even though they're likely to have been appointed by one or the other and probably remunerated by them. This situation can often be a challenging requirement.

ANECDOTE

An experienced forensic psychologist once told me about a case in which, although he wasn't sure whether the person he'd examined was guilty. He was certain that the individual was a dangerous man and should be locked up for a long time. Fortunately, he didn't say this in court because he'd have gotten into serious trouble.

Most legal systems are aware of the overly influential nature that an expert's testimony can bring to the court's decisions and, as I explain in the earlier section

"Being called as an expert in criminal proceedings," go to some trouble to try to neutralize that opinion. Often, this requires disallowing evidence that the expert thinks is exactly what the jury needs to know. This problem is particularly significant in much forensic psychology evidence.

Unlike the evaluation of physical evidence, such as a blood sample or a fingerprint, psychologists are never dealing with a distinctly separate aspect of an individual. No matter how hard you try to divide up a person and only deal with a particular aspect of their mental state, you're always commenting in a way that's relevant to the person as a whole.

Therefore, a jury can take even the most limited comment on the characteristics of an individual as indicating something important that spills over into other deliberations. A defendant, for example, may be a good worker and highly intelligent, but if the forensic psychologist lets slip that the person has psychopathic tendencies, the court may reinterpret many aspects of the defendant's activities in that light and in a negative way.

A major reason for the caution is the undue influence that expert testimony may have over the jury. Many jurors may be in a daunting courtroom for the first time, and reaching a decision about guilt or innocence can make people anxious. If an assured, articulate, authoritative person confidently presents information to the court that implies guilt on the basis of their expertise, especially if that expertise is rather difficult to fathom and seems to come from the particular genius of that expert, many jurors may accept that expert's opinion rather than worry about working out their own. At least, courts believe this can happen, hence their caution.

Accepting the restrictions of being an expert in court

The potential significance of a forensic psychologist's expert testimony was brought home to me by a prisoner I spoke to, who told me that he avoided psychologists like the plague. His reason was understandable. From his point of view, a psychologist could form an opinion about him and his actions, but he would have no possibility of influencing that opinion. He may have determined to give up any future criminal activity and lead a totally honest life, but if the psychologist formed a view that this stated intention was all window dressing and that the man was inherently criminal, he'd have extreme difficulty in challenging that opinion.

The problem for the psychologist is compounded by the fact that they're not investigators and so may have great difficulty gathering all the details of a case. If called in by the defense, for example, information that doesn't support the defense case may not be given to the psychologist.

THE FRUSTRATIONS OF A NEED-TO-KNOW BASIS

In one case, I was asked to assess the written material of a man who was accused of killing his wife. I wanted to talk to him in person to get to understand more of his way of thinking, but because the prosecution had called me in, the defense wouldn't allow me to talk to him.

From the other side, when called in by the defense in a suspicious suicide, I wasn't allowed to interview prosecution witnesses who knew the deceased, and who may have helped me understand the victim's mental state. By denying me that access, the prosecution made sure that my opinion wouldn't be put before the jury, because I didn't have all the facts.

REMEMBER

Experienced forensic psychology experts learn to discover what may be hidden from them and seek ways of obtaining all the crucial information.

In my early days providing expert testimony, I naïvely assumed that everything would be laid out before me. That I'd be able to offer the court an opinion on anything I thought I was competent to comment on. I soon realized after just a few cases that the rules of legal proceedings are somewhat different from those that guide academic research. The expert in court isn't playing by the same rules they would in other areas of professional life. Experienced experts find ways of using the court process to get their message across, as I eventually did. Less experienced ones may be bamboozled by the legal process. Not all experts are the same. If you're seeking an expert to provide evidence on your behalf, the expert you end up with can be crucial. You don't always get the expert you deserve.

Criticizing the role of forensic psychology experts in court

Some people have raised the following criticisms about the use of forensic psychologists as experts in court:

>> Their opinions are so powerful that they inappropriately dominate the legal proceedings.

>> They can offer opinions on the ultimate issue, something that the court should determine.

>> They're biased by the financial incentives of giving evidence (experts are paid for their time, often quite handsomely).

>> They may have professional relationships with defendants or witnesses that are external to the court process — for example, via therapy or consultancy.

>> They're under pressure from the lawyers to offer evidence that suits their side of the case.

>> They can fall into the trap of competing with an opposing expert and so overstate their case.

>> They may display a lack of awareness of sources of bias in the evidence.

2
Examining the Criminal Mind

Central to the day-to-day work of many forensic psychologists is the assessment of defendants and offenders. At the heart of this assessment is understanding what causes criminality. This process involves discerning why people commit crimes.

On that basis, a variety of assessments have been developed to help provide guidance on how to deal with offenders in various contexts. This may be, for example, to see whether they're mentally fit to stand trial or to determine the risk of their reoffending if they're let out of prison. Deciding whether a person is a psychopath is another example of such assessments. Over the years, a variety of standard procedures, often called *psychological tests* or *psychological instruments*, have been developed to ensure that the assessments are as objective as possible. To understand what forensic psychologists contribute to assessment, it's useful to understand how these measuring instruments are created. In this part, I describe the basics of building psychological assessments and give some examples of what they consist of and the ways in which they're used. One central challenge is understanding the criminals' thought processes.

Chapter **4**

Why Do People Become Criminals?

When I first ventured into a prison (with a colleague who worked there, to interview some inmates, I hasten to add), I was struck by the fact that my colleague stored in a special leather pouch all her keys for unlocking various doors. The idea was to foil the clever prisoner who might note a key dangling from a belt and memorize it and then secretly set about making a copy to aid their escape. It's a highly unlikely scenario, but even so, a picture flashed through my mind of the dangling key and a brilliantly demonic criminal who needed to be second-guessed at every turn.

Forensic psychology doesn't focus on this sort of offender, for the simple reason that you so rarely meet them in real life. In this chapter, I look at the different sorts of *real* people who become criminals and then offer reasons that offenders get that way. I show the limitations of the overly simplistic nature-or-nurture debate and suggest that much more is involved when people become offenders than how their genes fit or whether they love their mothers. A particularly important aspect of someone becoming an offender is the difference between personality disorders and mental illness and how both relate, or don't. Of course, not everyone turns to a life of crime, so I also talk about what stops the majority of people, or even those with criminal backgrounds, from breaking the law.

Are Criminals Just Evil?

The easy explanation for criminality, which dates back centuries, is that criminals are possessed by some malign force that makes them evil. Many assumptions are clear in this assertion — first, that all criminals are the same. As clearly stated throughout this book, criminals are as different from one another as all the rest of us are. Another assumption is that a single destructive force creates all criminals. Again, it's clear in this chapter and others that this is not the case. Of course, the other assumption can be thought of as religious or spiritual: This is the assumption, prevalent in many cultures, that leads to painful procedures to drive out whatever kind of devil people believe in. No evidence exists that these tortures had any more effect than killing or, at best, severely maiming the victim. One further challenge is that the assumption of criminals being driven by a force beyond themselves ignores human agency. It doesn't recognize the choices people make and their personal responsibility for their acts.

I have to admit, though, that, stripped of the idea that some crimes are created by a person being possessed by a devil, some crimes are so inhuman, depraved, and devoid of feeling that describing them as evil seems a reasonable way of characterizing them. Sadly, these are too often crimes committed by world leaders.

Getting the nature-versus-nurture debate out of the way

One apparently simple explanation for criminality derives from asking whether it's caused by a person's biological makeup — their *nature* — or something to do with their circumstances, especially their upbringing — or *nurture*. The question assumes that these are two independent processes. Yet a moment's thought demonstrates that they're inextricably entwined.

Consider one clear example. A person who isn't very bright finds themselves in a poorly run school, and nothing is done to help them. They grow bored and drop out of formal education. The dropout finds that the only way to get on in the world, survive financially, and get some feeling of self-worth is to join a criminal gang. In another context, the same person may find a teacher who recognizes some particular skills they have and encourages a pathway to success.

As a social psychologist, I personally put more weight on upbringing, experience, and culture than on any innate characteristics — these are the dominant causes of the great majority of criminality. Some individuals, who are extremely impulsive and violent likely would always have ended up criminals, no matter what they experienced. But I think they are rare indeed.

Later in this chapter, in the section "Defining Criminals and Crimes," I talk about how various legal systems define crime differently and the many different sorts of crimes that exist, from impulsive and violent crimes to crimes requiring intelligent planning in order to avoid violence. Some criminals may work alone. Some criminals operate in a group. Therefore, stating a general cause for criminality that holds true around the world and that gives rise to many different types of crime is impossible.

Giving birth to criminals

The causes of crime lie partly in inherited characteristics and partly in upbringing and circumstances. Both aspects of a person can combine to produce an offender. For example, consider someone with little intellectual ability, for whom school is one big turnoff, who finds more interest and excitement in mixing with their older siblings who are already committing crimes. Is it nature or nurture that makes that person a criminal?

More likely, some general personality characteristics — such as impulsivity, low intelligence, and the desire for excitement — open up the social pathways that can lead to becoming a criminal. Tendencies such as seeking excitement can also be channeled into more productive activities, such as sports (although sporting activities also need factors such as self-discipline and hard work). Similarly, plenty of capable, resourceful people grow up in a criminal culture and become gang bosses when, in a different situation and having alternatives, they may well have become politicians (assuming that you accept the wide difference between the two occupations). Wanting money can play a part in someone being drawn into criminal activities. Crimes involving financial gain, especially theft, can be caused by financial need. However, the average burglar generally makes little money from a burglary (what is made from selling stolen goods is invariably only a fraction of the true value of the items). Many thieves see burglary as an exciting opportunity and not a carefully considered way of making money.

REMEMBER

Calculating the actual financial rewards of burglary is difficult. The opportunity exists for insurance claims to be distorted by the victim of a burglary exaggerating their claim (crime feeding on crime).

In contrast to burglary, a carefully planned identity theft is more likely to attract a criminal looking to acquire a steady income. The criminal needs no direct contact with the victim, who's more than likely in a different country. Such criminals typically care nothing about the victim's feelings. They may believe that if the victim is so vulnerable to the fraud, they deserve to have their money stolen.

Defining Criminals and Crimes

How do people become identified as criminals? They commit crimes! But that response begs the question of what's illegal. For example, in some countries today, as in many countries in the past, consensual homosexual activity is against the law, inviting imprisonment or even execution. Another example is the world of financial management, where acceptable business practices can vary significantly from one country to another. What is daily behavior in one country is considered fraud in another.

People are labeled as *criminals* because they break the law, not because of some inherent characteristics of the person.

Getting caught (or not)

Being labeled a criminal means getting caught and convicted of a crime. I'm always amused by the TV police drama where the story ends with the roll of dramatic music as the culprit gives himself away quite unintentionally during the police interview or in the way they tied the victim's shoelaces. Rarely does the storyline consider whether the evidence will stand up in a court of law, or whether a good defense attorney can show that the evidence means something quite different from what the detective claims.

EARLY IDEAS ABOUT IDENTIFYING CRIMINALS

Cesare Lombroso (1835–1909) was one of the first people in modern times to study criminals and criminality, and although many of his ideas are now discredited, he left a mark on how people think of criminals even today. Lombroso tried to identify what's distinct about criminals, and his efforts contributed to the (of course, wrong) idea that criminals are some sort of subspecies of society. He also claimed that criminals had distinct bodily features, being above or below average height and with "projecting ears, thick hair, thin beard, . . . enormous jaws, square and protruding chin, [and] large cheek bones . . ." Lombroso suggested that criminals were heavier than non-criminals or markedly lighter, pigeon-breasted, with an imperfectly developed chest and stooping shoulders. Criminals were also flat-footed! He even produced *Atlas of Criminal Types,* showing what a poisoner, for example, or an assassin looked like.

A few careful studies comparing non-criminals (university students) with criminals soon showed how mistaken Lombroso was. But the idea that criminals are of a certain type and can be characterized in obvious ways still hangs on, as is obvious every time a journalist asks the silly question, "Can you just tell me the typical profile of a serial killer/robber/rapist/fraudster?"

In real life, the situation is somewhat different. In most countries, statistics show that, of burglaries reported to the police, only one in every ten burglars is caught; and possibly as many as six of every ten burglaries aren't even reported. An even smaller proportion of rape allegations leads to a rapist being convicted. The figures for murders are more encouraging in that only a handful of every hundred murders remain unsolved, at least in most Western countries. (In the US, the proportion of unsolved murders is much higher.) This success often comes because the murderer is known to the victim and can be readily tracked down and may even confess. It's not unusual that it's the killer who calls the police and admits the crime.

Experts call unreported and unsolved crimes the *dark figure* of crime — a bit like dark matter in the universe that astrophysicists know exists but cannot see. These hidden crimes may be committed by the same people who commit unsolved crimes. Or they may be quite different. It's difficult to know, although the poor clearance rate for many crimes does suggest that those convicted are convicted for only a small proportion of their criminal activities.

The crucial point for understanding the psychology of criminality is that many explanations of crime are based on studies of convicted criminals. They can thus be distorted by the characteristics of the offenders whose crimes are reported. The fact is that not all criminals share these characteristics. No doubt some astute, capable people do turn to crime — like the Tom Ripley character in Patricia Highsmith's novels — and repeatedly get away with it. They're unlikely, therefore, to feature regularly in criminal psychology research.

REMEMBER

When studying the personality of criminals, experts usually deal with people who are convicted. The offenders have been caught and (typically) are in prison because that's where researchers can find them and ask them to fill in questionnaires or complete psychological tests. Therefore, psychologists can't always tell you what the characteristics are of every person committing a crime. They only know about those they have access to.

Actions that are deemed to be crimes, the sheer diversity of crimes, and who gets caught and convicted have significant implications for the forensic psychologist. Under the right circumstances, just about anyone can be labeled a criminal. In certain cultures, even committing adultery can result in someone being treated as a serious criminal. Yet that act is the basis of much Western fiction. Therefore, great care is needed when discussing the causes of criminality, because there are so many ways and reasons for a person to become designated as a criminal.

Careering toward criminality

Sometimes people refer to persistent offenders as *career criminals*. This term is misleading because it implies that a life of crime is similar, say, to working your way up in a legal organization. Films about the Mafia can give you the idea that members climb a ladder of criminality, like starting as an office boy running errands for the boss and ending up in charge of the whole mob. Although some highly organized criminal groups do exist (such as the Chinese triads), the vast majority of criminals experience nothing like a career.

A more useful way to think of career criminals is as persons living on ill-gotten gains. Such criminals have no legitimate way of earning a living. They devote themselves to crime in the same way as most people have conventional jobs. The term *criminal career* is therefore more usefully thought of as the range of crimes a person commits over an extended period.

You won't find a criminal starting off in a criminality training course, although prison can provide training in how to commit crimes as youngsters mix with more experienced offenders. Fortunately, there's no such thing as becoming junior management of a criminal gang and then being promoted to sales manager and eventually joining the board.

Identifying various forms of similar crimes

There's generally a difference between crimes involving the taking of property (*property crimes*) and those involving direct interaction with other people (*crimes against the person*). Although this separation is a helpful summary, try asking your friends whether arson is a property crime or a crime against the person, and the answers you hear are likely to show the limitations of the separation. You need to know much more about certain crimes before you can accurately place that crime into a category.

ARE CRIMINALS SPECIALISTS OR VERSATILE?

MYTH
BUSTER

Criminals aren't usually specialist offenders, choosing to concentrate on being a devious fraudster, an ax-wielding maniac, a cat burglar who climbs up drainpipes to enter a house, or a bank robber, for example. Studies show that the great majority of people (particularly youngsters) who commit enough crimes to end up in prison are pretty versatile. When I looked into the criminal backgrounds of convicted rapists, for example, I found that eight of every ten had previously been convicted of a nonviolent crime — notably, burglary (though the vast majority of burglars don't commit sexual assaults). Older criminals can be a bit more specialized, but even an experienced cat burglar doesn't climb up a drainpipe if the front door is left open.

Studies of criminals show that those willing to get involved in violent crime form a distinct subset of the general mass of offenders — some criminals simply have more aggressive and confrontational personalities. The majority of offenders, especially burglars, prefer not to take on the occupants of a house.

CRIMINAL CHARACTERISTICS

Criminals are a varied bunch of people (as discussed in more detail in Chapter 2), but research shows that some general characteristics are typical of the average criminal, no matter what the crime:

- They're most often men (about 80 per cent for most crime types).
- They're usually in their mid- to late teens.
- They come from dysfunctional family backgrounds.
- They have family or friends who've been convicted of crimes.
- They probably didn't do well in school.

Of course, plenty of convicted criminals don't have these characteristics (and they sometimes write their autobiographies, just to show how capable and misunderstood they are). People from good family backgrounds can end up as murderers or major fraudsters, but they're the exception rather than the rule.

Without a doubt, social, economic, political, and cultural influences affect the prevalence of crime, but, hey, I'm a forensic psychologist, and I want you to know about the factors relating to *characteristics* of individuals. To find out more about criminals and crimes, check out *Criminology For Dummies,* written by Steven Briggs (Wiley).

Committing a Crime: What Leads Someone to Break the Law

Stephen Sondheim's tongue-in-cheek lyric from that outstanding musical *West Side Story,* and used to such brilliant effect, seeks to boldly shift any blame squarely onto society for the seriously bad behavior of the youthful hooligans and delinquents. (The full lyrics are available at https://www.westsidestory.com/gee-officer-krupke.)

Sondheim enjoys sending up the argument so often put forward for excusing criminal behavior. But as with all explanations for crime, the fact that plenty of people from similar circumstances never become criminals exposes its flaws. In this section, I take a look at several of the suggested causes of crime and try to find out what gives rise to a person becoming a habitual criminal, committing one sort of crime after another over a few hours, days, or number of years.

REMEMBER

Almost anyone is capable of committing a crime in a given situation — and probably everyone does from time to time, like filching the colored paper from the office stationery cupboard to make party hats or driving over the speed limit. However, most people, most of the time, avoid doing anything seriously criminal. Even in quite difficult circumstances, when survival may depend on breaking the law, many people resist.

ANECDOTE

It's surprising how people act in an emergency, such as being caught in a building on fire. I've seen people put their lives in danger so as not to break the law. For example, when a fire alarm sounds in shops or a restaurant, and even with smoke visible, many people queue up or wait to pay their bill rather than just run for the exit.

Keeping bad company

Mixing with bad company can easily lead a person off the straight and narrow. The interesting question, though, is what leads some people into bad company in the first place?

Of course, some people are "born" into a life of crime. Family and close friends are criminals, so people discover how to be criminal as they grow up, whatever their own psychological makeup.

Crime movies are fond of depicting the dark underworld of the criminal community and the difficulty of quitting and becoming a law-abiding citizen. A type of moral code exists within the criminal community, but the code is a distortion of what's legally acceptable. The many countries in which corruption is endemic show clearly that what a community accepts can vary with what the law requires.

In some cases, certain aspects of personality may make a person more prone to accept the opportunities provided by criminal contacts. The person joins in because of the excitement or status a life of crime provides, when a more cautious person likely turns away. This is particularly true of young offenders, as I show in Chapter 17.

Abusing substances

Alcoholism and drug abuse are problems closely associated with criminals and crime, though neither condition is usually regarded as a form of mental illness and certainly isn't a defense in law. However, alcoholism and drug abuse can rapidly lead to crime, by encouraging these results:

>> Needing lots of money to feed the habit

>> Making the addict more impulsive, violent, or disinhibited

>> Bringing addicts into contact with criminals for the supply of the substances

HOW FEMALE OFFENDERS DIFFER FROM MALES

Statistics record that men commit eight out of every ten crimes. The crimes that women commit are generally different from those of men. Women commit far fewer violent crimes and are less likely to be involved in gang crimes or have long careers as criminals. If a woman commits a crime, it's more likely to be fraud of one sort or another, except of course for the illegal activity dominated by women — prostitution (although in this case, who ends up convicted of prostitution varies enormously depending on the local laws).

The criminal justice system tends to deal with convicted women differently from convicted men, with court decisions often more lenient for women. This leniency occurs sometimes because of the effect on a child of being separated from their mother while she's in prison, or even the assumption that women aren't inherently wicked and that certain exonerating circumstances can lower the severity of a woman's sentence. Not uncommonly, people assume that for a woman to commit a crime, she must be mentally disturbed, so she may receive a sentence that's regarded as a form of treatment. Courts accept a whole host of psychological conditions as explanations for a woman's illegal actions, which I talk about in Chapter 13.

Sometimes the leniency of the courts can be attributed only to a form of chivalry, with the judge taking pity on an apparently defenseless and seemingly harmless woman against the glowering, burly, tattooed man!

Not everyone addicted to alcohol or drugs becomes a criminal. If people who are addicted can afford to pay for drugs by legitimate means or because they have easy access — as with medical professionals — and manage their intake so that it doesn't interfere with work, they may never become a criminal other than in the act of purchasing illegal drugs. These addicts are more likely to destroy their relationships and health, becoming a social burden rather than a criminal.

REMEMBER

As well as alcoholism or drug addiction causing crime, the opposite may also be true: criminals becoming addicts. From the proceeds of crime, a criminal can afford to get hold of substances previously out of reach and, by mixing with addicted criminals, get drawn into addiction. Unfortunately, in some countries, drugs are easier to obtain in prison than outside, so a term inside can open the way to addiction.

Passing it on in the blood

Every now and then, a pundit comes up with yet another attempt to explain the causes of crime by citing some aspect of the criminals' biological or physiological makeup. These include

>> Brain damage or dysfunction

>> Genetic inheritance

>> Hormones, especially testosterone or low serotonin levels

>> Physical stature

Blaming Darwin

A curious idea that's sometimes aired is that an evolutionary advantage exists to many forms of crime, especially crimes against the person: Violent humans are more likely to survive and pass on their genes.

The claim is that when men in prehistory raped someone, that behavior increased the likelihood of offspring being conceived and born. This would strengthen the genetic availability of whatever genes made rape more likely in the first case. Some criminologists even claim that murder is part of the human evolutionary makeup because when limited food is available for hunter-gatherers or fertile women are scarce, killing off competitive males increases the chances of survival.

Fascinating though these evolutionary theories may be, they still don't explain away the most prevalent types of crime, burglary, and other forms of theft. I believe the evolutionary arguments to be amoral: pseudoscience dressed up in Darwinian clothes. Although evolution may have some general validity in terms of the prevalence of violence throughout human history, the theories never tell you why one sibling can be a murderer and another an upright citizen, nor why the great majority of people never commit violent crimes.

IT WASN'T THE SYNDROME THAT DID IT

Some men have an added X chromosome (XXY), known as *Klinefelter syndrome*. Although some males with this syndrome may appear slightly more effeminate and, sadly, may suffer from illnesses that are rare in men, no evidence exists that a person with this syndrome is more docile or less criminal than other men. Indeed, in one tragic case, a man with Klinefelter syndrome killed two children. They had been teasing him mercilessly because of his appearance, and he hit out at them more violently than intended, with disastrous consequences.

This idea of the Y chromosome causing aggressive behavior seems overly simplistic, but it didn't stop some experts of a biological turn of mind from getting excited when they discovered that some offenders were endowed with the additional Y chromosome. "Aha!" they shouted. "That explains why they're criminal — they're wearing unusual genes." When the excitement died down and serious research was carried out, researchers found that plenty of violent criminals had perfectly normal chromosomes and that most people with the XYY anomaly would never hurt a fly.

Investigating the case of the extra chromosome

Other biological influences that are argued to be the cause of criminality are the basic components of inheritance: chromosomes.

As you probably know, women have two X chromosomes (so named because they're X-shaped when viewed under a microscope), but men are different (glad you noticed). They are missing one of the X chromosomes and have a Y chromosome instead. Therefore, what makes men aggressive by nature is often assumed to be caused by the Y chromosome.

Thinking about crime

Psychologists are fond of the term *cognition*, which refers to a person's thought processes and includes how they think about themselves and others and the world around them. The particular way a person or group thinks is sometimes called a *cognitive style*, and some experts say that it's what gives rise to becoming a criminal. Studies of persistent criminals show that they often have a particular way of thinking about themselves and their crimes, as described here:

>> **Denial of criminality:** This is the direct statement that it didn't happen, or at least not as the victim claimed. For example, "She wanted sex — it was consensual" or, in many cases, simply, "I didn't kill her."

>> **Justification:** "It was them or me." This type of thinking is that the criminal owes it to their associates to show who's in charge, or even that they're entitled to take what they believe society owes them. An example is the excessive insurance claim, such as "The insurance companies are all scoundrels, and I've been paying my premiums for years without making any claims, so I have a right to get some money back from them."

>> **Hostile attribution bias:** For example, "Who are you looking at!" Many criminals seem highly sensitive to ambiguous comments or gestures that assume they're aggressive when no accusation of aggression is intended.

>> **Minimization:** "I didn't really hurt her." This thinking seeks to minimize the impact or severity of the crime.

ANECDOTE

A rape survivor told me that after she was attacked, and before the rapist climbed back out of the window of her apartment, he said to her: "You shouldn't have left your window open. Someone could've come in and attacked you," thus denying to himself that he had done anything wrong or had in any way injured or traumatized the survivor of his assault.

>> **Rationalization:** "Never give a sucker an even break." Rationalizing in this way shifts the blame onto the target because they were asking for the crime to happen — for example, by leaving a purse where anyone can take it.

>> **Personal narratives:** Another intriguing suggestion that's gaining in popularity is that criminals develop a personal narrative in which they see themselves as heroes or victims, professionals or adventurers. This way of thinking — which seems to mix aspects of self-denial and justification — allows them to maintain their criminal lifestyle.

The thought processes of people who commit crimes are revealed by what they say about their crimes and how they think about their actions. Those things tend to be along the lines of what people often say to themselves in lesser situations. For example, have you ever told yourself that your employer won't miss a couple of paper clips, and anyway, the company made a huge profit this year?

What makes these thought processes part of the cognitive style of criminals is the application of them to more extreme situations in which various denials can never be defended.

Getting personal with the personality of many criminals

Many criminals show a number of common personality traits as well as having shared thought processes (which I list in the earlier section "Thinking about crime").

Psychologists use the term *personality* specifically to describe the distinguishing characteristics of a person (not to be confused with a TV personality or a celebrity). In psychology, everyone has a personality that can be studied and assessed, like other characteristics I describe in Part 4.

REMEMBER

When talking about the personality traits of criminals, I'm referring to aspects of personality that everyone shares to some degree, but which in criminals are, on average, more exaggerated. For example, research shows that many criminals are more extrovert and neurotic than the law-abiding general population.

Here are some shared aspects of the personality of many criminals:

>> **External locus of control:** People differ in their thinking on whether fate rules their lives or whether they have control over what happens to them. Psychologists call that dominant influence on a person's life the *locus of control.* Research has identified criminals not taking responsibility for their actions as having an *external locus of control*, claiming that their actions are someone else's fault. The research results aren't clear-cut, however, because some criminals are the opposite and believe that they have a right to take what they want (that is, to create their own destiny). This belief is particularly true of another Hollywood favorite, the bank robber.

>> **Lack of empathy:** Some criminals lack the ability to feel what others are feeling. The consequences can be that the criminal doesn't realize the effects of their actions; for example, a burglar or rapist not realizing the trauma they are causing the victims. This concept is similar to *denial of criminality* (which I mention in the earlier section "Thinking about crime") except that lack of empathy is an aspect of personality rather than a thought process. The person is unable to appreciate what others are going through.

>> **Lack of self-control:** *Impulsivity*, or the reluctance to delay gratification, has often been associated with criminality, especially among younger offenders and drug users. But then again, lack of self-control doesn't apply to someone who spends months planning a bank robbery or a complex financial fraud.

>> **Search for excitement:** Do you thirst to go bungee jumping or racing fast cars? Do you prefer wild parties over staying at home and reading a book? Do you grow bored seeing the same old faces and would never dream of seeing the same film twice? If you answer yes to all these questions, you're a *sensation seeker* and possibly a risk taker, too. Many criminals are sensation seekers, especially the younger ones. They enjoy the excitement of committing the crime and getting away with it. When you think about it, the boredom of prison must be particularly punishing for the sensation seeker.

Such personality characteristics are present in people in all walks of life but do seem to be more common in criminals than in non-criminals.

Investigating Mental Disorder and Crime

Having a *mental disorder* is about how a person feels, thinks, or acts that reflects some abnormal distress or disability that's not part of normal development or usual within any given culture. (As mentioned, *personality* describes a normal range of ways of dealing with the world. I talk about personality characteristics typical of many criminals in the earlier section "Getting personal with the personality of many criminals.")

A mental disorder has one of two main forms:

>> **A mental illness in which the person's thoughts and feelings are deeply disturbed:** This can take on a milder form that's usually referred to as a *neurosis.* Conditions such as anxiety and depression, and many phobias, are all thought of as neurotic. A more extreme form of mental illness occurs when the person is out of contact with reality: They hear voices *(hallucinate)* and believe that people are trying to control their mind or even kill them. These are aspects of *psychosis,* considered in a little more detail later in this chapter.

>> **A personality disorder:** This means having an extreme type of personality that marks a person as not dealing with others in the way most people think of as normal or acceptable.

Here are a few examples to highlight the different forms:

>> A person who thinks that external issues, such as upbringing, shape life isn't in any way "disordered." That's just exhibiting an aspect of *personality*, like being an extrovert or a neurotic (see the earlier section "Getting personal with the personality of many criminals").

>> A person (like Daniel McNaughton, whom I mention in Chapter 1) who thinks that members of a political party want to destroy them and so tries to kill a leading member of that party is suffering from a *mental illness*. This person is likely to be regarded by the courts as insane and therefore not guilty by reason of insanity.

Note that *psychopathy* is a term applied to people who are impulsive and who lack empathy or self-control; some may jump quickly to violence. Or in a different form, the person may be superficially charming and ready to take advantage of another's weaknesses. I discuss the term in more detail in Chapter 5, when I look at how psychopathy can be assessed.

However, labels such as sadism, narcissism, and borderline personality disorder are used in court to explain why a person was unable to stop doing what they did, as though they have a disease.

REMEMBER

Having a personality disorder doesn't label someone as a potential criminal, but a higher proportion of people with a personality disorder are likely to get into trouble than people whose personalities aren't thought to be disordered.

In Chapter 5, I discuss how experts assess psychopathy and its implications for understanding criminality and the different types of personality disorders. For now, my aim is to help you wrap your mind around some of the major terms that come into play in this area. Also, try to clear your mind of the single-minded killer of the movies, who's completely devoid of any emotion and just wants to wander around killing people, more or less for the sake of it.

Sadism: Enjoying the urge to hurt

Sadism is a sexual preference in which consenting adults enjoy inflicting pain on one another. One party, a *masochist,* enjoys being hurt, and the other, a *sadist,* enjoys doing the hurting — hence the activity of sadomasochism. Although not my idea of fun, the activity is legal and practiced, given the opportunity for the masochist to say, "Enough is enough" and the other party, the sadist, to stop.

You have to be careful using the term *sadism* in a criminal sense. Consensual sado-masochism is rather different from the personality disorder clinically described as *sadism,* in which being cruel and demeaning to another person, humiliating them, and causing them suffering gives pleasure to the sadist. A person with sadistic personality disorder is likely to be fascinated by weapons and violence and find aggression toward others amusing. Although the term comes from the writings of the Marquis de Sade (who put forward the abuse of others as a philosophical argument, for which he was appropriately imprisoned), people with sadistic personality disorder don't dress their predilection in such abstract clothing.

Sadism arises when investigating the causes of serial killing, which often involves sexual attacks as well as killing, and the victim is killed so that they can't be a witness to the crime. These are different serial killers from those who are sadists in the true sense and enjoy hurting others.

Narcissism: Loving yourself

You may remember the Greek myth in which the beautiful youth Narcissus falls deeply in love with his own reflection in a pool and, after hopelessly trying time and again to get hold of his image, eventually pines away. The idea that someone is so in love with their own image that they shun all other relationships became known as narcissism, and such a person as *narcissistic.*

Experts have turned this useful, mildly disparaging word into a nasty clinical condition. Narcissism is now a recognized personality disorder that describes someone wholly preoccupied with success and hypersensitive to criticism and who feels self-important and entitled to admiration. At the extreme, a person who's narcissistic can be so furious with being ignored or their desires not being satisfied that they attack or rape to get what they think is their due.

Although the majority of those identified as having *narcissistic personality disorder* (NPD) are men, women may also exhibit this behavior. Women tend to reveal their narcissism rather differently from men. Their desire for admiration and preoccupation with their own worth is more likely to use feminine wiles, using sexuality to charm others rather than the more bombastic, hypersensitive style of male narcissism.

If you know someone like that and want a peaceful life, best not tell them that they have a personality disorder called narcissism!

Borderline personality disorder: Sitting on the fence

A *borderline personality disorder* (BPD) is the label given to someone who has unstable moods, experiences difficulty forming relationships, grows intensely angry with no obvious reason, and fears abandonment. A person with borderline personality disorder isn't obviously mentally ill. They often can cope reasonably well on a day-to-day basis. They are likely to be often unhappy because those around them aren't relating to them the way they want. For this reason, they may drift in and out of various criminal activities, violent and nonviolent, as a way of trying to cope with their emotional confusions.

Psychosis: Out of touch with reality

People who know that they're doing something wrong and are clearly in touch with reality are described in law as having *mens rea* (described in detail in Chapter 1). That means that when committing a crime, the criminal is fully aware that their actions are illegal. (Some professionals are unsure whether a person with a personality disorder does have *mens rea*, but that's an issue to be sorted out in court.)

The general public sometimes assumes that a person who commits a horrific crime for no obvious reason, and which is therefore mindless or pointless, must be out of touch with reality, insane, mad, or suffering from a mental illness.

Yet the most inexplicable of criminals — such as serial killers who appear to wander around, killing people more or less at random for no obvious reason — are rarely regarded in court as mentally ill and are therefore unfit to face a trial. This situation is difficult to understand until you realize that the courts' definition of mental illness is rather different and more specific than what the term means in everyday life. For most courts (as with the anecdote about Daniel McNaughton in Chapter 1), the 150-year-old idea that the person has to exhibit a disease of the mind to be declared criminally insane still exists. This section discusses what counts as insane in court.

Psychosis is the legally accepted mental illness that goes beyond the person feeling anxious, confused, depressed or sad. Broadly, the psychotic person must have at least one of these symptoms:

>> **Intense paranoia:** Believing that others, sometimes unknown and invisible, are seeking to hurt them and *disturb* them, and possibly even controlling their mind.

>> **Hallucinations:** Seeing or hearing things that don't exist and believing that they're present.

>> **Delusions:** Believing in some unlikely set of circumstances — most notably, that they are the prime minister or Napoleon (although the latter is unlikely because Napoleon has been dead a long time).

Although a person may experience some of the symptoms of psychosis some of the time, the symptoms are considered significant and part of an underlying illness only when they become extreme and/or deeply disturbing, such as having schizophrenia.

SORTING OUT JEKYLL FROM HYDE

MYTH BUSTER

The term *schizophrenia* is widely misused in day-to-day conversation to suggest a split personality, as illustrated in the famous novella *The Strange Case of Dr. Jekyll and Mr. Hyde,* by Robert Louis Stevenson, describing the character who was pleasant, civilized Dr. Jekyll by day and dangerous, destructive Mr. Hyde by night. *Schizophrenia* is a psychosis, which can be paranoid, hallucinatory, delusional, or any combination. Schizophrenia isn't *bipolar disorder*, in which the person has extreme mood swings, which used to be called *manic depressive psychosis*. The mood can swing from deep depression to hyperactive, irrationally optimistic behavior.

(continued)

(continued)

Multiple personality — in which a person behaves as a completely different person from one occasion to the next, each character apparently unaware of the other — is extremely rare. Its exotic and potentially dramatic nature, however, caused the few recorded occurrences to take on mythical properties, giving rise to books and films. Many experts are deeply suspicious of the phenomenon of multiple personality as a mental illness, especially when used as a defense in court.

If I had to place a psychiatric diagnosis on the main character in Stevenson's classic tale, it would be multiple personality.

REMEMBER

Extreme depression can also be a psychotic state. It's far more than just feeling quite sad. Severe depression can be associated with intense feelings of despair and lack of self-worth. It can even lead to being suicidal.

A form of mental illness that courts sometimes accept is *automatism*. Here the person acts automatically without being aware of what they're doing, such as what's commonly called *sleepwalking*. Automatism has been allowed as a defense in some challenging cases.

ANECDOTE

A former soldier claimed that he saw a man hurting a child, and it caused him to relive an experience in battle that moved him into involuntary automatic mode and killed the man.

A person who commits a crime whom the courts deem to be psychotic, not responsible for their actions, may be sent to a special institution that can manage, and possibly treat, the condition rather than send the person to prison. In general, psychoses such as schizophrenia aren't a major cause of crime. The mass media are ready to point out that a killer is schizophrenic, implying that's why the person acted violently, but they ignore the fact that the vast majority of people with a psychosis are much more of a danger to themselves than to anyone else. Although many people in prison have some form of mental illness, only a small percentage are suffering from a psychosis. That number may be higher than in the population at large, but who's to say that this isn't because of how people with psychosis are treated by the rest of society, instead of psychosis being a direct cause of crime.

The Dark Triad

Some psychologists suggest that there's a combination of characteristics of individuals that form a particularly manipulative personality style. It consists of a combination of two personality disorders already mentioned in this chapter:

narcissism and psychopathy. In addition, a third aspect of personality makes up what is known as the dark triad.

The third aspect is *Machiavellianism*, a concept named after the 15th century political commentator (and poet!) who wrote a book about how kings and princes could manipulate others. Some years ago, psychologists developed a test based on Machiavelli's writing. A score on this test was taken as an indication of a person's Machiavellian leanings. Machiavellianism as an aspect of personality is thus taken as an indication of the use of strategic manipulation, deceit, cynicism, and a focus on self-interest.

These three aspects of personality overlap, although they have distinctly different emphases. You can therefore easily see that anyone who has this toxic cocktail may be prone to antisocial and criminal activities.

Understanding Why Not Everyone Is a Criminal

Most of the population shuns a life of crime. Even in some social subgroups where criminals are widespread — and accepting that social and psychological factors may increase the risk of criminality — the great majority of people (including those from the most underprivileged communities) don't commit serious crimes. In this section, I take a look at why there aren't more criminals in society.

Perhaps you argue that most people don't commit crimes because they're afraid of being caught. Evidence exists that property crimes can be cut by making burglary and robbery more difficult to carry out and easier to detect, a topic I talk about in Chapter 11. Violent crime is more likely to be a product of the personality of the offender and the culture they're part of, including having some of the personality disorders I discuss in the section "Investigating Mental Disorder and Crime," earlier in this chapter. People who relate well to others and can control their temper, in a society where violence isn't tolerated, aren't likely to commit violent crimes.

Of course, most people are good citizens because they've been brought up to observe the law and so avoid committing crimes. However, some people out there committing crimes are never caught and charged. So, exactly what proportion of the community is likely to commit a crime in the knowledge that they can get away with it, despite knowing right from wrong, is an open question.

MYTH BUSTER

Just about every psychological aspect of criminality I talk about in this chapter is present to some degree in most of the population — and with the majority of people having been convicted of nothing more than a traffic offense.

Protective factors

Many factors can cause a person to become a criminal — the list is long. For a broader sociological perspective, get hold of *Criminology For Dummies*, by Steven Briggs (Wiley) where you can find out much more about the causes of crime, such as deprivation and class conflicts. Yet not everyone earmarked as a potential criminal turns out bad. Certain aspects of daily life — known as *protective factors* — help to cut the pernicious influences that can give rise to a person becoming a criminal:

>> **Close relationship with a family member:** Feeling alone in the world is an ingredient for believing that you don't need to accept society's restraints. A close relationship with a family member, or an admired teacher, provides roots in the community and the feeling of self-respect that can prevent someone from drifting into crime.

>> **Good educational environment:** A good education is the key to so much progress in a person's development, even for someone not brilliantly clever. Enjoying a level of educational attainment gives a person self-respect; the ability to express their own capabilities protects them from a life of crime. It also opens up opportunities to be successful without needing to offend.

>> **Job satisfaction:** Someone who likes their job is more likely to experience self-worth *and* less likely to want to risk losing that job by committing a crime.

>> **Positive relationships with non-criminals:** Beyond the satisfaction that comes from having good relationships with individual family members and teachers, or other mentors, being part of a group of law-abiding individuals is as much a barrier to criminality as being part of a criminal gang is a pathway into the underworld of crime (see the earlier section "Keeping bad company").

>> **Sociability:** If you get along well with other people and relate to them well, you feel confident in yourself and are more able to resist the temptations of bad company and undesirable behavior. Crime becomes less attractive as an option.

Of course, knowing right from wrong helps keep people on the straight and narrow. But that knowledge comes from the people you mix with and the models you learn from in your family.

Lacking the opportunity

Absence of opportunity is a good way to prevent a crime from being committed. One school of thought argues that society can tackle crime by using *target hardening*: reducing to a minimum the opportunities and possibilities for crime. Target hardening is about making a crime more difficult to carry out, such as having measures in place to make it harder to steal and defraud. I explore target hardening in more detail in Chapter 11.

Fearing being caught

Punishments for crime exist to deter people from committing the crime. But the punishment has power only if people think that they're going to get caught. Therefore, the effectiveness of law enforcement is important in stopping people from becoming criminals.

REMEMBER

When people commit crimes and get away with them, they develop criminal skills and are more likely to be on the path to a criminal career. Some people have similar characteristics to a criminal but direct these personal traits into more socially acceptable behaviors — for example, the hard-headed businessperson who takes advantage of others while having no feelings of guilt for the consequences. The suggestion has been widely canvassed that some people who are successful in the cutthroat world of big business are best thought of as *psychopaths* — people lacking in empathy who callously and without remorse insist on getting their own way. In other contexts, they would be dangerous, probably violent, criminals.

Aging: "I'm too old for all this!"

The good news is that aging can act as a deterrent to crime. At a certain stage in life, people feel that committing crimes simply isn't worth the effort. Crime is a young person's activity (see Figure 4-1). Physical prowess, risk-taking, and believing you can get away with it and not end up in prison is typical of young people, especially young men. It's a way of thinking not nearly so common in older people.

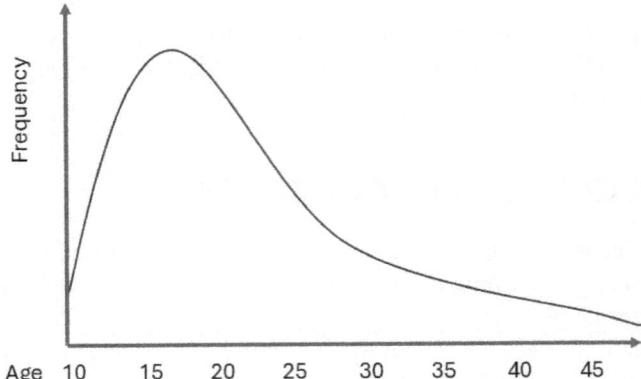

If people commit crime early in life and suffer the consequences, it's likely to cause them to want to put that experience behind them. A settled lifestyle with a spouse and children is often enough reason to avoid taking risks and avoid any possibility of doing time in prison.

Chapter **5**

Measuring, Testing, and Assessing the Psychology of Offenders

As part of their job, forensic psychologists often need to form a view of someone's psychology and personality — usually, a suspect or known offender — and guide that individual directly or advise others on how to deal with the person. Doing so requires forensic psychologists to be able to assess that individual — for example, the person's ability to understand the legal process well enough to participate effectively, or perhaps diagnosing particular mental or behavioral problems (with the associated implications for how the person should be dealt with and treated).

To accomplish this aim, forensic psychologists use measuring instruments (known generally as *psychological tests*) to assess clients. In this chapter, I describe some general psychological test methods, what areas they measure, and how to evaluate their effectiveness. The forms of assessment that I consider apply to the general population, but of course are relevant in forensic psychology because criminals are drawn from the general public. (For psychology assessment methods connected specifically to criminals, flip to Chapter 6.)

Introducing Psychological Measurement

People have been exploring ways of assessing psychological characteristics for over 150 years. These efforts produced a variety of psychological *measuring instruments* (assessment procedures, in other words). They are, in essence, standardized processes that have been carefully developed and evaluated to ensure that they give some consistently useful information. The idea is that any trained professionals who use these procedures will come up with more or less the same results. The procedures are hooked into an agreed set of ideas about what's being measured, an agreed theory or set of defined concepts, and how the psychology of the individual is revealed through the use of the particular instruments.

The tests used by psychologists to form an objective judgment of any person or group are more scientifically called *psychometric procedures* (from *psyche* for the mind and *metron* for measure). The best-known psychological tests are intelligence tests, which assess how a person's intelligence compares with that of people of a similar age, resulting in an *intelligence quotient* (IQ). (See the later section "Standardizing psychological tests" for more.)

Loads of other psychological tests exist, used with the general population, and can also be of value to legal proceedings, including assessment of various intellectual abilities, such as problem-solving, educational attainment, or particular cognitive skills such as logical reasoning. Some tests are specifically established to diagnose brain damage, such as that associated with Alzheimer's. Other tests measure various aspects of personality, such as styles of interpersonal interaction, extraversion/introversion, or ways of coping with stress.

REMEMBER

The central idea behind all psychological assessments is that the result they produce isn't biased by the assessor's particular way of seeing the world; in other words, the result of the assessment must be objective. This requirement is quite challenging and not always fully achieved, but the processes of assessment are constructed to be as free from personal bias as possible. After all, if two psychologists assess the IQ or personality of the same individual and come up with totally different answers, no one would have faith that what they're doing is scientific, objective, and therefore useful in any way.

In this chapter, I consider general psychological tests because criminals are members of the overall population, and understanding them requires knowing what sort of people they are, as it would be for anyone else. Therefore, to help offenders and understand more fully their circumstances, it's important to assess their general psychological characteristics. Intelligence level, personality, and any indications of mental disorder can all be crucial for determining the nature of a person's involvement in crime as well as how the law courts should treat them, as I discuss in more detail in Chapters 3 and 12.

Coming to Grips with Psychological Measurement Methods

Psychological tests take many different forms and aren't restricted to box-ticking questionnaires. The easiest way to think about the differences between various tests is in terms of what the respondents are asked to do. Are they just answering questions or being asked to complete a task? Is the psychologist listening to what they say or observing what they do? In this section, I describe just a few methods to give you more of an idea of what psychological assessment is like.

REMEMBER

Thousands of psychological assessment possibilities exist, and many major organizations are devoted to developing and selling them.

In Table 5-1, I give an overview of general psychological assessment procedures. (Procedures developed specifically for use with offenders are discussed in Chapter 6.)

TABLE 5-1	A Few Psychological Assessment Procedures
Projective procedures (see the later section "Saying what you see: Projective techniques"):	**Rorschach Inkblot Test:** Interpretation of accounts of what's seen in ambiguous images to indicate aspects of their subconscious mind.
	Thematic Apperception Test (TAT): Interpretation of stories told about ambiguous pictures to indicate the underlying needs and motivations that characterize a person.
	Szondi Test: A curious test in which the respondent indicates which drawing of a face is preferred. The drawings are of people with various mental illnesses and problems. The selection is meant to indicate the testee's mental state. This one isn't used much these days, but I mention it because of its novelty.

(continued)

TABLE 5-1 *(continued)*

Objective questionnaire-style tests (see the later section "Standardizing psychological tests"):	**Minnesota Multiphasic Personality Inventory (MMPI):** A wide-ranging exploration of personality, by answering whether nearly 600 questions about yourself are true or false.
	Millon Clinical Multiaxial Inventory (MCMI): An assessment of mental illness developed using people in psychiatric hospitals who already have diagnoses for mental problems.
	Personality Assessment Inventory (PAI): Consists of 344 questions developed to assess a person's problems in a way that can aid treatment planning; takes about an hour to complete.
Measures of intellect/cognition:	**Wechsler Adult Intelligence Scale (WAIS):** The standard test to measure intelligence. It has undergone many revisions and spawned many variants, including versions for special populations, such as children.
	Trail Making Tests A and B: A simple test to administer that assesses how quickly a person can carry out visual tasks such as joining up numbers in sequence; used to diagnose various forms of dementia.
	Luria-Nebraska Neurophysiological Battery: Consists of 269 items (that can take a couple of hours to complete) covering many aspects of brain functioning; used to assess the nature and extent of any brain damage.

Talking with people: Interview protocols

Sometimes the assessment takes the form of talking with the person to be assessed and listening carefully to their account of themselves and their experiences. Such interviews are more than informal chats, although, if done properly, the experience can feel like that to the person being interviewed. These interviews are usually based on a standard framework that's often called a *protocol*, which can be thought of as a fixed agenda for the meeting with the client.

The protocol varies according to the purpose of the assessment — for example, whether the person is being assessed for competence to stand trial or risk of future offending (as I discuss in Chapter 12) — but in general, the following issues are explored:

>> Early upbringing and family relationships

>> Education and educational achievement

>> Personal relationships, especially any intimate relationships

>> Work experience

>> Offending history

>> Any medical or psychiatric history of relevance

Much of the gleaned information relies on a personal account from the interviewee, which is open to bias and can be self-serving, especially if the answers are directly relevant to the charges against a defendant. The possibility of malingering also exists (a topic I cover in Chapter 8). The forensic psychologist therefore tries to validate the related information against any available records, such as medical or prison or earlier police reports. In serious cases, the psychologist may also interview the defendant's family and associates. They, of course, function as essential informants if the focus of the interview is deceased (such as when determining the cause of an apparent suicide), a procedure known as a *psychological autopsy* (turn to Chapter 12 for more info on this process).

As well as listening to the verbal answers, the psychologist carefully observes the way the respondent behaves in the interview because doing so can reveal aspects of the person's way of dealing with other people (and offer indicators of deception, as I mention in Chapter 8).

REMEMBER

The open nature of interviews is vulnerable to distortion by an offender wanting to hide personal aspects, or to bias by the interviewer in interpreting what's said. For this reason, many psychologists prefer to use more structured procedures, such as the ones I discuss in the following three sections.

Saying what you see: Projective techniques

Projective techniques have their origins in Freudian ideas of the unconscious and consist of presenting ambiguous images for the client to interpret. The idea is that when people interpret such images, they project onto them their unconscious desires and feelings, and so they reveal aspects of themselves that they may be trying to hide or are even unaware of.

The *Rorschach inkblot test* is the best-known projective test: a standard set of symmetrical smudges, initially produced by folding an inkblot into a piece of paper. Respondents have to describe what they see in the ambiguous image. Some of the blots are monochrome; others, colored. The psychologist carefully records everything that's said. This record is analyzed by considering which part of the blot was mentioned, any themes in what the respondent described seeing, and any references to colors or movement in the image.

STRANGE BUT TRUE

FINDING MEANING IN BLOTS

The Rorschach inkblot test (and no, not everyone sees a butterfly) has its origins in the parlor game of Blotto, which was popular over a hundred years ago. The game consists of giving meaning to indeterminate smudged blots, providing a hilarious evening of entertainment in the days before TV game shows.

Another commonly used projective procedure is the *Thematic Apperception Test* (TAT), in which a set of ambiguous pictures is presented and the respondent is asked to tell a story that each picture illustrates. The pictures may include, for example, a young man sitting on a bed with a woman sitting on the other side of the bed with her back to him, or a young boy on his own with a violin. The themes of the stories created are considered in relation to what they reveal about the needs or desires of the respondent. For example, are the man and woman described as just having had riotous sex, or as a couple who've been married for many years and no longer talk to each other? Is the boy described as aspiring to become a concert soloist or as being sad because he can never afford his own violin?

In all projective techniques, the idea is that respondents reveal something about their unconscious or hidden desires and thoughts by way of how they interpret the images. Detailed scoring procedures analyze the responses. A simplified example is that someone describing sex and violence in the images may be thought to be revealing the significance of this aspect in their life. By contrast, a person building an interpretation around future aspirations may be assumed to have a mature and forward-looking approach to life.

REMEMBER

Many challenges exist to the scientific value of projective techniques. The problem is that if the test is assessing unconscious aspects of the individuals, which they may not even be aware of themselves, what suitable external criteria are available to test the test? The issues that the tester claims are being revealed may never become manifest because, after all, they're unconscious. An ensuing problem is how anyone can know whether the test is revealing anything other than the tester's speculations about the person being tested.

Even more challenging is deciding which aspects of the answers to use to generate a sense of what the responses mean. When the given response is open-ended, such as telling a TAT story or interpreting an inkblot, a real possibility exists that different testers (or even the same tester on different occasions) may identify different aspects of the comments as being important. For example, should the tester give emphasis to the specific part of the inkblot that's mentioned (for example, the movement or color) or focus on the content of the meaning? In addition, with what population or sample should the responses be compared to determine whether they're unusual or significant?

Despite these problems, the Rorschach inkblot test is still popular and used widely to give court assessments. Psychologists like the idea that an offender can't know what answers are expected and that any extreme attempts to distort the responses may well be detectable. Also, the American psychologist John E. Exner claims to have developed a procedure to overcome challenges to the subjective nature of the Rorschach by providing a precise process for interpreting responses that's supported by computing technology. A major weakness in this more precise approach, though, is that not every tester follows it, and so courts may be ignorant of the consequences of such negligence on the part of the tester.

ANECDOTE

As part of my training as a psychologist, I was required to carry out a Rorschach test with a friend. I wrote down everything my friend said and took those notes to a Rorschach expert. He immediately spotted that my friend was intelligent (after there were pages of notes, all quite inventive) and described his psychology. When I told my friend what the expert had said, he was surprised at how much he agreed with it.

Assessing intelligence and skills through performance on tasks

Intelligence tests require respondents to complete a number of tasks, usually examining aspects such as verbal skills, mathematical skills, and spatial skills. Their distinct quality is that firm right or wrong answers are involved. Respondents can be assessed on the number of correct answers they give in each area being tested, in turn allowing the comparison of intelligence across each of the areas. If a great disparity results, for example, showing great verbal ability but poor spatial ability, it may indicate some neurological problem, disturbances in educational background, or another aspect of the person that requires more intensive examination.

REMEMBER

Psychologists can use simple forms of intelligence tests to estimate brain damage and intellectual competence. Even discovering whether a person has a clear idea of the date, day, and time can be a useful indicator, especially if the test is combined with simple arithmetic tasks such as subtracting, say, seven from a series of numbers.

Short-term memory is also a useful pointer to severe mental problems, and psychologists can test for this problem by mentioning three objects and then asking a few minutes later what they were. Psychologists can also incorporate motor movements into such assessments, such as those that were once used to test how drunk a driver was before breathalyzers became common — for example, touching the nose with a finger or grabbing the left ear with the right hand. (Close your eyes and try these tasks yourself after a few drinks!)

Many psychologists carry with them specially designed blocks of different shapes and colors and other test equipment, such as components of pictures, which are parts of standard testing procedures. These kits have been developed to explore particular aspects of a person's abilities and are often used in conjunction with neurological measurements such as brain scans.

Standardizing psychological tests

The most structured and rigid of psychological assessment methods are known as *standardized* tests, in which the standardization process consists of having the test completed initially by hundreds of people, sometimes thousands, in order to create a starting point for comparison. Their responses are then analyzed in relation to each other and to other external criteria.

The classic illustration is the development of IQ tests. The number of correct answers given by children of each age is calculated so that any given child can be compared with others of the same age. To make a child's score on the test easily interpretable, the average score for each age group is set at 100 so that a score of 59 (as in Daryl Atkins's case, which I describe in the nearby sidebar) can be seen as far below average. The statistics allow the precise calculation that less than 1 in 100 of the population has an IQ of 59 or below. A value this low has been found to be typical of people who can't truly take advantage of most schooling and are generally regarded as unable to make much sense of what goes on around them. (I talk more about IQs in the later section "Achieving precision: The need for norms.")

Standardized measuring instruments provide the backbone to a great deal of forensic psychology activity, not least because the courts are more comfortable with a view based on a standard procedure that many professionals agree is appropriate. Tests also provide a standardized framework for describing a person, thus making the preparation of a report much easier than searching afresh for relevant and appropriate terms.

A standardized psychological test widely used in the forensic context, especially in the US, is the Minnesota Multiphasic Personality Inventory (MMPI). This test comes in a number of versions, but the standard form consists of 567 statements, which respondents have to determine are true or false in regard to themselves. The MMPI takes between 60 and 90 minutes to complete and features statements such as these:

>> My daily life is full of things that keep me engrossed.

>> There often seems to be a lump in my throat.

>> I enjoy detective stories.

>> Once in a while, I think of things too bad to speak about.

>> My sex life is pleasing.

TAKING IQ INTO ACCOUNT

This case illustrates the highly significant role that a psychological assessment of the defendant can play (whether a person lives or dies), as well as the ethical and professional challenges faced by any psychologist giving evidence in court (expert evidence is given to assist the court in its decision, whether or not the expert agrees with that decision).

In August 1996, Daryl Atkins was sentenced to death in the state of Virginia for shooting Eric Nesbitt as part of a robbery. Before the death sentence was carried out, a psychologist who assessed Atkins determined that he had an IQ of 59. This result categorized him in the UK as learning-disabled. This result was used as the basis for an appeal under the Eighth Amendment to the American Constitution, which disallows punishment that is "cruel and unusual." The Supreme Court upheld this appeal and accepted that people with such low IQs aren't mentally capable enough to be executed.

Forensic psychologists then apply a complex and highly developed scoring system to the answers in order to indicate a wide range of potential problems the person may have, including schizophrenia, hypochondria, depression, and the sort of psychopathy (described in Chapter 6) that relates to disrespect for society's rules.

The test also includes measures of whether the respondent is faking good or faking bad, or generally lying, but as with all attempts to tell how honest respondents are being, considerable debate remains about the validity of these measures. The MMPI's detailed range of questions is probably one reason it's so often used as the basis for forensic evidence, despite continuing debate on its effectiveness.

Identifying the Different Aspects That Measurement Methods Assess

In this section, I look at the different areas of psychological functioning that the methods from the earlier section "Coming to Grips with Psychological Measurement Methods" typically assess. Most of the methods can investigate all the following areas, but some are better suited than others to certain aspects. The details that follow relate to the general population as well as to offenders. (For a description of assessment methods specifically and directly related to forensic issues, turn to Chapter 6.)

APTITUDE TESTS

Loads of tests are tuned to determining a person's skills and talents. They tend to focus on specific tasks that are relevant to particular jobs, such as making sense of diagrams or having a relevant vocabulary or numeracy skills. They're rarely relevant in forensic settings, so I don't discuss these any further. I suppose they could be of significance in an employment tribunal where a person complained of unfair dismissal, but I've never heard of them being used in that situation.

Thinking ability: Cognitive tests

Mental ability and *cognition* (that is, the way a person thinks and how effectively) are such a significant part of human functioning that many tests have been developed to explore different aspects of it. The ubiquitous intelligence test is only one of the many examples of cognitive tests that exist. In general, they explore these three aspects of intellectual performance:

>> **Attention:** Some forms of mental disturbance can have a direct influence on the ability to attend to specific tasks, or the readiness with which a person can be distracted from concentrating.

>> **Memory:** Many different aspects of memory can be assessed. I discuss the nature of memory in Chapter 7 (because an interview really relies on getting someone to remember), but that tends to be longer-term memory. With certain mental conditions, short-term (or immediate) memory can fail, a problem that becomes more common as people age.

>> **Reasoning:** People's ability to draw logical conclusions from presented information or to formulate reasonable concepts about various matters is an indication of both their intellectual ability and mental state. These tests can consist, for example, of a set of differently shaped blocks that respondents have to arrange in some logical groupings.

Discerning a person's personality

In this context, *personality* is the enduring aspect of people (and not how fascinating they are or how much personality they have). Personality has been measured for many years by asking people questions about what they like to do and how they act in various situations.

Such assessments can include questions along the lines of, "Do other people include you in their activities?" or "Would you rather go to a party or stay at home and read a book?" These questionnaires (often known as *inventories*) are then analyzed to determine people's scores on a number of different aspects (called *dimensions*) of their personalities, in order to give a profile of scores across the various dimensions.

In general, most psychologists agree that it's useful to recognize five major aspects of personality, known as the Big Five, with the acronym OCEAN:

>> **Openness:** Creative and original thinking; open to new ideas

>> **Conscientiousness:** Dependable, systematic, and punctual; well-organized and wanting to achieve

>> **Extraversion:** Outgoing and talkative; enjoys social situations

>> **Agreeableness:** Kind and warm, sensitive and trusting; affable and tolerant

>> **Neuroticism:** Moody and temperamental; anxious and irritable

REMEMBER

A number of personality questionnaires measure these five dimensions: Some are short and easy to complete and freely available over the Internet. Take a look at www.outofservice.com/bigfive.

Personality tests can be helpful in many forensic settings because they give you a systematic overview of the person you're dealing with. This can help with treatment or deciding which activities will be helpful to a person, as described in Part 5.

One major criticism of personality inventories is that they tell you only what you'd find out from a casual meeting with someone — they reveal what the person wants you to know. To understand people's innermost thoughts and feelings, you'd need to spend more time with them and talk with them more intensively.

Discovering beliefs: Attitude scales

By *attitudes,* psychologists mean people's thoughts, feelings, or intended actions toward some person, object, or situation. As with so many other areas of psychology, questionnaires are the most frequent way of assessing people's attitudes. Such questionnaires can be developed for specific purposes, such as attitudes toward religion. They can also explore belief systems, a common one being the beliefs that people hold about the conditions under which rape occurs, called *rape myths.* So, for example, knowing what a convicted rapist's attitudes are toward the conditions under which rape occurs can be a crucial starting point in helping him change his behavior. (Have a look at the whole process of treating sex offenders in Chapter 16 if you want some more details on how this works.)

Classifying mental disorders

The classification of mental disorders is fraught with difficulties because they don't line up as distinct diseases like measles or tuberculosis. Therefore, procedures for assessing what mental problems a person has are often used only in combination with a careful clinical interview and information from other sources. However, some major organizations have carried out brave, if somewhat controversial, attempts at the classification of mental disturbances.

Two approaches to classification dominate these considerations:

>> ***Diagnostic and Statistical Manual of Mental Disorders,*** which is produced and regularly revised by the American Psychiatric Association. Having reached a revised text version of its fifth edition, it's known as DSM-5-TR. This also provided a framework to guide professionals in using its classification system as summarized in the sidebar.

>> ***International Statistical Classification of Diseases and Related Health Problems: Mental Disorders,*** compiled by the World Health Organization (WHO), and now in its tenth edition and hence known as ICD-10-CM.

These classification schemes are widely drawn on, especially in legal proceedings, when the mental state of a defendant can be a crucial issue to determine, despite their authors being at pains to warn against their use in court. They are, nonetheless, used in this way because they give a *framework* (or useful shorthand) for typifying bundles of a person's features.

REMEMBER

Fitting individuals into the classifications on offer can sometimes feel like packing smoke into boxes. The classifications deal with complex and changing aspects of how people interact with others and live their lives; they don't identify particular bacteria or damage to distinct parts of the brain.

Various questionnaires have been developed to help in the assignment of people to the different diagnostic categories (refer to the MCMI and PAI entries in Table 5-1).

REMEMBER

All the authorities who produced these classification schemes emphasize that the DSM and ICD systems are guidelines that can be used only by clinically trained individuals. They aren't "cookbooks" to be followed without carefully guided experience. This salutary warning indicates that the diagnosis of these mental disorders is more of a craft than an objective scientific procedure.

CORE COMPONENTS OF DSM-5 ASSESSMENTS

Each of the mental disorders in a specific diagnostic category is presented be careful definition of both the criteria that must be achieved for a person to be labeled with that disorder, the related assessments that need to be considered, and consideration of how people from different cultural contexts exhibit the criteria in different ways.

Diagnostic criteria

- Every disorder has defined criteria for diagnosis.

- That criteria covers symptoms, duration, and severity.

- Other possible conditions need to be ruled out.

- Structured interviews and clinical judgment are used to establish whether these requirements are met.

- Changes over time are monitored to enable treatment to be tailored.

Cross-cutting symptom measures

- Standardized tests assess symptoms that span multiple disorders (for example, anxiety, depression, sleep issues).

- Level 1: Measures screen for a broad range of symptoms across domains.

- Level 2: Measures provide more detailed assessments for specific issues such as anger, mania, or substance misuse.

Cultural guidelines

- To consider the cultural factors that influence symptom expression, diagnosis, and treatment.

- The Cultural Formulation Interview (CFI) helps clinicians explore cultural identity, explanatory models, and psychosocial stressors.

Testing the Tests

The effectiveness of psychological tests varies enormously. To evaluate their utility and value a number of characteristics of tests have been identified that give an indication of their qualities. Recognizing a test's good and bad points is essential because it helps to evaluate how worthwhile a test is likely to be and what weight you can put on its results.

Imagine a ruler that's made out of flexible elastic for measuring length, which gives you a different result every time you use it for measuring the same piece of metal — that's not a measuring tool you'll trust again.

Aiming for test reliability

The most basic quality any assessment instrument must have is a high degree of reliability.

REMEMBER

Reliability is the likelihood that carrying out the same test under similar conditions, on more than one occasion, gives the same results.

The establishment of reliability is more difficult for psychological measurements than for measures of physical objects, but broadly the same process is used — the test is given under similar conditions to the same people on different occasions to see how close the measurements are to each other. Of course, people change more than a lump of wood does, and they may even learn something from carrying out the test the first time; and so various ways around this have been devised, such as having two similar tests administered at the same time.

In general, perfect reliability is never expected. A measure that varies between 0.0 and 1.0 is used to assess reliability. Anything higher than 0.9 is regarded as excellent, but tests that achieve around 0.8 are in common use, and even reliabilities as low as 0.6 aren't unusual.

Evaluating a test's validity

A test can be reliable and produce consistent results (see the preceding section), yet still not truly measure what it claims to measure. For example, a thermometer gives you a reliable measure of temperature, but isn't accurate if you use it to measure altitude! The problem with testing psychological characteristics is that (unlike physical objects) determining what you're actually measuring isn't easy. A measure that claims to be assessing how authoritarian people are, for example, may just be measuring their conventionality.

REMEMBER

The degree to which a test measures what it claims to measure is known as its *validity*.

You can evaluate a test's validity in two broad ways. One is the simple process of seeing what it does, called *face validity.* If the test asks questions that can be right or wrong, it's measuring intelligence or some aspect of general knowledge. If it asks about your feelings toward religion, it's measuring attitudes toward religion. If it asks about your drinking habits, it's probably picking up behavior relevant to alcoholism.

But face validity can be misleading. For example, measuring instruments that look as though they're of great relevance to criminality can turn out to be quite invalid. An interesting illustration of this problem is that many people assume that a lack of sophistication in moral reasoning is the hallmark of a criminal, but until this belief is proven, it's merely a hypothesis. Many tests show that criminals can have their own moral perspective, which you may not share, but it's not necessarily less sophisticated than yours.

Therefore, a second way to evaluate a test's validity is known as *construct validity.* What ideas, or *constructs*, is the test claiming to measure? This can be examined by comparing results using it with results from associated procedures that have similar constructs. For example, intelligence tests are supposed to give some indication of how well a person does at school or college, and so the results can be compared with examination marks. A perfect relationship isn't expected, because many other factors besides your intelligence can interfere with how well you do at school, but at least some reasonable relationship indicates whether the test does what it says on the tin. An IQ test wouldn't be of academic interest if the scores people obtained on it didn't relate reasonably closely to a person's educational achievements.

To take a more extreme example, if serial criminals didn't have, on average, higher psychopathy scores than people who lead blameless lives, you wouldn't take seriously the measure of psychopathy (described in Chapter 6).

Measuring validity by comparison with other assessments is a bit of a chicken-and-egg problem. If a newly developed test has a strong relationship to other measures of something similar it raises questions about whether it is of any additional value. Only over time, as the test becomes more widely used, does a history of associations with other tests and external criteria (like examination success for an IQ measure) build up to show its utility in a variety of different situations.

The tests listed in Table 5-1 (with the exception of the peculiar Szondi test) have been used over many years and in many different situations. Consequently, plenty of examples exist of how useful they've been as well as illustrations of what they assess beyond the face validity of the test items themselves.

Standing up over time: Test robustness

Although you don't find test robustness listed in textbooks on psychological tests, I think that it's the attribute that leads to tests being used instead of being left on the shelf. By *test robustness*, I mean how easy they are to use and how difficult to misuse. Can they really and truly stand up to being used in many different situations by many hundreds of different sorts of people without the results being compromised?

REMEMBER

Although thousands of psychological tests have been developed over the past century or more, relatively few are in wide use. These tests have demonstrated reliability, validity, and robustness and are the ones that people have found most useful.

Achieving precision: The need for norms

Achieving precision in something as subjective and fluid as a person's psychology is clearly problematic. With temperature, for example, you can define fixed points for the benchmarks of measurement, such as when water freezes or boils. Variations have obvious meanings and have well-understood implications. But how do you weigh how intelligent, extroverted, or psychotic a person is? Faced with these questions, psychologists came up with a deceptively simple answer: Compare the person's results on the test with others in the relevant population.

REMEMBER

The distribution of scores achieved on a test by a population of people who've taken it is called the *norms* for a test.

This process of comparing an individual's scores with norms is what makes these measuring instruments different from the sorts of informal questionnaires found in magazines, where journalists create arbitrary score values and give interpretations. The use of norms also distinguishes these measuring instruments from public opinion polls in which the interest is solely in the proportion of a given population who agree with a specified opinion.

The determination of the norms for a test and the establishment of how scores vary from the average for a particular population is known as the *standardization* of a test. I describe this aspect in more detail in the earlier section "Standardizing psychological tests," where I illustrate how IQ norms were used in the defense of Daryl Atkins. IQ measures are a good example of standardized psychological tests because they're so highly developed and widely used. Many of the principles of their use, especially the calibration of scores by comparison with norms, are applied to other forms of psychological measurement.

To understand the applicability and utility of any psychological measurement, therefore, you need to know what norms are being used to calibrate it. Unlike IQ measures, some tests aren't calibrated against the average for a relevant population but by comparison with one or more subgroups. This comparison may be done, for example, by establishing the scores of people diagnosed with particular mental illnesses, or people who've done well in particular jobs. Those comparison scores provide benchmarks for assessing other people.

REMEMBER

The appropriateness of a given test's norms and how well their validity is established is a crucial aspect of their value. In particular, norms may not be appropriate for people different from those who were used to develop the test. For instance, an indicator of psychopathy developed in the USA may have little value in countries with wildly different cultures, such as India, Nigeria, or Russia. Until the test is translated and standardized in those different contexts, its use may be counterproductive.

Creating and Giving Psychological Tests

Not just anyone can invent a psychological test or administer it. Creating such measuring instruments isn't the same as a journalist thinking up questions for a magazine to indicate the headline-grabbing question, "How good are you in bed?" Nor are psychological tests like opinion poll surveys in which a single question is asked, such as "Would you vote for the president if he ran again?" from which percentages across representative samples are used to test the public mood.

Anyone giving a psychological test has to know something about how it was developed and how the results can be interpreted. The test has to be given under special conditions that relate to its intended use and the background to the test. A major industry is involved in creating tests and standardizing them and then setting up training courses for people who want to use the tests.

Broadly, three categories of tests exist that determine who can administer them:

>> Tests that can be used by anyone with some background knowledge, such as general attitude surveys.

>> Tests that require some university qualification in psychology, such as general personality measures.

>> Tests that require specific training in their use and application. (All the tests listed earlier, in Table 5-1, are of this kind.) Some tests may require intensive training over many months, whereas others may require only a few days of training.

For important tests that require considerable expertise, people have to achieve a special license to be allowed to administer them, which is usually awarded when certain standards are achieved on the training course. For these tests, people are allowed to administer them only if they have an up-to-date certificate.

Training in the application and administration of a psychological assessment covers, at the very least, these points:

>> **Choosing the appropriate test for the purpose at hand:** This requires an understanding of the psychological theory that underpins the test and the situations in which it has been used that reveal its validity.

>> **Understanding how to administer the test:** Often, specific procedures apply that the tester is required to carry out for the test to maintain its reliability and validity.

>> **Knowing how to score the test:** The way in which answers are combined to derive scores may not be a simple addition. Different answers may get different weights in various ways. Training explains how this is done, sometimes involving special guides to assist in calculating the scores on the test. That may also include guidance on the different components of the test that can generate separate scores. For instance, in the intelligence test, respondents may earn different scores for verbal, numerical, and spatial intelligence.

>> **Writing reports:** These determine how the report of the test should be prepared and what headings are required for each test.

>> **Recognizing the sorts of ethical and professional issues (such as those I describe in Chapter 18):** They include abiding by aspects of privacy and confidentiality, and how and what the person being assessed should be told.

Chapter **6**

Diagnosing Evil: How (or whether) Criminals Think

There are special challenges for a psychologist when interviewing or trying to help offenders. They often regard the psychologist with suspicion. There are also likely to be many reasons offenders will not tell the truth, or perform as they would normally on any tests they are given.

Nonetheless, over the years, psychologists have developed many assessment methods that help them to overcome these challenges. They have been developed specifically to reveal the psychological make-up of offenders. Most commonly, these procedures assess the risk of the individual committing another crime in the near or distant future. Other tests have been developed to explore offenders' sexual attitudes and preferences or an offender's competency to understand the trial process.

Forensic psychologists nearly always use these procedures alongside in-depth interviews. The tests provide a way to describe important psychological aspects of a criminal and compare those characteristics with other known offenders and the population at large. Also, these tests are of value in looking back to the original offense and helping to understand those aspects of the person who contributed to the crime occurring. The results of these assessment procedures can therefore be of great significance in the lives of offenders.

Difficulties in Assessing an Offender's Psychology

A forensic psychologist can be required to assess an offender as part of their defense or prosecution, or in relation to appropriate sentencing for their crime and/or subsequent treatment. That makes the relationship between psychologist and client potentially much more fraught than is usually the case in a clinical consulting room. For a start, the setting of the meeting is likely to be a prison or another secure setting, which isn't conducive to forming a comfortable rapport with the offender.

If the assessment is part of the case a defendant wants to make, there are likely to be pressures on the defendant to indicate psychological problems that could help the court look at the case more leniently. This is a double-edged sword, though. In some jurisdictions, notably in the UK, if a person is found guilty of a serious crime because of some mental illness, such as psychotic paranoia, typically associated with the verdict of "not guilty on the grounds of insanity," they may be given an indeterminate sentence and sent to a prison called a *special hospital.* They can be kept there until the medical staff and a parole board decide they are well enough to leave. This could mean, for example, that rather than receive a sentence of 12 years for a murder, they can spend 20 years in a special hospital, rather euphemistically known in the UK as "at his majesty's pleasure." This is one reason many offenders want nothing to do with psychologists or psychiatrists.

The situation is even more fraught if a defendant is being assessed on behalf of the prosecution. A defendant might feel pretty uneasy about being interviewed by a prosecution psychologist because they have a real fear that their words, behavior, or emotional reactions could be given a meaning that weakens their defense. They might worry about being unfairly labeled. On top of that, the psychologist isn't just there to observe; they're working for the prosecution, the side trying to prove guilt, so it's natural for the person being interviewed to feel like the interview is less about understanding and more about gathering ammunition. And since psychological evaluations can carry serious weight in court — especially when it comes to mental health, competency, or assessing risk — a negative report can end up making things much worse for the defendant when it comes to sentencing. All of this can make the interview a tense one in which the offender tries hard to avoid providing any responses that would be detrimental to their case.

Also, of course, whether the interview is for the defense or the prosecution, an offender may just lie to defend their innocence — or because lying is a natural mode of dealing with any authority.

Uncovering Possible Malingering

As a consequence of the potential for dishonesty in a forensic interview, one crucial challenge when assessing an offender, which isn't usually a concern with other people, is whether the person is telling the truth. This may be lying about the events surrounding the crime (which I discuss in Chapter 8), but in this section, I consider the use of psychological tests in discerning whether offenders are lying about their mental state.

The use of the polygraph and other aspects of lie detection that I discuss in Chapter 8 are relevant to many aspects of crime, especially in determining whether offenders' reports of their actions are truthful, but a quite different set of requirements emerges when a suspect claims to have some sort of mental disturbance.

As I mention in Chapter 1, one strand of forensic psychology grew out of the defense that a person was so mentally disturbed that they didn't understand what they were doing or that it was wrong. As lawyers put it, the defendant didn't have *mens rea*. Therefore, a strong defense can be that a person was, in common language, mad or insane (although, as I discuss in Chapter 12, the law doesn't define insanity the way common language does) at the time they carried out the criminal actions, which clearly gives an incentive for criminals to malinger.

Malingering is a way of giving information that deliberately fabricates or grossly exaggerates symptoms. Malingerers may also feign symptoms, whether physical, such as a limp, or psychological, such as pretending to hear voices.

Defendants often think they can have the trial postponed or stopped altogether, or at least receive a shorter sentence, if they're thought to be mentally ill. Malingering isn't limited to criminal cases. A person claiming compensation for injuries resulting from a car accident or an incident at work — especially when these injuries are difficult to observe, as in a psychological disorder — may also be motivated to exaggerate or fake symptoms. People claiming benefits from the state may also distort their symptoms. But as far as I know, psychologists have never been used to help assess their claims.

MALINGERING GOES TO HOLLYWOOD

One exotic illustration of how a criminal can mislead experts about their mental state is the case of the malingering Kenneth Bianchi, who pretended to have multiple personalities. (Chapter 12 has more details.) And because Hollywood loves a battle of wits between a clever criminal and a psychologist, in a movie based on the case, called *Primal Fear*, Richard Gear plays the hoodwinked attorney in the same way that Bianchi initially fooled psychiatrists.

As a consequence, any assessment of mental state needs to take account of the possibility that a mental illness is being invented or faked in some way. Forensic psychologists often use special procedures to establish how honest any claims of mental illness may be. The most common such method is an intensive clinical interview. In this, people are asked in a relaxed atmosphere to talk about their lives and any mental issues that have affected them. The interviewer isn't listening carefully only to the content of what's being said but also to the way in which the account is being given.

These are some indications of possible malingering:

>> Dramatic or exaggerated presentation of the experiences or symptoms

>> Overly careful or deliberate recounting of what has happened

>> Inconsistency in what's described compared with what's known about the claimed psychological problems

>> Reporting only well-known aspects of a recognized psychological syndrome, such as hearing voices

You can't use these aspects definitively to determine malingering, but they can be an indication that a more systematic examination is necessary using standardized tests (which I describe in Chapter 5).

Evaluating reported symptoms

One of the most highly regarded standardized procedures for assessing malingering is the Structured Interview of Reported Symptoms (SIRS). The latest version has 172 items and takes about half an hour to complete. Some of the questions are subtly repeated to check consistency in responses. The following issues illustrate some aspects of how the SIRS procedure works:

>> If rare symptoms are described that are known to occur in less than one of every ten patients, the tester's suspicions are aroused. Claims about many of these rare symptoms are a useful indicator of some sort of malingering.

>> Claiming a large number of symptoms has to be treated with caution. Severely mentally ill patients typically have rather few symptoms, and malingerers tend to over-egg the pudding.

>> If an offender claims lots of well-known obvious symptoms but few less-obvious ones, the tester may suspect malingering.

>> The claim of odd, unlikely symptoms is also a pointer to faking. Preposterous symptoms are extremely rare, and if a person claims to have lots of them, the tester will question the individual's honesty.

>> The tester carefully examines whether the reported symptoms are consistent with each other and with observations available from other people. For example, someone claiming to be quite depressed who has a healthy appetite may well be faking, as is a person claiming he's suffering from tremors that no one has ever seen.

Testing memory

Memories are highly malleable and subject to being distorted. One understandable problem, therefore, is determining whether someone genuinely believes the memories even if the events didn't happen (as I describe in Chapter 7). A different problem arises, however, when a suspect claims not to remember what happened. Such amnesia or other forms of memory loss may be relevant to claims of brain injury or the inability to give an account of what happened in a crime for which the person is accused.

Various procedures have been developed to assess memory impairment. One of the most widely used is the Test of Memory Malingering (TOMM). This test was developed by comparing how people with known brain injuries perform against what's typical of responses from the population at large. The person with an unusually low score, but a pattern of responses that doesn't relate to known brain injuries, may be thought to be feigning memory problems.

REMEMBER

This clever test appears to be an ordinary test of memory that seems more difficult than it actually is. It has the paradoxical benefit that if the person being tested earns an exceedingly low score, the individual is likely trying to pull the wool over the tester's eyes. But someone who receives a high score also doesn't have the claimed memory problem. Getting the appropriate score and pattern of answers that do relate to genuine memory problems is difficult to feign without knowing the inner workings of the test.

Exploring Cognitive Distortions, Justifications, and Sexual Deviance

One challenging feature of many offenders is that they see other people and their own actions in distorted and sometimes warped ways. Their thoughts don't follow the logic that non-offenders would think appropriate (as I discuss in Chapter 2).

A particularly challenging group of criminals in this regard is those convicted of sexual offenses, whether the crime is the abuse of children or rape or other criminal sexual activities. These criminals' activities and experiences are caught up with particular ways of thinking about sex, including the sort of sometimes bizarre fantasies they have (that can shape their desires) and how they justify their actions. A child molester, for example, may claim that the 4-year-old victim wore suggestive clothing and so initiated the seduction, or that because their spouse wouldn't accept their sexual advances, raping their daughter was acceptable.

Such individuals tend to think about their offending in ways that the great majority of people would think were odd and irrational. These cognitive distortions contribute to their justifying the crime to themselves and anyone else who asks them about it. They don't think of what they've done as wrong. Their justifications shape their criminal activity. Therefore, psychologists developed special procedures to explore these aspects of offenders' thoughts and attitudes. These tests allow the clinician to develop a profile of the offender's sexual orientation and psychology that is of value in developing treatment programs (as I discuss in Chapter 15) and predicting whether the individual is likely to continue to be dangerous to other people. In some cases, these assessments can be used in court to form a view of the accused and the nature of their crime, as in the nearby sidebar, "A Psychosexual test in action."

One widely used assessment of a person's psychosexual characteristics is the Multiphasic Sex Inventory, which consists of 300 questions describing aspects of a person. Respondents have to indicate whether the questions are true or false for themselves. The test takes about an hour and a half to complete and is analyzed under a number of different headings that provide the profile of scores. These analyzed areas include

>> The person's normal sex drives and interests, to determine whether the respondent is telling the truth or trying to present what sounds like normal behavior — in other words, what the respondent believes the tester thinks is acceptable.

» An obsession with sex, giving it a prominence that goes beyond normal adult interest.

» Any attempt to deny involvement in illegal sexual activity, or an unwillingness to accept that certain sexual behaviors are inappropriate.

» Any justifications that may be offered for sexual offending, including minimizing the seriousness of an offense or its consequences for the victim.

» Any sexual fantasies and the role they play in the offender's actions, including the exploration of the stages an offender may undergo from fantasy to justification, and then on to planning and carrying out the assault.

» Any *paraphilias*, which are unusual objects or situations that cause sexual arousal, such as shoe fetish, bondage, making obscene phone calls, or voyeurism.

» Any sexual dysfunction, such as physical disabilities, impotence, or premature ejaculation.

» Any knowledge and beliefs about sexual matters.

ANECDOTE

A PSYCHOSEXUAL TEST IN ACTION

A 20-year-old man was accused, in Northern Ireland, of raping and killing a young woman he'd met at a nightclub and taken back to her house. The police called in an FBI agent to comment on whether the assault was part of a sexually deviant fantasy. The agent looked at the crime scene photographs and autopsy report and said that the killing was sexually sadistic: In other words, the offender had gotten sexual excitement from the killing. This assessment implied that the offender was extremely dangerous. In the particular jurisdiction, the person would have had to spend perhaps 12 years in prison if found guilty of murder, but much longer, 20 or 30 years, if the killing was thought to be part of sexually sadistic fantasies. Indeed, he may have been regarded as so dangerous that he would never be let out of prison.

I was called in by the defense to establish whether the individual was a deviant, sexually sadistic person. I interviewed him carefully, exploring his life history and giving him a standardized test of his sexual fantasies. From the results, I formed the view that he came from a background in which outbursts of violence were to be expected, but that he had no deviant sexual fantasies or experiences. Therefore, I argued that the FBI report was mistaken and the offender wasn't a sexual killer. On the basis of my report, the prosecution withdrew the FBI report from the court and the defendant admitted to the murder. He was given a life sentence, which meant he would spend a minimum of ten years in prison.

Examining the Inability to Relate: Psychopathy

A crucial aspect of assessing the psychology of offenders connects to their personality — that is, their enduring characteristics and the broad way in which they relate to other people and deal with the world. (Flip to Chapter 5 for a fuller discussion on personality.)

REMEMBER

Some people's personality is so unusual that their personality is regarded as being disordered in some way (which is different from the person having a mental illness). Of course, not all such people necessarily commit crimes. They may just be regarded as strange and perhaps quite distressed about why, as they see it, other people don't relate to them effectively.

The nearby sidebar "Some personality disorders as listed in DSM" contains a few labels given to different types of personality disorders in the Diagnostic and Statistical Manual (DSM) of the American Psychiatric Association (which I describe in more detail in Chapter 5).

The type of personality disorder particularly relevant to criminality, and which has found its way into popular discourse and court use, is *psychopathic disorder,* or *psychopathy.* People with this label are lucid and coherent with no signs of any learning disability or psychotic symptoms. Some of them can be superficially charming and are intelligent enough to be plausible on first acquaintance. They don't hear voices or think that they're commanded by forces beyond their power. Yet over and over again, they abuse people, lie with no compunction or remorse, can be unpredictably violent, and seem unable to relate effectively to others over any extended period.

REMEMBER

Labels such as psychopath, psychopathy, and antisocial personality disorder aren't medical diagnoses that can be linked to a bacterium or even a specific brain disorder — they're summary descriptions of the person in question. Some experts have even commented that these labels are moral judgments masquerading as medical explanations. The personality disorder and psychopath labels are useful as condensed descriptions of some rather difficult (and often nasty) people.

Getting to grips with psychopathy

Rather than require the offender to fill in a questionnaire, psychologists use checklists when assessing a person's level of *psychopathy,* for this reason: A psychopath, if questioned themselves, can be expected to lie. In addition, the person is interviewed and their associates are also questioned so that a number of pointers can be indicated on the special checklist in the section "The psychopathy checklist," later in this chapter. The scores the person receives are then used to decide whether an individual is a psychopath.

Various forms of criminality often reflect an aspect of psychopathic individuals' lifestyles. If they commit crimes, they understand what they're doing and that it's illegal. But these same aspects of their personality have been cited in court to claim that, although not mentally ill, they are mentally disturbed and that this should be taken into account during any legal proceedings.

The term *psychopath* itself is hotly debated. It isn't part of any formal list of medical diagnoses. The DSM that I discuss in Chapter 5 prefers the term *antisocial personality disorder.* In the US, some people prefer to talk about *sociopaths.* But it's such a useful way of summarizing particular bundles of characteristics that clinicians still like to use it, drawing on the psychopathy checklist that you can jump to later in this chapter.

A FEW PERSONALITY DISORDERS, AS LISTED IN DSM

Here are just some of the personality disorders that DSM specifies:

- **Paranoid:** Sees other people as generally demeaning, threatening, and untrustworthy

- **Schizoid:** Solitary, indifferent to others; limited emotional expression or experiences

- **Borderline:** Rapid mood changes, intense anger, impulsive, self-mutilations; fears abandonment

- **Histrionic:** Great excess of emotional reactions, although often superficial; seeks attention

- **Narcissistic:** Extremely self-important, feels entitled to admiration from others; upset when criticized

- **Antisocial:** Displays irresponsibility and behavior disorders, at least from the age of 15, including fights, defaulting on debts, recklessness, and lack of remorse

REGIONAL TIP-OFF

The term *psychopathic disorder* isn't a medical diagnosis but rather a legal term under English and Welsh law that refers to a "persistent disorder or disability of the mind." It's not that far removed from the McNaughton rule, which first emerged over 150 years ago and which I discuss in Chapter 1. Thus, some debate exists regarding which of the psychiatric diagnoses of personality disorder listed in the earlier sidebar "A few personality disorders, as listed in DSM" are closest to the legal definition of psychopathic disorder, and whether any of them relates to the popular conception of a psychopath.

After you've met someone who you know has committed horrific violent crimes and yet can be charming and helpful, continuing to believe in the Hollywood stereotype of the psychopath (described in the nearby sidebar "Beyond the Hollywood stereotypes") becomes difficult. Without a doubt, though, some people seem pleasant and plausible in one situation but can quickly turn to viciousness. Some people can never connect with others and are constantly, from an early age, at war with those with whom they come into contact.

REMEMBER

Not all psychopaths end up as vicious criminals. Some experienced businessmen and politicians would probably receive a diagnosis of psychopath if they were clinically assessed. For example, Bernard Madoff, who defrauded thousands of investors out of billions of dollars, had many of the characteristics of the Type 1 psychopath, as listed later in this chapter. Some have even suggested that certain people in senior positions in many government administrations fit the description of a psychopath or personality disorder.

The psychopathy checklist

The many ideas surrounding the notion of the psychopath led Robert Hare to develop a standard checklist that can be used to measure the degree to which a person exhibits psychopathic traits. It consists of 20 items that can be given a score of 0 if they don't exist and a score of 2 if they do, with a score of 1 for the possibility that they exist. These scores are then added up. A score higher than 30 is generally considered to indicate a full-blown psychopath.

A further refinement is that two different styles of psychopath can be identified from the scores:

>> **Type 1:** These people have superficial charm but are pathological liars and are callous, remorseless, and manipulative. The clearest fictional example of this sort of psychopath is Tom Ripley, who has the central role in many of Patricia Highsmith's amoral novels.

>> **Type 2:** These people are more obviously criminal, impulsive, and irresponsible, with a history of juvenile delinquency, antisocial tendencies, and early behavioral problems — and whose lives are chronically unstable.

BEYOND THE HOLLYWOOD STEREOTYPES

The Hollywood psychopath is inevitably a merciless serial killer, often some sort of cross between Dracula and Frankenstein's monster! Films from the silent 1920s cinema, such as *The Cabinet of Dr Caligari* and *Kalifornia* and *No Country for Old Men*, or the even more recent *Joker*, never really provide any deep psychological insights into the actions of the monsters who are the antiheroes of their dramas — they're presented as pure evil. The rather more psychologically interesting films, such as *Psycho* or *The Boston Strangler*, do provide explanations for the nastiness of their villains (drawn from a simplistic use of the theories of Sigmund Freud), but still present their antiheroes as alien individuals who can appear unthreatening but deep down are extremely malevolent.

These types are captured in the following items in Hare's checklist:

>> **Selfish, callous psychopathy (Type 1):**

- Glibly, but superficially, charming
- Grandiose feeling of self-importance
- Pathological liar — lies even when no need to exists
- Manipulates others; cunning
- Lacks remorse or any feelings of guilt
- Doesn't feel strongly about anything
- Lacks empathy
- Doesn't accept responsibility for own actions

>> **Deviant psychopathy (Type 2):**

- Easily bored, needs excitement
- Feeds off other people
- No realistic, long-term goals
- Impulsive
- Irresponsible
- Lack of control over actions
- Behavioral problems in childhood
- Juvenile delinquency

- Different types of offending
- Abuses any conditions set by the courts

Perhaps not surprisingly, both styles of psychopathy are also related to

» Promiscuous sexual behavior

» Many short-term relationships

Assessing the Risk of Future Offending

A vital area of forensic psychological assessment is the determination of how likely a person is to reoffend and whether they're likely to be violent in the near or distant future. This form of assessment is quite common when deciding the court's sentence and whether, after undergoing some sort of treatment, a person should be allowed back into the community. This process is called *risk assessment* and relates to the risk that a person may be a danger to themselves or other people.

Dangerousness covers everything from the possibility of attempting suicide to being abusive to a neighbor. A high probability exists that many offenders will continue to offend, but that isn't a reason under most legal systems for keeping them locked up. Under the law once people have served their sentence they must be allowed to walk free. The issue in risk assessment is whether any indications exist that the person will be seriously dangerous.

REMEMBER

Predicting the risk of future offending is, well, risky. The process can never be foolproof, for the simple reason that predicting what a person may experience, and the unfolding circumstances of their future life, is impossible.

Forensic psychologists usually take into account three general aspects when predicting the risk of an offender's future dangerousness:

» **Dynamic factors:** These characteristics of the individual can, potentially, be changed by way of experience or direct intervention, including the person's attitudes and compliance with treatment, their views of their crimes, and their indicators of mental illness.

» **Static factors:** This is information about a person that isn't open to change, including previous history of violence, age and ethnicity, previous relationships, and education and employment experience.

>> **Protective factors:** Some aspects of a person and their circumstances can reduce the risk of future violence, including a supportive social network, a feeling of responsibility for a family, or a satisfying job.

Appraising risk of sexual violence

A number of standardized procedures have been developed for use in assessing the risk of future violence, especially of further sexual offenses. A well-known instrument is the Structured Assessment of Risk and Need (SARN). In addition to evaluating static and dynamic factors (see the preceding section), it examines issues relevant to formulating treatment programs for individuals. The SARN covers these issues:

>> **Sexual interests:**

- Preoccupation with sex and related activities
- Sexual preferences for children and prepubescent individuals over adults
- Sexual violence — preference for coerced rather than consensual sex
- Sexual deviance of relevance — other aspects of original offenses that were socially deviant

>> **Distorted attitudes:**

- Regarding dominance as a significant part of sexual relations
- The entitlement to sexual activity as one desires it
- Minimizing the seriousness of sexual activity with children
- Justification of rape
- Viewing sexuality as corrupting or exploitive based on gender identity

>> **Social and emotional aspects:**

- Feeling lonely and inadequate
- Preferring emotional intimacy with children
- Suspicious, angry, and vengeful
- Lack of intimate relationships as an adult

>> **Self-management:**

- Impulsive and irresponsible
- Difficulty in dealing with challenges
- Uncontrolled outbursts of emotion

Women, of course, can also have distorted attitudes and beliefs about sexuality and violence, but the great majority of assessments of these are carried out with men.

Many of the aspects that are evaluated in the SARN reflect aspects of personality disorder that are also explored in other protocols. The main difference from assessing a person using the SARN and, for example, Hare's Psychopathy Checklist (which I describe in the earlier section "Using the psychopathy checklist") is that the checklist assigns a person to a particular *personality type,* whereas the SARN gives a profile of the psychology of the individual in various areas of functioning. By combining this with what is known about the person and their circumstances, forensic psychologists can make predictions of future risk and the appropriate forms of treatment.

Working with the young: Juvenile Sexual Offender Protocol

Youngsters who become involved in violence, especially sexual assaults, pose a particular risk assessment challenge for the authorities. The young people may not be regarded as having *mens rea* (knowing what they're doing), and so the law may not allow them to be imprisoned as a form of punishment, but instead recommends treatment. Greater potential may exist for successfully treating juveniles than for adults, who are already set in their ways. This has been demonstrated by the lifetime work of internationally renowned David Farrington. Professor Farrington established that young people who find their way into any form of illegal activity have an increased risk of drifting into a life of crime (and so present a risk to the public). For this reason, any successful interventions early in an offender's development can be of great significance.

Forensic psychologists have given lots of attention to assessing the nature of the risk of reoffending by juveniles. A typical example of a number of developed procedures is the Juvenile Sex Offender Assessment Protocol (J-SOAP), which is designed for use with 12- to 18-year-olds. It draws on as much objective information as possible so that the personal, subjective judgment of the assessor is kept to a minimum.

REMEMBER

J-SOAP covers these four crucial aspects of the offender:

>> **Adjustment in the community:** These are the protective factors, including the stability of the current living situation and experience of schooling. Other positive support systems are also of relevance.

>> **Antisocial activity:** This one focuses on what I refer to as *static* factors earlier in this section: the variety of offenses for which the offender was arrested before the age of 16, but also the inconsistency of experience with caregivers.

>> **Effects of intervention:** An exploration of any lack of empathy for victims or remorse for crimes is considered in relation to any treatment the offender may have received. This aspect relates to the possibility of personality disorder of psychopathy, which I discuss in the earlier section "Examining the Inability to Relate: Psychopathy."

>> **Sexual offense history:** This includes the number of offenses for which the young person has been convicted, including the extent to which they personally have been a victim. Their preoccupation with sexual activity is also assessed.

The seductions of crime

A rather different approach to examining criminals' psychology is to explore the reasons they themselves have for committing crimes. Note has already been taken of the distortions in the thinking of many offenders, minimizing the severity of what they've done or blaming the victim. A further development of this is to examine the benefits crime gives to the offender. A famous sociologist, Jack Katz, called this "the seductions of crime." Those benefits to the offender include moral outrage, thrill-seeking, defiance, and desire for control.

These are rather different from the motives so delighted by detective fiction writers and often drawn on in court cases as explanations for committing offenses. They are rather simple-minded reasons for committing a crime, such as greed, jealousy, revenge, desperation, or obsessive control — or to hide the evidence of another crime. Some fictional accounts, often oddly called psychological thrillers, draw on some sort of mental illness. That does relate to features of criminals considered earlier.

ANECDOTE

MY LIFE AS A FILM

A rather unusual way of exploring how offenders see themselves and their criminal actions is to ask them to describe what a film would be like that covered their life story. They might even specify which actor would play them and other important characters in the film. A close examination of the film described reveals who is important in their lives — possibly their parents or siblings, but more notoriously,

(continued)

their partners in crime. How they became involved in offending is also an indication of how they exonerate themselves or regard themselves as just unlucky. Their excitement from their illegal actions or other seductions as mentioned is also a good indication of possible future criminality. How they end the film is also of interest, revealing what they think lies in their future.

The great advantage of this approach is that the offenders enjoy it and don't find it as threatening as many of the procedures mentioned earlier in this chapter. Of course, if they insist they are innocent, their autobiographic film may take quite a different turn.

3

Assisting Law Enforcement

Sometimes psychologists move into areas that most people think are really the provenance of the police; interviewing witnesses, deciding if a suspect is lying, helping victims or even considering how to prevent crime. The role in this area that has caught the public imagination is offender profiling, which is usually presented as some almost magical skill of a gifted individual. In all of these areas psychological processes can help the police to be more effective. In this part the psychological theories and methods that underpin these contributions are described and I blow away some of the myths that fiction writers live by.

Chapter **7**

How to Ask Questions of Witnesses, Victims, and Suspects

C ommitting a crime and not being detected is thought of as the perfect crime (well, at least in crime fiction). Until someone reports a crime, it doesn't appear on the radar. When you see the report of a crime on TV, you're almost always given what appears to be a clear picture of what's happened and when. Yet even a video recording of a crime is open to interpretation. It is from one viewpoint only. Another view may offer a different perspective. For example, you return home to find that your house has been burgled and the furniture and your possessions are in a topsy-turvy mess. But the purpose of the crime is open to question until you can give law enforcement an accurate description of what's been taken. At every stage of the legal process, a description of what has actually happened is required — usually, by a witness or witnesses making a statement to the police or lawyers. But confusion about the details of the offence can also emerge from a suspect being interviewed and being asked where they were and what they were doing at the time of the crime.

In this chapter, I walk you through the psychology of interviewing people as part of an investigation (talking to a patient in therapy, for example, is something quite different). When a witness has seen something or someone that may be a crimes they are likely to be asked to identify the object or person. I also consider this eyewitness testimony. I don't worry in this chapter about the complicating factor of deliberate lying and deception (a topic I cover in Chapter 8). I discuss the process and experience of interviewing witnesses, suspects, and (alleged) victims by investigators. *Interviews* are accounts of what people remember. So I also examine how human memory works, including the ways in which memory can be unreliable, and I describe the issues of helping people remember what may be traumatic incidents, particularly when the person is distressed.

Interviewing and its connection to other sources of information

Interviews with victims, witnesses, and suspects aren't the only sources of information available to an investigation and to the courts. All the sorts of forensic science information that TV shows like "CSI" and "Silent Witness" draw on are used in real cases, too. I don't discuss those here because you can glean a great deal about forensic science from those shows as well as from many other books.

REMEMBER

You can also use these types of sources when they're available:

>> **Biological evidence:** Blood stains, semen, and excreta, for example

>> **Crime scene records:** Especially photos or videos

>> **Geographical information:** Plus related location information

>> **Impressions:** Fingerprints, tire tracks, or "ear prints" (which are marks left by pressing an ear to a window or other smooth surface)

>> **Personal records:** Diaries, suicide notes, and computer information, like emails or Facebook pages

>> **Records:** From hospitals, birth and death records, and medical treatments

>> **Traces:** Fibers, soil particles, and gunshot residue, for example

Any or all of these pieces of evidence can be used to form a fuller picture of the crime and those involved, and, together with the interview, for example, can test the claims made by victims, witnesses, or suspects.

Managing the process: Interviews as conversations

When you're carrying out an interview, you're making use of the witness's memory. The purpose of an interview is to draw out facts about a crime from a person who has some special connection with it; the crime interview is a live event and not just a theoretical exercise, as in a laboratory experiment.

REMEMBER

An interview consists of two or more people involved in a dialogue, so one way of thinking about the process is as *conversation management:* By forming a friendly, but professional, working relationship with the person being interviewed, the interviewer can encourage confidence and honesty.

Establishing rapport is important, but you also need to have the flexibility to change what is being asked in response to the answers being given rather than bulldoze through the questions you think you *ought* to be asking. Doing so can be difficult with a reluctant witness, or one who's anxious about what's going on. A traumatized victim may be in an emotional state that makes answering questions clearly difficult. They may need careful encouragement and time to respond.

As an interviewer, you can develop rapport by:

>> Explaining clearly what the interview is for and how you're carrying it out

>> Listening carefully

>> Showing respect

>> Being nonconfrontational

>> Acknowledging the respondent's anxieties

The Ethical Interview

Interviewing suspects has particular challenges. There have consequently been many attempts to obtain information from them by means that are not ethical, such as torture, misleading statements, and other forms of coercion. These are discussed in Chapter 8, where I describe the guidelines on ethical interviewing provided by Professor Ray Bull and his colleagues to the Special Rapporteurs's report that was eventually accepted by the United Nations.

REMEMBER

Responses to questions can also be influenced by social pressures, such as the desire by people being interviewed to please the interviewer, wanting to help because of the seriousness of a situation despite having little to offer, or when rapport or a relationship develops with police officers involved in the case, so they go out of their way to imply their memory is clear when it's really very vague.

Pressure on a witness to remember the details of an event can cause mistaken recollections because of the witness desiring to appear correct, observant, helpful, and not foolish. For example, a witness who's eager to help may be trying hard to guess what the police want to hear and then persuade themselves that what they're remembering corresponds with what's required.

Combating the possibility of witnesses saying what they think the interviewer wants to hear rather than what they authentically remember is a subtle business. Letting the person give an account of what they remember without too much direct prompting — saying things like "Tell me what happened" rather than "Did you see him punch her?" — is part of good interview technique. But there's much more to it than that, which is why all sorts of interview frameworks have been developed, which I discuss later in this chapter and in Chapter 8.

Remembering That Memory Can Mislead

Researching how the memory works is a hot topic in psychology and has been for over 150 years. No surprise, therefore, that forensic psychologists have been exploring witness and victim memories since the earliest days. (In Chapter 21, I give ten examples of the role and significance of memory in an internationally famous trial.)

Try this little test. Can you remember the last time you ate at a restaurant you've eaten at a few times before? If I ask you to describe what the table looked like are you likely to give me a different answer if I provide a list of possible settings and ask you to tick a box? Or how do you go about explaining to someone who often eats in a rather different type of restaurant?

What I'm getting at is that your account takes on two crucial aspects:

>> **The act of remembering:** You have to remember what happened, which isn't simply a matter of taking out some sort of mind-movie and playing it to the person who's asking the questions. Then you need to put together a description, drawing on your verbal skills and what you can dig out of your memory.

>> **The situation:** What you say depends on who's asking the questions. You may relate an account to a close friend that's different from the one you would give to a police officer. How questions are asked also influences how you answer. If you're given a list of possible answers to choose from, you may choose one even though none of them quite fits the situation you remember; but if you're asked to describe what you remember in your own words, you may struggle to find the exact words.

MYTH
BUSTER

You may think that a question is a question is a question, but not so. How you phrase a question can help you unwittingly direct the answer. An *open question* is one that gives no hint of supplying an answer: for example, "What did you have for breakfast?" In contrast, a *closed question* gives the respondent possible answers, such as the yes or no kind ("Did you have breakfast today?") or more detailed, such as "Which of the following did you have for breakfast: cereal, eggs, coffee, juice?" The problem with the closed question is that the questioner is assuming what the possible answers can be. If you had chapati and a banana for breakfast, a closed question won't reveal that fact.

REMEMBER

Asking open-ended questions is the art of good investigative questioning.

Going back over a crime with a witness and encouraging them to remember the details relies heavily on their working memory, which is often less than perfectly reliable. Psychological studies of witness memories show that things can go wrong in many different ways, not least because a witness is lying. (Turn to Chapter 8 for more on lying and detecting deception.) *Interrogation* (asking a question) is a word you often hear when referring to police interviews, implying a challenging confrontation with a suspect. But the main purpose of an interview with a witness, victim, or suspect is to draw forth a description of who did what, where, and when. The event you're asking about is in the past, and it's rare to have an on-the-spot record of what happened. An *explanation* of what happened may also be needed to determine whether a crime has been committed and whether the suspect being interviewed knew what they were doing: remembering why they did what they did. This explanation may be arrived at after the event, opening the way for the witness's statement to be legally challenged.

Recalling past events

Research shows that memory isn't like taking an old photograph out of a box, which may have just faded a bit with age.

REQUIRING A PHOTOGRAPHIC MEMORY

ANECDOTE

Courts of law are good at assuming that all witnesses and defendants have a good memory of what happened. Here's one example. I was giving evidence in a trial in which a report I'd written 20 years earlier was drawn on, but I hadn't been given advance notice of this fact. I was expected to remember the details of the report without being allowed to look over the document itself. Also, in the same trial, something I said in the morning was raised with me in the afternoon, as if I had total recall of everything I was saying and the exact words I was using.

The earliest studies of memory show how quickly ordinary memories decay and fade away, but the attorneys questioning me were eager to act as though no such memory decay exists. As a witness, I was expected to remember everything with no prompting. Of course, not all courts work exactly like this, but any admission of a lack of clarity of memory can be used to challenge the veracity of what the witness is saying. (Skip to Chapter 13 if you want to see how this works in court proceedings.)

You have two types of memory, working quite differently from each other:

>> **Long-term memory:** You're drawing on your long-term memory when remembering a past event, such as a crime.

>> **Short-term memory:** Your short-term memory is your immediate memory — your *working* memory — like a scratch pad where you make a note or jot down a phone number before throwing it away.

The effectiveness of your long-term memory for an event or experience depends on these factors:

>> How long ago the event was

>> How much attention you were paying to the event at the time

>> How memorable the event was

>> Whether there are any cues to help you in remembering

You can help a witness or victim remember the event by offering useful cues such as taking them back to the context of the event (called *context reinstatement*). For example, if you're being asked to recall what you ate in a particular restaurant, it's much easier to remember if you return to the restaurant rather than try to remember from a distance. Returning to where you were at the time of the crime is useful for jogging your memory of the event. The process can add detail and clarity rather than change the fundamental aspects of the memory itself.

Sometimes a significant event has an overwhelming and emotional impact on you, called a *flashbulb memory*, such as how and where you heard about the 9/11 twin towers attacks or, if you're my age, how and where you heard of the death of John F. Kennedy or John Lennon.

A difference exists between identification testimony and other forms of testimony. When you're asked to select (say, from a police lineup or a set of photographs) a person you saw and who's associated with a crime, it's usually referred to as *eyewitness testimony* (see the later section "Looking into Eyewitness Testimony"). Choosing from a presented selection in this way is different from generating your own account of what happened in a police interview.

Forgetting: Why do people fail to remember?

Forgetting the details of an event involves two processes:

>> **Recording the memory:** If you didn't notice or pay much attention to the initial information, you tend not to store the information effectively. The more unusual, memorable, or emotionally significant the event, the more it attracts your attention, so you're more likely to remember the details.

>> **Retrieving the memory:** After committing the information to memory, you then need to retrieve that information. The process of retrieval is vulnerable because your memories can be distorted — delving into your memory isn't simply like playing a record. Remembering is an active process of generating a report of the bits of information that are stored. There may even be some assistance from general experience and logic of what is possible: "I usually have eggs for breakfast, so I suppose I did three days ago. I have no eggs left in the fridge, so I guess I ate them all."

Remembering anything you experienced more than a few moments ago means *reconstructing* past events (a topic I talk about more fully in the later section "Filling in the gaps: Errors in memory"). Reconstructing draws on various strategies, which psychologists call *scripts*, based on your knowledge and assumptions of what happens where and when (your preconceptions, in other words). The more the event follows your day-to-day expectations, the more you're reconstructing what you *think* happened rather than any direct memory of what really *did* happen. The result is that you may inadvertently alter the facts and leave some out.

Decaying over time

Psychologists studying memory found that memories of a past event often become rapidly worse and less detailed over time. This *decay over time* starts soon after the event, and then the loss of memory levels off. The longer the delay between an event and your attempt to remember it, the less complete and accurate your account is generally likely to be. For example, this decay can easily apply to a witness now taking part in a police lineup or viewing a set of identification photographs.

The decay isn't the same for everything, though. I can still remember that I was washing dishes and listening to the radio when I heard of John Lennon's death. (It wasn't the unusualness of my washing up, but being at Liverpool University when The Beatles were in their prime meant that they were part of my formative years.) However, I can't even remember if it was my turn to do the dishes last Wednesday. Regular actions and events don't stick out in the same way as special or unusual ones.

REMEMBER

Your memory doesn't normally improve over time, and most of your forgetting takes place close in time to the event. Within a few days, most of the forgetting that's going to take place has already happened. This forgetting occurs even when you've taken pains to "store" the memory by rehearsing it. Also, as you grow older, retrieving information from memory becomes slower, without a doubt. However, what you forget, and what you have difficulty remembering, does depend on the many aspects I mention throughout this chapter.

Filling in the gaps: Errors in memory

You deal with the incremental loss of memory for events over time by *reconstructing* what happened. The process of reconstructing those memories that don't stand out for the sorts of special emotional or distinct qualities I mention earlier can include:

>> Connections you're holding between places and events

>> Your experiences of patterns typical of various sorts of activities

>> What you know about people and activities

Memories are open to distortion from existing preconceptions, and from information discovered and events occurring after the experiences now being remembered. Typically, these distortions aren't deliberate or conscious: You genuinely believe that what you're remembering is what actually occurred.

Post-event information can affect a witness's memory and even cause the person to include nonexistent details into a previously acquired memory.

One unexpected consequence of these distortions is that a witness's report in a criminal case can become more complete and less ambiguous each time the witness repeats what (allegedly) happened. So the account being heard in court appears to be more accurate, perhaps many months after the initial somewhat confused report that was given to the police. This process of *filling in* can be an efficient way of remembering, but can also be unreliable. The witness may be distorting or reconstructing the memory to fit information that becomes available after the event, such as who's suspected of the crime. The witness may be doing so for the best of intentions, conscientiously constructing parts of an unclear memory to make it seem more plausible.

Facing up to false memories

False memories occur when you remember something but getting one or more details wrong, or in extreme circumstances thinking you remember something that didn't in fact happen. In a crime investigation, one of the most direct ways in which false memories occur is when a witness is offered an answer, which is implied by the phrasing of the question.

Elizabeth Loftus, a leading psychologist, carried out experiments showing that people can come to believe that they remember something by being led to believe it happened (see the nearby sidebar "Example of a Loftus experiment").

The law recognizes false memory by limiting the use of leading questions that imply what answer the witness is expected to give. The most extreme leading questions are those implying guilt, such as this famous example: "When did you stop beating your wife?" But a subtler leading question that implies the answer, "What did you see the defendant carrying from the shop?" is likely to be challenged by any good defense lawyer. The question implies that the defendant was indeed carrying something, possibly leading the witness in trying to think of something they *may* have seen. A better question is, "Did you see the defendant leaving the shop?" or, even better, "What did you see?"

AN EXPERIMENT IN ENCOURAGING FALSE MEMORIES

Spend 30 seconds memorizing the 14 words in this list; after 30 seconds, cover the list and write down as many of the words as you can remember:

Wheel	Road
Driving	Traffic
Travel	Passenger
Engine	Fuel
Highway	Tire
Steering	Journey
Van	Train

Compare the words you've written down against the list of words. Are any words on your list not on my list? Did you add extra words, such as *auto* or *car* or any other term having to do with road travel? If so, they're false memories. This exercise shows that your added words tend to be connected with vehicles or road travel because each of the listed words is associated with such traveling. When recalling the words from the list, you draw on the commonly associated meanings of these words to help you in remembering. But by using that as a cue, you add words that are *not* on the list, though you possibly thought they should have been. To test this idea, you could ask "did you recall the word 'train'?" Not creating that word demonstrates that it was road travel that was the central memory device you were drawing on to remember the words from the list.

Recovered memories are another aspect of false memories that are contentious. These particular forms of false memory came to the fore with a number of well-publicized accounts of people supposedly remembering that they'd been abused as children many years earlier, although they'd apparently long forgotten that abuse. Such memories usually emerge during the course of psychotherapy. Of course, as I mention earlier, certain processes can also improve the details of what is remembered — that's different from what I'm calling recovered memories here.

EXTREME EXAMPLE OF FALSE MEMORIES

The daughters of Paul Ingram *recovered* memories of their father abusing them. Ingram was a Christian fundamentalist and the chief civil deputy in a sheriff's department. He agreed to be intensively interrogated, using techniques similar to those used in hypnosis (which I describe in the later section "Using investigative hypnosis"). During investigative hypnosis, Ingram recovered memories of having brutally raped his daughters over a long time and of having led a satanic cult that sacrificially murdered hundreds of babies. He was sentenced to 20 years in prison, although there was no evidence that he had committed any of the crimes. No babies were missing, and no bodies found. Ingram later denied his confession but was released only after serving his sentence.

Assisting Witnesses and Victims to Remember

Gathering as much relevant information as you can from an interview in a criminal investigation is vitally important. Psychologists have developed ways of maximizing the information you find during an interview. In this section, I describe two such approaches (cognitive interviews and hypnosis) and give you guidelines on how children are best interviewed.

Letting someone speak: The cognitive interview

To carry out a successful and effective interview, consider these actions:

>> Helping the interviewee try to remember what happened. Anything that can help the memory process is of value.

>> Establishing a good relationship between the interviewer and the interviewee (known as conversation management, which I talk about in the earlier section "Managing the process: Interviews as conversations"). You need to be as supportive and helpful as possible so that more effective information is likely to be obtained.

The *cognitive interview* has been developed to enhance both of these aspects of interviewing by suggesting that you try these strategies:

>> Establishing rapport

>> Listening actively

>> Encouraging spontaneous recall

>> Asking open-ended questions

>> Pausing after responses

>> Avoiding interrupting

>> Asking for detailed descriptions

>> Encouraging the person to concentrate on the question

>> Encouraging the use of imagery

>> Re-creating the original context of the event

>> Adopting the witness's perspective

>> Asking relevant questions

>> Encouraging multiple retrieval attempts

Cognitive interviewing stresses the importance of making full use of various mental processes. Therefore, you need training and preparation before carrying out a cognitive interview. This type of interview is also time-consuming and sometimes difficult to put into practice. For these reasons, cognitive interviewing is being used more in research studies than in real-life police investigations.

Interviewing suspects

Questioning someone who's suspected of a crime is rather different from interviewing a victim or witness. What the person says may be used in evidence against them. (The more challenging matter of whether they may *not* be telling the truth is dealt with in Chapter 8.) The law in most countries tries to control how those interviews take place. One problem, though, is that police interrogators may believe that the purpose of their questioning is to gain a confession. This can lead to people admitting to crimes they have not committed.

Dealing with false confessions

Sometimes a person confesses to committing a crime when they're innocent. This strange situation can come about for a number of reasons:

>> **Substance abuse:** Being drunk or on drugs at the time of the crime can mean having no actual memory of what happened and therefore being susceptible to suggestions.

>> **Mental illness:** Schizophrenia, for example, makes it difficult for the person to distinguish fantasy from reality.

>> **Learning disability:** This might mean the person is unable to understand what's happening.

>> **Cultural differences:** An authority figure's statements may be accepted without question, causing a person from this culture to accept that they have done whatever they've been told they've done.

>> **Coercion:** A person can be threatened or coerced into making a confession.

>> **Submissive personality:** Someone with a personality that's susceptible to the influence of others, which is shown by recognized personality tests.

In the UK, police officers are trained in an interview procedure that emphasizes that the point of questioning a suspect is to find the truth, not necessarily to get a confession. It is not true elsewhere. In the US, there is still a culture of interrogation to get a confession. This is changing around the world with the introduction of the UN guidelines mentioned earlier and explored further in Chapter 8.

REGIONAL
TIP-OFF

Recognizing the importance of improving police interview procedures, authorities in England and Wales in 1992 introduced the PEACE system, which draws on research similar to the cognitive interview: The PEACE acronym summarizes five stages:

>> **P**reparation and planning

>> **E**ngage and explain the purpose of the interview and process

>> **A**ccount: Free recall

>> **C**larify, challenge, conclude

>> **E**valuate the quality of the interview and perhaps seek new lines of inquiry

PEACE gives weight to what the police do before and after the interview and highlights the importance of engaging with the respondent: building rapport and listening carefully. The aim is to encourage the interviewee to give an uninterrupted account in response to open questions, such as "Tell me what you remember."

Although the use of PEACE has had beneficial effects on police interviewing, some police officers still interrupt and ask focused rather than closed questions. In part, this seems to be because the PEACE framework goes against the grain of police culture, which is to make forceful assumptions about an event and then use the interview to confirm that assumption.

Using investigative hypnosis

What is hypnosis? Now, that's a big question! You may believe it's a special trance-like state that reaches aspects of consciousness that aren't reached any other way. Or you may think it's just a form of relaxed concentration that allows people to focus on certain things more clearly.

Experts frown on the stage hypnotist, who's apparently making people do silly things against their will. Research studies show that it's difficult to persuade someone to take actions against their will while under hypnosis, but you can certainly confuse the person. Also, not everyone can be readily hypnotized. As part of my forensic psychology training, I attended hypnosis sessions, but I never delved into anything other than a slightly edgy, quiet state (yet I can fall asleep during a classical music concert with no difficulty).

But whatever hypnosis really is, some researchers claim that in special circumstances, it can help witnesses or victims remember more clearly what they saw. Hypnosis is used only rarely when it's thought that a person may be able to remember some crucial detail if carefully helped. It holds the risk, like any intensive interview process, of distorting what is remembered; therefore, many safeguards are recommended if hypnosis is being used in a criminal investigation. For example, the hypnotist has to be fully trained and must have no other involvement in the investigation, and the hypnosis session must always be fully recorded by audio or, preferably, video.

Follow these stages in investigative hypnosis:

1. **Preparation:** Reviewing what's already known about the crime and the witness or victim and finding out what needs to be known.

2. **Introduction:** Telling the person being hypnotized what's going to happen and why.

3. **Induction of the hypnotic state:** Taking actions that include eye fixation, looking upward while closing the eyes, deep breathing, muscle relaxation, and repeated instructions to relax.

4. **Deepening the state:** Increasing the comfort of the person being hypnotized, using images of being on a sunny beach or another relaxing location.

5. **Drawing out information:** Reminding the witness of the crime scene and then encouraging the person to give a further account of what happened.

   A witness can be prompted at this stage to go into even more detail. A posthypnotic suggestion can also be used to help the witness remember other material, to help any further interview.

6. **Bringing the person out of the hypnotic state:** Using instructions to make the person feel calm, relaxed, fully awake, and normal in every way.

Investigative hypnosis is a potentially powerful procedure, but is open to all the problems, confusion, and influences I discuss in the earlier section "Facing up to false memories." It can generate, or seem to generate, memories of events that did not actually happen. Because of this, many courts disallow information obtained under hypnosis to be used as evidence.

Helping children tell what happened

Children become involved in criminal proceedings for many reasons: as victims, witnesses, and defendants. There have been historical swings of opinion on whether children should be allowed to give evidence and much debate about how to involve them in court. These days, young children (often, *young* depends on the maturity of the child and the views of the judge) rarely appear in the actual courtroom. In many places. This may be a video-recorded interview in a special room in a police station, or by video link in a court case where they're generally interviewed in a separate room. This arrangement makes for less intimidating surroundings and, likely, a more successful interview.

An interview supporter, interpreter, or intermediary may be used in an earlier interview or during the trial to make sure that the child understands what's being asked of them.

Interviewing children, follows these four main stages:

1. **Establish rapport with the child.**

2. **Encourage the child to provide a free-flowing, uninterrupted narrative of what happened, in their own words.**

3. **Ask specific questions based on that free narrative, only then followed by other necessary and appropriate questions.**

4. **Obtain closure (for example, post-interview counseling).**

If questioned effectively by skilled, trained interviewers children can be reliable witnesses, giving detailed, valid information. In Chapter 8, I look at how experts examine children's statements for validity. This is an important issue because, in certain cases (for example, sexual or physical abuse), children are the only witnesses.

Looking into Eyewitness Testimony

Even with the increasing use by law enforcement of digital evidence from cellphones, and computers witnesses are e still essential in many criminal investigation, providing on-the-spot and relevant evidence in court proceedings. *Eyewitness testimony* is often vitally important in catching a criminal, yet problems can arise over the accuracy of eyewitness evidence.

The reasons for errors in identifications are complex and not fully understood, but many academic studies point to relevant factors such as the length of time between the alleged event and the identification.

A witness can feel pressure to perform. The witness is also likely to assume that the police have a suspect in mind or even in custody. They therefore feel they have to identify someone, even if the officer asking the questions is careful not to force the issue. Police interviewing the witness can sometimes unintentionally communicate their knowledge about who is the suspect.

Such inadvertent influence, often by conveying verbal and nonverbal cues, was found to be particularly problematic in the old system of lining up a number of people including the suspect. The eyewitness was then required to identify which participant in the row of people being viewed is the person they saw. Many studies have shown the power of the inadvertent influence of the administrator of the identification task. It has been found that when some administrators were given assumptions that one person was the culprit, and others the assumption that it was a different person, the person identified by a witness varied, depending on the assumption the administrator had been given.

That process organizing a row of people into which the suspect is places for iden-tification by an eyewitness is illustrated in many fiction films and documenta-ries. However, that is now very unusual. Some countries have replaced this with a set of photographs rather than a n actual line up of people. More generally through, the ready availability of video recording has given rise to a widely used procedure known in the UK as the VIPER procedure — *Video Identification Parade Electronic Recording,* developed to reduce stress for witnesses and streamline the identification process. VIPER involves:

- **Digital Line-Up:** Instead of a live line-up, witnesses view a short video showing the suspect alongside several volunteers. Each person turns their head from left to right in a neutral setting.

- **Standardized Presentation:** All individuals appear against a grey background, wearing similar clothing, and performing the same movements to minimize bias.

- **Volunteer Database:** The system uses a large database of volunteer video clips representing diverse ages, genders, and ethnicities. These clips are recorded under controlled conditions and stored securely.

- **Witness Experience:** Witnesses view the parade on a screen at a police station, often with support from trained officers. They can replay the video if needed, and the suspect is never physically present.

REMEMBER

The term *remember* covers different kinds of processes. One process is *recalling* which requires generating a memory with little help or guidance. That is different from *recognizing* that relies on selecting from cues offered. As mentioned *recalling* an event draws heavily on the need to reconstruct what happened (as I discuss in the earlier section "Remembering That Memory Can Mislead"). *Recognition* is illustrated, for example, by the fact that you may be unable to recall a name but can readily choose the correct name from a list.

Although recognition is generally more accurate than recall, recognition is still open to distortions, as shown in these examples:

- **Age:** Witnesses are most accurate when calculating the age of someone of a similar age because they're already familiar with that age group. And the greater the difference between the age of the witness and the age of the offender, the less accurate a witness's estimate of the offender's age is likely to be.

- **Height:** Witnesses are often poor at judging heights, and as with age, the greater the difference in height between the offender and the eyewitness, the less accurate the estimate.

- **Build:** Witnesses have difficulty judging the build of a person, with judgments heavily influenced by clothing.

- **Clothing:** Witnesses' descriptions of clothing *styles* are usually reasonably accurate, but descriptions of clothing *colors* are often less accurate.

Eyewitness identifications aren't nearly as accurate and reliable as members of the public and the courts believe. For example, in one experiment, a person draws attention to themselves by paying only with pennies for their purchases at a convenience store. Soon afterward, the salesperson views a photo spread and identifies the "customer." The percentage of correct identifications in this type of exercise ranges from 34 to 48 percent; the percentage of false identifications, from 34 to 38 percent. Even after quite a short interval, an eyewitness is as likely to be incorrect as correct when attempting to identify strangers.

Eyewitnesses are most accurate when identifying someone from a familiar and similar situation to themselves.

REGIONAL TIP-OFF

THE INNOCENCE PROJECT

Scary but horribly true! In 1999, in the US, eyewitness identifications led to 75,000 prosecutions. DNA, which now offers a much more reliable way of identifying a suspect, shows just how dodgy many legal eyewitness identifications are. One study shows that of the 62 persons acquitted by DNA evidence, 52 had been imprisoned on the basis of faulty eyewitness identification. These early findings have now contributed to an ever more widespread follow-up of the findings that the majority of false convictions are caused by mistaken eyewitness testimony. As a consequence, there's an increasing uptake of reforms to eyewitness testimony procedures in many US states and in other countries, as discussed in the section "Minimizing bias: Good practice recommendations," later in this chapter.

MYTH BUSTER

LACK OF RELATIONSHIP BETWEEN CONFIDENCE AND ACCURACY

A witness talking with great confidence about what they can remember doesn't mean they're any more accurate in what they're saying than someone who seems much less confident. There's no evidence of a simple link between confidence and accuracy, although that does depend on the person. Some witnesses will only speak with confidence when what they say is actually valid. Furthermore, confidence increases over time, especially if the witness is giving the same account to different people, so any relationship between confidence and accuracy grows less and less.

Also, if a police officer confirms to a witness that what the witness says agrees with other facts known to the police, the witness's confidence increases further, although the accuracy of what's being said doesn't.

A person is more likely to be recognized by a witness, or an event to be accurately described, if the happening was particularly memorable or striking. For example, you're more likely to remember a person's clothing, race, or age if it stands out in contrast to that of other bystanders. Unusual events — such as a ballerina tripping during a performance or, even more memorable, a politician admitting that they made a mistake — are more readily noted and remembered because the event is rare and unusual.

Assessing eyewitness accuracy

Mnemonics, in which a memorable word is used to summarize a set of other facts, is a powerful aid to memory. Two colleagues of mine, Graham Wagstaff and Mark Kebbell, have created the mnemonic *ADVOKATE* to summarize the key factors influencing a witness's ability to remember the details of an event:

>> **A**mount of time under observation: The longer a witness observes an event, the better the event is remembered.

>> **D**istance of the witness from the person or event: Being closer to the person or the event means that a witness is likely to be better at storing and remembering details.

>> **V**isibility: The more visible the event, the better the witness is likely to recall it.

>> **O**bstruction: The fewer obstructions to a witness's view, the better the event is remembered.

>> **K**nown or seen before: If a witness has seen the offender before, they're more likely to remember when they see that person again in a different situation.

>> **A**ny reason to remember: If something is striking or novel, it's more likely to make a strong impression on the witness.

>> **T**ime lapse: The greater the length of time between an event and the witness's attempts to recall it, the worse their memory for that event is likely to be.

>> **E**rrors or discrepancies: If parts of a witness's testimony are inaccurate, other aspects of the testimony are also likely to be inaccurate.

REMEMBER

If someone's pointing a knife or gun at you, the chances are good that you're looking at the weapon rather than at the face of the attacker. Stress, fear, violence, or the presence of a weapon will help you remember more clearly what is happening, but some of the details may be left out because you're noticing what's important to your survival and not the information that can help identify your attacker.

Understanding unconscious transference

Human memory is much more readily influenced than you may realize, and it constantly strives to make events and happenings fit together and make sense. Memory can be distorted by exposure to similar situations or people between the event and its later recall. Also, because recognition is helped by being in the situation where the events being recalled took place, an out-of-context witness can be aware that a person seems familiar but be confused about where they may have seen or met that person. This process is called *unconscious transference*, where the witness remembers seeing a person but wrongly assigns that person to the criminal context.

How widely unconscious transference occurs is unclear, as is what degree of familiarity with the other person is necessary — and under what circumstances — for it to surface. Many psychologists agree that unconscious transference needs to be watched out for when considering eyewitness testimony.

In an experiment to demonstrate unconscious transference, 50 students were told a story with six characters, one of whom was a criminal. The students were shown pictures of each character, who were all generally similar in appearance. Three days later, the students were asked to choose the criminal at the center of the story from a set of photos. In the sets of photos that didn't include the criminal's picture, 60 per cent of the students chose a photo of a character whose face seemed familiar but wasn't the criminal of the story.

ANECDOTE

Here's an example of unconscious transference in an actual case. At the railway station, the ticket clerk was robbed at gunpoint. He later identified a sailor as his assailant. On the day of the robbery, however, the sailor was away at sea. The forensic psychologist reviewing the case realized that the sailor had been an obvious victim of unconscious transference. The ticket clerk picked him out from the police lineup because his face was familiar. As it turned out, the sailor was based near the railway station and had bought train tickets from the same clerk on three different occasions before the robbery took place.

Minimizing bias: Good practice recommendations

To cut the risk of bias in police lineup identifications, the American Psychological Association (APA) recommends these strategies:

>> **Double-blind testing:** The person managing the lineup should have no knowledge of the identities of the persons in the lineup or of the culprit.

>> **Keeping eyewitnesses informed:** The eyewitnesses should not be told whether the culprit will be present in the lineup.

>> **Look-alikes:** Make sure that the persons selected in the lineup resemble the description of the suspect given by the eyewitness.

>> **Confidence of the eyewitness:** To be assessed and recorded at the time of identification.

>> **Impartiality:** Make no comment about the person the eyewitness chooses.

Sometimes, the recommendations of the APA on bias are completely disregarded by the court. For example, a judge or an attorney may ask the witness, "Is the person who you saw leaving the premises with the stolen goods here in court?" And the witness is face-to-face with the accused, who is standing in in front of the court. This is a situation in which these statements are true:

>> The suspect is put at a disadvantage.

>> The court assumes that the suspect appeared in the police identification process.

>> Only the lone suspect is presented to the witness in the court proceedings.

>> A witness who's feeling insecure or unsure about their testimony can hide behind the legal formalities.

REMEMBER

Asking a witness to identify the person standing in the dock as the person spotted at the time of the crime is an unsafe and unsound means of seeking witness corroboration, yet many jurisdictions around the world use this procedure with great confidence.

Chapter **8**

Exposing Liars and Detecting Deception

A lthough most people tell the truth, deceptions do occur every now and then, such as telling that little white lie, from the highest of motives, because you want to avoid hurting your best friend's feelings. Or you may even hide the truth because life would become just too complicated if you had to explain all the details. But dishonesty isn't the default characteristic of the majority of people in most situations.

This situation is a bit different, though, in the world of crime and criminal investigations. You can't assume that everyone is trying their best to tell the truth and nothing but the truth. Police investigators have to assume that suspects may try to weave a web of lies. They may deny guilt or, even more problematically for detectives and prosecutors, falsely confess to being guilty.

Filtering out the truth and detecting deception is a major challenge for any investigation. In this chapter, I take a look at the nature of lying, the ways that people set out to deceive, and the tools available to help disentangle truth from lies. I also delve into the business of interviewing criminals and the difficulties faced when trying to get at the truth when examining documents.

Understanding the Nature of Lying

It's not that easy to lie. (See the next section to discover the difficulties.) So people lie in many different ways:

>> Saying something false as if it were true (the most obvious way)

>> Leaving out key facts in an account when those facts are likely to reveal the truth

>> Hiding the truth by giving misleading information

>> Providing a partial account by omitting certain facts

>> Telling the truth in an exaggerated way and making it sound unbelievable

Surprisingly, many suspects will admit to their crimes. The majority of convictions come because the culprit confesses. But you also need to understand that certain suspects are *more likely* to tell lies than tell you the truth, simply because of the type of person they are, such as the ones described in this list:

>> **Psychopath:** This person lies even when telling the truth won't harm them or cause them any problems. Telling lies can be just a habit they have without thinking about it.

STRANGE BUT TRUE

In extreme forms of psychosis, the person has difficulty distinguishing between what's real and what's imaginary. This situation raises an interesting philosophical question: Can a person who believes that their neighbors are reading their thoughts and poisoning their cat and complains about it to the police be regarded as a liar? This question poses a challenge for investigators if they have no understanding of psychosis. It can also make legal proceedings fraught because the defense can challenge anything the person claims, even though some of it may be genuine.

>> **Adults with a learning or mental disability or a young child:** Both of these may be unable to tell the difference between the actual facts and what they want the facts to be. Also, as any parent can tell you, a child from a remarkably young age is quite clever at deceiving you if it serves their purpose or they think it's fun. Because of this problem, it's possible that such individuals may not be allowed to give evidence in court.

ANECDOTE

Before my grandson was even a year old, he liked to play a game of putting out his hand to me and pretending he was giving me a present, and then pulling his hand away, giggling furiously as I tried to grab hold of it. An example of deception being practiced from a very early age?

>> In certain social groups, there's a deep-seated fear, or respect, of figures of authority, believing they must agree with anything the authority figure says. Therefore, a suspect may agree to having been in a particular place simply because a police officer is telling them that's the case. This tendency raises issues about more forceful techniques of discovering lying and deceit, which I discuss later in this chapter, in "Interrogating suspects."

Discovering the difficulties of successful deception

You may be surprised to find that being a successful liar isn't all that easy. This fact becomes clear when you think about the emotional and intellectual demands that people who are lying place upon themselves:

>> A liar has to create a lie, requiring imagination.

>> A liar has to combine the untruth together with the known facts.

>> A liar has to develop the untruth around plausible possibilities.

>> A liar has to think through how to make the deception plausible, which can be intellectually challenging.

>> A liar has to be careful not to give themselves away when they're believed, by some response, such as smirking, that may seem inappropriate to the interviewer.

Sticking fast to the lie is the most difficult aspect of lying. For example, if someone offers you a vast sum of money in exchange for doing nothing, you don't need any sophisticated lie-detecting equipment to know there's a catch. You simply know that the world doesn't work like that — providing free lunches willy-nilly.

Experienced fraudsters know that people may be suspicious of what they're offering, which is why the fraudster couches their claims in plausible scenarios (such as, "Your address came up in a lottery that you didn't know about"). In the later section "Plausibility," I describe the procedures you can follow for testing the truth and reliability of a statement being given in court.

Recognizing why detecting deception is extremely difficult

Any lie detection procedure should take into account the intellectual and emotional demands that lying requires (as I describe in the earlier section

"Discovering the difficulties of successful deception"). The nitty-gritty of detecting a lie is in testing the plausibility of the claims the suspect is making. But if a liar truly believes that they're telling you the truth, none of the intellectual or emotional aspects of lying exist, and the usual procedures for detecting deception are unlikely to work.

Hardened liars are experts in using strategies to reduce the likelihood of being detected:

>> The lie is rehearsed so that there's no need to invent a lie on the spot with all the associated risks of getting details wrong or saying something implausible.

>> The lie is built on an event that actually happened, so most of the details are true and plausible and don't need to be invented. Only some crucial aspects of the lie are untruthful.

>> The liar avoids giving any details to eliminate the risk of tripping themselves up.

REMEMBER

You can make things much harder for a suspect you think is lying by asking for as much detail as possible. The more the liar has to invent, the more chance they'll reveal inconsistencies in their story.

Detecting Lies: Some Procedures

Lie detection procedures have been developed for interviewing suspects in a criminal investigation, helping to weed out the lies and leaving the truth exposed. They are also relevant for considering whether witnesses or (alleged) victims may be lying.

REMEMBER

You have to bear in mind that none of the lie detection procedures I describe in this section is completely accurate or foolproof. Indeed, some procedures can mislead you into thinking you've detected lying when the opposite is the case.

You can take one of these four general approaches in detecting lying or deceit:

>> **Physiological approach:** Records the physiological changes in a person's body when answering specific questions.

>> **Behavioral approach:** Examines the way a person is behaving to see whether the person is showing any of the emotional or stressful aspects of lying (see the earlier section "Discovering the difficulties of successful deception").

>> **Semantic assessment:** Evaluates the words the person is using and the possible meanings in the answers they're giving under questioning.

>> **Legal approach:** Questions a person in a court of law and undertakes a detailed examination of the plausibility of their statement.

Lie detector procedures — such as physiological, behavioral, semantic, and legal approaches — are concerned with testing the truthfulness of what the person is saying while giving an account of a significant event. These procedures don't include a careful investigation that can show that a person's *alibi* — the claim not to have been at the crime scene — is false. Nor do these procedures have the means of examining the impossibility of the person doing what is claimed — for example, because that person has a physical disability or the journey they claimed to have taken could not have been completed in the time available. You need to independently test the credibility of what the person is claiming to find out whether the person's story is true.

Testing the validity of a lie detector procedure can be problematic. For example, you set up an experiment in which you get a person to simulate committing a crime. Then the person is questioned using a lie detection procedure. But in an artificial situation, the reactions of the suspect and the truthfulness or otherwise of the suspect's statement don't carry the same high stakes as in real life, where not being believed can mean a long prison sentence.

REMEMBER

Getting true-life examples of the validity of lie detector procedures can throw up many ethical and legal problems. In the real world, getting adequate comparisons with what is likely to have happened in a criminal investigation if the lie detector procedure hadn't been used is often impossible. Companies selling lie detection equipment or software typically avoid providing important comparison data. Although the company claims their product can show that many deceptions were uncovered using their (often expensive) system, no one can tell you whether the lie detector system truly did add value. I discuss this anomaly in more detail later in this chapter, in the section "Combating insurance fraud."

Using physiological approaches

Monitoring the physiological reactions of suspects to detect whether they're telling the truth or lying has been in use for some years (a topic I talk about in Chapter 1). The aim of the physiological approach is to pick up on what's technically known as *arousal*: a heightened energizing of the nervous system and muscles. Arousal is shown by an increase in heart rate and the rate of breathing, as well as by a change in the skin's ability to conduct electricity because of an increase in sweating. The person's voice can also become higher-pitched and more erratic. The person may also move around a bit more and squirm.

The problem for the forensic psychologist is that the heightened responses can also be a sign of general emotional reactions produced by the anxiety of being questioned, especially if the person fears being wrongly thought of as a liar.

ANECDOTE

Recently, a TV show demonstrated the unreliability of the physiological approach for testing lying. Celebrities were asked tricky questions to find out whether the answers they were giving were true or false. The interrogator maintained that the lie detection system showed that some of the celebrities were lying — but the celebrities hotly denied the accusation.

The celebrities were likely reacting emotionally to the crassness of the questions being asked — in front of millions of viewers on live TV. The experiment was dropped from further shows.

Companies selling physiological lie detector tests often claim that the lie detector can tell the difference between testing normal anxiety and the anxiety associated with lying. For example, the claim is that as the test continues, normal anxiety disappears and the emotions associated with lying show at particular points when lies are being told. But variations between individuals in their response to the questioning can mask such subtleties.

REMEMBER

Displaying heightened emotional responses isn't the same as lying. All physiological lie detection procedures are, in fact, detecting only emotional responses, such as the anxiety of the person being interviewed, from believing that they won't be believed. Because physiological lie detectors can be unreliable in detecting whether a person is lying, few courts allow their findings as evidence.

The polygraph

The *polygraph* is a machine used for measuring a number of small physiological changes in the body at one and the same time: heart rate, breathing, and sweating, for example. It's the best-known type of equipment for detecting lying (and is usually just called a *lie detector*). Originally, the polygraph recorded these physiological changes using pens running across a moving sheet of paper, which is where the name *polygraph* comes from, meaning "many lines." Polygraph machines have since been computerized, so the magic of pens bouncing across paper with a dramatic, crunchy upsurge when a "lie" was being told is no more.

In an attempt to separate normal heightened emotional responses from the responses associated with lying, the polygraph is used alongside the *guilty knowledge procedure.* Under this procedure, the suspect is asked to give yes or no answers to questions that contain a mixture of information, some of which is common knowledge, and some that only the suspect can possibly know about (the "guilty knowledge"). The comparison between the physiological responses to the questions containing the guilty knowledge and the unbiased questions is used to indicate whether the person is lying.

Scientific studies show that the guilty knowledge procedure is the most reliable procedure on the market for detecting lying. It typically correctly identifies liars in about three out of four cases. Importantly, the guilty knowledge procedure is much better at showing when a person *isn't* lying than showing when they are, doing that correctly in as many as eight out of ten cases.

As long as the guilty knowledge procedure spots no suspicious reactions, that person is likely to be telling the truth. So, although most courts don't allow a polygraph test to be presented as evidence of guilt, it can sometimes be a useful way of eliminating a suspect from the investigation because of the person being shown probably to be telling the truth.

When setting up a polygraph test using the guilty knowledge procedure, you need to know about the circumstances of the crime as well as understand how much only the suspect can possibly know (which is difficult if lots of information about the crime has become public knowledge). Also, the suspect has to be carefully briefed about what happens during a polygraph test and how the procedure works.

There may not be much that only the suspect would know, so other types of polygraph procedures are sometimes used. For example, a suspect's physiological reactions when presented with incriminating information may be compared with their reactions when asked innocent questions about things that many people do wrong. This is far less reliable than the guilty knowledge test. Consider your likely reaction to being wired up to a polygraph and being asked bluntly, "Have you ever lied to avoid being found out about something you did wrong?" Like me, I think your heart is likely to start thumping and you're gasping for breath, even though most people would be expected to say yes to this question. Yet a hardened criminal is quite capable of responding in a relaxed manner: "Yeah. Sure. Haven't you?"

There are many ways of cheating on the polygraph test (entire websites are devoted to telling you how to do so). If a person's emotional responses are haphazard or they set up some distraction, such as having a stone in their shoe that's hurting them or having difficulty focusing on the question, the polygraph machine is generally unable to detect the difference in responses to crucial questions.

Anyone making a living out of polygraph testing can tell you that the key to a valid test is establishing a working relationship with the person being tested. Having rapport with your subjects determines how much they believe in the result of the procedure, sometimes to the point of admitting to guilt without even needing to read the output from the equipment.

Voice stress analysis

Voice stress analysis is a computer product on the market supposedly for detecting whether a person is telling you the truth while speaking on the phone. The product is controversial. It may be used, for example, by companies dealing with insurance claims for detecting whether the customer is making a false claim. The idea behind voice stress analysis is that stress is indicated in the voice by fluctuations in how quickly a person is speaking, with the voice higher in pitch or hesitant or using rhythms unnatural to how the person is talking, including long pauses. The sounds of the person speaking therefore undergo some sort of computer analysis to determine whether any of these aspects is greater than usual.

Voice stress analysis faces lots of problems (hence the controversy). You know yourself that the pitch of your voice changes if you have a cold, or at different times of day. Women generally have higher-pitched voices than men, as well as pitch changing with age. Voice stress analysis also suffers from the same problems as the polygraph: It mainly measures heightened stress, or confusion, not lying. A person whose house was recently burgled and who phones in to claim insurance might well be stressed.

Developments in artificially intelligent computer algorithms are being applied to these issues. They attempt to overcome some of the false conclusions that an innocent person isn't telling the truth. But, as in all attempts to develop a machine that will detect truths and lies, the jury is still out on whether they're truly reliable.

My concern is that voice stress analysis can be used by inexperienced and untrained call handlers, who simply watch the indicator on their screen (that's supposedly indicating whether a person is telling the truth) instead of the call handler listening carefully to what the customer is saying and how plausible they sound. In other words, does the use of voice stress analysis distract from the less high-tech approach of carefully challenging what the person is claiming? (As considered in the later section, "Studying semantic assessment.")

Truth drugs

Administering *truth drugs* to detect lying and deceit was popular for a short while in the second half of the 20th century. The favored drugs were sodium amytal or sodium pentothal, which are essentially sedatives. The idea was that they would make the person being questioned less wary when replying because they're in a highly relaxed state, induced by the drugs. However, the reliability of truth drugs is questionable because a person in a dreamlike state is just as likely to be fantasizing as telling the truth. In effect, it's like having plenty to drink: The person is likely to become more chatty, but no more likely to reveal whether they're lying.

Under international law, using truth drugs to detect lying is regarded as a form of torture. Judges forbid evidence gained from using truth drugs.

Brain fingerprinting

Scientists are now able to produce a map of the electrical and related activity in the different parts of the brain, which commercial companies call *brain fingerprinting.* Mapping electrical activity in the brain is a more sophisticated lie detection procedure than those I've already talked about (see the earlier sections "The polygraph" and "Voice stress analysis"). Brain fingerprinting consists of placing a number of electrical detectors on a suspect's head and mapping the pattern of electrical activity across the brain while the person is answering questions during a crime investigation.

The technique of brain fingerprinting is similar to the guilty knowledge procedure used with polygraph testing, except that this time the person being interviewed is shown pictures relevant to the crime mixed up with unrelated images, with the technique picking up on the images the suspect is particularly sensitive to. It's also being enhanced by computer analyses as artificial intelligence takes hold.

Growing evidence suggests that, under carefully controlled conditions, brain-mapping has a part to play in determining a suspect's innocence or guilt because those suspects who do have trust or faith in the procedure, are likely to be inclined to confess. Brain-mapping, an advanced version of physiological testing, is likely to be used more and more as the equipment becomes cheaper and less cumbersome, as well as being integrated into computer analyses.

BRAIN-MAPPING RESEARCH

Early research studies show that some parts of the brain are particularly active during lying — for example, when a group of people were told they would be paid a small sum if they were successful in lying about the cards they were holding in their hands. The results of these studies allowed the researchers to decide with a high degree of accuracy whether a person was lying. Studies since then claim 100 per cent accuracy in detecting lying. Brain-mapping evidence has been used in India to support the guilt of a person accused of murder, as well as the innocence of others. But it is not accepted as evidence in most European countries.

Observing carefully: Behavioral approaches

You can find out a great deal about what a person is thinking and saying from the way they're behaving. In the game of poker, where you have to decide whether another player is bluffing or has a great hand, a nonverbal clue is called a *tell* (such as shuffling their feet or scratching an ear, suggesting that they're lying). Using these clues to detect deception is fraught with difficulties. Studies show that looking at the way a person is behaving, and what they're saying, as a means of determining whether they're lying is more complicated than it first appears.

Nonverbal leakage (body language)

You can't help thinking the term *nonverbal leakage* sounds a bit rude (conjuring up the image of a young child squirming because of needing the toilet but denying it furiously — although, come to think of it, the squirming *is* a form of nonverbal leakage and, if correctly understood, can indeed stop other forms of leakage). The idea is that people show you what they're feeling from the way they behave, but they aren't doing this consciously — as when a person threatens you by waving their fist in your face — they're doing it inadvertently. It's leaking from them without them being aware that it's happening.

This nonverbal leakage is an aspect of *body language.* You express many things without the use of words, sometimes deliberately: a shrug of the shoulders, looking away, glaring into someone's eyes. There are claims that some aspects of this nonverbal communication can be used to indicate lying.

Using body language to determine lying is unreliable, in that everyone has their own way of behaving when telling a lie, and that behavior can change from situation to situation. Even poker players are aware that not every player has the same tell; you have to watch a person playing over time to spot whether the tell is special to that individual.

STRANGE BUT TRUE

HOW WELL DO THE EXPERTS DETECT DECEPTION?

Regarding body language studies show that professionals, such as police officers, are not much better at detecting deception than the person in the street. Typically, both groups have success in detecting truth or lying accurately in just over half the cases studied (only marginally better than guessing by tossing a coin). The only professional groups that do significantly better at detecting lying are members of the secret services, that employ spies. Some studies indicate that spies seem to get it right in nearly two out of every three cases.

Some people assume that a guilty person is likely to be more nervous when lying and show stress by displaying more hand movements, slower speech, and general fidgeting. But studies show that the opposite is the case: A person under pressure of maintaining the lie is concentrating harder on the lie, with the result that there is *less* nonverbal leakage displayed than you may expect. On the other hand, a person who's telling the truth is so often concerned to show that they're telling the truth that their body language may become more animated and exaggerated.

Body language is a gripping metaphor for communicating by way of gestures, facial expressions, and other bodily movements. But these movements are not a language in the same way the written and spoken word are. They can add emphasis, as when people thump the table, but these movements and gestures don't provide an account of what is claimed. They aren't open to logical scrutiny of how plausible they are. You need to consider the words themselves and what they mean. (See the section, "Studying semantic assessment.")

Micro-twitches

Paul Ekman has spent more than 40 years studying how people express emotions, focusing on the small changes in facial muscles that go with what a person is feeling. These *micro-twitches* often last only a fraction of a second, and you can see them best by watching a slowed-down video recording. Ekman claims that micro-twitches show what a person is feeling even when trying to hide their emotions. They aren't really part of body language, because they're visible only under special scrutiny.

Giving a false smile to hide what you're really feeling is the most obvious micro-twitch. Ekman's theory claims that although the muscles around the mouth are indicating pleasure, the facial muscles around your eyes are showing the opposite.

As a result of Ekman's research, micro-twitches are now being used for trying to detect lying and deceit. The problem is that these tiny facial muscles can show only strong emotions, such as anger, fear, or surprise. If strong emotions can be proved to link directly to truthfulness or lying, micro-twitches can be valuable in detecting deception. For example, the suspect may be asked how they feel about the victim and say that they liked the person while their wrinkling nose indicates disgust. Or the suspect is asked directly whether they're lying and they deny it, but the micro-twitches around their mouth are showing that even *they* don't believe in what they're saying.

Paul Ekman warns against the danger of ignoring the value of micro-twitches as a way of detecting lying, calling it the *Othello error:* Othello in Shakespeare's play refuses to believe Desdemona's protestations of innocence, totally ignoring her anguished face, and then killing her out of jealousy. So the investigator needs to bear in mind that the workings of the facial muscles have a part to play in helping get at the truth when you're interviewing a suspect in a crime investigation. The practice of observing micro-twitches as a way of detecting malicious intent is now being used in public places such as airports. However, this practice is being questioned on the grounds that a particular facial expression can be caused because of a person's culture in which such expressions are normal as much as being a sign of what the person is thinking and feeling. Some people also have a general dislike of authority and show this dislike in their facial expressions, despite being innocent of any crime.

**STRANGE
BUT TRUE**

Aldert Vrij and his colleagues have explored many ways of detecting deception. In one study, they carried out an experiment observing the rate of blinks before and after a person is telling a lie. Vrij found that the relative differences in the rates were much larger for liars than truth-tellers.

Paralinguistic cues

What a person's telling you, and the actual meaning of what they're saying, often has less to do with *what's* being said than *how* it's being said. Because these aspects of speech run parallel to one another, they're called *paralinguistic cues*, such as:

>> Pauses of varying length and frequency

>> The number of mispronunciations or inappropriate words

>> The speed of delivery — either very fast or very slow

>> Inappropriate nonverbal utterances, such as laughter

>> Filled pauses — for example, saying "uh" and "um"

Computer programs have been set up to measure the frequency of paralinguistic cues and the relationship to a person's emotional state. Researchers have found that big differences exist between people in their paralinguistic characteristics. If these variations are allowed for, paralinguistic cues can produce results that give a reasonably accurate indication of a person's emotional response — most notably, fear. But whether this relates to lying depends on the individual and whether the circumstances of their utterances are so demanding that these cues will be revealing.

Studying semantic assessment

When you're looking closely at a suspect's statement and you believe that they're deliberately setting out to deceive, you're dealing with what I call the semantic assessment of deception. *Semantic assessment* involves examining each significant word in the statement for meaning and how that word is being expressed. In this section, I look at what you need to do when you're carrying out a semantic assessment, the difficulties you can come up against when trying to get to grips with what's being said, and the plausibility of the statement.

Experts have drawn up useful checklists setting out the valid points you need to keep in mind when carrying out a semantic assessment of a suspect's, witness or alleged victim's statement. Some countries — notably, Germany — use these checklists for examining children's accounts of sexual abuse. The idea behind these checklists is that what you describe from actual experience will contain information that usually isn't present when you invent a description.

Here are the sorts of signs you should look for to determine whether a statement is an imaginative creation or the truth:

» Is there an overall logic to the account in which each aspect makes sense with every other aspect?

» Is the way the statement is given disorganized, or does it have a clear unfolding structure to it?

» Does it have enough convincing detail?

» Is the context in which the event occurred clear?

» Where other people are present, how well are the interactions with them described?

» Is any conversation reproduced in a plausible way?

» Are unexpected complications described?

» Are there any unusual details?

» Are some of the details given superfluous to the main account?

» Does the person giving the statement describe aspects of what they were thinking or feeling at the time?

» Are there spontaneous corrections?

» Is there an admission of lack of memory?

» Does the person making the statement raise doubts about what happened?

DON'T DO THAT — DO THIS!

ANECDOTE

Aldert Vrij and his colleagues have been looking into ways of exploiting the intellectual demands made on a person when inventing and maintaining a lie. Vrij claims that if you ask a suspect to carry out two separate tasks at the same time, putting pressure on their thought processes, more signs of lying become apparent. For example, the suspect might be asked to play a computer game while making a statement or giving an account of what happened in reverse chronological order. When this additional pressure is applied, many of the weaknesses in the plausibility of what is being said can rise to the surface.

This list of questions isn't without its critics and certainly isn't foolproof. It doesn't, for example, show the difference between a partially truthful account and an untruthful one, especially if the untruthful version is built on an event that actually happened, but not to the suspect or witness or not at the time claimed. As discussed in Chapter 7, memory fades quickly over time, so the lack of clarity in what a liar says can be mistaken for a sign that they're telling the truth. Plus, memories of a traumatic event can leave an indelible mark and can be much sharper than the answers to these questions may lead you to expect.

Looking at legal approaches

For the forensic psychologist, the most common way of finding out the truth of a suspect's statement and detecting deception is during court proceedings. Courts rely heavily on their own tried-and-tested approaches to getting at the truth, despite research showing the many difficulties associated with detecting lying and deceit.

Power of court proceedings

Lawyers have great confidence in the ritual of the court as the best way of extracting the truth from the person taking the witness stand. The witness or defendant has to swear an oath and is then examined closely in front of the judge, jury (if one is present), members of the public, and sometimes even victims. This confidence comes partly from the belief that if a ritual is powerful enough, a person feels compelled to tell the truth. Indeed, the swearing of an oath comes from times in which a belief in God's wrath was so strong that a person feared divine punishment if they lied under that oath.

Getting to the truth in a court of law relies on the effectiveness of the questioning of witnesses and the defendant. In many jurisdictions, the defendant may not be open to questioning, which was the case in British courts until quite recently because of the belief that defendants can't be expected to tell the truth or to inadvertently incriminate themselves.

In the US, the view that a person is never put in a position where they can incriminate themselves is enshrined in the Fifth Amendment to the US Constitution: ". . . nor shall be compelled in any criminal case to be a witness against himself."

Plausibility

Court proceedings, and increasingly the training of police officers and other investigators, put a great deal of emphasis on the plausibility of a person's statement. To establish the truth of a statement, the court has to refer to what's generally expected to be possible or typical for a person's lifestyle or set of circumstances. Forensic psychologists, therefore, look at statements in terms of what the person may be expected to know and how ready the person is in giving that information, including:

>> Assessing the clarity or vagueness of the evidence

>> Working out whether the evidence is being presented in a logical sequence

>> Deciding whether the witness or defendant is willing to answer questions directly

>> Considering how the evidence relates to the general pattern of similar events

>> Assessing whether irrelevant information is likely to distract from the central issue

>> Looking at whether the evidence contains too many references to people in general rather than specific persons

>> Checking to see whether the witness or defendant's evidence contains lots of modifiers, such as the words *sometimes* and *probably*

Discovering false allegations

Bringing a false allegation against a person is a particularly pernicious form of deception, especially when someone is accusing another person of a heinous crime such as sexual abuse or rape. Some research evidence shows that false accusations of rape may occur in at least one out of every ten allegations. Concern that stating such probabilities may make genuine victims reluctant to report the crime has meant that the crime may not even be reported.

REMEMBER

In the case of rape, making a false allegation is quite a separate problem from determining whether consent to sexual activity took place. A false allegation is the dishonest claim that unwanted sexual activity occurred when there's clear evidence that both parties consented to the activity or that the activity never took place.

These are some reasons for making false allegations of rape:

>> Looking for financial gain: for example, compensation

>> Seeking to gain support from other people by being seen as a "victim" who needs help

>> Needing to excuse inappropriate behavior, such as getting drunk and having a fling that's later regretted

>> Hoping the authorities can change the person's circumstances (for example, when wanting to secure different welfare housing)

>> Wanting to hurt or discredit a person or an institution

>> Creating difficulties in a relationship or as part of a job (as a form of blackmail)

>> Claiming false (as in recovered) memory, a topic I discuss in Chapter 7

REMEMBER

The major problem with rape investigations is, as mentioned, that victims are often reluctant to come forward. A high proportion of rape victims never report that they have been sexually assaulted. They may fear that they won't be believed. Being aware that only a small minority of rape allegations are false helps the police take all allegations seriously. In fact, in many jurisdictions, the police assume the allegation is true unless they see overwhelming evidence that it isn't. The crucial point to keep in mind is that, in the absence of any other evidence, the determination of whether a crime took place relies in part on establishing *consent*. That is rarely something that leaves a record after the event. Huge swings in Western culture, such as the MeToo movement, have made women more likely to be believed than was once the case. However, in many countries around the world, that is still not the case.

Tackling extortion

Extortion is illegally getting hold of money by compulsion — for example, a well-known company receives an anonymous letter threatening to poison the company's products unless money is paid or some other action is taken. The threat can have a major impact on the company if any hint that the company is being threatened reaches the public. This situation falls under the category of *extortion*. Therefore, careful examination of the threatening communication is crucial in deciding what steps to take.

Fortunately, the majority of people writing threatening letters never follow through on their threats. Often, the act of writing is just an expression of anger or frustration, malice, or spite. Against that backdrop, the task is to detect the minority of letters indicating a real determination to put the threat into action.

I've been involved in several cases of threatening letters and now know the signs to look for in establishing whether the threat is genuine or false. Clearly, making these signs available to the general public is inappropriate, but I can say that the signs draw upon a careful analysis of the credibility of the threat and the benefits and costs to the writer of carrying out the threat. Meticulous study of the form of words in which a threat is expressed can be of great value in understanding the sort of person the writer is and their background and knowledge. For instance, consider what the writer's really trying to achieve. Is it really money they're after or havoc? What sort of person the writer's likely to be can also be gleaned from the way they write. The crucial question, though, is the probability of the person actually carrying out the threat (check out the later section "Examining Documents to Help Solve Crimes" for more information).

Interviewing Suspects to Sort Truth from Lies

Witnesses are generally in the habit of trying to tell the truth, as they understand it, when being interviewed, although in certain circumstances, even witnesses will lie or hide crucial information. When interviewing suspects, you can't start by making the assumption that they're telling the truth. Interviewing procedures are established in some places that make it easier to find out whether the suspect is telling the truth. However, you need to keep in mind that such interviewing procedures can be fraught with problems.

Dealing with false confessions

A suspect confessing to a crime they didn't commit is a serious problem for police investigators. You have to get at the truth to avoid seeing the person be wrongly imprisoned (often, the person is vulnerable and needing help, such as psychiatric treatment, rather than custody) and, of course, wrongful imprisonment means letting the guilty person go free.

ANECDOTE

In 1980, when Sean Hodgson was 30 years old, he told a prison chaplain that he'd murdered a barmaid. He withdrew the confession at his trial a year later, saying he was a pathological liar who'd falsely confessed to countless crimes. But Hodgson spent nearly 30 years in prison until DNA evidence cleared him.

You may think that a person who's being tortured or coerced is more than likely to confess to a crime of which they're innocent. But many examples exist of people confessing (some falsely) with no such pressures. Police investigators have to be on the alert all the time for such possibilities in even fairly common crimes such as burglary. False confessions can happen because the person is:

>> **Craving attention,** believing that they can gain notoriety or glory from admitting to a crime.

>> **Feeling confused about what they did** or where they were at the time of the crime, especially if the person is a habitual criminal and was under the influence of alcohol or drugs.

>> **Suffering from a serious mental condition** and possibly unaware of the true situation. This is different from something they imagined or interpreted wrongly.

>> **Accepting what they're being told.** Ghisli Gudjonsson, a forensic psychologist who has made a special study of how some people will accept what they've been told, calls this tendency *suggestibility.* He has developed a special way of measuring how prone someone is to suggestibility, consisting of asking people questions and then giving them suggestions in relation to their answers and seeing whether they accept them. This procedure has been used in court cases to support the innocence of people who initially confess.

>> **Wanting to end an awkward situation,** like having been put in a cell and just wanting to go home, possibly not realizing the serious consequences of confessing.

In many parts of the world today, and in the past in most places, the main cause of false confessions was physical or mental intimidation or torture. The whole basis of the Inquisition in the Middle Ages was to torture people until they confessed their sins. This is less so now in the UK since the introduction of the PEACE interview process (described in Chapter 7) and the tape-recording of interviews of suspects.

STRANGE
BUT TRUE

Curiously, in high-profile murder cases or other crimes hitting the headlines, you find people confessing to the crime who couldn't possibly have done it. For example, in 1932, when the son of the famous aviator Charles Lindbergh was kidnapped, nearly 200 people confessed to the crime. In 1986, more than 100 people confessed to the murder of the Swedish prime minister, Olaf Palme.

Police investigators are aware of this phenomenon, which is why crucial facts about a case are kept secret, so that anyone confessing to the crime is required to show knowledge of these decisive facts.

Encountering the IEE approach in the United States

Paul Ekman and his colleagues in the US have drawn up a set of pointers called Improving Interpersonal Evaluations for Law Enforcement and Evaluations — better known as the *IEE approach* — for helping the police interviewer decide the truthfulness of what's being said. A simple ABC list summarizes what's involved in IEE:

>> **A**wareness: Gain knowledge of ways in which information can be inaccurate.

>> **B**aselines: Study the normal mode of behavior of the respondent.

>> **C**hanges: Note reactions of the respondent that are different from the baseline.

>> **D**iscrepancies: Observe variations in reactions in different channels of communication.

>> **E**ngagement: Create a comfortable context for continuing rapport.

>> **F**ollow-up: Explore corroborating evidence from other sources.

The IEE is a set of guidelines for establishing the truth in a police interview and draws on Ekman's work showing how people reveal their emotions while under stress, which I describe in more detail in the earlier section "Micro-twitches."

REGIONAL TIP-OFF

CONFESSIONS AROUND THE WORLD

People being presented with (false) evidence are sometimes willing to confess; teenagers are particularly vulnerable to this pressure. Although not exactly coercion, such subterfuge isn't allowed under UK law but is acceptable in the US.

In many countries, corroborative evidence is required before a confession is acceptable in court. One notable exception is China, where a large number of convictions are based on confessions.

In India, for many years, it was common practice by the police to beat or threaten a confession out of a suspect. But now a law has been passed whereby no confession obtained in the presence of a police officer is allowed as evidence in court.

The nearest equivalent UK police interview guidelines to the IEE is the English and Welsh PEACE, created with the help of forensic psychologists to improve the quality of interviews and combat false confessions.

Interrogating suspects

REGIONAL TIP-OFF

In the US, there are fewer constraints on police practice when obtaining a confession or getting vital information out of a suspect than in the UK. Certain US police procedures would raise eyebrows if they were tried out in a British court. Results from those procedures would not be allowed as evidence. For example, in the US, there are *interrogations* as well as the more benign-sounding *interviews*; these are the differences:

>> An *interrogation* aims at obtaining a confession or evidence leading to a conviction.

>> A *police interview* aims at revealing the truth in as much detail as possible.

Before the introduction of the PEACE procedure, which I describe in Chapter 7, the UK police also had a confession culture in which the purpose of interviewing a suspect was to gain a confession.

During an interrogation, the interviewer works at persuading the suspect that it's in their best interests to confess, by direct challenges or using spurious techniques (like trying to uncover lies by using lies), which can include these actions:

>> **Using undercover police officers to obtain a confession:** In Britain, it's illegal for undercover police officers to entrap people or force a confession, but in Canada and the US, such undercover operations are often used to try to elicit a confession from a suspect.

>> **Underplaying or even lying on the part of the police about the seriousness of the offense:** For example, saying the murder victim survived or offering the possibility that the killing was an accident.

>> **Telling downright lies:** For example, saying that uncontroversial evidence of guilt exists or that a codefendant has already confessed.

ANECDOTE

When an undercover law enforcement agent pretends to be a convict to obtain a confession in a jailhouse investigation they are called Perkins operations because of the landmark U.S. Supreme Court case *Illinois v. Perkins* (1990) in which a police officer pretending to be another convict befriended a suspect in his cell in order to obtain a confession.

The Reid interrogation technique

Fred Inbau and John Reid, two experienced US law enforcement officers, developed a procedure and an associated training organization, used in North America, laying out nine steps for carrying out a persuasive interrogation:

1. **Being confrontational:** The suspect is told positively that they committed the alleged crime. The idea is that an innocent person immediately and without hesitation denies the offense, whereas a guilty person is evasive.

2. **Developing a theme:** The suspect is given reasons for thinking that the crime is less serious than they believe. This is an attempt to let the suspect "off the hook" psychologically, making them feel more secure and less intimidated.

3. **Handling denials:** Denials are stopped short in their tracks, and the suspect is told to listen to what the interrogator has to say. This is a way of preventing the suspect from believing that their denials carry any weight or of hitting their stride in advancing those denials.

4. **Overcoming objections:** The interrogator overcomes the objections the suspect is giving as an explanation or reason for their innocence and therefore undermines the suspect's confidence in their own innocence, making them more vulnerable to the assertions of the interrogator.

5. **Getting hold of and keeping the suspect's attention:** When the suspect shows signs of fatigue, the interrogator reduces the psychological (and, if necessary, physical) distance between themselves and the suspect to regain the suspect's full attention.

6. **Handling suspect's passive mode:** When a suspect's resistance looks about to break down, the interrogator focuses on the suspect's main reasons for committing the crime, to show signs of understanding and sympathy. The interrogator appeals to the suspect's sense of decency and honor and possibly religious convictions, using the well-established psychological principle of rewarding behavior that you want to encourage.

7. **Presenting an alternative question:** The suspect is presented with two possible alternatives for committing the crime, one face-saving and the other a repulsive or callous motivation.

8. **Having the suspect tell in their own words various details of the offense:** When the suspect accepts one of the alternatives, they're asked to go into the story in further detail.

9. **Converting an oral confession into a written confession:** This gives a further opportunity for ensuring that the confession is clear and legally watertight.

Lots of controversy surrounds the use of the Inbau and Reid technique. Some challenges relate to the legality of the whole process of misleading a suspect. Others relate to its likelihood of inducing false confessions. But perhaps the greatest challenge to its usefulness is the claim by some who have studied the technique closely that it just doesn't work. As a consequence its use is diminishing as the Mendez principles are gaining ground.

UN Guidance on Ethical Interviewing

In contrast to the Inbau and Reid approach, the United Nations High Commission for Human Rights has put forward comprehensive guidance on ethical interviewing in police investigations. It provides standards that can be used globally for noncoercive interviewing that respects the person being interviewed and is firmly based on evidence. The person overseeing the development of this protocol gives his name to it as the Méndez principles, but it was actually some authoritative forensic psychologists who provided the key guidance (including one who had studied with me).

Extreme procedures

Although the UN protocol is specifically set up to avoid the use of torture in interviews, sometimes you still hear an interrogation being described as "extreme." In reality, this is another way of saying that torture is being used: Someone is being beaten or physically abused as a way of getting them to give up information. The moral dilemma put forward is whether torture is acceptable if the information obtained can save one or many lives. However, this argument assumes that torture is a productive way of actually obtaining the truth. Growing evidence shows that it's a weak and inefficient way of getting at the truth.

THE MÉNDEZ PRINCIPLES IN A NUTSHELL

Here is a summary of the Méndez principles for carrying out ethical interviewing in criminal investigations:

Principle	Summary
Foundation	Interviewing must be grounded in science, law, and ethics.
Practice	Effective interviewing gathers accurate information while respecting legal safeguards.
Vulnerability	Interviewers must identify and accommodate the needs of vulnerable individuals.
Training	Interviewing is a professional skill requiring specialized training.
Accountability	Institutions must ensure transparency and oversight of interviewing practices.
Implementation	States must adopt robust national measures to embed these principles in law enforcement and justice systems.

Most experts agree that using torture as a means of getting at the truth is counterproductive. Inflicting extreme physical or mental pain can result in obtaining misleading information or nothing of use at all. Everyone involved is alienated, often including the interrogator, making it extremely difficult to build any future rapport that may lead to opening up to the truth. Developing a relationship, or *rapport*, with the person being interviewed is far more likely to get the information being sought.

Chapter **9**

Beyond Offender Profiling

I n Thomas Harris's bestselling thriller *The Silence of the Lambs*, which became a 1991 blockbuster film, Clarice Starling is a novice FBI agent trying to catch a serial killer. She visits the brilliant, but disturbingly violent, Dr. Hannibal Lecter in prison to discover from him the likely characteristics of the serial killer. For many people (including me), this film was their introduction to the notion of *offender profiling*. Lecter was portrayed as having brilliant insights into the killer's mind because, well, he was a killer himself and, um, he was brilliant. The fun bit, though, is that, if you read the book carefully or look beyond the fabulous acting in the film, Harris, cleverly, has Lecter give no clear indications about the serial killer that are much help to Clarice.

A considerable amount of misunderstanding has been drawn from fictional accounts of how psychologists could help the police.

In this chapter, I spell out the facts of *offender profiling*: the fascinating questions that are at the heart of what psychologists offer to criminal investigations, and how the struggle to answer these questions opens up the new field of investigative psychology. However, to contribute to investigations, you need to be aware of how crimes and criminals differ, so in this chapter, I also guide you through the various types of crimes.

Investigating Offender Profiling

An experienced homicide detective used to say to people who asked him for a profile of the killer, "Do ya want a profile, or do ya want me to help you catch the bad guy?" This statement neatly demonstrates the confusion over what a profile is.

The popular notion is that an offender profile gives police investigators pointers on where to target their investigations, describing the likely personality, lifestyle, motivations, and other characteristics of an offender: in other words, a sort of speculative pen picture of the perpetrator. But although that notion may seem fun in fiction, it isn't much use in an investigation. What detectives need are specific directions to channel their search or guide how they interview a suspect, not general chat about the unknown criminal's personality or family relationships. In this section, I provide the facts about offender profiling, using a number of real-life cases as illustrations, including the one that dragged me into this whole murky area.

MYTH BUSTER

I suppose, if the detectives have no idea where to look or who the criminal is likely to be, a pen picture may get them started. But look at the issue this way: Surely a much more useful approach is to ask, "Have you asked around at any local hostels where offenders recently released from prison are staying?" Though hardly a detailed profile of the possible offender, this suggestion may be the only pointer the police need. Giving this type of advice on where to find the criminal, rather than describing the individual's characteristics, has always been a large part of the contributions of experts in helping the police, and part of good detective training.

OFFENDERS' CHARACTERISTICS TYPICALLY MENTIONED IN BIA REPORTS

- Their probable gender
- An indication of their likely age range
- Some suggestion of their motivation
- Likely previous offenses
- Probable future offenses
- Any violent history
- Whether they were known to the victim
- Whether the offense was planned or spontaneous
- Whether the crime involved more than one offender

A BRIEF HISTORY OF OFFENDER PROFILING

People have always been ready to draw on their own particular expertise to tell detectives about the criminal they're looking for — particularly, crime writers.

An early instance of someone profiling a case was Edgar Allan Poe, famous for his dark stories of murder and mayhem. In 1850, he wrote *The Mystery of Marie Roget*, which, although presented as a fiction set in Paris, was intended to be a contribution to the investigation of the murder of Mary Rogers in New York in 1842. From the crime scene details, Poe concluded that a gang of villains killed the hapless Mary, which contrasted with the police view that it was suicide. They didn't take kindly to his suggestions, but because the case was never conclusively solved, it's still anyone's guess who was correct.

Conan Doyle also offered profiles on various real-life crimes that were troubling the police, although no indication exists that they took any notice of his advice or that it was ever of much use. Yet this shows, as with Poe, that helping the police was regarded as an act of imagination rather than as some scientific endeavor. This belief lingers, adding to the general mythology that profiling is a dark art, which owes more to the brilliance of the person producing the profile rather than to any systematic procedure.

These advisors may have a background in forensic psychology, but often won't be the sort of qualified forensic psychologists I describe in Chapter 18. They may even avoid the term *psychologist* altogether and just call themselves behavioral scientists. Yes, I realize that this topic is growing complicated, but the problem is that the term *offender profiler* is neither a legal nor professional label. It has more currency in the mass media and in fiction than in any professional gathering. People who want to claim they have special powers may call themselves profilers, but that doesn't mean that they are forensic psychologists, or even criminologists, or know much about the sorts of topics I describe in all the other chapters in this book.

Jack the Ripper

Perhaps the first true professional offender profile in modern times was a report from a medical officer, Dr. Thomas Bond, who carried out autopsies and advised the police on the murders that became known as the work of Jack the Ripper (the killer of at least five women working as street sex workers in the Whitechapel area of London in 1888). Bond offered the following opinion:

The murderer must have been a man of physical strength and great coolness and daring. There is no evidence he had an accomplice. He must, in my opinion, be a man subject to periodic attacks of homicidal and erotic mania. The character of the mutilations indicates that the man may be in a condition sexually that may be called **satyriasis.** *It is, of course, possible that the homicidal impulse may have developed from a revengeful or brooding condition of mind, or that religious mania may have been the original disease, but I do not think either hypothesis is likely. The murderer in external appearance is quite likely to be a quiet, inoffensive-looking man, probably middle-aged and neatly and respectably dressed. I think he might be in the habit of wearing a cloak or overcoat, or he could hardly have escaped notice in the streets if the blood on his hands or clothes was visible.*

NOTES OF EXAMINATION OF BODY OF WOMAN FOUND
MURDERED AND MUTILATED IN DORSET STREET,
DATE-STAMPED 16 NOVEMBER 1888, MEPO 3/3153

By modern standards, this description is quite sensible, except for the allusion to *satyriasis* and erotic mania, which aren't common medical terms these days (although *heightened sex drive* may be an acceptable substitute term). Today's experts may also debate whether the violent mutilations that gave the killer the nickname Ripper are more likely to relate to sadism or, indeed, psychosis (which I discuss in Chapter 6) rather than sexual desires.

There is pressure to reduce the overall length of the book and this is a long chapter. So I am deleting everything that I deem unnecessary for the central argument.

The Jack the Ripper murders have never been solved to everyone's satisfaction, although theories abound. Until the crimes are solved, no one can tell how valid the profiles were. One thing is certain, though: They weren't much use in getting the villain caught!

The Mad Bomber of New York

The most well-known modern offender profile was of the Mad Bomber of New York. This instance stimulated the myths of the power of profiles because it was claimed to have solved a serious crime series.

Over a 16-year period in the 1940s and 1950s, homemade bombs were left in public places around New York City. Letters claiming to come from the bomber were sent to the *New York Herald Tribune,* saying that the bombs would continue until the Consolidated Edison Company "brought justice for the bomber." The letters didn't specify exactly what sort of justice, but it was clear that the writer of the letters felt he'd been badly treated by Consolidated Edison. The police kept information about these bombings relatively quiet, but when they called in the psychiatrist James Brussel, he recommended that they use the news media to see whether anyone was able to identify the bomber. You didn't need to be a genius (or even a psychiatrist) to realize that the perpetrator was somewhat peeved with Consolidated Edison, but Brussel gave this simple idea some impetus. From an examination of the letters the bomber had sent, and other information about his actions, Brussel proposed that the person possessed the following characteristics:

>> Is male (because most bombers are male)

>> Has knowledge of metalworking, pipefitting, and electricity

>> Suffered an injustice by Consolidated Edison, rendering him chronically ill

>> Suffers from an insidious paranoia

>> Is pathologically self-centered

>> Is a loner who has no friends, male or female

>> Has a symmetric athletic body type, neither fat nor skinny

>> Is middle-aged (due to onset of illness and duration of bombings)

>> Has a good education: likely high school educated, but not college

>> Is unmarried, and possibly a virgin

>> Distrusts and despises male authority; hates father

>> Never progressed past the Oedipal stage of love for his mother due to her early death or separation from him

>> Lives alone or with a female, mother-like relative

>> Lives in Connecticut, attends church, and is Roman Catholic and of Slavic descent

>> Is neat, tidy, and clean-shaven

>> Is quiet, polite, methodical, and prompt

>> Has a chronic illness, cancer, tuberculosis, or, most probably, heart disease

>> Was wearing a buttoned, double-breasted suit when caught

MYTH
BUSTER

Despite Brussel's rich description, it was an assiduous clerk at Consolidated Edison, Alice Kelly, who led to the bomber's capture. She read the newspaper reports and decided to look through the company's special files on those employees who had earlier made threats as part of their requests for compensation. This search drew attention to George Metesky, who'd been injured at the factory in 1931. The correspondence in these files showed similarities of wording to the anonymous letters the bomber had been sending to the police, leading the police to him and his eventual conviction.

The Railway Murderer

This case is the one that set me on the path to writing this book, when I produced an offender profile for a major investigation into many rapes, and three murders, that took place near railway stations and were committed across London between 1982 and 1985.

The police claimed they had a number of possible suspects, but only one, John Frances Duffy, fit my profile. They therefore put him under surveillance and obtained enough evidence for a conviction. The success of the profile that helped to identify John Duffy as the offender thus opened the way to the new science of investigative psychology, which I describe in the later section "Delving into Investigative Psychology."

Here's a summary of the profile I produced to assist the police investigation:

>> Lived in the area of early offenses in 1983

>> Arrested after October 1983 for violence, not necessarily sexual

>> Lives with wife or girlfriend — childless

>> Aged mid- to late 20s

>> Light hair

>> 5 feet 9 inches tall

>> Righthanded

>> Has blood type A (in the days before DNA testing)

>> Semiskilled

>> In a job with no public contact

>> Keeps to himself and has only one or two close friends

The ideas I used to produce the profile of John Duffy are all derived from my *consistency principle:* What an offender does in a crime is an expression of how that person behaves in other, noncriminal situations. Actions during a crime are likely to be more extreme than in other situations, but they're still consistent with them. Therefore, whatever the criminal does in a crime can be taken as a direct indication of the sort of person they are.

Various, more detailed, aspects follow from this conclusion:

>> The *familiarity* a person exhibits in the crime reveals what they're normally familiar with. So, in this case, the area of criminal activity would relate to places known from usual activity. (This concept relates to the routine activity theory I describe in the later sidebar "Staying close to home.") Duffy's crimes spread out across London; however, I hypothesized that initially he had attacked near areas he was familiar with and then began to look for opportunities farther afield, where he wouldn't be recognized. His behavior, as described by his victims, had become more planned and determined, which also fit this idea. This insight led to the conclusion that his earliest attacks would be the best indicators of where he was based. This process is an early development of geographical offender profiling, which I discuss in the later section "Locating offenders geographically."

>> His *emotional responses* in the crime would be an indicator of his emotions in other situations. This offender was a man violently attacking young women, so it was reasonable to assume that he would be known as a violent person. The point here was to draw attention to his violence rather than to the sexual nature of the crimes. Such violence was likely to have previously brought him to police attention.

>> His *social interaction* in the crime revealed that he was able to relate to his victims initially before he attacked them. This suggested that he was able to have a relationship with a woman that wasn't entirely vicious. Perhaps naïvely on my part, I assumed he wouldn't have had any children; otherwise, he wouldn't have attacked young women as he did. Since that time (a quarter of a century ago), I've realized that married men with children can be much nastier than I ever thought possible.

>> His *intellectual ability,* as revealed in his planning of the crimes, indicated that he would have a job that wasn't a low-level manual one but had some skill associated with it, like being a carpenter (which he was).

>> His *skills* may also have been relevant — for example, in understanding the details of how he bound and controlled his victims — but were less obvious in this case than in many others.

>> His *criminal habits,* that were the crimes themselves, suggested that the suspect didn't normally relate well to other people, and, like many violent sex offenders, had few friends and little contact with other people.

I drew the other information in the profile from witness descriptions and the forensic results the police had. They were carefully summarized to provide a coherent set of the most probable information the police could work with.

For the record, none of the following claims is true:

>> Offender profiling is an invention of the late 20th century.

>> Offender profiling was created by the FBI.

>> American FBI agents are the current world leaders in profiling. (People may assume this is true because so much publicity is given to what goes on in the US, especially in movies emanating from Hollywood.)

>> The emergence of offender profiling was isolated from any other scientific developments.

>> Only odd crimes with curious psychological aspects are open to profiling.

>> Offender profiling can be applied only to serious serial crimes — notably, serial murder and serial rape.

>> Offender profiling is essentially an art dependent on the intellectual gifts of the person producing the profile.

>> The FBI carried out serious scientific studies on which they base their profiles.

>> Serial killers are always educated white men.

>> Serial killers can be categorized as organized or disorganized.

>> Offender profilers solve crimes.

STAYING CLOSE TO HOME

Routine activity theory, a common idea in criminology, means that criminals often choose their crime locations from places in which the criminal is routinely located: on the way to work or near the pubs they use, for example. They're thought to see the opportunities for crime when going about their noncriminal activities. Although this idea has much to recommend it, from a psychologist's point of view, it's the familiarity they have with an area that's crucial. This familiarity can even come from other sources, such as maps or even criminal colleagues.

In addition, of course, habitual criminals may seek out areas beyond where they're based in order to find opportunities for crime. One burglar interviewed had been stealing golfing equipment from golf clubs around the UK. When I asked how he knew where to go, he said that he simply used maps for golf enthusiasts (that show where all the golfing establishments are) to find opportunities for thieving.

Delving into Investigative Psychology

As I describe in the earlier section "Investigating Offender Profiling," giving a detailed account of an offender's inner psychology isn't much help to investigators (although it can be useful in guiding how to approach interviewing a suspect and sometimes helps detectives develop a feel for the sort of person they're looking for). However, some knowledge of the offender's psychology can be useful to prosecuting lawyers in court because they can use this insight to help the jury understand how and why a crime was committed. (Of course, the defense can use similar information to argue that the defendant couldn't have committed the crime.)

The myths surrounding the whole idea of profiling and its weaknesses led me to identify a branch of psychology that would be the scientific basis for contributing to police investigations on a much broader front than just producing pen pictures of unknown villains. I call this area of research *investigative psychology,* which is the subject of this section.

Think of it this way: Creating a profile of an offender requires gathering the details of the crime and then making some if-then assumptions. For example, as I did in the Railway Murderer case, you may say, "If a man has been violent to women in these crimes, then the police may know someone who has been violent to women on other occasions." This if-then conjecture is an *inference.* You are *inferring* features of the culprit from aspects of the crime. Making this type of inference requires an understanding of criminals and how they act, which makes it part of forensic psychology. Developing these inferences requires much more than some clever insights into the criminal mind. It draws on the many different aspects of scientific psychology that I describe in the rest of this chapter, as well as other chapters in this book.

When you're making inferences about offenders, you're using what is known about their actions. But as a scientist, you cannot just accept the information you're given — you want it to be as reliable and valid as possible. An important part of investigative psychology is developing and improving ways of acquiring information in investigations. (Yes, the topics discussed in Chapters 7 and 8 on interviewing and detecting deception are aspects of investigative psychology.)

Following the investigative cycle

To see how psychology can contribute to all aspects of police investigations, recognizing how they unfold is useful. They usually follow this cycle of activity (see Figure 9-1):

1. ***Information* comes to the notice of the police that a crime has been committed.** How the police gather the best information by interviewing and dealing with deceit is a matter that investigative psychologists can help with (as I describe in Chapters 7 and 8).

2. ***Inferences* are made on the basis of that information.** This is the development by psychologists of the if-then propositions I discuss in the preceding section.

3. **Actions that may generate more information result from these inferences.** Investigative psychologists can guide these actions and produce techniques the police can use, like the geographical profiling systems I describe in the later section "Locating offenders geographically."

FIGURE 9-1:
A simplified illustration of the stages of an investigation.

The cycle continues until enough information is obtained to take a suspect to court.

To help in the criminal investigative cycle, psychologists need to have a full understanding of the sorts of information detectives need to know, which various psychological sources can answer (see Table 9-1).

Profiling equations

The inferences that make up offender profiles can be thought of as similar to mathematical equations that link the actions in a crime to characteristics of the offenders. I call them A→C equations. The arrow (→) here implies that there may be any of a number of relationships between actions and characteristics. One important aspect of investigative psychology is trying to solve these equations with data from actual offenses.

TABLE 9-1 **Questions That Detectives Need Answered**

Aspect	Question
Salience	Of all the events that happen in any crime, what are the aspects that are most important in determining the precise nature of the crime, on which any inferences can be made?
Differentiating cases	What aspects of a crime are distinct about it and help to separate it from other similar crimes?
Linking cases	What cases can be linked together as likely to be the work of the same individual(s)? This may be achieved by forensic evidence, witness descriptions, or similarities in the pattern of the criminal's actions.
Eliciting suspects	Where can possible suspects be found? This may imply targeted searches of police records or hunting on the ground through house-to-house inquiries (see "Locating offenders geographically," later in this chapter) or from police informants.
Prioritizing suspects	Which of the suspects should be closely examined first? Limited police resources mean that suspects have to be put in some sort of order.

MYTH BUSTER

It's rare for one simple aspect of a crime to imply one simple characteristic of the offender. The clue so favored by fiction writers that opens the way to the offender (such as a suspect referring to a cellphone as a mobile phone, showing that they lived in the UK, where that term is common) may come from various types of forensic evidence, such as fibers and body fluids; when dealing with criminal actions, however, it's usually the pattern of actions that points the way, not one specific action.

REMEMBER

» **Actions** in the profiling equations represent all the information about the crime that the police have (before they know who did it): for example, the place and time of the offense, as well as the details of the victim and what actually happened.

» **Characteristics** in the profiling equations mean all the information that's of use to the police in solving the crime, such as where the offender may be living or which other crimes they may have been convicted of that will be recorded in police databases.

ANECDOTE

INFERRING ISN'T AN EXACT SCIENCE

In one rape case I worked on, the victim reported that the offender had long fingernails on his right hand but short ones on his left hand. Detectives became excited when they remembered that some guitar players have nails like these. So were we looking for a sexually violent guitarist? No. When he was caught, police found that he had no musical talents, but in fact worked a job replacing tires on cars, which seemed to result in his wearing down the nails on one hand more than on the other.

Unfortunately, no simple equation exists in which one action can always be used reliably to infer one characteristic. The anecdote in the nearby sidebar "Inferring isn't an exact science" illustrates this point. Sometimes, combinations of actions offer the possibility of various likely characteristics. Possessing a firearm and using it with accuracy and confidence, for example, may imply that a person is a firearm enthusiast or has had military training. But here, again, context needs to be taken into account. In many areas of the US, most people know how to use a firearm and have ready access to one. That is most definitely not the case in the UK. (I have never held an actual firearm.)

Facing the challenge of contingencies

Contingencies are those aspects of the circumstances in which a crime occurs that can influence what inferences can be made about that crime. Any investigative psychologist trying to derive inferences needs to consider these. The following aspects challenge the possibility of developing a simple profiling equation (see the preceding section):

>> One feature of a crime can change the implications of many others. For example, the actions during a burglary committed at night, when the occupant is likely to be in the house, have rather different implications from a daytime burglary.

>> Combinations of features can change each other's implications. For example, setting fire to a building after it has been burgled suggests a different inference (such as the fire being set to destroy evidence) from setting fire to a building that has symbolic significance, such as a school.

>> Events outside the control of the offender may distort what inferences can be made. This would be the case where a victim unexpectedly fights back, so the offender's actions are in part a reaction to the victim. Or if the offender is disturbed during the crime, the actions may not fully indicate what was intended.

>> Opportunities may occur for the crime that the offender may not have anticipated. Someone may have intended to climb a drainpipe to enter the building, thus allowing inference of their particular skills and age, for example, but found the front door open and then didn't need to.

Hearing the stories people tell themselves: Criminal narratives

One interesting way of understanding what criminals are doing that investigative psychologists have been developing is to think of the personal stories that criminals themselves tell about their lives. These narratives can be used as a basis for inferences as well as assisting in guiding interview strategies.

The following four criminal narratives have been suggested as being prevalent in the minds of different criminals:

» **Being on an adventure:** The offender sees crime as an exciting escapade in which adversity is overcome to win the rewards that are due to the victor.

» **Being on a heroic mission:** The mission may be avenging an insult to someone's honor or even fighting for the honor of family or others. Whatever the precise nature, offenders cast themselves in the role of justified hero.

» **Being a tragic victim:** The offender feels that they're always the scapegoat and that their crime was simply their attempt to cope, but it all went wrong. They don't see themselves as criminals, but rather as misunderstood and picked-on people.

» **Doing a professional job:** Some criminals I talk to, usually older ones, say that crime is just what they do: It may even have lost some of its excitement for them. But they're proud of committing their crimes effectively — for instance, pulling off a bank robbery without anyone getting hurt.

NARRATIVE NOT MOTIVE

Criminal narratives are rather different from the idea of *motive*, which is enjoyed immensely by fiction writers. In fact, courts don't need to know the motive for a crime. The judge and jury just need to know that the crime was committed by the defendant, who knew what they were doing and its implications. The term *motive* is such a slippery one that I avoid using it throughout this book. It can mean an explanation, a purpose, a reason, an urge, the set of actions it was part of (such as "We were all drunk and having a laugh"), or some form of narrative (as in "I don't let people push me around"). The term's ambiguity also makes it difficult to establish what the motive may have been for a crime.

(continued)

(continued)

The classic motives in thrillers — such as revenge, jealousy, or greed — never go the whole way in explaining why the particular crime was the way of achieving that motive. Furthermore, in real life, more than one such explanation exists, and the criminal themselves may not be fully aware of why they committed the crime.

Locating offenders geographically

One of the most useful pieces of information that detectives can find is the geographical location where the culprit may be found. This information allows the prioritization of suspects by putting them in order of how near they are to that location. It facilitates linking different crimes to one offender and also enables the police to install surveillance in designated locations or to carry out careful house-to-house inquiries in a targeted area. When they need to search for possible suspects by using DNA matches, an indication of the area in which the offender may have lived at the time of the offense can help to limit the number of people whose DNA needs to be matched. For all these reasons, investigative psychologists' research has explored *where* a crime occurs as well as what happens in the crime. They can use this information to make inferences about where criminals may be based.

I did an elementary form of geographical offender profiling when I proposed that John Duffy had lived in the area circumscribed by the first three crimes of the series (see the earlier section "The Railway Murderer"). However, since that time, computer programs have been developed to indicate the likelihood of an offender living in any particular location.

As an example, take a look at Figure 9-2, which shows the locations of bombs left in an extortion campaign across London. The points are the locations on a map of where the bombs were left. By looking at the distances criminals typically travel to commit their crimes, a computer program calculates the likelihood of where on the map the bomber's home might be and then joins up the areas that have the same probability. This is similar to height contours on an ordinary map, but rather than height, this map shows how probable it is that the offender is living in any location. The figure shows two areas that have high probabilities: one to the east and one to the west. The police placed surveillance on ATM points in the west and caught the culprit, Edgar Pearce, who lived near the location where he was caught. The high-probability area to the east surrounds where his former wife lived, whom he still visited.

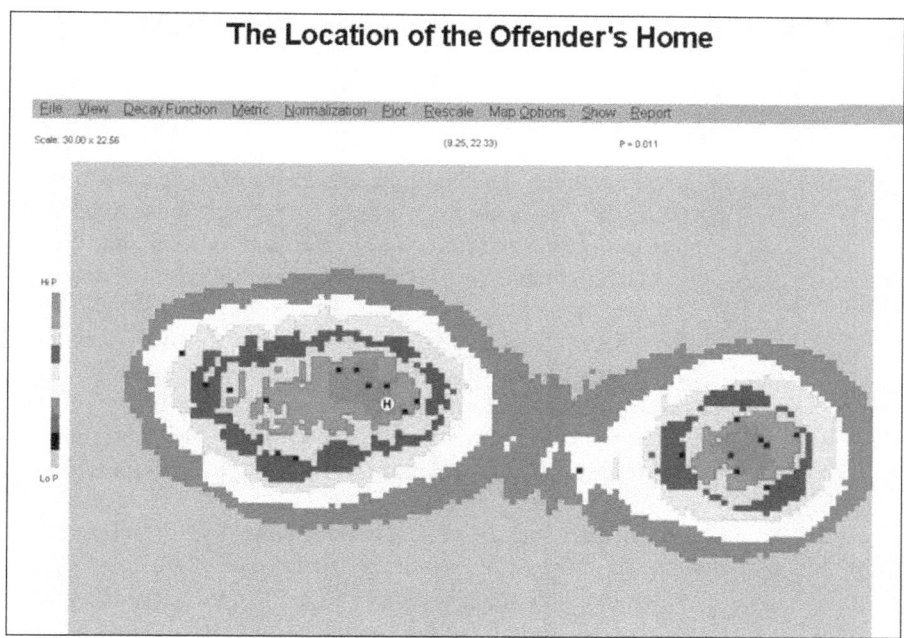

FIGURE 9-2:
A map showing the locations of bombs left in the London extortion campaign.

Distinguishing between Crimes

Crucial to profiling an offender is gaining an understanding of the type of criminal acts the person carries out. Therefore, as part of profiling offenders directly (a subject I cover in the earlier sections of this chapter), forensic psychologists have to examine and understand the various sorts of crimes people commit, identifying the distinguishing characteristics of a crime. For example, the willingness (or not) of a person to use violence is central to making an investigative inference. Doing so requires an understanding of how crimes that notionally appear similar (and may even have the same legal label) differ from each other in important behavioral ways.

REMEMBER

Of course, certain basic aspects remain common across most crimes of a certain type (a burglary involves stealing from a property, whereas a rape involves a sexual assault). But the forensic psychologist needs to be able to distinguish more subtly between crimes, identifying the *less* common actions of different styles of behavior. These are the actions that will be indicative of the characteristics of the person committing the crimes.

Dealing with property crimes

Experts often use the technical term *acquisitive crime* to describe all those crimes in which something of value is taken without the permission of the owner. In such cases, the owner is always directly or indirectly caught up in the crime. The most crucial difference between crimes is whether only property is taken or a victim is confronted by the criminal. This distinction between property crimes and crimes against a person is central to understanding criminal actions.

The consistency principle I describe earlier in this chapter (in "The Railway Murderer") draws attention, for instance, to familiarity and the typical way of dealing with other people that you'd expect to be common in criminal and noncriminal situations. Consequently, whether the offender engages directly with the victim or avoids such contact has key psychological implications.

Within the category of acquisitive crime, a wide range of variations exists. For example, a span of scenarios can be identified, from having contact with the victim (as is characteristic of robbery) to burglary (in which the victim may or may not be present) to the modification of documents in which no direct contact is ever made (as may be the case in many frauds). This set of stages implies a reduction in the willingness to use physical threats to obtain the property and an increase in the skills of manipulation of opportunities.

Forensic psychologists need to proceed with caution, though, because many combinations are possible. For example, some fraudsters start off distant from their victims, but having made contact, can start using threats of violence.

Fraud

Broadly speaking, people become major fraudsters via one of three dominant routes. In one they spot loopholes in systems and then gain access to them to obtain large sums of money. The second it the development of that which is now prevalent on the internet. That is scams where criminals find ways of taking advantage of weaknesses in how the internet works. This helps them to gain access to their victims bank accounts, and in many other ways. A third route is when people who are in a position of trust find that they need some money, which isn't readily available from personal funds. You may be surprised to know that the first group is in the minority. Notorious examples such as Frank Abagnale do exist (see the nearby sidebar "Catch me if you can — oh, you did!"), but they're very unusual.

It used to be the case that the usual way in which serious fraud happened was people abusing positions of trust and, say, steals from a company or an organization. While that still happens by far the most prevalent forms of fraud these days happen over the internet. That is now such a vast area of criminal activity that it would take a whole other book to discuss properly. There is *Cybersecurity for Dummies* by Joseph Steinberg if you want to explore this in depth.

ANECDOTE

One fraudster said that his business collapsed when apartheid suddenly came to an end in South Africa. He employed many people and didn't want them to lose their jobs. To continue to employ them, he therefore took a little money from a source he shouldn't have, hoping that the business would get better and he could pay it back. But things got worse, and he took more money. Eventually, he'd acquired nearly $70,000 fraudulently before he was caught.

Forensic psychologists know that this sequence of small betrayals of trust leading to bigger and bigger fraud until it spins out of control is a common pattern.

Burglary

An important psychological difference exists between a burglar who takes precautions to avoid contact with the occupant of a building and one who doesn't mind or even relishes such confrontation. In general, the former is most common. The majority of burglars go to a great deal of trouble: They watch a house to make sure that everyone has left and then knock on the door first to make sure no one answers. If someone does, they just ask for a fictitious person and then apologize and leave, saying they have the wrong address.

MYTH
BUSTER

Some burglars who avoid confrontation are nonetheless interested in the occupants of the building. They rummage through drawers without taking anything and may even destroy property unnecessarily, just to insult the occupants. The courts take account of this behavior, treating it as a more serious form of burglary than just stealing a handbag left by an open window.

Arson

The key to understanding arson is the nature of the target that's set on fire. Broadly, five sorts of targets exist, and each carries different implications for the inferences that a forensic psychologist makes:

>> **Domestic buildings in which people may be present:** The people are likely to be the target, and the arsonist is acting out a narrative of a heroic mission to redress some hurt they suffered.

>> **Institutions such as schools or hospitals:** These places have symbolic significance for the arsonist and may often be related to some mental disturbance experienced.

The term *pyromaniac* is sometimes used to describe someone who gets pleasure from watching buildings on fire and so carries out a series of arson attacks. The person may feel excitement from the arrival of the firefighters and the whole dramatic event. Some experts even think that sexual arousal may be involved in this excitement.

>> **Vehicles and other locations related to crimes committed:** Here, arson is a strategy of the criminal who sees himself as a professional getting rid of the forensic evidence.

>> **The arsonist:** A fire in which the arsonist gets hurt or even killed may well be a painful form of (attempted) suicide, most likely carried out by someone known to be mentally ill.

>> **Arson for profit:** This is the term given to setting fire to buildings to claim the insurance payout, especially for failing businesses or unwanted buildings that nobody wants to buy.

Working on violent crimes

Experts make a general distinction between different kinds of violence that's crucial to the forensic psychologist's work:

>> **Expressive violence:** The act is an outburst of some emotional feelings.

>> **Instrumental violence:** Violence is being used as a means to an end.

People's relationship to violence can be heavily connected to the culture in which they're raised. Without a doubt, certain subcultures exist in which violence is seen as a dominant means of communication and an expected form of interaction. It may surprise you to know that even in modern developed countries like the US and UK, there are subcultures for which violence is a normal aspect of daily life. This is grippingly illustrated in Mikey Walsh's bestselling autobiography *Gypsy Boy* (St. Martin's Griffen), but this is just one of many books that lift the lid on the violent worlds into which some people are born.

Rape

The significance of the victim to the offender takes on a different perspective when considering sexual assaults than it does in burglary or arson (crimes I discuss in the earlier section "Dealing with property crimes"). As in other types of crime, there are many different aspects to rape. Although rapists use their victims to achieve sexual gratification, this isn't the only, or even necessarily the psychologically most significant, aspect of rape. Sexual assaults are often infused with anger and frustration and the desire to control the victim. They may even be mainly an attempt to show where the power lies in a relationship. In fact, most rapes occur between people who are acquaintances.

Although some individuals are sexually aroused by the control they exert over their victims, and the pain they produce (as I mention in Chapter 2, in my discussion on sadism), that isn't what usually drives a rapist to be violent to his victim. Some rapists mistakenly believe that the victim will enjoy the violent encounter. They think they're involved in an acceptable relationship with a woman. In fact, it's not unknown for potential rapists to run away from a victim who fights and screams, but many victims are so traumatized by the attack that they're unable to do that.

**STRANGE
BUT TRUE**

Many rapists have regular sexual partners and aren't obviously sexually frustrated, although they're likely to have been violent to that partner even if that person doesn't report it. A few rapists do have a high sex drive that they have difficulty controlling, but that's not an explanation for why they rape women.

Forensic psychologists consider three ways in which rapists make use of their victims:

>> **Victim as object:** When the attacker treats the victim as just an opportunity for sexual gratification, it matters little to the offender who the victim is or what her reactions are. All he wants to do is to control her enough to be able to carry out the sexual act. This rapist may well have a broad-ranging criminal background as a thief or involvement in other forms of criminality.

>> **Victim as vehicle:** The victim represents some aspect of womanhood that the offender wants to control or have power over. Victims may represent women he feels slighted him in the past or women he believes are unavailable to him in any other way. Typically, these attackers have little ability to relate to women and may not have a regular sexual partner.

>> **Victim as person:** These are rapists for whom the victim is a significant person, perhaps their regular sexual partner or someone they've been stalking. The rapist may totally misunderstand the nature of his own actions, believing the victim wants the sexual act to take place.

REMEMBER

Men can be victims of rape too, by other men or even by women. Such victims may be quite reluctant to report the crime because of public attitudes. Such men and their male attackers aren't necessarily homosexual.

I explore attempts to treat sexual offenders in Chapter 16.

Murder

Murder is a catchall term, and it's more useful in forensic psychology work to understand and use more precise terms:

REGIONAL
TIP-OFF

>> **Homicide** is the killing of one person by another. This act may not be murder if the killing is lawful, such as in self-defense.

Apparently, in the state of Texas, ten or more legal ways exist of killing someone.

>> **Contract killing** occurs when a third party is hired or urged to kill a person on behalf of another person. Cinematic films make much of the professional contract killer who's anonymous to the person who hires them and who moves around the world, killing to order. Although such people undoubtedly exist in organized crime syndicates, more usually, the contract killer is someone known to the person hiring him or at least known to someone they know. Quite often, though, unwittingly, the friend-of-a-friend is actually an undercover police officer who has insinuated himself into a criminal network in order to find out who's trying to supply contract killers. He then has the evidence to convict the person who asked him to kill. (By the way, I've not come across any female contract killers except in the TV series 'Killing Eve'.)

>> **Serial killers** kill a number of people over a specific period (most experts require three murders before they place a criminal into this unattractive league), with so-called cooling-off periods in between. These cooling-off periods can be as short as a day or so or as long as a number of years.

>> **Spree killers** kill a number of people in one intense activity. They walk into a store and shoot everyone they can before being stopped. School shootings, like the one at Columbine, Colorado, in 1999, are typical of the activities of spree killers.

>> **Mass murder** is the sort of thing that violent dictators perpetrate, killing hundreds, thousands, or even millions of people. They can't carry out this slaughter on their own, of course. It tends to be part of an organized process in which many killers participate. Sometimes it's a cult that kills all its followers, as happened at Jonestown, Guyana, in 1978, or the cult may set out to kill members of the public, like the sarin gas attack on the Tokyo subway transport system in 1995.

Murder can occur in a number of different situations, and understanding these helps to clarify the nature of the particular killing:

>> **Domestic violence:** Although this type usually involves the man killing the woman, vice versa also happens. This violence can arise out of an enduring violent relationship in which both people involved attack each other from time

to time, or circumstances in which one partner is habitually violent. The violent person's behavior may be aggravated by the use of alcohol or other drugs that reduce normal inhibitions.

>> **Juvenile homicide:** This typically emerges out of a group event in which the victim and the killer could just as readily be the other way round, if one had been quicker or slower to react. Of course, this can happen with adults too, but usually it happens with gangs of youths. These homicides often emerge out of masculine competitiveness, perceived defense of reputation, and the quest for respect.

>> **Confrontational homicide:** This one can result from criminal challenges and is often embedded in violent subcultures in which honor and machismo are at a premium. The offenders can be directly instrumental in the desire to remove a competitor or to demonstrate power over others.

>> **Crime-related homicide:** This one occurs when a significant witness, such as to a rape or a bank robbery, is killed in the belief that this act reduces the likelihood of being caught and convicted. Sometimes this category of murder involves a threat that gets out of control.

Organized crime

Terrorist groups are the most obvious examples of organized criminals. They have a network of contacts that work together in a coordinated way to carry out crimes. But don't fall into the trap of thinking that all criminal networks have similar strict hierarchies and structures; in fact, growing evidence suggests that not even terrorist groups are as tidily organized as is often assumed.

MYTH BUSTER

Maintaining an illegal organization is rather difficult: Everything has to be secret. No one can be trusted unless they're close family members or part of a powerfully coercive subculture, such as the Chinese triads. As a consequence, the notorious criminal organizations such as the Mafia are a rarity among criminal networks, and even they aren't as tightly structured as the movies would have you believe.

The idea that illegal organizations have the same sort of structure as legal ones — with a chief executive, board of directors, managers of departments, and clear lines of command — is misleading. They tend to be volatile groupings that draw on different mixes of individuals for different crimes. The individuals involved have all the variations in their personalities and styles that I discuss throughout this chapter. Consequently, the actions that occur in a crime known to be part of a particular criminal network tell you something about the individuals carrying out that crime.

One interesting way of studying criminal networks is to look at who's in contact with whom and to represent the result as a network chart (as shown in Figure 9-3). This approach allows investigators to identify the key individuals and cliques as well as determine who's on the periphery of the network and so may be willing to act as an informer to the police. Investigative psychologists can also establish the coherence of the network and how tight and interconnected it is to help determine its vulnerability to police interference.

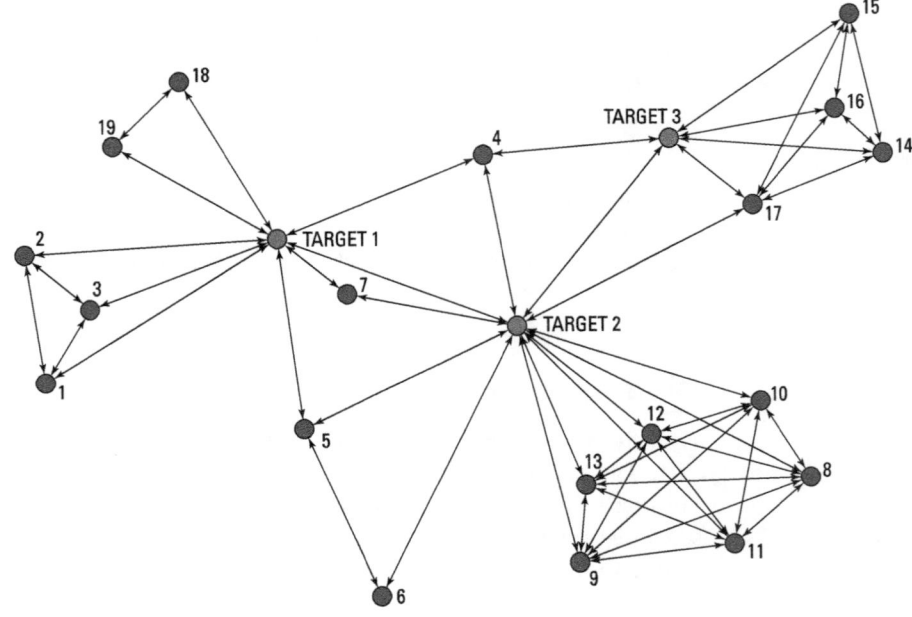

FIGURE 9-3:
A network of
associates in a
criminal gang.
The light gray
circles named
Targets 1, 2, and
3 are well-known
prolific offenders.
The lines join
them to other
individuals with
whom they have
been arrested.

For the example in Figure 9-3, the three target individuals provide the basis for a loosely knit gang that incorporates 19 people in total. Putting these three people out of action — say, by imprisonment — would drastically reduce the network's ability to function.

Investigative psychologists can also provide inferences about the characteristics of those involved in terrorist attacks in much the same way they can for any other crime. This can be particularly helpful in identifying who in a terrorist group may be least committed to the terrorist cause and so may be willing to withdraw from the group and help the police.

Questioning whether This Chapter Should Be Published

One question I'm often asked is whether I'm revealing too much by publishing accounts of how investigative psychology works. I still remember the row I had with a government official who said that publishing would just make criminals savvier and more difficult to catch. In reply, I asked her whether she'd have kept the potential use of fingerprints to solve crimes a secret if she could. Without hesitation, she said yes!

I disagree with her for many reasons, but the main one is that in a democratic society, it's essential that no group has secret control of information that can be used to entrap others. Another reason is that secret science is inevitably bad science: If people disagree with what I write in this book, they can test their ideas and mine, show which are correct, and allow everyone to benefit from the published results.

Perhaps the most important reason, though, is that crime grows from criminals' lack of awareness and insight into the implications and consequences of what they're doing. When informed, criminals can change their activities. For example, out of the blue, I received a letter from a prisoner in a South African prison who had read my book *Criminal Shadows: Inside the Mind of the Serial Killer* (on which I draw throughout this book). This man had a long history of violence in and out of prison. He wrote that, after reading my book, he realized that he had always thought of himself as a tragic victim and that the thought was inappropriate. Having gained that insight, he was now on the road to a productive, violence-free life.

Chapter **10**

Victims of Crime and Their Experiences

A ll too often, writing about crime — in fact and in fiction — focuses on the criminal. Open any of the thousands of academic books about crime, and all too rarely is there a section on the victims and how to help them. Similarly, crime fiction nearly always focuses on catching the villain: The consequences for the victims of the criminal's actions and for their families are usually mentioned only briefly (unless the plot has a vengeful hero seeking retribution).

Fortunately, experts are now redressing this imbalance by considering the consequences of being a victim and how to help those who experience crimes. Although forensic psychologists are often part of these considerations, they work with many other professional groups. These include criminologists, psychotherapists, psychiatrists, police officers, and social workers, all of whom bring their own particular perspectives to bear on helping victims. These groups draw on the insights from forensic psychology that I describe in this chapter, whether or not they have a professional forensic psychologist who is part of their team and who is qualified, as I describe in Chapter 19.

The study of victims, known as *victimology,* covers issues such as who becomes a victim and the resulting social and political implications, while also examining the legal processes that are in place, in some countries, to assist victims.

In this chapter, I generally write about victims of crimes. But the experiences of victims of accidents overlap with these. If you have the great misfortune to be struck by a car, the police will probably assume that it was a crime. The driver will be charged with dangerous driving or a similar charge.

You will be appropriately angry at what you have suffered. If you're unlucky, you may experience some trauma similar to that experienced by people who are assaulted by a thief who steals their belongings. There's no simple distinction between victims of crimes and victims of accidents. Therefore, in some parts of this chapter, I comment on the forensic psychology of accident victims, although mainly focusing on crime victims.

Understanding the experiences of victims helps to clarify the psychological assistance they may need. In this chapter, therefore, I focus on the typical victims of crime and the impact on them of suffering from the acts of criminals. This approach is relevant for all the professional groups who seek to help them. Effective interviewing of victims is described in Chapter 7.

REMEMBER

When I identify what typifies people who are victims of crime, I am, of course, in no way blaming them for what they suffer (though the media and other people sometimes do). My hope is that by understanding their vulnerabilities, the many different professionals who help victims (as well as society in general) can do more to assist them and reduce crime.

Who Becomes a Victim of Crime?

Determining with accuracy how many crimes take place or who's most likely to be a victim isn't easy, mainly because not all crimes are reported to the police, and the way in which reported crimes are recorded varies considerably from one law enforcement area to another. For example, some police officers may identify and therefore record certain criminal acts that the public would see as serious in such a way that they go into a category of minor offenses.

REMEMBER

Experts believe that only two sorts of crime are always reported to the police, so reasonably accurate figures are available only for the following:

>> **Murder:** Because it's a crime that's hard to avoid if a body is found

>> **Car theft:** Because the owner wants the insurance money, and usually has insurance because of legal requirements

To nail down more accurate figures, therefore, many countries carry out crime surveys in which a carefully selected sample of the population is asked to indicate in confidence whether they experienced any crimes in the previous year. These surveys invariably show a much larger number of crimes than are officially recorded. Researchers estimate that, on average, only about half of all crimes find their way into official records. Crime surveys pick up on otherwise unreported crimes, such as less serious crimes and criminal acts in areas where people see no point in reporting them, because they believe that nothing will be done about it. These surveys therefore help forensic psychologists develop a better picture of which crimes actually occur and the sorts of people who are victims but may not be recorded in official statistics.

REMEMBER

To identify victims of crimes — which is the aim of this section — crime surveys, and not official police reports, provide the most accurate information.

Identifying the victims

ANECDOTE

Although crime surveys provide descriptions of who is likely to be vulnerable to crime, these should not be taken to mean that no other people are at risk of suffering from a crime. I experienced a telephone scam that drained lots of money from my bank account. Fortunately, I quickly realized what had happened and was able to get the money back from the bank. When I made my experience public, I heard from a number of professionals, such as doctors and even people who studied online fraud, who had also been scammed. Online fraud is becoming so sophisticated that a high-level university education doesn't necessarily protect you from being a victim. Nor does it protect you from the trauma of suffering the type of crime I experienced.

Crime surveys show that not everyone is equally likely to be on the receiving end of a crime. In general, two contributory factors influence how likely people are to become victims:

>> **Personal characteristics and vulnerabilities:** If you live a disorganized lifestyle, fail to look after your property, or are less able to look after yourself, criminals may take advantage of that situation.

>> **Location:** Inevitably, if you live in, or often visit, a high-crime area, you're more likely to get caught up in a crime.

More specifically, here's a list of attributes, locations, and circumstances that increase the likelihood of becoming a victim of crime:

>> **Attractiveness:** Where the target object is so valued that the offender can sell it to others — for example, an expensive car or the latest cellphone. Clearly, the items in this category are ever-changing as new, desirable objects come onto the market.

You may think that attractiveness can also apply to victims of sexual assaults, but no clear evidence suggests that women who are generally regarded as attractive have a higher probability of being victims of such crimes. Although younger women are more likely than older women to be victims of rape, this is just as likely to be a consequence of lifestyle — that is, being out and about, mixing with a variety of people — than any special attractiveness to rapists.

>> **Deviant place:** Locations where crime, especially minor offending, can flourish, such as where high numbers of people meet at the same time and place. For example, in busy markets or around crowds entering baseball matches.

If the police don't patrol such places, they can become known as *crime hot spots,* where people are at a higher risk of victimization.

>> **Proximity:** Where the offender can access the target geographically or by person-to-person interaction.

Criminals select some victims simply because they're near the location where the offender operates. (This fact is the other side of the coin to locating offenders from knowing where the crimes are, geographic profiling which I discuss in Chapter 9.)

>> **Vulnerability:** Where a lack of protection of property exists or the reduced ability of a person to resist an attack increases the risk of being a victim. The elderly, the very young or infirm, or those with learning disabilities may all be more at risk if they're in the wrong place at the wrong time.

REGIONAL TIP-OFF

The following groups are generally more than twice as likely to be burgled than the average household:

>> Households of young people

>> Single parents

>> People who are unemployed

In the US and UK, teenagers and young adults are twice as likely to experience violent crime compared with the rest of the population. As people grow older, they're less likely to experience violent crime. For example, a teenager in the US is ten times more likely to experience some sort of assault than a person over 65 years old. In addition, Black people in the US are almost twice as likely as White people to experience a violent crime.

Large variations in the prevalence of crimes also exist in different regions of a country, especially property crimes. As is widely known, you're more likely to become a victim of crime in cities than in the countryside, although the types of crime vary, so you have to be cautious about comparisons. For example, not much cattle-rustling takes place in New York or London, and not many fraudulent bankers are roaming the Yorkshire moors or Indiana farmland!

MYTH BUSTER

Interestingly, violent crime tends to have the same frequency per head of population — whether in cities, small towns, or rural areas — which contradicts the general assumption that violence has a higher rate of incidence in the inner cities. Of course, many more people — and more vulnerable people — live in inner cities than in small towns, so the actual number of violent crimes is much higher. After all, the London Metropolitan Police Service has to deal with about a quarter of all crime that occur in the UK, but the population they serve accounts for about a third of the people who live in the UK.

REMEMBER

Fear of crime and the actual experience of crime aren't always closely related. Fear of crime is often highest in those people who feel vulnerable, such as the infirm and elderly. In fact, this group is the least likely to have directly suffered a crime unless they happen to be in the wrong place at the wrong time.

Over the past decade, a growing number of people think that crime is increasing, but in fact, both reported crime and crime surveys show that crime has generally been decreasing in most Western nations.

THE EFFECT OF LOCAL SITUATIONS ON CRIME

The relative incidence of crimes can be quite different in different locations. For example, violent crime is much higher among street gangs in Chicago and Detroit, in vendettas between organized crime groups, and within social groups for whom violence is a way of life (as I describe in Chapter 4). Although these crimes capture the attention of the mass media and raise public concern, the simple fact is that in Western countries, the number of crimes reported overall has been dropping steadily for the past 20 years or so.

MYTH BUSTER

Some believe that we live in particularly violent times. But the murder rate in Oxford in the late 16th century (at the time of William Shakespeare) was many times higher than it is anywhere in the UK today.

Breaking the cycle: Criminals becoming victims and victims becoming criminals

In this section, I want to emphasize an important point that's often missed: Many criminals are also victims of crime. Consequently, when forensic psychologists are helping prisoners (as I describe in Part 5), they have to keep in mind that they're also dealing with people who are likely to have been victims of crime. The typical victim of crime is a young man living in a poor inner-city area, possibly with a lone, unemployed parent, in rented accommodation. But that's also a description of a typical criminal offender. These young men are likely to have been part of a subculture in which theft isn't unusual and using violence to defend oneself is expected.

REMEMBER

I hasten to add that the great majority of young people living in these circumstances don't commit crimes; such behavior is by no means an inevitable consequence of their situation.

The factors that can increase the possibility of a person becoming a victim of crime (for a list, flip to the earlier section "Identifying the victims") are particularly relevant within a community of criminals, especially within a prison. Therefore, one challenge of imprisonment that forensic psychologists who work in prisons (or prison psychologists, as they're sometimes called) have to deal with is to create an environment in which vulnerable individuals don't become victims, with all the traumatic and destructive consequences that can entail.

SECONDARY VICTIMS

Many crimes cause fallout beyond the immediate victim; family, friends, and neighbors can all be secondary victims. A criminal event can disturb even passers-by and witnesses. Major criminal events, such as the destruction of the Twin Towers in New York on 9/11, can cause trauma that spreads around the world. In New York itself, reports indicate a 25 per cent increase in alcohol consumption after 9/11, a sure sign of an increase in fear and anxiety.

One particularly vulnerable group of people are those who work as street-level sex workers. Of course, people who sell sex on the streets of cities have a lifestyle that's quite different from the misleadingly romantic image of the film *Pretty Woman*. For most sex workers, prostitution isn't a favored career choice; the great majority are under pressure from pimps or drug addiction to earn money in the way they do.

Those who work the streets are more vulnerable to assault and homicide. Their vulnerability illustrates the circumstances that can combine to increase the risk of suffering crime:

>> **Dangerous locations:** Sex work is illegal in most places, so it has to be carried out away from the relative safety of public settings. This situation is especially hazardous outdoors with no recourse to others for help.

>> **Reluctance to talk:** When crimes are committed against sex workers, investigators have difficulty gaining information from the victims or their associates because of the way revelations about their activities open them up to prosecution. The women often may also have been brought into the country illegally and lack the requisite papers, work permits, or visas to stay. Because they may fear deportation to much worse conditions back home, they're reluctant to report an assault to the police. Furthermore, their clients are also committing an illegal act that they don't want others to know about, so they're extremely reluctant to volunteer information to help the police. Identifying clients in the first place is also difficult for detectives.

>> **Lack of public sympathy:** The general public is less likely to be concerned about these victims, so they may be unwilling to come forward with information that may help the police.

>> **Associated drug and alcohol problems:** Many, or probably most, street sex workers have alcohol or drug dependency, which makes them desperate to obtain money to maintain their addiction. This encourages them to take risks relating to where they go and with whom. If under the influence of drugs or alcohol, they're probably less able to defend themselves or remember the details to report to the police.

>> **A well-known vulnerability:** Criminals are aware of these vulnerabilities, so they might prey on street sex workers, which is why they're the favored victims of serial killers.

Criminals can also start out as victims — typically, of violent crimes, especially physical and sexual abuse. Often, the offender was the direct victim of such assaults within a family or institutional setting when young. Therefore, helping victims, as discussed in Part 5, is often an important way of reducing the cycle of crime from one generation to the next. (Take a look at the nearby sidebar, "A criminal who started out as a victim".)

Establishing who's at risk of repeat victimization

Many of the conditions that make certain people more at risk of being a victim of a crime than others (check out the earlier section "Identifying the victims") don't go away after a crime has happened. As a consequence, some people are unfortunate enough to experience repeated crimes over a relatively short period of, say, a year. Yet, although this fact seems obvious, only in the past two decades has law enforcement, in some countries, recognized this susceptibility and developed a policy for tackling it. This recognition of the prevalence of repeat victimization comes from criminology studies of general patterns of crime, but forensic psychologists do take the possibility into account when working with offenders or victims.

Studies show that more than one in ten people who suffer a crime, such as burglary, are likely to experience a similar crime within 12 months if they don't take direct efforts to reduce the risks. In fact, the chances of suffering another similar crime are greatest in the days and weeks immediately following the original crime.

A CRIMINAL WHO STARTED OUT AS A VICTIM

ANECDOTE

Joe Thomson pleaded guilty to 129 crimes in South Auckland, New Zealand, committed over a 12-year period starting in 1983. These offenses included many rapes, abductions, burglaries, and instances of incest. When arrested, Thomson described how his earliest memories, from the age of 4 onward, were of being sexually abused by his older sisters and cousins. He said his parents were never around, so that he and his siblings were just "let loose to do what we wanted whenever we wanted." His parents brought their friends home to rape him, and his sisters had been raped by his parents. He seemed relieved at last to be arrested, although his relief stemmed from the fear that he would be killed during one of his assaults. In the controlled, organized environment of prison, he was a model prisoner, although his lack of participation in sex-offender treatment programs (see Chapter 14) means he has not been granted parole.

Efforts by the police and local authorities to reduce the future risk of crime need to account for the following factors, which make people particularly prone to repeat victimization:

>> Living in an area where many criminals live or where they visit.

>> Having chaotic lifestyles or leisure activities that put them at risk of crime, such as spending a great deal of time out late at night and getting drunk enough not to remember where they've been.

>> Displaying a lack of concern to control the crime, as sometimes happens with theft from shops or petty vandalism.

>> Being part of destructive relationships — most notably, domestic violence, which I examine in Chapter 15 — continue as long as the relationship does or until an outside agent intervenes to stop the violence.

Therefore, reducing repeat victimization consists of dealing with the context that supports the crime, whether from the locality or from the weakness of the target of crime. This concept, referred to as *target hardening,* may be as simple as making sure that buildings are securely locked or one that's more complex, such as introducing careful stock control in a business. This may not sound like an aspect of forensic psychology. Often it's not, but sometimes a psychologist needs to consider why some people have vulnerable lifestyles or keep taking the sorts of risks that make them open to crime, like not locking doors when they leave their home.

REMEMBER

When the roots of repeat victimization are within the person's own personality, helping them to understand what they can do themselves to reduce the risk is crucial.

The Effects of Crimes on Victims

All forms of crime, from burglary to rape, can have lasting psychological effects on the victims, far beyond any economic or physical consequences. In this section, I take a look at these psychological issues, which forensic psychologists and other professional groups who help victims often find they have to untangle. The emotional effects can influence the victims' behavior and social lives, including nervousness, anxiety, and worry that can last for months or even years.

Viewing burglary as violation

Studies by forensic psychologists, criminologists, and others show that, after burglaries, many victims feel distress from the violation and intrusion into the place they regard as their private, sacrosanct dwelling. One in five such victims reports severe emotional upset that nearly always includes anger and often shock. These emotions are often expressed in tears and increased fear of future victimization. This distress is frequently accompanied by insomnia.

These effects are strongest when the burglar delves into the most personal parts of the house, such as bedrooms and cupboards, especially when this intrusion also involves ransacking the property and other forms of physical intrusion.

REMEMBER

Some burglary victims compare the violation as having parallels to being raped. Most people see their home as an integral part of who they are and how they present themselves to others. When it's abused, they feel personally attacked, as though the assault was made against their person and body, not just against their property. Many victims relocate so that they aren't reminded of the way the burglar violated them.

Experiencing uncertainty: The worst part is not knowing

Not surprisingly, the experience of suffering property crime, physical assault, or rape often induces an increased feeling of vulnerability in victims. The fixed beliefs in the stability of daily routine, free from threat, are eroded, and the trust in relationships is jeopardized. This in turn increases the fear of possible future victimization and a lack of confidence in people and places that had earlier been regarded as nonthreatening. In addition, the offender still being at large adds considerably to the victim's anxiety.

In many areas of human activity, stress is partly a product of a lack of control over what a person is trying to do. Not knowing whether an attack or a burglary is likely to recur consequently generates considerable stress.

In the particular case of a crime relating to a family member or friend who disappears, the inability to clarify the emotional relationship to the missing person (for example, whether to mourn the person) can cause even more anguish, which is why such victims often say that they'd rather know whether their loved one is dead than be kept in the dark.

Suffering from the trauma of rape

In this section, I discuss some of the details of how victims respond to the shock of a sexual assault. Two stages are often identified in response to rape:

>> **In the hours immediately after the assault:** Victims may experience shock, disbelief, anger, and general anxiety, which is likely to be accompanied by confusion and disorganization in their activities with considerable general fear.

>> **In the days, weeks, or months after the assault:** As victims begin to put their lives back together, they're likely to feel humiliation, embarrassment, and a growing desire for revenge.

Rape victims often feel that they've lost control of social situations and sexual encounters, as well as their autonomy over their intimate relationships. One of the most debilitating psychological aspects is when victims blame themselves, at least in part, for what happened. They may think they gave the wrong signals through their actions, the words they said, or the clothes they wore. In some cultures, the tendency to blame the victims can be so strong that, quite inappropriately, they accept their culpability.

Women in particular often experience rape as life-threatening, even in cases where no direct physical or verbal threats were present, which naturally aggravates all the other anxieties associated with unwanted sexual activity. Large variations do exist, though, in how victims react to sexual assaults: Some manage to find the ability to pull through and deal with the trauma. Family and social support is significant in helping victims cope.

Men who experience rape can suffer particular traumas, whether their assailants are women (as I illustrate in the earlier sidebar "A criminal who started out as a victim") or men. Men may feel that the attack challenges their identity as men, causing them to feel especially vulnerable and even guilty in some ill-defined way for not being "manly enough."

When the victims experience violence, especially including rape and sexual abuse as a child, many more severe effects than those experienced from suffering a property crime are common. These can persist for many years and include:

>> Emotional disturbance

>> Sleep disorders

>> Eating disorders

>> Feelings of insecurity

>> Low self-esteem

>> Difficulties in relating to others

People from minority ethnic communities; lesbians, gay men, and transsexuals; and the elderly suffer more profoundly from violent crime than others in the population.

Forensic psychologists need to recognize the various situations in which male rape can occur, although of course these situations also have parallels when the victims are women:

>> **The victim may be overwhelmed by physical force that he's unable to resist.** This can challenge his view of himself as a capable man, whereas women may sometimes accept that they're physically weaker than their assailant.

>> **A friendly, mild homosexual encounter may be taken further than the victim wants.** Men may feel their heterosexuality has been questioned, which they can find deeply hurtful, in contrast to women, who may have more unwanted sexual approaches from men.

>> **The victim may be trapped in a situation he can't manage because of substance abuse or unwanted drugs.** This can also apply to women, of course, but men may be less aware of the risks of getting into such situations.

>> **Threats may be used to coerce the victim.** Men are more likely to believe they can deal with coercion than women, so they feel especially demeaned if they can't.

REMEMBER

Surveys show that men are just as likely to report having been assaulted by a partner as women, although women report more frequent assaults and suffer greater injuries. I discuss domestic violence in more detail in Chapter 15.

For details on how the trauma of a violent crime is handled in court, turn to Chapter 12.

Examining the effects of physical abuse on children

Children are especially psychologically vulnerable to the effects of physical or sexual abuse because they're still forming an understanding of who they are and how they can relate to others. At the early stage in their development, abuse can have a profound effect on their personalities and create a lack of trust of others and lowered feelings of self-worth. The likely consequences of such abuse are listed here:

>> Beyond the immediate pain and suffering, children are likely to develop medical problems, which can be anything from severe bed-wetting to skin disorders or extreme anxiety. Young children have less physical capability to cope with physical assault and, as a result, death can result from a physical injury in some cases, such as blows to the head, that may not have so severe an impact on an adult.

>> Children are likely to express emotional problems through recurring anger, hostility, or anxiety. They may be fearful of adult contact, which can also involve an inability to express their feelings.

>> Children can experience physical assault as humiliation and thus have lowered self-esteem.

>> Their relationships with other children may become problematic, expressed as aggression toward others, hyperactivity, truancy, inability to form friendships, or poor social skills. Self-destructive behavior, including excessive risk-taking and self-harm, may also be present.

>> Their inability to be part of a social group or to relate to others can make the educational process challenging for abused children, with the outcome of poorer cognitive and language skills.

These are the long-term consequences of child physical abuse:

>> Possible development of physical disabilities; for example, brain damage or eye damage

>> A tendency not to get along with others easily — for example, difficulty trusting others within adult relationships or having violent relationships

>> A predisposition to emotional disturbance, feelings of low self-esteem, and depression

>> An increased potential for abusing their own children when they become a parent, although this isn't inevitable if they're given help early on

>> Possible development of drug or alcohol abuse

Identifying and handling traumatic brain injury

Traumatic brain injury, such as when part of the brain is damaged, is most often caused by accidents, but it can be the result of violent assault. Such injuries become relevant when forensic psychologists are considering victims from two points of view:

>> The effects on those victims that may be relevant in trying to help them, such as seeking medical support and medication or considering the way the brain damage has impaired cognitive abilities

>> The basis that it can provide for understanding how, in some cases, such victims can become criminals, such as changes in their ability to control their emotions or to fully understand the consequences of their actions

Many possible consequences of injury to the brain can result. This depends on which part of the brain is injured. In addition, the forensic psychologist needs to recognize that the event may have had a psychological effect in making the person fearful and anxious quite independently of any brain injury. If the injury results from an assault, the psychological consequences that I discuss earlier in this chapter with regard to rape (see the section "Suffering from the trauma of rape") may be the main cause of any psychological disturbance. Therefore, disentangling the influences of organic brain damage from the emotions associated with the violent crime can often be difficult for anyone trying to help the victim.

REMEMBER

Children are particularly vulnerable to the effects of brain injury and can display:

>> Lower levels of self-esteem and the inability to cope with challenging circumstances, such as the first day at a new school

>> Higher levels of loneliness

>> Maladaptive behavior, such as avoiding any problem faced rather than trying to deal with it, like running away from home because of a family row

>> Aggressive or antisocial behavior

For adults, similar problems may be apparent, but because their involvement in the community at large is more demanding than for children, brain injury can be psychologically debilitating because it reduces the victim's social contact, which may increase feelings of loneliness and related depression. These problems can remain long after the physical consequences of the injury have improved. Social isolation and decreased leisure activities create a renewed dependence on such victims' families to meet these needs.

REMEMBER

A real fear is that traumatic injuries increase the likelihood of a person slipping into criminal behavior (see the earlier section "Breaking the cycle: Criminals becoming victims and victims becoming criminals").

These are the consequences of traumatic brain injury that can increase the susceptibility to commit criminal acts:

>> Decrease in friendships and social support

>> Lack of opportunity for establishing new social contacts and friends

>> Reduced leisure activities

>> Anxiety and depression for prolonged periods

A particularly important effect of severe brain trauma is the loss of memory, known as *post-traumatic amnesia.* This problem can affect victims of brain trauma, making it difficult for them to assist a police inquiry into the nature and cause of the trauma. This is sometimes claimed by offenders as a reason for being unable to give any account of what they did. This memory loss is typically exhibited as a state of confusion or disorientation. Victims may be unable to say their names, where they are, or the current time or the day of the week. (Refer to Chapter 8 to see how forensic psychologists assess whether amnesia is genuine or faked.)

The loss of memories can be those that were formed shortly before the injury. This loss may exist for only an hour or so, or the person may never be able to remember what happened just before the injury. They may also have problems in creating new memories after the injury has taken place. In some cases, this inability to form further memories may not develop until several hours after the injury. Awareness of these processes is crucial for any therapy a psychologist may attempt to carry out with a victim. They may not wish to face up to what they experienced, or they may genuinely forget it because of the brain trauma. Knowledge of these processes is relevant to everyone who works with victims: police, social workers, and the courts.

Criminals' awareness of post-traumatic amnesia can be drawn on as a defense. They can claim that they can't remember what happened leading up to the crime or soon after. It can be difficult to determine whether this is genuine memory loss (as I make clear in Chapter 5, where I describe how memory loss is assessed). Assessment requires a full understanding of how memory works and what is, and isn't, likely to be forgotten. Forensic psychologists with this special knowledge may be called in to determine whether the defendant is malingering or truly is a victim of a crime.

Helping victims deal with trauma

Providing support for people who have suffered the impact of traumatic experiences — whether from violence, abuse, wrongful conviction, disaster, or any of the other experiences of crime dealt with earlier in this chapter — requires a caring, compassionate approach that increasingly draws on some special forms of psychological support.

One form of psychological therapy that's gaining ground in helping people who have experienced trauma is EMDR — *eye movement desensitization and reprocessing*. It consists of getting people to concentrate on their memory of distressing events while being distracted by rapid side-to-side eye movements and other activities, such as rapid tapping. Some evidence shows that this strategy helps reprocess these memories so that they become less vivid, less emotionally intense, and more integrated into the person's way of thinking about themselves.

But, like all such forms of psychotherapeutic support, they need to take place within the context of careful, nonjudgmental listening to the client. That has to happen within an environment where the person feels safe. It also helps if they come to understand the nature of post-traumatic responses, such as hypervigilance and flashbacks as well as lowered self-esteem and inappropriate shame. In addition, social support of various kinds can be of great benefit. This includes support groups that bring together people with similar experiences. They may share accounts of their traumatic events, helping them all not to feel isolated, fostering resilience, and reducing any stigma the survivors may feel.

Assessing the Psychological Effects of a Crime on a Victim

Psychologists — whether they're general clinical psychologists who provide therapy for many different types of patients with mental health problems or more specialized forensic psychologists who are helping victims, along with family doctors, psychiatrists, and other professionals (even the local priest) — may also be called on to assess the extent of the effect of the experience of a crime. This may be done to determine how the therapy should be conducted and to identify the particular problems the victim needs help with.

But assessment of the victim of a crime may also be carried out to establish exactly what the effects are, so that other forms of help beyond counselling and psychological therapy can be provided. This can include compensation from the state or the culprit or from insurance or other forms of support for disabilities. These assessments often require psychological expertise as well as medical expertise. The forensic psychologist assesses the victim in much the same way as if the person had experience an accident. Although crimes generate fears and anxieties that may not be so prevalent as a consequence of accidents, the psychological issues are similar.

Part of the challenge of making accurate assessments about crime victims is that sometimes the person wants to appear as damaged as possible, perhaps to increase the chance (or amount) of an insurance payment. In addition, in court cases, the victims may be determined to ensure that culprits are seen to have caused deep psychological damage and thus avoid the judge or jury being lenient. Consequently, psychologists assessing the victim have to find ways of determining the true nature of the situation.

REMEMBER

Here are the main ways in which forensic psychologists assess the experience of a crime victim:

>> Seeking objective information from as wide a range of sources as possible, including medical and employment records and, wherever possible, interviewing people who knew the victim before and after the critical event, such as family friends and work colleagues

>> Getting the details of the incident as clear as possible to determine how it may have had any effects

>> Considering the person's capabilities and emotional tendencies before the incident

>> Assessing the official interviews of the victim in the light of other evidence

>> Using psychological tests (as I discuss in Chapter 5)

One particular aspect is to consider how the victim deals with the interview process itself, sometimes called the *response style*. These responses can display a number of different characteristics:

>> **Malingering,** especially the deliberate fabrication of symptoms or greatly exaggerating them

>> **Minimization,** the denial of any symptoms or the reduction in the account of their seriousness

>> **Distraction,** or dealing with questions by going off at a tangent to talk about irrelevant issues, probably indicating an unwillingness to engage directly with the interview procedure

>> **Lack of effort** in performing any tasks because part of the assessment may be caused by weariness or frustration, but can also indicate other symptoms the victim isn't totally aware of — notably, depression

>> **Lack of cooperation,** such as when the victim refuses to answer questions or gives only minimal answers

The forensic psychologist uses these response styles to form a view of the disabilities of the victim and the effect of the incident. Alone, they don't imply whether the victim's account of the incident's effect is valid. Taken together with all the other information, the response styles provide a valuable basis to any opinion the psychologist can offer.

Dealing with post-traumatic stress disorder

I discuss post-traumatic stress disorder (PTSD) in some detail in Chapter 12, where I consider expert testimony in court because it's one of the most common forms of psychological disturbance used as evidence. Take a look at that chapter for details of the symptoms that comprise PTSD. In this section, I focus on identifying and treating PTSD, a common component of any assessment of a victim of a crime or an accident.

To be sure that any incident has given rise to PTSD, whether it's a violent assault or an event that looks like an accident, the forensic psychologist needs to establish that the symptoms arose close in time to the event. In some cases, PTSD has been diagnosed as many as 30 years after the event (check out the nearby sidebar "Assessing for PTSD years after the event"), but being sure that the symptoms are related to the event under such conditions is extremely difficult.

To make matters more complicated, considerable evidence suggests that a person's psychological state and makeup before the traumatic event, taken together with the support and other helpful aspects of lifestyle (or lack of), can have a considerable influence on whether PTSD occurs and the form it takes. The emotional reactions the person is having — anxiety, avoidance of people or places, and the other general aspects of PTSD — may have been generated by something other than the particular trauma for which the person is claiming. Or these other experiences may have made a mild shock more significant.

ANECDOTE

ASSESSING FOR PTSD YEARS AFTER THE EVENT

The problem of disentangling causes when PTSD is delayed is demonstrated by the Australian disaster in 1964 when an aircraft carrier collided with a destroyer that then sank. Eighty-one people drowned. More than 35 years later, hundreds of people claimed PTSD. Assessing these claims required consideration of the individual's psychological state immediately after the disaster and what had happened to that person over the intervening years, particularly identifying any other stressors that may have occurred during this time.

Studies in the US indicate that about half the population claims to have experienced some sort of serious traumatic event during their lifetime. If they experience another such event, are the effects magnified, or has the person developed coping strategies that make them less vulnerable? The answer is yes or no, depending on the person.

If a person is psychologically stable before the event and in a supportive environment after it, that person is likely to be able to cope with what appears to be serious trauma. A number of examples exist of studies of children who have lived through wars — in Lebanon or Bosnia, for instance — who show no signs of PTSD. They were part of warm and loving families and had no psychological problems before the war. These preexisting circumstances protected them from PTSD.

Sadly, in recent years, immensely destructive wars have killed the parents and other relatives of children who survived. This denies those children the sort of support that would have helped them cope with the intense traumas they are suffering. They experience not only the impact of the war and the deep, deep challenge of dealing with the loss of parents and family but also the loss of support that would have been of some assistance in handling these profound tragedies.

The various professions that offer help to victims, including clinical and forensic psychologists, draw on a variety of different approaches for treating PTSD, some of which I mention earlier in this chapter. People's reactions to events and the nature of those events vary enormously. Any help or support for someone suffering from PTSD therefore has to be adjusted to the person. (Much of the work on this syndrome emerged out of the recognition that soldiers can suffer great traumas.) In general, the following activities are involved in treating PTSD:

» The nature of the problem and what the client particularly wants help with is identified; for example, fear of particular locations, difficulty of being with other people, or intimate relationships.

» Ways of relaxing are explored with the person, perhaps involving forms of self-hypnosis or other techniques widely used throughout psychotherapy.

» Victims are encouraged to develop ways of relaxing in relation to particular aspects of their problem, perhaps focusing on particular places or occasions, or even back to the traumatic event. Various procedures can be used, such as requiring the client to do the homework of trying to deal with some small aspect of the difficult circumstance one tiny step at a time, or guided imagery in which the person thinks carefully about particular stressful circumstances (when calm) and considers how to act effectively in those situations in the future.

>> A follow-up is organized to address the current concerns of the individual to help maintain any improvements in the person's psychological state.

Offering restorative justice

Identifying the traumatic consequences of crime and developing accounts of victims' experiences can imply that they have something close to a medical problem. This approach can lead to their being assigned a clinical label that ignores their unique experiences and ways of dealing with those experiences. They may find themselves being treated as a medical case rather than a person, with expectations of how they should act being influenced by general ideas about those sorts of cases rather than by the individual person's behavior.

To counteract this problem, many victims are encouraged to think of themselves not as victims but as survivors of an awful event. This change in labeling also gives people the confidence to take back control of their lives and not allow the offender to continue exerting an influence over what they do by continuing to give rise to their fears and anxieties.

One way of helping victims feel empowered is by confronting the person who attacked them or stole from them, such as testifying in court or being part of a *restorative justice* process. This approach focuses not on the clinical problems but on the fact that crime involves an explicit or implicit relationship between the offender and the victim. This situation needs to be dealt with. Restorative justice emphasizes repairing the harm that has been caused by the crime, or going to the essence of the crime. Connecting the offender and the victim can also have beneficial effects on the criminal.

MYTH
BUSTER

Restorative justice gives the victim (or survivor) a significant role in the judicial process. That person's suffering is placed center stage. This differs considerably from most legal systems in which the state punishes the criminal, and the victim is just one more witness to provide evidence for the state.

At the heart of restorative justice processes is offenders acknowledging their wrongdoing and apologizing for it. Studies show that this humane acceptance is beneficial to victims. It helps them accept the validity of their own suffering and understand more fully the reasons that the crime occurred, which also helps them come to terms with it.

Victims offer the following reasons for requesting a restorative justice procedure:

>> To find out from the offender why the crime was committed in that way with that particular victim

>> To make the offender understand and accept the effect the crime has had on the victim and to accept and apologize for that effect

>> To have the opportunity to forgive the offender and thus bring the experience to a resolution

The restorative justice process can employ many different formats, such as small-group meetings, more formal conferences, and mediation through a third party. These formats can include support from legal or psychotherapeutic professionals or even ex-offenders. In general, restorative justice involves these stages:

>> **Meeting:** Bringing together all those affected by the crime to talk about the crime and its consequences

>> **Recompense:** Exploring how the offender can help repair the harm caused, including clear indications of remorse, apology, and acceptance of the impact of the offense

>> **Reintegration:** Setting in motion the restoration of victims and offenders as full, positive members of society

>> **Inclusion:** Ensuring that all those for whom the crime has particular relevance participate in the agreed-on actions

MYTH
BUSTER

Restorative justice isn't a soft option for criminals. Many of them refuse to accept responsibility for their crimes, drawing on the justifications I discuss in Chapter 4. Nor do they want to face their victims or set in motion anything that would redress the damage they have done. In many cases, offenders have preferred to go to prison rather than participate in restorative justice. This reaction reveals the central weakness of what's otherwise a good idea: it requires the offender's full and open participation.

WHEN THE VICTIM IS A WHOLE NATION

Forensic psychologists tend to deal with individuals, but unfortunately, situations also exist in which large groups of people, possibly even whole nations, suffer crimes. In those cases, the principles of forensic psychology are just as relevant for these large numbers of people as they would be for one person. In such tragedies, many thousands, often millions, of victims exist, and each individual may suffer the consequences I discuss throughout this chapter. In most cases, the poor and dispossessed are the ones who suffer, along with those with limited or no resources for coping. This suffering can readily set in motion the cycle of criminality I discuss earlier in this

(continued)

(continued)

chapter, in the section "Breaking the cycle: Criminals becoming victims and victims becoming criminals." When countries come through these traumas, they sometimes work with forensic psychologists and those who draw on forensic psychology to help heal the nation.

Unsurprisingly, given its traumatic history when generations had their families torn apart by apartheid, South Africa is an example of such problems. Young men and women were born into families in which the father was forced away from home and in which the police and legal system focused on depriving of their rights those with the least resources. Such daily traumas may have predicted that many of them would be unable to relate to others and see criminality as a natural form of existence. The miracle of South Africa as it moved into multiracial democracy is that it didn't explode into a criminal bloodbath. This achievement is due, at least in part, to the social and political processes of reconciliation used to reconstruct the social fabric of that society.

In a form of restorative justice, people from the different sides of the earlier conflict were brought together and an attempt made to balance remorse with forgiveness. (The danger was that some victims were left feeling as though their suffering wasn't taken seriously.)

One interesting finding in this area is that religious institutions can play a powerfully positive role, perhaps because they provide individuals with the possibility of reconstructing themselves as members of an ethical, even magnanimous, community guided by civilizing principles. They can think of themselves as builders of a new world rather than as sufferers from the misdeeds of others. In other words, they can reinvent their personal narratives so that they don't see themselves as victims who seek revenge but rather as pioneers creating a born-again country. Like a rape victim who refuses to continue to suffer from fear, individuals in post-conflict societies can use the fundamental forensic psychology idea of the value of taking control of their lives and making the future work for them.

Chapter **11**

Preventing Crime: Problems, Processes, and Perseverance

You may wonder what forensic psychologists have to do with preventing crime. Don't they just help clear up the mess and damage afterward? Well, preventing crime is about influencing the actions of individual criminals. Anything known about them psychologically contributes to more effective crime prevention and reduction. Therefore, when forensic psychologists increase their understanding of criminals and help provide a framework for their rehabilitation or stop them from continuing a life of crime, they're carrying out steps toward preventing future crime.

As I discuss in Chapter 4, the great majority of criminals aren't bizarre individuals — they're people whose psychology can be understood. Making sense of their influences, and how they see the world and the opportunities for crime, provides the starting point for prevention.

In this chapter, I focus on those aspects of crime prevention that have a psychological focus: an emphasis on criminals and their actions. I discuss the difficulties involved in preventing crime, some different attempts that have been suggested and tried, and the foreseen and unforeseen consequences of applying these techniques. More specifically, I investigate how psychology can help combat the particular criminal areas of kidnappings, street gangs, and organized crime.

Facing Up to the Difficulties of Preventing Crime

I've never come across a society that experiences no crime. One of the first acts of human beings described in the Bible is Cain killing his brother Abel. So you have to face the fact that humans have always committed crime in one form or another, and that the chances of eliminating it are rather slim. This section looks at the problems involved in preventing crime, the psychological knowledge that can help, and the fact that society may well have to accept that reducing the severity and frequency of crime is the best that can be achieved.

REMEMBER

Throughout this section, one question about the causes of criminal behavior arises repeatedly: Is committing crime the result of people's inherent characteristics or their social circumstances? (I discuss this subject in more detail in Chapter 4.) Most experts accept the premise that crime results from a mixture of these causes. But people in power tend to be more simple-minded. They decide whether it is social processes that cause crime or something inherent in the individual. Either way, that belief will influence their views about the best way to prevent crime. That in turn will influence how they use psychological knowledge, insights, and approaches.

REGIONAL TIP-OFF

The prevalence of crime is reflected in the surprising statistic that 34 percent of the UK male population will have a criminal conviction by the time they're 30 years old. That doesn't mean they've been in prison — just that they've committed a crime and have been caught. This includes a range of various crimes from the most serious to the most trivial. The statistics for the US are more difficult to pin down and are much more disproportionately distributed across subcultures, but they do seem to be on a par with the UK figures. Obviously, the number of people who commit crimes and don't get caught is much higher. Self-reported criminal activity in anonymous surveys indicates that every man and a high proportion of women have likely broken the law in one way or another by the time they're 30. These crimes can include buying illegal drugs, shoplifting, and more serious crimes like burglary and rape. The figures show that criminality isn't limited to a small subset of the population, although prolific offenders are rare.

A major challenge is to stop criminals from committing more than one crime. *Recidivist* is the term given to a person who's arrested and convicted again within a given period — say, three years. These days, in general terms and round figures, about two-thirds of people convicted of crimes reoffend within three years. These figures vary greatly, depending on the type of crime and the sentence a person receives. People who are locked up for ten years don't reoffend for quite some time — outside prison, at least.

Politicians complain about these high reoffending figures. They put many schemes in place to stop reoffending and sometimes claim success in reducing the recidivism figures. But the truth is that many schemes don't do much better than the general one-third reduction, which is what happens if you do nothing. And guess what? In the fascinating book *The Criminal,* published in 1901, Havelock Ellis complains about the fact that about two out of every three criminals soon reoffend. In other words, the rates of repeat criminality are remarkably consistent.

MYTH BUSTER

Although the number of people who become criminals (or at least who are caught) has fallen over the past three decades, those who are convicted of an offense are just as likely to reoffend today as was the case a hundred years ago.

REMEMBER

Being charged with an offense depends on what is illegal in that jurisdiction. Many actions (or even thoughts) may be against the law in one country but totally acceptable in another, which affects the calculation of crime rates enormously.

Keeping pace with the evolution of crime

One challenge in preventing crime is that it continues to develop and evolve. For example, one new type of criminal is the offender with information technology skills, who uses the internet to commit crimes that in the past may have been carried out by door-to-door fraudsters (or further back in time, by highwaymen). Table 11-1 gives some insight into how changes are opening up ever-new areas in which criminals can prosper.

New types of criminality are turning up in illegal activities, and existing criminals are finding their opportunities in different ways today from those available a century ago. Experts — including forensic psychologists — therefore need to consider whether existing approaches to crime prevention are still relevant. For instance, is the psychology of the internet-based thief different from someone prepared to rob a person physically? If so, preventing that crime requires a different approach.

Each of the developments in Table 11-1, and many others, raises new challenges to preventing or reducing opportunities for offending. People still need to make life as difficult as possible for potential criminals (the target-hardening that I discuss in the later section "Making crime more difficult"), but much of this attempted prevention will be in cyberspace rather than on main street.

TABLE 11-1   **Developments and Emerging Opportunities for Crime**

Developments	Opportunities for Criminals
Increased wealth throughout the world (although big differences remain between rich and poor)	More wealth to be stolen or fought over, with plenty of people experiencing injustices
Greater number of portable consumer goods	More desirable objects that are easier to steal
Information stored and transmitted electronically	Access to confidential, personal information, such as identities and bank accounts, with no need for physical contact
Developments in technology	Technology that becomes a target as well as a tool for criminality
Easier global travel and more open borders between many countries	Criminals who are able to move without hindrance and over greater distances
Improved crime prevention	Paradoxically, may in some cases cause more violent crime in order to overcome protective devices

Despite the changing nature of crime, being alert to the psychological characteristics of offenders and their attitudes to what they're doing (in order to discern their weaknesses) remains central to crime prevention strategies. (Check out the later section "Examining Ways to Prevent or Combat Crime.")

As well as the changes listed in Table 11-1, authorities need to consider widespread social changes that present new types of criminal behavior (see Table 11-2).

TABLE 11-2   **Social Changes Relevant to Understanding Criminals**

Social Changes	Implications for Criminals	Breakdown of Traditional Religious and Ethical Frameworks
Offenders now come from wider areas of society than in the past and from unusual backgrounds.	Reduction in the positive influence of family and family discipline across social groups.	Criminals' backgrounds are becoming more widely dispersed, by way of social groups.
Wider education and availability of better technological skills.	The increasing ease of use of many emerging technologies, especially by younger people, means that more people have the skills to abuse them.	Increased cultural mix of many cities.
Offenders are now drawn from wider ethnic and cultural backgrounds.	The greater increase in inequality around the world and in many Western nations.	The seeds of alienation and distress are planted, which can lead to certain criminal thought processes.

PUSHING TO INCREASE THE CRIME RATE

Crime is rather like the adaptation of a species when a change in habitat occurs — criminal actions evolve to fit into the new opportunities. Here's just one example: Las Vegas has well over 100 thousand hotel rooms, each inhabited for a few days by people who may have never stayed in a hotel. Some of these guests are careless about shutting and locking their room door. As a consequence, a special type of burglar evolved in Las Vegas: These *door-pushers* wander around the endless hotel corridors simply pushing on room doors until they find one that's not secured and then entering and stealing the belongings. This type of burglar is possibly unique to cities with large numbers of hotels located near each other.

In many senses, criminals don't change themselves — just their methods. (See the nearby sidebar "Pushing to increase the crime rate.") People who conned vulnerable members of the public a hundred years ago — say, by selling snake oil as a panacea — now sell equally useless products from websites. Stalkers who used to confront estranged lovers physically or bombard them with endless letters now threaten them via the internet with streams of emails or abuse on Facebook or X. Perhaps the modern-day equivalent of the young pickpockets whom Charles Dickens portrays in *Oliver Twist* now work at computer terminals, stealing and using fake websites and fraudulent emails.

Asking whether prison works

If authorities believe that some people are inherently criminal, these people have to be discouraged from their errant ways, which can be quite difficult in a free society. Often, they're imprisoned, which worldwide is a common process for trying to prevent crime.

Clearly, this approach reduces the possibility of people committing crimes for the period they're in prison — at least on the streets — although they can influence crimes indirectly and, of course, offend within the prison. But beyond the short-term objective of taking offenders out of circulation, does prison reduce their risk of reoffending after they're let out?

Although the recidivism figures paint a pessimistic picture of imprisonment — around two out of every three people reoffend within three years — the prison experience does change certain offenders' behavior permanently.

Viewing prison as just one type of experience, however, is perhaps misleading because the inmates' experiences can vary a great deal. Some prisons are boring, violence-ridden places, full of aggressive gangs and drugs, that so delight

Hollywood. Many others provide training and support activities that enable people to reconstruct their views of themselves and their lives. These approaches can help offenders return to society, provided the stigma of imprisonment can be overcome and they have effective support after their release.

Around the world, many other attempts at punishment that can also rehabilitate are in use. Such procedures as electronic tagging, community service orders, and various forms of open imprisonment have had mixed success. These approaches seek to reduce the negative effects associated with incarceration while making clear to individuals that their offending is both unacceptable and unproductive. The challenge is to help offenders deal with the causes of their crimes (perhaps rooted in the social networks and/or their personality characteristics) while simultaneously meting out appropriate punishment, which is an extremely tall order.

Getting tough on the causes of crime

If those in power believe that social settings and upbringing are predominantly responsible for crime, it follows that some possibility of rehabilitation exists, so treatment and support projects may be worthwhile (as I consider in Part 5). In this case, authorities are likely to support programs that help people become better parents or that try to move children out of the conditions of poverty that foster crime.

As I explore in Chapter 10, many offenders who commit violent crimes have been victims of physical or sexual abuse. Consequently, any reduction in those initial crimes, and efforts to help those who suffer from them, is likely to reduce the number of people in subsequent generations who carry out similar offenses.

This last point indicates one of the difficulties in dealing with the causes of crime, however, which is that any positive effects can take decades to appear. Such social programs are expensive to put in place and run, and the results are often subjective and difficult to prove (at a time when displaying value-for-money public expenditure is crucial).

REMEMBER

One area that's often undervalued in reducing crime is education. Many people drift into criminal activity because they haven't received the knowledge and skills from schooling to enable them to find a productive place in society. The reality is that many people in prison have low levels of educational achievement, often being unable to read or write effectively.

Although academics may argue whether the lack of education is the cause or consequence of an involvement in truancy and related criminality, this chicken-and-egg question doesn't matter when the aim is to reduce crime. These are the important objectives:

>> Keep youngsters in school.

>> Give offenders the skills to survive legally outside of prison.

Succeeding only in displacing crime

Efforts to prevent or reduce criminal activities often face the difficulty of *displacement*, where the crime simply moves to another jurisdiction or no longer shows up in official statistics under previously used headings. Superficially, the crime figures appear to have improved, but the overall crime rate (and people's suffering from it) remains the same.

Experts have identified the following changes in features of crime as a result of crime prevention initiatives, all of which contain a psychological element:

>> **Criminals move from one area to another.** For example, muggings stop where Closed-Circuit Television (CCTV) or other forms of security cameras are present, but increase away from the cameras.

>> **Criminals change their timing.** Office burglaries happen when security guards are away, for example.

>> **Criminals change how they operate.** They start to wear hoods to avoid being identified on security systems.

>> **Criminals alter their behavior.** An improvement in vehicle security reduced the number of cars stolen from the street, but instances of *carjacking* (stealing cars at gunpoint) slightly increased.

>> **Criminals change the nature of their crimes while maintaining the same objectives.** Aircraft hijacking is much rarer due to the great increase in security checks of passengers, but terrorists have changed their tactics to kidnapping and suicide bombing.

>> **Criminals change their targets.** Terrorists move away from attacking highly protected consulates and embassies to striking more vulnerable tourist locations.

Of course, I'm not saying that society shouldn't use all the crime prevention strategies at its disposal, but an understanding of criminal psychology can help to recognize and anticipate some of the consequences. The fact is that new crime prevention measures change the landscape for criminals. As a result, offenders adapt to the new surroundings and take advantage of new opportunities.

Some attempts at crime prevention can increase crime, if not handled carefully. For example, when a policy of arresting anyone accused of domestic violence shames offenders into less violent behavior, others may respond by becoming more defiant, more dangerous, and more violent toward their victims.

The possibility of displacement, and of even more serious crimes resulting from attempts at crime prevention, shows the need to understand criminals' psychologies and points of view when trying to change their actions. If due attention is paid and prevention procedures aren't introduced blindly, research suggests that many new initiatives can be successful in reducing the overall crime rate.

Examining Ways to Combat Crime

This section covers just a few ways in which authorities try to combat crime: Most involve psychology. Some may be simpler than you'd suspect.

Understanding the weaknesses of criminals in their use of new technologies opens up new directions for law enforcement. The use of mobile phones is widespread among criminals in South Africa — even those who live in informal settlements *(shantytowns)*. Yet many of these criminals are unaware of how the police can now use mobile phone networks to locate the offenders. Police have caught serial rapists and murderers by using the simple device of calling them on a mobile phone they've stolen from a victim! This is an instance of police using psychology in the battle against crime — or more simply, outthinking offenders. Indeed, the great majority of crimes are now solved in many countries via digital information. We all leave a similar record of what we've done and where and even why we've done it.

Making crime more difficult

The central idea of all attempts to reduce crime, rather than the more optimistic goal of preventing it completely, is to make criminal activity less attractive to the criminal. This reduction can be done in a number of ways:

>> **Target-hardening:** This is the most common way of thinking about making crimes more difficult to carry out. It can include everything from making sure people lock their cars to putting hooks under tables in busy places so that handbags can be hung there to make them less vulnerable to being snatched, all the way through to placing concrete slabs outside embassies and airports to stop terrorists from driving car bombs into them. Increased lighting and

other design developments that make any nefarious activity easier to see can also be part of this approach.

» **Dampening:** If it becomes apparent that a particular form of crime is developing, such as a spate of pickpocketing or break-ins to schools, authorities may set in motion attempts at dampening the criminal actions. Methods include campaigns to make people more aware of the problem, increased surveillance, or even increased direct attempts to arrest the main culprits.

» **Zero tolerance:** This approach, which seeks to disrupt the development of an individual's criminal career, assumes that people often start offending by committing minor crimes such as painting graffiti or breaking windows. If they can be made aware early on that their behavior is unacceptable and that they risk becoming more heavily involved in the criminal justice system, this awareness may reduce the likelihood of further, more serious criminality.

The added benefit of zero tolerance — if it also includes removing from the streets burned-out cars, rubbish, and other signs that a neighborhood tolerates antisocial behavior and criminality — is that it sends a message to would-be criminals that their offenses won't be tolerated. This sets in motion a virtuous cycle that produces fewer signs of crime and areas less attractive to possible offenders.

» **Gated communities:** This direct environmental, or even architectural, approach seeks to restrict access to potential criminal targets. Gated communities have been established in the richer parts of South American cities for many years and are becoming increasingly popular in the US and a few locations around Europe.

In the UK, attempts have been made to make access to houses more difficult for burglars. For example, the small alleys at the back of houses in layouts, such as row houses are especially conducive to illegal activity. Cutting them off with gates to which only residents have keys (called *alleygating*) removes this problem. The interesting psychological benefit, beyond reducing crime, is that people feel they have more ownership of their area and an enhanced community spirit. This feeds into the virtuous cycle I note earlier in relation to zero tolerance.

In general, research shows that alleygating reduces crime in a particular area. In one circumstance, however, it can increase crime: If persistent burglars live within the area surrounded by the gates, they may be unable to get out easily to offend elsewhere, with a resulting increase in their committing crimes locally.

Ensuring that crime doesn't pay

Many studies of criminals point to the deterrent effect of getting caught. The risk of the punishment isn't what stops them, however — it's the challenge and the potential embarrassment that comes with being detected. Consequently, improvement in policing and detection (to which psychology can contribute, as I discuss in Chapter 8) is a way of reducing crime.

The problem is that many criminals don't fully understand the risks of being caught, believing that they're impervious to detection. Also, with police resolving only around one in ten burglaries, burglars have reason to make this assumption. Therefore, increased effectiveness of detection not only brings criminals into the justice system where they can be punished, or helped to see the error of their ways, but also discourages other criminals from taking the risk of getting caught.

Disrupting criminal careers

One approach of crime prevention is to work directly with offenders to diminish their likelihood of committing further crimes, or at least reduce the prevalence of their crimes. For much more on the various programs in place, especially for violent offenders and those who've committed sex crimes, check out Part 5 of this book.

REMEMBER

Addressing some of the background contributions to an individual committing crimes can help reduce or even prevent crime. One obvious example is drug abuse: The expense of high levels of illegal drug use, as well as the way buying and selling these drugs becomes part of criminal activities, doubtless fosters many forms of theft — as well as violence. Whether drug addiction itself causes crime is open to debate, but I've certainly spoken to criminals who say they began using illegal drugs only after they became involved in property crime that gave them the money to buy the drugs or were introduced to substance abuse via their association with other criminals.

Alcohol abuse also contributes to many forms of crime, especially outbursts of violence. Helping people deal with alcoholism can reduce criminality. This process is demanding, however, because of peer pressure and the institutionalized popular amusement and even attractiveness associated with drunkenness.

**STRANGE
BUT TRUE**

Treating people for alcohol addiction requires helping them cope with the temptations to have a drink. In prisons where no alcohol is available, it's difficult to provide the experiences that will develop these coping mechanisms.

Changing the law

At the risk of stating the obvious, crime is what is proscribed (or prohibited, in other words) by law. Politicians often ignore the fact that crime can be prevented by changing the law so that certain actions are no longer illegal.

One obvious example is the impact of prohibition on the manufacture or sale of alcohol. Although best known in 1920s America, many countries have had similar laws in the past, and some Islamic countries still impose the prohibition. Such restrictions generate illegal activity because significant proportions of the population don't regard the activity as criminal. When many people want to do things that they don't regard as wrong, but that the law prohibits, the result is increased criminal activity.

Here's my list of activities that are illegal in many countries, often attracting severe penalties, but that many people don't think of as wrong. You can probably think of others:

>> Adultery

>> Exaggerating insurance claims

>> Prostitution

>> Smuggling widely used products, such as cigarettes, to avoid import duties

>> Tax evasion

>> Underage drinking

>> Homosexual acts

Of course, many behaviors that are legal for adults are illegal for children, too. Some activities are crimes if a 14-year-old is involved, but are not illegal for an adult. In most countries, this includes many forms of sexual activity as well as buying cigarettes and alcohol.

REMEMBER

An important aspect of crime prevention is educating the public to understand the reasons for laws being in place, accept the consequences of breaking those laws, and believe that the legal system is reasonable and just.

Using Psychological Knowledge to Combat Specific Types of Crime

In this section, I take a look at three different types of crime and show how psychological knowledge and approaches can be invaluable in combating them: hostage-taking, street gangs, and organized crime.

Negotiating in hostage situations

The circumstances in which a person is held hostage can quickly turn into an even more serious crime of murder. The handling of hostage situations, therefore, requires psychological insight into each particular hostage event and the development of negotiation skills that enable the least destructive conclusion possible.

Identifying types of hostage-taking and kidnapping

Hostage situations fall into three general groups, each of which requires different psychological approaches:

>> **Siege:** In the US and UK, the most common form of hostage event is one in which a person barricades himself (it's usually a man) in a room or house with a hostage — often a partner, spouse, or an acquaintance. These hostage-takers are often mentally disturbed, depressed, or even psychotic, so any approach to managing the situation needs to appreciate their special way of seeing the world. Occasionally, such hostage-takers may be so mentally disturbed that they even have to discuss their actions with a nonexistent, imaginary person before they respond to any law enforcement suggestions.

REMEMBER

An offender who has a criminal background may feel that they have more to lose by giving themselves up. Anyone negotiating needs to take this into account by presenting options the offender may not have considered.

>> **Criminal kidnapping for ransom:** Kidnapping people for financial gain is quite different from a siege in which an angry husband threatens his estranged wife to stop her from leaving him. The ransom element creates a negotiation built around threats in which the kidnapper and the negotiator each tries to control the situation. Threats to harm the victim are used to persuade the authorities to pay up, but the negotiator can offer safe passage or other inducements to the kidnapper. Although a kidnapping for ransom may seem like a straightforward business deal, this situation requires a delicate negotiation recognizing that the kidnappers may not be rational

businesspeople. They may have other reasons for the kidnapping than just trying to obtain money, such as showing the authorities to be incompetent.

REMEMBER

The sad fact is that, more often than not, hostages in ransom kidnappings are killed, particularly — and tragically — if the hostage is a child. This may be because keeping a child for any length of time is difficult. As a result, attempts to release hostages by using force may be more appropriate than is often believed.

The business plan of gang members who make money frequently from ransom requires that they hold on to their franchise and keep other gangs out of their territory. Some drug cartels in Mexico, such as the notorious Los Zetas, maintain a strong identity and kill people in other gangs who have the temerity to carry out kidnappings in their domain.

Countries differ considerably in handling kidnapping and hostage-taking incidents, with pervasive attitudes toward criminals influencing their methods. Some authorities strive, at all costs, to avoid loss of life — even of the kidnapper. For others, the primary need is to make a stand against such events — the kidnapper is regarded as an outlaw who deserves to die.

STRANGE BUT TRUE

In some countries (especially in South America and, notably, Cuba), organized gangs have taken to abducting pet dogs — especially rare expensive breeds, which have to be walked outdoors — and demanding large ransoms for their release.

>> **Political:** When the hostage-taking is part of a political act, in which negotiations may concern the release of prisoners or other concessions, authorities face considerable challenges — primarily, that any concessions may be regarded as political weakness or simply encouraging future kidnappings. In addition, the kidnap itself can have symbolic significance and great propaganda value. Consequently, some countries refuse to entertain any consideration of negotiating with kidnappers, whereas others have a history of conceding to political kidnappers' requests.

Dealing with kidnapping

The negotiation process requires contact with the kidnappers or their agents, which in itself can be difficult to achieve. The kidnappers want to avoid revealing their location, and the negotiators have to verify that the hostage-takers' are who they claim to be. Many people may falsely claim to be the kidnappers. In fact, the film *Proof of Life* is based on the initial demand from any negotiator — that the victim is indeed still alive and under the control of the agents with whom negotiations are taking place.

PREVENTION IS BETTER THAN CURE

Obviously, avoiding hostage situations altogether is the best situation, which requires an understanding and awareness of the circumstances under which someone may be abducted, held hostage, or kidnapped. Although not possible in sieges with a domestic background, ransom requests and political kidnappings can be tackled in areas where kidnapping is virtually an industry on its own. The procedure is well known — in some countries in South America, for instance, networks exist where one group does the actual kidnapping. The victims are then passed on to a sort of wholesaler who keeps them while a third group does the ransom negotiation. In such circumstances, people who are at risk must have armed guards and live in protected gated communities.

The negotiation is then a struggle for power in which the negotiator tries to convince the kidnappers that they're in control while moving their decision-making in the negotiator's desired direction. Here are four strategies they use:

>> **Confirming:** The negotiator acknowledges that the kidnappers have authority over the hostage, which leads them to feel confident that they have room to maneuver. For example, the negotiator may say, "I know you're determined to follow through on this, but I don't want you to do anything that will make matters worse."

>> **Authorizing:** This strategy unites the negotiator and the hostage-takers as part of the same group against a third party, such as the political masters or negotiator's superiors. It builds some level of relationship between the negotiator and kidnappers and makes the latter aware that they're part of a much bigger picture over which neither may have control. The negotiator may say, "I'd like to get you out of here in a car, but my boss won't allow it."

>> **Complicating:** The negotiator introduces issues that the kidnappers may not have thought of that undermine their assumptions of what's possible. This approach can loosen their belief in what they can achieve. For instance, the negotiator may point out that being outdoors with the victim may make them prey to snipers or becoming snarled in traffic.

>> **Testing:** The negotiator directly challenges the hostage-takers about their threats so that other ways of seeing themselves can surface. The most direct test of this would be to tell the kidnappers that they're clearly not going to harm the hostage if a peaceful solution can be found.

Tackling criminal street gangs

Crime statistics show that most members of delinquent street groups are likely to be involved in crime. These youngsters are more likely to have carried knives or even guns and have consumed illegal drugs. Some calculations, particularly from the US, suggest that about 5 per cent of gang members account for 25 percent of crimes committed by youngsters. All this adds to the need to combat illegal gangs and their activities as a direct form of crime prevention.

Gangs provide a clear social role for young people who feel alienated from their families and those around them — and often serve as substitute families. But gang membership can be more than that in an area in which territories are marked out by rival groups; it becomes a form of protection. Gangs also give status to individuals by way of direct membership and by the positions individuals can obtain or aspire to within the group.

Therefore, attempts to reduce the impact of gangs need to take into account the social psychology involved, subvert these perceived benefits, and provide attractive alternatives. Here are some such approaches:

>> Provide exciting, positive activities for youngsters.

>> Ensure that schools and associated educational activities are safe.

>> Provide mentoring for youngsters so that they can relate to individuals whom they admire and who are achieving significance legally.

>> Help parents understand their role and be more effective in it.

Using social psychology against criminal networks

Some criminals are part of networks of contacts. For example, to make illegal drugs available, the drugs have to be obtained, smuggled across borders, sold on to middlemen, who then sell them to individuals who sell them on the street. This network may involve dozens or even hundreds of people. Undermining this arrangement requires an understanding of how criminal networks operate, which I explore in this section.

FEMALE GANGS

Men commit the majority of crimes, as noted throughout this book. Although most street gangs still consist of young men, female gang members also exist and carry out the full range of criminal activities. Make no mistake: Female gang members aren't just an adjunct to male gangs. Some groups of young women have formed their own independent gangs.

As I considered how authorities can combat the activities of illegal, criminal networks, I wondered whether they can perhaps take advantage of the principles of the discipline known as *organizational psychology*, which was developed to improve the effectiveness of organizations and the satisfaction of their workforce. Could a hundred years of this research into *improving* how organizations work together productively be turned on its head to *undermine* organized criminal enterprises? In other words, surely crime prevention can develop a *destructive organizational psychology*. In this section, I suggest some ideas on which to base this approach.

Appreciating the difficulties facing illegal networks

Although films and novels often depict criminal networks as being arranged like legitimate companies, such highly structured criminal groups are quite unusual. Even the Mafia and the Triads operate quite differently from Coca-Cola or Microsoft. The reason is that maintaining and managing a criminal organization is difficult — something that destructive organizational psychology can take advantage of. Here are some of the problems in setting up an illegal venture:

>> Maintaining secret communications is the most difficult part of keeping an illegal organization active. Communication requires that people contact each other, and it helps if they know whom they're contacting. If everything that the criminals do and plan is to be kept secret for fear of it being discovered, communication becomes extremely open to confusion and misinformation.

>> Most legitimate organizations inform the market of their products by some form of advertising, which isn't a good idea if you want to keep the police away! Word of mouth is usually the only way open to criminal networks, and it's slow and prone to misunderstanding.

>> As criminal networks grow, their problems increase. Their lines of communication become stretched, making it more difficult for communications and contacts to be controlled, as well as giving increased opportunities for

mistakes. Furthermore, a larger organization is likely to have a higher proportion of individuals on the periphery of the network. These people may have less commitment to it.

» Larger networks demand more complex organization. Those trying to lead these networks can be pushed beyond what they can cope with. Also, lieutenants and others in less powerful positions may want more of the action and so challenge the positions of the "bosses."

All these processes create difficulty in maintaining commitment to the illegal organization, especially if it can't deliver direct financial (or other types of) benefits. Therefore, a strong tendency exists for criminal groups to keep people involved by way of violence and coercion.

These challenges are the key to how the authorities can destroy or damage criminal networks.

One consequence of the difficulty in maintaining an illegal enterprise is that such criminals are rarely formed into neat organizational hierarchies, such as the police, the army, or a major corporation. They're more likely to be a loose network of contacts that constantly change. In fact, even the Mafia in its heyday consisted of many different "families" that were constantly in competition with each other, with defections from one group to another and little trust among them.

Understanding the social psychological reality of criminal networks helps to give pointers on how they can be undermined, which I describe in the next section.

Swindling the leader

You may think that taking out the boss is the obvious way to undermine a criminal network. But organizational psychology analysis of these networks indicates that this may not always be the most effective strategy.

The network shown in Figure 11-1 illustrates why the popular idea that a criminal network can be destroyed by taking out "Mr. Big" may be a delusion. Many illegal networks — whether they deal in drugs or traffic human beings, handle stolen goods, or set up fraudulent banking schemes — are constantly changing in a complex *ad hoc* arrangement of individuals. Even those involved directly in such team activities as bank robberies or hit-and-run crimes are unlikely to maintain the same group for every crime. The various members of the gang change, depending on contacts and circumstances.

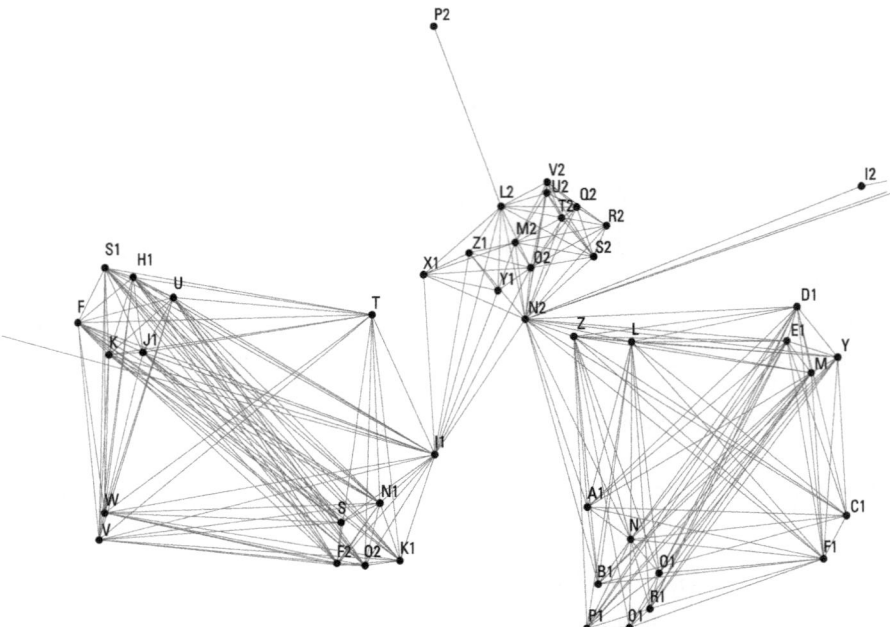

FIGURE 11-1:
A network of contacts between people involved in staging car accidents to fraudulently claim insurance.

Attacking communication links

The psychological understanding of how groups work (some of which I describe in the earlier section "Appreciating the difficulties facing illegal networks") can be used to disrupt the activities of organized crime groups. One productive possibility is to gain access to their communication system and use its inherent vulnerability to identify key facts that can lead to investigative actions.

ANECDOTE

The militant group Al-Qaeda was aware of this possibility and went to great pains to avoid electronic communication that may have given away the location of Osama bin Laden. Nonetheless, to continue to influence his network, he had to communicate with his followers. Eventually, one of them used a mobile phone carelessly, enabling the security services to locate the courier and follow him to bin Laden's lair.

Organizational studies show that people on the edge of communication networks may have less commitment to the organization and be more likely to become dissatisfied with it. Authorities can make use of this insight because such people may be open to providing information, overtly or inadvertently, that can help law enforcement undermine the criminals' activities. In addition, criminals often keep people within the crime network via coercion. If members feel safe in giving evidence, that can be the key to unraveling the whole illegal organization.

Getting to the root of the problem

Organized crime can flourish only when it has a home within a community. It can't survive without contact with clients or funders: It has to connect to and be part of a group of more or less law-abiding citizens. The psychology of these citizens, therefore, becomes important. Through fear or ignorance, or an inability to see things happening any other way, the community implicitly or explicitly colludes with the criminals. People in pubs may buy goods that "fell off the back of a truck," for example. Pop stars and their fans may buy illegal drugs. Famous sports stars may think that forcing themselves sexually on female followers is acceptable, and the victims feel unable to report the rape. If the local culture accepts this type of illegal activity, it encourages the emergence of organized crime. Therefore, many aspects of organized crime prevention require tackling public awareness of what's being supported by actions that may seem to be only minor violations of the law or unworthy of reporting — for example, making people aware of what's involved in buying diamonds that were illegally obtained or involved many abuses of human rights to acquire them.

4

Psychology in Court and Beyond

Forensic psychology started off as a service to the courts around the 1900s. That is still a central part of the area, although probably more forensic psychologists these days work in other settings. Over the years, their contribution to the legal process has broadened. What started as assessments of defendants to determine whether they had the mental capability to deal with the legal process has expanded into considerations of jury selection (most notably in the US) and advising attorneys on how to ask questions. Many of these contributions to the work of the courts raise challenging issues about what is the appropriate due process and whether psychologists are overstepping the mark with these contributions. By gaining a fuller understanding of these issues in this part, you will be in a better position to join in this important debate.

IN THIS CHAPTER

» Appraising the legal aspects
  of insanity

» Understanding the assessment
  of competence in court

» Discovering the psychological
  syndromes used in legal defenses

» Advising on risk assessment

» Seeing how forensic psychology
  contributes to civil proceedings

Chapter **12**

Giving Guidance in Legal Proceedings

s I mention in Chapter 1, the *forensic* aspect of forensic psychology indicates a professional activity that provides guidance to the courts. So, although the current reach of forensic psychologists extends well beyond the courts into many secure settings, such as prisons, a common activity is offering guidance to legal proceedings. Traditionally, this activity started with comments on the reliability of testimony (often dealing with the erratic nature of memory, which I explore in Chapter 7), but soon blossomed to include comments on the mental state of defendants.

Some forensic psychologists become associated with particular points of view and consequently offer opinions solely for the prosecution or for the defense. However, as in all other areas of expert evidence, the legal process forces the development of standard procedures in order to reach conclusions. Over time, frequently challenged evidence disappears from the courts, and accepted procedures become better established.

In this chapter, I explore some of these standard procedures, including issues of competency; factors that constitute insanity in criminal cases; what to do about people after they're convicted (especially assessing how dangerous they're likely to be); how to form an opinion about someone's mental state at the time of their death; and ways in which forensic psychologists can contribute to civil court cases.

Assessing Insanity Pleas in Court

Forensic psychologists may be called as expert court witnesses to provide testimony concerning a defendant's claim of insanity. Other professionals, especially psychiatrists, are likely to be called as well. Whether it's a psychiatrist or a psychologist varies from place to place, depending sometimes on who happens to be available.

REMEMBER

Forensic psychologists face certain particular problems when giving evidence in court arising from the fact that they're assessing people rather than objects. Crucially, as court experts, forensic psychologists are privileged witnesses who are allowed to offer their opinions rather than just the facts as they know them.

Legal casebooks are full of defendants who exhibit the most bizarre behavior, even when giving evidence in court (behavior that most people would agree indicates that they're obviously mad), but who are still found guilty and whom the courts don't classify as insane. I touch on this subject briefly in Chapter 2, but because it's the starting point for lots of forensic psychology advice to the courts, I examine the issue more closely in this section.

Forensic psychologists may be required to provide some sort of psychological assessment of the defendant at three broad stages in the legal process:

>> **Before the trial,** when issues of the person's competence to stand trial are considered

>> **During the trial,** when the issue of the defendant's mental state at the time of the crime may be significant

>> **Before sentencing,** when the convicted person's likelihood of changing — and particularly, how dangerous the person is — can be crucial to determining what form of sentencing is applied

A court of law isn't much interested in whether a person charged with murder, robbery, arson, or any other crime believes that he's Napoleon, that computer hackers are controlling his mind, or that he has to rid the planet of aliens masquerading as traffic wardens. The concern of the legal system is whether the person had a guilty mind, or (to use the Latin phrase I introduce in Chapter 1) *mens rea.* In other words, did defendants know at the time the crime was committed that what they were doing was wrong; did they know that he was doing it; and did they have voluntary control over their actions? If they didn't, they can offer the court the insanity defense: the plea of not guilty by reason of insanity. Establishing this defense in reality, however, turns out to be much trickier than you may expect.

Contrary to popular belief, people claiming that they're not guilty by reason of insanity is extremely rare. Only about 1 in 100 serious cases in the US involves a person making this plea, and on average, just one in four of those is successful.

Claiming diminished responsibility

Many people have tried to define insanity in legally acceptable ways. In fact, a sign of a civilized society is that it doesn't want to find a person guilty only for what they did but also based on their intentions. But probing into anyone's mind is extremely difficult, and doing so in a way that fits the requirements of legal advocates is even more challenging. For this reason, continuous debate rages about the legal definition of insanity, with the variations briefly summarized in the nearby sidebar "A brief history of defining insanity."

REGIONAL
TIP-OFF

With the developed understanding during the middle of the 20th century that mental illness can take many forms, a further refinement was added to legal codes in many countries. In the US, the new term was *diminished capacity*; in the UK, *diminished responsibility.*

A BRIEF HISTORY OF DEFINING INSANITY

The legal definition of insanity has varied over the centuries as the understanding of mental illness has changed:

- **18th century, the wild-beast test:** For a person to be regarded as insane in law, they would have to act like a brute or an infant, completely unaware of what they were doing and with no memory of it or understanding of its implications.

- **19th century, the McNaughton rules:** These rules, mentioned in Chapter 1, were the start of the modern concept that the person can suffer from a disease of the mind, causing the defendant not to understand the nature of what they did and that it was wrong.

- **20th century, various modifications:** These included:

  - Weakening the understanding requirement to *lacking substantial capacity to appreciate* that what the person did was wrong

  - Putting emphasis on a person's inability to control their actions

  - The defendant's need to prove that they're insane with clear and convincing evidence, instead of the prosecution demonstrating that they're sane beyond a reasonable doubt

In some jurisdictions, the verdict of guilty but mentally ill was introduced in addition to not guilty by reason of insanity. The intention was to allow the person to be assigned to a treatment program and, when or if it was successful, to be moved to a standard prison.

The result was to weaken the requirement that the accused had *mens rea*. A person who pleads diminished responsibility can claim that they didn't intend to commit the crime, although accepting they did it. In murder cases, the person may be charged with the lesser crime of manslaughter or its equivalent and then receive a lesser sentence. Defendants and their lawyers can draw on a number of different mental disorders to support the claim of diminished responsibility:

>> **Amnesia:** The accused claim of being unable to remember significant events to an extent that's far more severe than normal forgetfulness, particularly if it's related to some physical or intense psychological trauma. Amnesia is particularly difficult to validate because a person can so readily claim to have forgotten something. Claims of amnesia occur in quite a few murder cases.

>> **Automatism:** In this condition, actions occur involuntarily and quite possibly without the person even being aware that he's doing them. The clearest examples are those in which a person is violent during his sleep without ever waking up. Automatism is a recognized clinical condition, so if it's assessed by a competent clinician (usually a psychiatrist, but can be a forensic psychologist), it's rather more difficult to fake than might be expected.

>> **Dissociative identity disorder:** Otherwise known as multiple personality disorder, this condition is reflected in Robert Louis Stevenson's famous tale, *Strange Case of Dr. Jekyll and Mr. Hyde.* Kenneth Bianchi claimed that he had an involuntary switch to a different identity, but he was discovered to be faking and was convicted of being the Hillside Strangler (see the later sidebar "Tricking the trickster").

>> **Intoxication:** This can be used as a defense, especially if the person can demonstrate that he was unaware of the possible impact of imbibing too much alcohol or other drugs in increasing the risk of committing the crime, and especially if he can demonstrate that his drinks were spiked. Just being drunk when committing a crime may attract a more severe punishment, but if the defendant can show he had not intended to get drunk, it can be a mitigating circumstance.

>> **Personality disorder:** This catchall concept is increasingly being used to claim diminished responsibility. The defendant is presented to the court as having an enduring set of characteristics that causes his behavior to be pervasively and inflexibly antisocial. Because of this condition, he can't fully control his actions and isn't fully responsible for them. I discuss aspects of this disorder in more detail in Chapter 6.

STRANGE BUT TRUE

THE TWINKIE DEFENSE

Dan White was accused of shooting the mayor of San Francisco, George Moscone, and a city supervisor, Harvey Milk, in 1978. As part of his defense, his lawyers claimed that White suffered from manic depression (now called bipolar disorder) and that his condition was made much worse when he binged on soft drinks and junk food. Although Twinkies (an American sugary snack that its manufacturer calls a "golden sponge cake with a creamy filling") weren't named in the proceedings, the tongue-in-cheek term of the Twinkie defense caught on (to indicate an improbable defense). White was convicted of involuntary manslaughter due to diminished capacity rather than murder.

Making sense of madness

If you're confused about the legal definition of insanity and diminished responsibility, don't worry: You're in good company. Intense debate continues to rage between experts about most of the issues I mention in the preceding section. Even more importantly, juries are often confused as well. Studies indicate that juries are often reluctant to accept an insanity defense, whereas judges are more inclined to do so. This tension puts pressure on the forensic psychologist or other expert witnesses to be able to provide an objective report that the court finds acceptable.

Exposing malingering

One of the most important aspects of any assessment of a defendant is to determine whether the symptoms described are genuine (which is somewhat different from detecting attempted deception, discussed in Chapter 8). If the defendant has no symptoms or is faking them in some way, it's known as *malingering*. In this case, the forensic psychologist is evaluating not the truthfulness of what the person says but whether the mental state of the individual and related experiences indicate some psychological condition of relevance to the trial. Some standardized tests (which I mention in Chapter 5) have been developed for determining this malingering. A carefully structured clinical interview has also been shown to be useful. More informally, malingering may be indicated by:

>> An exaggerated and dramatic account of symptoms

>> Unusual care and deliberation in answering questions

>> A mix of symptoms inconsistent with known diagnoses

>> Generally inconsistent statements

>> The presentation of only the most well-known and obvious symptoms

Assessing insanity

Other than the determination of malingering that I discuss in the preceding section, surprisingly little standardization exists in assessing a person's mental state at the time of the crime. The clinician has to determine, as best as possible, which dysfunctions, if any, were present in intellectual, emotional, and behavioral aspects of the defendant at that key time when the crime happened, and how those disturbances relate to the criminal act.

These assessments are usually made on as wide a range of information as possible, not just a carefully structured interview of the person concerned. This information usually includes:

- » Employment records

- » Medical records

- » Police reports

- » Previous psychological tests (as I discuss in Chapters 5 and 6)

- » Witness statements

The aim is to determine whether a consistent pattern of actions and reports about the defendant exists that is in accord with that person's own account of his experiences.

Examining Issues of Competency

As well as having to testify in connection with a person's plea of not guilty by reason of insanity or diminished responsibility (see the preceding section), a far more common form of assessment that may be made is whether the person has the mental and emotional ability to stand trial. This idea of the *competence* of the defendant is based on the ethical requirement that no person should be subjected to a trial if, at the time, they have the ability to:

- » Interact effectively with their lawyers

- » Understand the legal proceedings they're a part of

ANECDOTE

TRICKING THE TRICKSTER

When Kenneth Bianchi was charged with a series of rapes and murders across Los Angeles in 1977 and 1978, which led to him being called the Hillside Strangler, he offered as part of his defense that he should be regarded as insane because he had multiple personality disorder, saying that his other identity, Steve Walker, had done the killing.

Two experts originally believed him, but the police were suspicious because Steve Walker was the name of the student Bianchi had used to fraudulently obtain a college certificate so that he could practice psychology; also, in interviews, he kept referring to Steve as *he* rather than *I*. The police called in Martin Orne, who had conducted many studies of how people behave when pretending to be hypnotized. Orne set about

(continued)

(continued)

hypnotizing Bianchi and decided that he was faking it. To test this suspicion further, Orne purposely misled Bianchi into believing that people with multiple personalities usually have more than one extra personality. Bianchi unwittingly fell for Orne's trick, soon generating a new personality, Bill, and a couple of others.

Realizing he had been caught out, Bianchi agreed to testify against his cousin Angelo Buono, who was charged with him, but Bianchi still was given multiple life sentences (though not one for each personality).

About one of every five people referred for a competency evaluation is eventually found to be not competent enough to undertake the legal process. These people tend to be those who:

>> Have a history of institutional treatment.

>> Are diagnosed with a mental disorder — typically, schizophrenia or other psychotic symptoms, although some authorities try to dissuade practitioners from using such diagnoses because a jury, and even a judge, may misinterpret it by believing that it means a split personality rather than a lack of contact with reality.

>> Are found to lack competence in the formal forensic mental health assessment of their cognitive and related abilities.

Courts generally hold no firm view on how old people must be before they're competent to give evidence or stand trial. The age has varied considerably over time and differs between jurisdictions. If any doubt exists, the person is assessed to demonstrate the ability to:

>> Accurately perceive, recall, and share facts

>> Distinguish truth from lies

>> Recognize that they must tell the truth

**REGIONAL
TIP-OFF**

ASSESSING COMPETENCY FOR EXECUTION

In the US, 38 states have the death penalty. But under US law, a person can be executed for a crime only if, at the time of his execution, he has the mental state to understand the reason for the execution and its implications. This situation generates challenges for forensic psychologists and psychiatrists who may be uncomfortable with the whole idea of executing people who have committed certain crimes. As a result, many professionals refuse to take part in the competency assessment of a person who may be executed for their crimes.

Assessing whether a convicted person, on death row, is competent to be executed is a challenging task. The American Constitution doesn't allow the execution of a person who isn't aware of the punishment they're about to receive or why they have to undergo it. The inability may be because of intellectual deficit, such as low intelligence, or extreme mental illness that gives one little contact with reality. Giving the court an opinion that will influence whether a person lives or dies is an extremely onerous task. If done properly, it's based on these factors:

- Detailed interviews with the convicted person

- Formal psychological assessment (using one of the personality inventories I describe in Chapter 9)

- Interviews with death row prison staff

- Observation of the person in his cell

- Interviews of family members, friends, and spiritual advisors

- Review of any legal, military, or health records available

- Consideration of any letter written in support of clemency

Getting Controversial: Examining Syndromes in Court

One controversial area of psychological guidance to the courts revolves around giving expert testimony on why the actions of key individuals, usually victims or defendants, aren't what would normally be expected. Such as a person claiming they've been raped calmly giving their testimony. Behavior that's unusual or difficult to comprehend is problematic for the courts to digest, partly because judges believe that they know a great deal about human beings and that juries should be allowed to draw on their own experience to make sense of what they're told.

Consequently, if a standardized test can be used to support a psychological conclusion, it adds an extra level of expertise beyond that available to the court from personal experience. Similarly, if a particular behavior can be presented as a sort of medical diagnosis, it may also be more acceptable and carry more weight than mere professional opinion.

For this reason, a burgeoning number of psychological syndromes to describe a defendant's actions have found their way into legal proceedings. In medical terms, a *syndrome* is a cluster of symptoms that occur together in some meaningful way and are usually kick-started by an identifiable event.

REMEMBER

Many lawyers and psychologists are uncomfortable with presenting patterns of behavior in this way, as though they were some sort of distinct disease, like measles or tuberculosis, with little or no individual variation, when in fact large differences exist between people in how they behave.

But this reluctance hasn't stopped such behavioral syndromes from becoming part of the vocabulary of forensic psychologists.

Post-traumatic stress disorder

The most common psychological syndrome to be used in evidence is *post-traumatic stress disorder* (PTSD). This syndrome has a long and checkered history, with its origins residing partly in the shell shock recognized during World War I and what was called battle fatigue during World War II. (A similar phenomenon was identified in the US Civil War, called *soldier's heart.*) As a distinct clinical diagnosis, it gained strength after the Vietnam War, when the difficulties that many veterans had in returning to civilian life were recognized.

Initially, all these extreme reactions to the experience of battle were dismissed by those in authority as cowardice or a weak personality. During World War I, some soldiers were even shot for cowardice or desertion who would now be recognized as suffering from PTSD. Indeed, many of them have been posthumously exonerated. Today's clinical understanding of the effects of severe trauma has helped produce a more enlightened understanding of what people experience in the heat of war, but this work has also provided a framework for evaluating the psychological impact of many other traumatic situations.

STRANGE
BUT TRUE

Some estimates suggest that as many as one in ten of the population suffers PTSD during their lifetimes. For example, if you are involved in a driving accident and thereafter are reluctant to drive again and are hypercautious when on the roads (responding with a sudden surge of anxiety whenever you become aware of squealing tires), you have the basis of at least a mild form of PTSD. If these symptoms last for two or three weeks, they may well be labeled *acute stress disorder*.

The diagnosis of PTSD requires a number of distinct components:

>> A clear cause of a traumatic event that can be regarded as beyond normal human experience, particularly if it involves intense fear, helplessness, or horror

>> Psychological consequences of the trauma shown to have lasted for longer than a month and to include upsetting memories or flashbacks or distressing dreams, or some mixture of these symptoms

>> The need to avoid anything associated with the trauma, such as places or people, or even with some of the memories

>> An increased sensitivity to potential threats, especially from anything linked to the cause of the trauma, with associated anxiety and anguish, often indicated by sleep disturbance

If some aspects of each of these four constituents are present, PTSD is diagnosed. The number, intensity, and longevity of the symptoms are drawn on to indicate the severity of the disorder.

PTSD has been accepted in US courts as a form of mental illness and thus can be used as mitigating circumstances for a violent attack.

ANECDOTE

The New Jersey Superior Court accepted that a violent attack on a police officer by a war veteran was a product of a flashback in which the police officer was mistaken for an enemy combatant.

The main use of PTSD is in accident claims, where it provides a well-tried and clear set of criteria for assessing the psychological impact of the accident. This can contribute to decisions about compensation, or even consideration of the punishment, if someone had caused the accident. However, even this apparently obvious application is open to question. Considerable evidence suggests that the impact of any trauma depends on the psychological well-being of the person who suffers the event before it occurs. Also, the experiences after the trauma, such as social support or loss of employment, can have an impact on the development of PTSD. Most problematic is the clear indication that PTSD may be more long-lasting and severe if ongoing litigation is involved in which it could play a role, as would be the case if a person is seeking compensation.

Battered woman syndrome

When a woman brings a charge of assault against her husband or partner, claiming that he frequently battered her, the defense may assert that the wife stayed with her husband over many years and so the assaults can't have been as bad as she claims. Consequently, opposing lawyers sometimes use *battered woman syndrome* to explain why a woman suffers extensive physical abuse over a certain period yet still fails to leave the relationship, even when the abuser is absent or asleep.

The characteristics of the syndrome revolve around the idea that the victim is taught by the offender to become helpless. *Learned helplessness* is a phenomenon first observed in animals that were unable to escape from electric shocks in unpleasant experiments. They eventually stop trying to avoid the shocks and just lie there listlessly. This passivity in relation to unavoidable, random abuse has since been found in many individuals.

As well as this feeling of helplessness, women suffering from battered woman syndrome also display these associated behaviors:

>> Development of ways of surviving (for example, by appeasement rather than escaping)

>> Low self-esteem

>> Depression

>> Self-blame (when the victim mistakenly believes the abuse is her fault and that she can do something to stop it from happening in the future)

>> A genuine fear for her life or her children's welfare

The abuse may well have psychological blackmail components too, such as telling the victim that her children will be taken from her if she reports the violence. All this abuse is often supported by an irrational belief that the perpetrator is all-powerful and all-knowing.

An important aspect of battered woman syndrome is that a cycle of abuse evolves: Tension builds up, the assault occurs, and then the offender is contrite and remorseful; tension increases again, another assault takes place, and so on. This cycle can occur many times before the victim reports what's happening and tries to get help from the authorities.

The acceptability of this syndrome, as for all the others described in this section, is dependent on the jurisdiction and the particular judge. In some US states and areas of the UK, there are general guidelines to judges for which syndromes are acceptable as mitigating evidence. However, because they are not illnesses caused by a bacterium that can be seen under a microscope, for example, but instead patterns of behavior that are interpreted by experts, people will always debate, in any legal proceeding, whether the syndrome is relevant to a particular case.

Parental alienation syndrome

In child custody cases in the US and Canada, usually as part of divorce proceedings, lawyers have identified cases in which a child exhibits extreme reactions against one parent. Dr Richard Gardner named this behavior *parental alienation syndrome,* which he describes as "a parental campaign of unjustified disparagement against another loving parent." This is usually inferred from various reports available to the court, especially what any children involved say or do.

These are the crucial aspects of this syndrome:

>> A lack of any apparent basis for the child's hostility to the parent

>> An active program of one parent influencing the child's opinion

>> The generation of strong negative opinions by the child in the dispute

Assessment of the existence of this syndrome is based on evaluating the child's behavior across the following areas:

>> Negative acts or statements toward the victimized parent

>> Criticisms based on absurd generalizations

>> Polarized emotions toward the parents

>> Claims that the reactions are the child's own ideas

>> Total loyalty to the parent carrying out the disparagement

>> No remorse for cruelty toward the victimized parent

>> Imagined or rehearsed scenarios

>> Extension of negative emotions to those associated with the victimized parent

A central difficulty in accepting the existence of parental alienation syndrome in any particular case is that, although it claims to be a comment on the child's state of mind, it is instead a way of indicating that the alienating parent is doing something pathological — that is, brainwashing the child. As a consequence, it's highly suspect. It has not found its way into any of the diagnostic lists I describe in Chapter 5, such as DSM. Even though many experts have challenged whether this syndrome is scientifically valid, parental alienation syndrome has found its way into civil proceedings as a way of challenging children's claims against the disparaged parent of physical or sexual abuse.

Premenstrual stress syndrome

Many syndromes that courts accept relate directly to women's actions, often to help juries understand the apparently surprising behavior of female victims (such as in the behavior of abused wives, described in the earlier section "Battered woman syndrome").

These syndromes based on women's behavior generate lively debate about whether they are forms of misogyny in disguise or not authentically established medical conditions.

One such syndrome is *premenstrual stress* (PMS), sometimes called *premenstrual tension* or *PMT,* in which women at a particular stage of the menstrual cycle may be more emotionally vulnerable and suffer a mixture of physical and psychological deficits. PMS has been accepted as a form of temporary insanity in a number of jurisdictions and also used as a defense in violent assaults (and even a few murder cases).

MYTH BUSTER

Although some evidence exists for monthly mood swings in males, this can't be related directly to major physiological changes. As a result, women have access to a legal defense that's unavailable to men. Therefore, one of the basic tenets of the law, that all are equal before it, isn't followed through by the acceptance of this defense.

Rape trauma syndrome

Rape trauma syndrome (RTS) is typically associated with rape victims who are women, but is potentially applicable to men. RTS has parallels to PTSD (see the earlier section "Post-traumatic stress disorder"), although its emphasis is rather different and less clearly defined. The use of RTS in court is to clarify why a rape victim delays reporting the assault; the claim is that this delay indicates some doubt about her role in the rape, even possibly blaming herself. This delay is claimed to be part of the psychological effects of the trauma of the attack, which often include depression, suicidal thoughts, and general fear and anxiety.

An important point about all the psychological consequences of various stressors and traumas that result from rape is that they can also result from events that don't involve obvious, extreme violence. Fear and profound psychological insult can be as traumatic as vicious physical aggression, or even more so. Many studies show that stress relates to a lack, or loss, of personal control. As a consequence, situations that take away the feelings of control from the individual can have a significant impact on feelings of self-worth and the ability to be in charge of one's life.

Munchausen syndrome by proxy

Munchausen syndrome is where a person displays a relentless determination to obtain medical treatment from self-inflicted injuries or nonexistent symptoms. *Munchausen syndrome by proxy* is a related behavior, a curious form of child abuse in which a parent (nearly always the mother) forces medical attention on her child frequently over an extended period with no medical cause for the child. The child is used as a surrogate (or proxy) and may have to endure falsely reported symptoms (perhaps by adding substances to the child's excreta to distort the laboratory tests) or even injuries or illnesses induced by the parent (such as starving the child or giving her toxic injections) to gain medical attention.

Experts disagree on the reasons for Munchausen syndrome by proxy behavior, but the following characteristics have been identified as common to those diagnosed with this syndrome:

>> The mother is highly involved with her child, and the father is emotionally distant.

>> The parent is emotionally empty, unable to feel for other people, and lonely.

>> The parent experienced childhood emotional, physical, or sexual abuse.

>> The parent appears as an ideal, concerned parent.

>> The parent is overprotective of the child.

>> The parent is obsessed with the child's illness.

REMEMBER

As these characteristics indicate, the parent can often be quite convincing. As a result, in the cases of reporting false symptoms, sometimes the modifications of samples sent to the laboratory may be the first indicator that something non-medical is wrong with the child because the test results are so unusual.

The sorts of false symptoms reported by the parent commonly include these:

>> Asthma/allergy

>> Diarrhea

>> Failure to thrive, such as claims of not putting on weight

>> Infection

>> Seizure

>> Vomiting

Some veterinarians report that a family pet may also be a proxy: Owners deliberately hurt a pet to garner sympathy and medical attention.

Making Judgments for Risk Assessment

At various stages throughout the legal process, before, during, or after the trial, a forensic psychologist may be called on to assess how dangerous the defendant is likely to be in any future situation. This process, called *risk assessment*, includes the possibility that they may harm themselves or others by way of violence or sexual assault.

Risk assessment is becoming a major and extremely challenging task in many different settings. Recommendations are generally based on reviews of static, relatively unchanging factors alongside more dynamic risk factors that are potentially open to change.

The static risk factors tend to be historical, such as:

>> Previous violence

>> Employment problems

>> Clear evidence of psychopathy

>> Substance abuse

The dynamic factors are more directly psychological issues:

>> Lack of insight

>> Impulsivity

>> Unfeasible plans for the future

>> Social support and how the individual dealt with any previous forms of remedial intervention

>> Potential stressors

To illustrate how risk assessment works, I compare two different offenders:

>> A married man in his mid-30s who pleads guilty to sexually abusing his teenage daughter since she was 4 years old

>> A single young man in his early 20s who was convicted of having sex with an underage boy a few years younger than himself, whom he had just met in a local park

According to some standard risk assessment procedures, the young man has a much higher risk of future offending than the married man. The reason is that statistics show that a married man, older than 25, who abuses a female family member is less likely to offend again than someone not in a cohabiting relationship who offends against a male stranger. This difference may come as some degree of surprise, but it's based on studies using these assessment procedures and following up on how accurately they predict what happens later.

Although such risk assessment procedures have a strong logic to them, and studies show that they're generally accurate, they're far from being foolproof. One reason is that, although it may be possible to characterize an individual, characterizing and predicting the situations in which that person may find themselves is much more difficult. Also, for many people who must be assessed, little reliable background information is available.

Courts may use risk assessments in the following circumstances:

>> If a decision needs to be made for involuntary committal to a hospital or another institution, this can't be made only on the grounds of mental illness. The person must also exhibit impending danger to themselves or others.

>> If an expert becomes aware that a person has the potential to be violent toward a specific person, they must provide a report that warns of this possibility.

>> If the person poses a serious risk of future criminal conduct, a risk assessment report can contribute to deciding on preventive detention.

>> To assess how dangerous a person is who has been convicted of predatory sexually violent behavior, and to provide background information in regard to sentencing and the form of institutional commitment.

REMEMBER

The general principle for risk assessment is that the more recently a person has been violent in the past, the more likely that person is to be violent in the near future. Consequently, risk assessment is more likely to predict with accuracy whether a person will be violent in the next 48 hours, or even 14 days, than over a longer period, such as 48 months or 14 years.

Psychological Autopsy

When the cause of a person's death is equivocal — for example, some doubt exists about whether someone committed suicide or suffered an accident or was murdered — a forensic psychologist may be asked to establish the characteristics of the deceased in order to throw light on what happened. In other words, an autopsy is conducted, but on the person's psychology and not on their body. This task is called a *psychological autopsy* (or, if you want a term that sounds more sophisticated, *reconstructive psychological evaluation*).

REMEMBER

The psychological autopsy process consists of trying to build a picture of the dead person's thoughts and feelings leading up to their death, as well as a detailed examination of exactly how the fatality happened. The psychologist uses documents (such as letters, diaries, blogs, or emails) that the deceased left behind, as well as interviews with people who knew the person.

The resulting reports can provide important information in murder trials where the defense is that the deceased committed suicide, but also in contested wills or other circumstances in which the mental state of the deceased is of significance.

Another term sometimes used is *equivocal death analysis,* but this one usually refers to an examination carried out by law enforcement agents rather than by forensic psychologists. Equivocal death analysis is particularly prevalent in military situations where the complexity and danger of what's going on, sometimes aggravated by "the fog of war," can raise many important questions about how someone died. I describe one notorious example in the nearby sidebar "Equivocal death analysis."

EQUIVOCAL DEATH ANALYSIS

One important example of the confusion that can surround inferences about a dead person is the examination of the explosion in the gun turret on the US Navy battleship *USS Ohio* in 1989, which killed 47 of the turret's crew. FBI agents carried out what they called an equivocal death analysis of the incident and those in the turret room. They concluded that one crew member, Clayton Hartwig, had exploded the gun in an act of suicide. Subsequently, the American Psychological Association set up a special working party to review what the FBI had done and the related evidence. The party was critical of the FBI report, and not all members supported the view that Hartwig had committed suicide. A further detailed technical examination of the turret concluded that an accidental over filling of the gun had occurred, which caused it to explode. Subsequent inquiries in turn challenged this conclusion, which shows just how complex the examination of equivocal deaths can be.

Conducting a psychological autopsy is fraught with difficulties, not least because the person who could answer many of the key questions is dead. In addition, if a murder inquiry is in progress, legal hurdles may be put in the way of interviewing all the people who have some knowledge of the dead person (and, of course, the prosecution and defense are likely to have access to different sets of witnesses, who may hold opposing views). If suicide is an issue, the people close to the dead person may be unwilling to give full and frank information. (They may feel some guilt if the person did commit suicide and then be eager to support a belief in some other cause that exonerates them.)

Conducting psychological autopsies into possible suicides

To help explain a psychological autopsy, in this section I discuss the various aspects that have to be considered in order to produce a report on a suicide. The psychological processes considered when examining the possibility of suicide draw on four dominant processes: stressors, exposure, availability of lethal agents, and psychopathology.

Stressors

An important consideration in any fatality is the circumstances surrounding the event — in particular, any indication of the stressors that the deceased may have suffered. Studies show that people who attempt suicide often experience significant life stressors in the four weeks before the attempt. The weakness in these studies, however, is the lack of careful exploration of people with similar stressors who don't attempt suicide, or of the surrounding social and family circumstances that may consistently be associated with the stressors. Without such knowledge, the preexistence of stressors in an examination of an equivocal death may be given too much weight.

Exposure

Police inquiries, as well as more systematic studies, suggest that teenage suicides in particular may be more likely after direct exposure to another suicide through family or friends, or indirect exposure from media coverage. If, for instance, the person had been consistently brooding on the event, a safe assumption is that, at the very least, it focused their thoughts. Such intense analysis may also provide ideas about the actual mechanics for carrying out their suicide.

Studies indicate that the latter situation sometimes seems to be the case when what may be considered unorthodox means of suicide are used, such as setting fire to oneself or laying one's head on a railway track. Enough examples exist of minor epidemics of suicides following initial, widely publicized incidents using the same method to support the contention that some individuals decide *how* to commit suicide from these exemplars.

A particularly disturbing illustration of this sort of copycat suicide is exhibited by the spree killers I mention in Chapter 6. These people almost invariably end up being killed or killing themselves as part of their killing spree. Evidence suggests that some increase in this sort of suicide occurs when a similar event is highly publicized, such as the Columbine school shootings in the US.

A morbid fascination with a suicide event can certainly be taken as an indication that the deceased had at least considered the implications of taking their own life. And if the experience of the suicide was more direct — or the deceased thought in some way that the original suicide was positively regarded or, in some senses, heroic — it can be considered to have had the effect of validating the planned action.

Psychopathology

One of the major assumptions made in guiding an equivocal death investigation is that any evidence of prior *psychopathology* (which is some form of mental illness or another psychological disturbance) can be taken as an indicator of the probability that a person took their own life. Because this area of interest is such a natural part of psychiatric assessment, the various structured protocols that have been developed to elicit indications of mental illness (described in Chapter 5) have been adapted for use with surviving parents and family in an attempt to complete a psychological autopsy as though the deceased is present.

Signs of depression, or previous acts of self-harm, provide support for suicide as opposed to accidental death — even if no direct signs of depression in the deceased are available. Many studies also show that if close relatives have had mental problems, it's important to consider the possibility of early-stage depression developing or unrecognized aspects of mental disturbance in the person whose death is equivocal.

What to make of a diagnosis of schizophrenia or personality disorder, however, is more difficult. Where a severe psychosis is apparent, the borderline between accidental and intentional self-destruction is wide and vague. Was the person lucid enough at the time to be aware of the *full* consequences of their actions? Even though the person had expressed a desire to commit suicide, were they *fully* cognizant of what that meant?

An extreme, but useful, example of the difficulties of using information on psychopathology in an equivocal death investigation is any case referred to as suicide by cop. In such situations, a person creates a confrontation with the police that inevitably leads to being gunned down in a shoot-out.

REMEMBER

The suicide by cop scenario illustrates the intense complexities involved in this area. The individual may even see himself as heroic and look to the agents of the state to enshrine his heroism. After all, many acts of suicide, across a variety of cultures, are typically regarded as heroic, often involving some confrontation with the state or a designated enemy, whether it's biblical heroes such as Samson, World War II kamikaze pilots, or present-day suicide bombers.

Contesting wills

A special aspect of the psychological autopsy is the consideration of whether a person was competent to make a will when they did so; *testamentary capacity* is the legal term used in the US. Most jurisdictions fail to set high standards for achieving this competence, requiring only that the person know:

>> That they were making a will

>> The extent and nature of their property

>> Who (or perhaps what) was to receive his property

>> How the property was being divided

A psychological assessment would consider appropriate indicators by obtaining information from records and from those who knew the person, ascertaining whether drugs, mental illness, or physical or emotional trauma may have so influenced his state of mind that he wasn't appropriately competent at the time he prepared and signed his will.

ANECDOTE

WHEN ECCENTRIC PEOPLE DIE

Howard Hughes, the famous millionaire, who had been a recluse for most of his later years, gave rise to the need for a psychological assessment of his mental capacity because of challenges to his will. Raymond Fowler, a past president of the American Psychological Association, carried out a psychological autopsy on Hughes and concluded that "psychological problems, numerous head injuries and drug misuse had changed a vibrant millionaire into an emaciated recluse." The possibly psychotic basis of his reclusiveness, rather than mere eccentricity, posed challenges to the probity of his estate. The many millions of dollars he left behind were divided between dozens of relatives and various causes.

Providing Expert Testimony in Civil Proceedings

An increasing variety of situations outside of criminal proceedings require some sort of psychological assessment to be drawn on to reach a legal decision. I mention some of these earlier in this chapter, but for tidiness, here are some legal circumstances in which a psychologist's report may be used in civil proceedings:

>> **Child custody cases** in which the parents, as well as the children and their relationships, are evaluated. This assessment can include recommendations of the conditions under which children should visit a parent or another guardian.

   Expert evidence can be crucial where there are issues of credibility regarding allegations of abuse or concerns over the child's evidence in such child custody issues.

>> **Civil rights claims** where the psychologist may comment on gender or racial stereotyping.

>> **Claims of breach of contract,** where the psychologist may comment on the traumatic effect of the breach.

>> **Sexual harassment,** where counselling or advice to a company may be part of the outcome of the case, as well as assessment of the parties involved.

REGIONAL
TIP-OFF

In Oregon, a mentally competent adult with less than six months to live may ask his physician to prescribe medication that would hasten death. An expert, such as a psychologist, may be called on to advise whether the individual is mentally competent to make this decision. Such laws are being put in place in other states and countries. In the UK, there has been great debate around passing such a law. But the professions allowed to advise are only those medically trained. Given that the mental state of the person wanting to end their life is a crucial issue, some may think that other professionals would be better placed to make that decision.

Examining the capacity to consent to treatment

In some jurisdictions, mentally disturbed individuals have to agree to any treatment they're given. This situation, in turn, requires a test of the decision-making competence of the patient in relation to their ability to:

» State a choice

» Understand relevant information

» Appreciate the nature of their own situation

» Reason with the information provided

As with many other attempts to provide standard procedures, these tests of competence have generated much debate about whether a test that seems sensible for one person (say, a young white woman) would be equally relevant for someone from a different generation and ethnic background.

For much more on this subject, flip to the earlier section "Examining Issues of Competency."

Assessing for compensation

In a range of situations (from possible negligence on the part of an employer to that of another person in a car accident), civil courts or similar settings may need to assess whether a person has suffered an injury at the hands of others and, if so, the degree of that injury. Although physical injury has long been accepted as a basis for claiming compensation, in recent years, courts in many countries have been willing to accept evidence of psychological or emotional damage as well.

Many of the assessments carried out for such claims are of a highly specialized kind, relying on neurological tests or exploring brain damage or other physiological defects. Beyond these examinations, many of the issues I mention earlier in this chapter in relation to mental state at the time of a crime are relevant. Any evidence of chronic mental health problems that predate the injury would be considered to throw light on what the consequence of the trauma was and what may be an enduring aspect on the person.

A crucial part of the assessment is an attempt to predict the longevity of any injury and its future consequences. This task is especially difficult with psychological examinations because the very fact that a compensation claim is pending may cause stress-related symptoms. The psychologist also needs to be alert to various forms of faking, as I discuss in the earlier section "Exposing malingering." Where significant financial gain is feasible, various forms of fraud are always possible.

Chapter **13**

Psychological Aspects of Court Procedures

Many of the forensic psychology activities I describe in this book revolve around assessing the mental state of offenders, or the practice of *clinical* psychologists who work with mentally ill or disturbed people who come to them via legal considerations. This chapter is a little different: It focuses on the psychology of people without problems, who aren't criminals. It covers the ways in which forensic psychologists illuminate court processes by drawing on the psychology of judges, lawyers, and jurors and how they interact with each other (that is, the practice of *social* psychology). In particular, the presence of people without legal training (the jury) taking an active role in court proceedings raises many interesting psychological questions.

In this chapter, therefore, I explore the court processes themselves and the attitudes and behavior of juries, lawyers, and expert psychologists, in order to throw light on the thought processes and behavior of the people involved in this most curious of human institutions.

Uncovering Psychology in the Courts

The adversarial legal process consists of judges and juries hearing witnesses being questioned and the prosecution and defense lawyers offering their account of the evidence. (I describe this process and other legal systems in Chapter 3.) All this activity takes place within a long-established framework, which many legal experts have developed and studied. Yet in all English-speaking countries and many other democracies, a central role is taken by ordinary people because they make crucial decisions as part of a jury. These juries operate in different ways in different countries, but in this chapter, I focus on the sorts of juries you find in the US, the UK, Australia, and Canada.

The jury is an unusual (and even unnatural) but fascinating social group. It consists of people who don't know each other, yet have to come to momentous decisions within legal constraints that are novel to them.

The power of the interpersonal processes that are active when a jury debates the evidence is brilliantly illustrated in the classic 1957 film *12 Angry Men,* in which Henry Fonda's character eventually persuades all 11 other jurors to change their minds. Yet the forms of influence that people exert on each other in the jury room are generally poorly understood. That is because of the secrecy of their deliberations as they interpret the evidence.

Examining existing legal rituals

Over many hundreds of years, the trial procedure in courts developed into a standard practice with many associated rituals. These rituals make psychological assumptions about how seriously everyone involved takes the legal proceedings, and how readily they accept the power and legitimacy of the courts. For this reason it's valuable to assess the assumptions.

The rituals are enshrined in the physical layout of most courts. This has changed over the years and varies from one place to another. US courts tend to have a more informal layout than in the UK. Courts that deal with families usually deliberately try to break down many of the formal barriers inherent in traditional layouts. But it's useful to be aware of the symbolic significance of the traditional layout because that reveals the symbolic and psychological significance of the various actors in the court proceedings.

In the traditional layout, the judge has the highest seat, usually in the center of the court, in order to reflect the position's supreme importance and high status (and ensure that the judge can see everything going on). Below the judge is likely to be a clerk to the court (who looks after proceedings) and often a stenographer or someone else who's recording the whole proceedings.

The rest of the layout also represents the significance of the other individuals in the legal process. If it's a court that has a jury, they will typically be to one side, on benches slightly lower than the judge or in their own boxed area. In the Crown Courts in the UK (where the most serious crimes are tried), the accused stands in what's known as the *dock* at a separate location, with direct access to the holding cells. Interestingly, in the US, the accused may often sit with their attorney, which gives them an opportunity to communicate during the trial, an arrangement a little more awkward in most UK Crown Courts, because it is not encouraged while the trial is in progress.

REMEMBER

The descriptions of courts and juries in this chapter relate to the courts that deal with the most serious crimes. In most countries, the great majority of crimes (as many as 97 percent) are dealt with in courts that have no juries but have only one judge — or, in the UK, three people who aren't qualified lawyers, known as *magistrates* — who make the legal decision. (More details are given in Chapter 3.)

Each witness stands, alone and in turn, often in a *witness box,* to show that the person in that location is playing a significant role on which the court is focused. In front of the judge, in the main body of the court, are seats or benches for the lawyers and behind them, for the solicitors who advise them. The area for the public is behind the lawyers because justice in a democracy "must be seen to be done." In courts that hold trials of public significance, special benches are set aside for reporters.

Many constraints are placed on how the proceedings are conducted. Witnesses aren't usually allowed in court until they give their evidence so that they aren't influenced by the evidence of other witnesses. The defendant is brought into the court after everyone else has assembled, except for the judge, who enters last. When the judge comes in, everyone stands as a sign of respect. In all criminal courts, the judges and often the lawyers wear some sort of distinguishing costume — usually, a gown. In the UK, these participants also wear wigs, whose length and style relate to their seniority. As with any costume, this system distinguishes the key players from the general mass of people and demonstrates that they're playing a special role. The wigs are claimed to make these people seem more neutral and less like ordinary citizens.

GETTING A HANDLE ON LEGAL DEFINITIONS

Loads of technical terms are used for all the various jobs associated with legal professions. Just about anyone with a legal qualification can be called a lawyer. An *advocate*, though, is someone who speaks on behalf of another person. Advocacy is usually taken to mean the ability to support someone else's case. In US courts, the person who presents the case for or against the charge is known as an advocate.

In the UK and British Commonwealth countries, a select group of lawyers are allowed to be advocates in the higher courts, known as *barristers, or counsels*. Junior and senior counsels work in most significant cases, but don't expect the juniors to wear shorts and chew gum; the term simply means that the person is an assistant to the senior counsel who manages the prosecution or defense case in court.

By legal definition, *attorneys* are people who can act on behalf of others, but the term is most common in the US. In the UK, people who help others with legal matters are called *solicitors*. They can't present cases in a higher court but appoint barristers to do so for their clients. In English-speaking legal systems, judges are typically selected from among experienced barristers or advocates, which is why they're often quite elderly, although this situation is changing now that they have to retire at 70. In other jurisdictions, such as France and Spain, being a judge is a direct career choice with its own training, so they're much more likely to be young and, yes, female. In some of the lower courts, the person presiding over the court is known as a *magistrate*, which is the term used in France and other countries for the person who English-speakers call the *judge*. (The French TV serial *Spiral (Engrenages)* is an excellent illustration of how the French legal system works. It shows the magistrate sometimes assisting with the investigation of crimes, which cannot happen in the UK. The highly acclaimed 2023 French film *Anatomy of a Fall* (*Anatomie d'une chute*) gives an excellent example of the French court proceedings, quite different from those in English-speaking countries.) The terms *magistrate* and *judge* are interchangeable for the issues I explore in this book.

The dramatic layout of the court exists to demonstrate the seriousness of the proceedings and create a psychological impact on all involved. You know you're not in a place of casual conversation, where any sort of informal behavior is acceptable. Many judges and lawyers believe that the rituals and setting increase the likelihood that the truth will be revealed in court. They believe that the power of the legal ceremony influences people to take the whole situation extremely seriously and to be honest.

These processes can be daunting for people who don't experience them daily. They can cause considerable confusion regarding what's considered appropriate behavior and what is being discussed. (Flip to the later section "Comprehending legal rituals and terms" for more.)

Taking stock of the court process: Order of ceremony

Besides the symbolic rituals and layout of the court that I describe in the preceding section, legal proceedings under the English-speaking adversarial system, and most other systems, also follow a standard process: an *order of ceremony.* You need to have some idea of this process to understand the various psychological issues that arise along the way:

1. **The judge and lawyers discuss what evidence can be acceptably introduced and how the trial will proceed** *before* **the jury is brought in.**
   This part is known as the *voir dire,* which is derived from the Latin term meaning to "tell the truth." In particular, there's a discussion of which evidence will be allowed and which experts will be called. The judge makes the final decision, but there's often lots of give-and-take between the opposing lawyers at this stage. In the US, it's also an opportunity for lawyers to object to particular jurors in the process of jury selection. (See the later section "Selecting the Desired Jury" for more on this practice.)

2. **The jury is selected and swears an oath to act honorably.**

3. **The judge explains its task to the jury.**

4. **The prosecution counsel presents a summary of the case and the evidence that is to be brought, followed by the defense counsel's summary of the evidence and the issues to be aware of.**

5. **The prosecution calls its witnesses to give evidence, in this sequence:**
   1. *The prosecution counsel questions the witness.*
   2. *The defense counsel cross-examines the witness.*

      (Check out the later section "Cross-Examining the Psychology of Cross-Examination.")
   3. *The prosecution counsel is allowed a few more questions for clarification.*

6. **The defense calls its witnesses to give evidence, following the same sequence of questioning as in Step 5.**

7. **The prosecution and defense counsels present their closing arguments.**

8. **The judge instructs the jury on what it needs to consider.** This stage often includes a recounting of the key points in the evidence and, for example, whether the jury needs to decide whether a key witness was telling the truth. The judge also draws the jury's attention to key points of law, such as the need for the defendant to have intended to commit the crime, especially for a verdict of murder.

9. **The jury is sent to the private jury room, where the members deliberate on what they've heard, with no contact with people outside.** This can take anything from a few minutes to many days. They are usually allowed to go home in between sessions, but are warned not to reveal anything about their discussions. When they've reached a decision, they return to the court and the person chosen by the jury to represent its view, *the foreperson,* reports the jury's conclusion to the judge.

REMEMBER

At every stage of this unfolding process, the lawyers have to determine how best to present the information and arguments to the judge and especially to the jury (if there is one). The jury, in turn, has to make sense of all that's going on and come to an informed decision. Psychological factors are relevant at every stage.

Delving into Jury Psychology

A joke goes as follows: A jury is a group of 12 men and women who have to decide whether the defense or prosecution has the best lawyer! This somewhat cynical take on court procedures is useful in drawing attention to the power of how evidence is presented in court, and the significance of the skills of the lawyers in laying the case before the jury.

People used to assume that judges were able to ensure that jury members knew, with only limited guidance, what they were doing and how to respond to the legal processes and make sense of the legal arguments. Many studies have shown that juries don't necessarily act in the logical, informed way that the law assumed. For this reason, psychologists started demonstrating to lawyers and judges the problems that members of the jury face and how best to inform them. I discuss some of these psychological issues in this section.

Facing decision time: How juries act and make decisions

In legal systems that place great emphasis on jury decisions, the jury members are kept protected from any outside influence. Their deliberations are secret. They aren't allowed to tell anyone what went on in the jury room. This level of secrecy makes it extremely difficult to study jury decision-making in real-life trials or to determine how individual members reach their conclusions. From necessity, what's known about jury decision-making comes from indirect sources (which therefore have to be treated with some caution), and from more general examinations of the relationships between personal characteristics and legally relevant decisions.

ANECDOTE

The consequence of the secrecy of what happens when a jury is deciding was revealed in one murder trial when a member of the jury eventually told the court that some people had used a Ouija board to try to contact the dead victim and ask him who had killed him!

One way of studying jury decision-making is to gather a group of people to simulate a jury (called a *mock jury*). Court proceedings can then be presented to the members, and they're observed coming to a decision. The main concern is to discover what makes the members more likely to decide in favor of guilt or innocence. Of course, one significant problem here is that the same pressures don't exist on these people as in a real case. For example, no one will be imprisoned for a long time, and members of the jury don't dip into legal hot water for misbehaving. They don't have the same pressures on them to do the right thing as there would be in a real court. Unsurprisingly, such results are far from a clear reflection of what happens in real-life practice. Such studies do tend to show that juries are rather more able to deal with the complexities of the legal process than may be expected.

REMEMBER

How juries decide the verdict is psychologically fascinating. Research shows that jurors do what anyone does when hearing about a crime: They try to work out the most plausible storyline that accounts for the facts; that is, they produce a cause-and-effect sequence that accords with their understanding of how events can occur. This sequence draws on assumptions about the evidence presented, judgments about the defendant, and about how and why such crimes happen.

The development of a plausible story by jurors often undergoes these three phases:

1. **The jury members individually construct various possible plots that tie together the evidence as it's presented.** The extent to which the evidence is covered by any proposed narrative is used to select from among the different stories on offer. The possible plots are also examined in terms of how internally consistent they are, how well the facts agree with each other, and how they fit into the narrative. All these aspects are checked against the juror's understanding of how things typically happen — in other words, how plausible they are.

2. **The jury members evaluate various storylines against the instructions given by the judge.** This step includes key legal issues and the various types of verdicts available.

3. **The jury members select the verdict that most closely matches the most plausible cause-and-effect narrative sequence of actions.** The result is a lengthy discussion or even a hung jury, one on which no overall agreement can be reached between all, or most, of the members of the jury. This is because no close match emerges, or members of the jury disagree with each other about the most plausible story or how well it fits the facts or implies a verdict.

THE CONTRAST EFFECT

An interesting phenomenon found with jury decisions is the *contrast effect,* which applies to many human judgments. If you're offered an expensive pair of shoes and then a cheaper pair that is still expensive, you're likely to think that the second pair is more reasonably priced than if you're offered an inexpensive pair and then the moderately expensive pair, which then seems quite expensive. In other words, people's judgments tend to be relative.

The contrast effect is found in studies of people making decisions about guilt or innocence in simulated legal decisions. If a rape case is presented followed by a vandalism case, a greater chance exists of the vandalism case receiving a guilty verdict; if the vandalism case is presented first, it has a lower probability of leading to a conviction.

This effect is most powerful if the jury — or the judge, even — is dealing with a series of cases one after another. Their idea of seriousness is influenced by what it's compared with. That's one reason there are guidelines on which crimes should receive what sentences. That is an attempt to try to make sentencing less influenced by these sorts of psychological effects.

Comprehending legal rituals and terms

The legal profession all over the world delights in its own vocabulary. The esoteric labels for the various participants in court (check out the earlier sidebar "Getting a handle on legal definitions") are only the tip of the topic of legal jargon. Even everyday terms such as *insanity* take on special meanings in law (as I discuss in Chapter 3). Concepts such as *mens rea*, which I describe in Chapter 1 and refer to throughout this book, and many other legal terms are used in court, and jurors need to understand them.

REMEMBER

A jury is deliberately a random sample of local residents who consequently have a mix of education and intellectual ability. This situation raises questions about how well juries truly understand what's going on in court and the instructions they're given. Studies in the US, mainly with mock juries (described earlier), indicate that as few as half the instructions given to a jury by the judge may actually be understood by the jury.

This list describes the sorts of issues that juries often struggle with or fail to understand:

>> The notion of *the burden of proof,* and especially the idea in criminal cases of *beyond a reasonable doubt.* These terms turn out to be somewhat ambiguous, and jurors may have difficulty agreeing on what they mean.

>> The requirement of *intent* before a person can be convicted of murder.

>> The fact that physical injury doesn't need to be present for an assault charge and the difference between *burglary* and *robbery* (the latter incorporates assault or the threat of it).

>> The aspects of a crime that make it particularly heinous (known as *aggravation*) or that help explain the defendant's actions and reduce the implications of its seriousness (called *mitigation*).

Such confusions and misunderstandings can have serious consequences. Research shows that the impact of legal jargon increases the likelihood of a defendant being found guilty when the charges are presented in archaic legal language. Jurors are less likely to find the defendant guilty when the instructions are translated into everyday language.

Other matters also make it difficult for jury members and put psychological pressures on them to come to a decision:

>> **How complex the trial is, especially if it lasts more than six months:** In these cases, jurors can have significant difficulty in understanding the judge's instructions.

>> **Low educational achievement of jurors:** Not surprisingly, people of a higher educational level can make more sense of what's going on in court.

>> **Willingness (or not) of specific jurors to accept authority and adhere to the instructions given because of aspects of their personality:** People concerned to present a good impression are more likely to follow instructions.

>> **Preexisting beliefs about how courts work and what goes on within them:** These ideas often draw on fictional accounts and also reduce a juror's ability to act in accordance with real-life legal frameworks. Such jury members may act on what they believe is common sense far more readily than observing the niceties of legal requirements.

Various attempts have been made to help lawyers and judges work more effectively with juries, including

>> Carefully analyzing the instructions to juries to take account of the educational level required to make sense of them

>> Giving written instructions to jurors

>> Presenting instructions to jurors before they hear the evidence

>> Repeating instructions to the jury

>> Providing special verdict forms for the jury to complete

>> Supplying diagrams and illustrations that lead the jury step-by-step through the evidence to reach a decision

Animated, computer-based illustrations have even been tried, for example, to help a jury understand which forms of self-defense are legally acceptable. But the power of legal precedence and accepted rituals puts a strong break on the acceptance of such innovations. In addition, the legal problem exists that, if instructions to juries differ from accepted practice, the way is opened for an appeal against any verdict.

Research findings aren't clear that any of the attempts listed inevitably improve jurors' understanding of what they need to do and how they should reach a verdict. Every case has unique qualities. What may be helpful in one case may hinder in another. Most experts believe, however, that lots of room still exists to improve how juries are helped to reach decisions.

Dealing with inadmissible evidence

At an early stage of the court process, an attempt is made to decide which evidence the jury will be allowed to hear (see my earlier description of the *voir dire* stage). Most typically, information about a defendant's previous crimes is kept out of court by the defense (if at all possible, although in the UK, changes in the law are making this more difficult for the defense to do). The argument is that the person should be tried only for the crime currently before the court, and not for previous misdemeanors. The defense claims that facts about previous offenses will *prejudice* the jurors — that is, lead them to make decisions in advance of, and probably ignoring, crucial facts of the case.

The influence of such prejudicial information is certainly powerful. I carried out a simple study in which a set of actions was described that was ambiguous and could perhaps imply a crime (or not). I had two sets of instructions, which differed only in one simple aspect: In one condition, the protagonist was described as having just come out of prison; in the other, the person was described as just coming home from work. People were given only one description and asked whether the person was guilty. An overwhelmingly larger number of people decided that the protagonist was guilty when a hint was included that he'd been in jail. Although they were not aware of it, people used the information about the protagonist's criminal background to reduce the ambiguity in the direction of criminality.

A similar problem may arise (that may lead to a jury giving a guilty verdict) when a person is tried for a number of similar crimes altogether. The reason may be to save time and money, but as you'd expect, if a person is charged with a string of offenses, the jury is likely to be rather suspicious about him and more likely to convict. For this reason, intense debate takes place before the court proceedings begin in front of the jury about whether cases are sufficiently linked to warrant being presented together.

Another problem is when jurors are at risk of finding out evidence that the judge decides isn't admissible in court. In the US, this evidence often comes from newspaper reports before or around the time of the trial. (In recent cases in the UK, this has been from searching online by smartphone for details!) In the UK and many other countries, after a person is charged with an offense, the offense becomes *sub judice*, meaning that it's now in the hands of the justice system and no one can mention anything that may influence potential jury members (which, before selection, can be almost any member of the general public). With its stronger commitment to a free press, the US doesn't have such strict *sub judice* rules.

ANECDOTE

Recent statements by President Donald Trump about people charged with crimes would break *sub judice* rules in the UK and lead to the charges being dropped. The defense would argue that a fair trial was not possible because the jury would already have been biased by hearing those statements.

The judge instructs jurors to put all emotional concerns out of their minds and to review the facts as objectively as possible based on the way they've been determined in court. They're also told to ignore anything they've heard about the case except the evidence they hear in court. Yet when jury decision-making is looked at closely, research often finds that jurors are unable to ignore what they may have heard outside the courtroom and to pay attention only to the facts as presented in court.

Making sense of the evidence

Particular challenges arise for a jury when it has to consider scientific or technical evidence. The following examples describe the sorts of matters that juries can have difficulty dealing with:

» **The probability of an occurrence:** For instance, if an expert says that 1 out of 100 cases would randomly produce the results found in this particular case, members of the jury may be unable to determine whether this means the results found are so unusual that they could have just happened by chance, or are so unusual that they have to be significant for the case. By contrast, eyewitnesses stating with confidence that they saw the defendant at the crime scene may be taken as strong evidence, even though (as discussed in Chapter 7) such a confident assertion may sometimes have little validity.

» **Large amounts of information:** If lots of information is available, especially when that information is complex scientific information, jurors may feel well-informed but then find it difficult to disentangle the different aspects of that information and come to a conclusion.

» **Requirement for a control group:** Often, jurors are unaware of the need for some sort of comparison against which to assess any scientific conclusion (what scientists call a *control* group of people or objects to whom the procedure hasn't been applied). For instance, being informed that a particular chemical was found in people who died would be suspicious only if the chemical wasn't found in people who did not die.

Cross-Examining the Psychology of Cross-Examination

In this section, I examine the psychology involved in the questioning of witnesses and the defendant in court.

Setting questions and giving answers

The legal process relies heavily on the questioning of witnesses. How well the lawyers asking questions understand the issues at hand is therefore central to how a case unfolds in court. If the lawyer goes off in a direction that the witness (whether an expert or not) thinks is misleading, getting back to what the witness considers crucial to understanding the matter at hand can be extremely difficult.

The whole legal process therefore depends on how effective the question-and-answer sessions are from which the evidence is drawn. This arrangement gives the lawyers considerable power in how evidence is presented to the judge and jury. They can guide the sequence in which information is presented and thus how readily it may be believed.

ANECDOTE

As a university teacher, I'm used to giving lectures on topics, using illustrations wherever possible. I was surprised, therefore, the first time I gave evidence in court and discovered that I wasn't expected to give a talk explaining my opinion and the reasons for it. Instead, the barrister led me through a series of questions as a way of revealing who I was and my opinion. Courts are rarely designed to allow easy presentation of illustrations, so most of what's explained comes in answers to questions. This means that it's difficult to develop elaborate explanations of subtle issues, and, as I describe in the following sections, the way the material is presented is open to strong influence from how the lawyers want to show it.

Avoiding leading questions

The rules of what's acceptable in court are shaped to avoid unfair bias in questioning that can influence answers unfairly. The most significant of these rules is the avoidance of *leading questions.* Here's the most well-known example: "When did you stop beating your wife?" The question assumes that the defendant did indeed beat his wife. A more acceptable question would be, "Have you ever been violent toward your wife?"

The assumption is that leading questions imply facts and may therefore influence a jury even if no evidence exists for those facts. They may also encourage witnesses to give positive answers because of the intimidating pressure of the legal rituals.

These assumptions about leading questions are valid and can be taken a stage further by building implicit suggestions into questions. In one study, when people were asked to estimate the speed of a vehicle, they gave much higher estimates when the question mentioned the cars smashing into each other than when the phrasing was contacting each other. Witnesses are also more likely to report seeing broken glass when the word *smash* is used, even though none was present. This research relates to the easy influencing of memory, which I explore in Chapter 7.

Although leading questions are improper when lawyers are questioning witnesses from their own side (for example, the prosecutor questioning prosecution witnesses), such questions may be tolerated, and indeed may be explicitly permitted in some jurisdictions, during cross-examination of the opposition's witnesses, sometimes causing distress and confusion in the witness.

Variations on leading questions are also acceptable in the forms I discuss in the following list; certain aspects of these questions, however, raise problems because, although they may seem innocent enough, they may implicitly distort the given answers or mislead the jury:

>> **Directed questions:** "What color cap was he wearing?" is a question that assumes the person was wearing a cap. In addition, it doesn't deal with anything else he was wearing, so it draws attention to only one aspect of the clothing. Witnesses are likely to be comfortable with such questions because they can appear supportive and encouraging, and so are more willing to answer them confidently even when their memories are less than clear.

>> **Directed choices:** When lawyers offer a set of options, this approach can distort the jury's perception of what's at issue, as well as put witnesses in a position where they can seem unhelpful or awkward if they don't choose one of the options. "Would you say the wounds caused death or were serious?" is a question that requires strong conviction to answer by saying that the wounds were neither. Yet the jury has already been led to believe that, at the very least, they were serious.

>> **Short questions:** The legal ritual often supports the use of short questions, especially those containing two sharply contrasting parts, such as, "Would you say this was a dangerous action?" Such questions imply that a simple answer to such a simple question must exist. Expert witnesses may want to quibble over being given such a simplistic choice, but any attempt to develop a more subtle answer — for example, along the lines of "It all depends on what you mean by dangerous" — can be seen as pedantic and unhelpful. Short questions, therefore, give the lawyer much more control over how the evidence is revealed to the court than may seem apparent at first sight. The lawyer can guide the direction in which the witness unfurls the facts without the jury necessarily being aware of what's happening.

>> **Casting doubt:** Because the law in criminal cases requires that the decision is beyond a reasonable doubt, any suggestion of doubt can be used, especially by the defense, to raise questions in the minds of the jurors. The most

prevalent way of doing this is to ask whether some alternative is possible, such as, "Is it possible these injuries occurred when paramedics examined the body?" Such a question can force experts or other witnesses into making categorical assertions or seeming wishy-washy if they admit to some doubt. If doubt exists, further questioning can give weight by asking whether this assumption is reasonable.

>> **Facts or opinions:** Courts allow only expert witnesses to give opinions (as I discuss in Chapter 12); other witnesses are supposed to limit themselves to the facts. So if a lawyer can imply that a witness is offering an opinion and not facts, this can persuade the jury not to take seriously what the witness says. The problem is that no simple division exists between facts and opinion when people are drawing on their memories. "Can you be sure the car was red?" leads to the possibility that what the witness is saying isn't a hard-and-fast fact, but rather is an opinion of what's likely to be the case.

>> **Exchanges:** The question-and-answer sequence is the essence of giving evidence in court. Although this approach can appear to be a cumbersome way of informing people of the facts as the witness sees them, it gives the lawyer the possibility of setting up a rhythm of questions and answers that can corner unsuspecting witnesses into revealing weaknesses in their evidence.

Here's an example from my own experience of giving evidence to challenge the opinion of another expert, whom I call Reverend Q:

>> Barrister: Is it true, Professor Canter, that you invited Reverend Q to give a presentation at a conference you organized?

>> Me: Yes.

>> Barrister: Is it also the case that you give lectures on Reverend Q's work on your postgraduate course?

>> Me: Yes.

>> Barrister: Yet you're now telling the court that his work is of no value.

>> The barrister was clearly expecting me to be flustered by this sequence of events and to give some less-than-convincing answer. However, I saw his trap coming and answered:

>> Me: Yes. I think it's important for my students to see poor science so that they can distinguish it from work to be trusted!

Seating the Desired Jury: Can Psychologists Help?

One area in which forensic psychology expertise is drawn on in the US is in giving guidance on how to select a jury, as I describe in this section. The use of juries in courts is to ensure that anyone accused of a crime is judged by similar people from the same community, on the assumption that they understand the defendant's way of life and can make sense of their actions. The belief is that members of a jury will make honest, objective judgments of the facts presented to them.

Remember that being "judged by one's peers" was a fundamental part of the 1215 *Magna Carta* (Clause 39), showing how embedded the idea is in Western legal systems.

Various legal systems accept that if a juror holds prejudices that are relevant to crucial issues in the case, that person can't make unbiased decisions on that case. For example, if a juror believes that female doctors can never be trusted, they should not be allowed to sit on a jury in any case involving a female doctor. Therefore, legal systems allow challenges, in various ways, to the presence of individual members of the jury on the grounds that they would be biased. This bias can be the simple matter of the juror knowing the defendant.

REGIONAL TIP-OFF

In the UK, requests by the defense or prosecution to challenge any member of the jury are rare and have to be based on clear legal issues, but in the US, the possibility of objecting to the presence of one or more people on the jury is accepted in many states. This objection may even be allowed without the need for any explicit or distinctly legal reason. This can become a major aspect of the court procedure in the US, requiring hundreds of jurors being asked to attend court for possible jury service (as happened in the trial of O. J. Simpson for murder).

Psychologists can offer some general principles on jury selection, such as older people being more willing to convict someone. Another suggestion is that people who have had previous experience of a trial are more likely to support a conviction. However, no strong evidence exists for any simple relationship between the characteristics of people and the decisions they'll make after they've heard the evidence and discussed it with other jury members. Even unexpected findings (for one such phenomenon, check out the later sidebar "The black sheep effect") can confound any simple assumptions about a jury.

REMEMBER

About the only aspect of a juror's characteristics that does predict an above-chance probability that the person is more likely to convict someone is the person's attitude toward the legal system. The more confident people are in the processes of law, the more likely they are to convict.

NO COACHING ALLOWED

A personal experience illustrates how cautious UK barristers are about any form of coaching or interaction with a witness. Some years ago, I gave evidence about audio recordings, the transcripts of which were read out in court. On the first day I gave evidence, it emerged that two of the recordings were quite similar. Overnight, I realized that I had inadvertently recorded the same material twice, but the transcribers hadn't produced identical versions, which is why the material read in court wasn't absolutely identical. I was to continue to give my evidence the next day, so I tried to speak to the barrister to explain the error before the court proceedings began. But he gently told me that he couldn't speak to me while I was still giving evidence. The court never heard why there were two similar transcripts!

The ploys described in the following section for preparing witnesses and other forms of scientific advice on how attorneys should behave are totally unacceptable in many jurisdictions outside the US. Therefore, much of the information in this section relates only to the US.

Selecting juries for scientific trials

A particular challenge to the judge and lawyer, as well as for juries, is how they deal with scientific and technical information in areas about which they may have had no formal training. In the US, where legal practice allows extensive selection of jury members, issues arise of how to select a jury that's most likely to give the desired verdict (from both sides' point of view). As a consequence, a special area of expertise has grown up to advise attorneys on how to do this, which inevitably raises ethical as well as legal and psychological questions (check out the later sidebar "The Runaway Jury").

The possibility of jury selection improving the chances of each side obtaining the verdict they desire encouraged the study of how jurors make decisions. This information has been included in the commercial practice of providing guidance, usually to the defense, on the selection of juries. It has become known as *scientific jury selection.* Employing this expertise is often quite expensive and is usually used only in high-profile cases.

An intensive, data-driven, psychological approach to jury selection was carried out on behalf of Donald Trump in a 2024–2025 New York trial. He was charged with falsifying business records to conceal a hush money payment made to the adult film actress Stormy Daniels during the 2016 presidential campaign, potentially violating election laws.

Donald Trump's defense team used scientific jury-selection tactics to screen jurors for potential bias. They analyzed jurors' social media activity, political affiliations, and media consumption habits. Extensive questionnaires probed views on Trump, law enforcement, and the justice system. The team aimed to identify jurors sympathetic to Trump or skeptical of the prosecution, delaying the process and shaping a jury perceived as more balanced.

As with other cases that use such intensive techniques, the results are not always what was intended. Donald Trump was found *guilty on 34 felony counts* of falsifying business records.

REGIONAL
TIP-OFF

For those cases in which the jury is required to determine the sentence after a person is convicted, or levels of compensation in civil proceedings, the significance of a juror's preexisting attitudes is particularly important. In the US, this issue comes to a head, especially when a jury is required to decide whether a convicted murderer should be executed. A person, opposed to the death penalty in principle, is often excluded from such a jury.

Coaching witnesses

One contribution that psychologists have made to major cases in the US is *witness preparation* — that is, coaching witnesses by reviewing what they're going to say and how they'll say it. The aim is to improve their effectiveness in convincing the jury. This practice is much more common in the US than in the UK, where it's frowned on (see the earlier anecdote "No coaching allowed").

MYTH
BUSTER

THE BLACK SHEEP EFFECT

You may think that jurors would be more lenient to defendants of their own ethnicity, but in fact, studies show that the opposite may be the case — this tendency is called *the black sheep effect*. The jurors believe that the defendant has let down their ethnic group and should be treated more harshly. Clearly, this research has implications for jury selection. Jury selection assisted by psychologists can also be part of a broader range of psychological support, the most intensive of which is the creation of a *shadow jury*. This consists of employing a group of people who closely match the actual jury in terms of age, ethnicity, and socioeconomic status. This parallel jury then listens to exactly the same evidence as the real jury, but is available for comment and discussion on the sense that the evidence is making to them. The attorneys can then modify how they present subsequent information to the actual jury.

Witness preparation involves educating the witnesses in courtroom procedures and reviewing their previous statements — for example, to the police — to ensure that no contradictions are included. If this preparation involves some form of rehearsal, it increases the witness's confidence and fluency in court, which in turn is likely to increase the credibility of the witness. Witness preparation further ensures that the attorney is totally familiar with what the witness knows and is likely to say.

THE RUNAWAY JURY

The various psychological interventions of coaching witnesses, studying jury decision-making, using shadow juries, and developing questioning strategies add up to a great deal of potential interference with how a court works. This problem is delightfully illustrated in John Grisham's book *The Runaway Jury* (made into a film starring Gene Hackman). In the movie, every possible psychological device is employed by the attorney to persuade the jury to accept his arguments. However, the plot twist (spoiler alert!) is that a member of the jury is even more sophisticated than the attorney and by a variety of clever ruses convinces the just jury to reach the opposite decision. This narrative device illustrates how problematic any attempt is to shape activities in court.

The Runaway Jury also draws attention to the ethical and legal dilemmas created by introducing psychological expertise into how the court processes should run. Not least is that the experts providing such services are usually quite expensive (although free online advice is increasingly becoming available). As a result, rich defendants are more likely to use them, especially a major corporation (which is the defendant in the John Grisham book), rather than ordinary folk who can't afford such advice. Another concern is that the advice can drift into distorting the evidence presented and how the legal procedure unfolds in ways that undermine basic principles of the law — notably, that it should be objective and its processes openly transparent.

5
Helping and Treating Offenders

The most important way to reduce crime is to stop it from happening in the first place or, if someone does commit a crime, to set in motion some intervention that will reduce the chances of the person doing it again. Psychologists are quite active in working with families to lower the probability that their children will become criminals *and* in providing interventions with offenders that are aimed at helping them out of future criminality. Violent and sexual crimes are the ones most obviously open to some form of treatment programs. In this part, I present illustrations of how they work and the principles on which they're based.

Chapter **14**

Can Offenders Be Rehabilitated?

I n this chapter, I explore the psychological issues surrounding punishment and other interventions with offenders. These issues deal with the commonly asked question of whether offenders can ever be rehabilitated. I examine the use of imprisonment and ways in which incarceration is helpful or otherwise. I also describe using psychological treatment programs with prisoners, some effective and others less so, and the associated challenges. Although there are many difficulties in providing successful interventions, including lack of resources, adequate training of staff and offenders' reluctance to participate in interventions, some do have benefits and reduce reoffending.

REMEMBER

In a variety of countries, a large proportion of convicted offenders don't go to prison. They have to attend probation sessions and carry out services in the community or suffer other forms of sentencing, such as a curfew verified by electronic tagging. Many of the interventions I mention in this chapter are relevant to people in prison as well as to those who aren't, although delivering therapeutic programs to offenders who aren't in the controlled environment of the prison can be difficult.

Examining the Challenges of Imprisonment

The sentence that a convicted criminal receives has a number of possible objectives, including these:

>> Retribution for wrongdoing

>> Removal of the offenders from society so that they can't commit further crimes while in prison

>> Deterrent to discourage others from committing similar crimes

>> Rehabilitation to encourage the offenders to desist from their criminal ways

For the widest possible benefit to both prisoners and the general public, the last entry is perhaps the most important one.

The overall objective of prisons is to combine reformation with punishment, which is why they can be called *correctional* establishments in the US and are called *reformatories* for young offenders in the UK. Yet this view raises questions about how successful prison sentences truly are in changing people for the better and whether other, more effective ways exist to enable offenders to find their way onto the straight and narrow.

Investigating the effectiveness of prison

A major form of legal punishment around the world these days is to serve time in prison, with debate revolving around how long a person's sentence needs to be for any given crime. However, a strong case exists for using alternatives to prison because the experience of prison can be destructive. For this reason, various forms of punishment, such as service in the community or in special secure units (including the therapeutic communities I describe in the later section "Treating in therapeutic communities") are increasingly being used in various judicial systems.

Prison was introduced as a major form of punishment relatively recently, about 150 years ago (not to be confused with the medieval practice of throwing people in dungeons or locking them in the Tower of London, which weren't legal punishments as such, but were ways of keeping awkward people out of circulation). The increased use or prison as a punishment in the 19th century drew on the idea that crime was a product of association with other criminals. The popular notion was that a person who was separated from other criminals and given the Bible to study would mend their ways. Physical exercise, such as walking on a treadmill or around an exercise yard, was allowed, but all imprisonment was, in effect, solitary confinement.

BANNING CRUEL PUNISHMENT

Throughout history, societies have used many different forms of punishment, including physical assault, such as whipping or binding with chains, and various types of execution, as well as fines, being forced to join the military, or being transported to the Americas or Australia (or another country).

In most countries, the more vicious forms of punishment have been stopped, and both the US and Europe have special constitutional requirements that disallow torture and demeaning and unusual forms of punishment.

In the US, the Eighth Amendment to the Constitution forbids excessive fines or cruel and unusual punishments.

The European Convention on Human Rights, Article 3, states that "No one shall be subjected to torture or to inhuman or degrading treatment or punishment."

This system was soon found to be debilitating to prisoners (see the later sidebar "Isolating a prisoner") and expensive to manage. As a result, the authorities changed it to today's prison system, in which inmates are allowed to mix with each other (known in prison jargon as *association*) and required to participate in any available work activities. Prisons now often aim to provide tasks to replace the traditional sewing of mailbags, however, so that the work provides both a sense of achievement for individuals and a social context in which habits of working productively with others can be developed. If possible, the work also gives the inmates skills they can use in legitimate jobs after they're released.

Can prison make offenders worse?

Prison can cause distinct, debilitating psychological effects on inmates, including these:

>> **Feelings of worthlessness, low self-esteem, and depression:** Incarceration denies people their basic right to privacy and forces them to relinquish control over everyday features of their daily lives that other people take for granted. They may live in small cells that are sometimes extremely confined and poorly lit and ventilated. They may have little or no say in choosing the person with whom they have to share that space. In addition, they have no option over when they get up or go to bed, when or what they eat, when they shower or exercise, or when they use the toilet. These degrading circumstances continually remind them of their stigmatized existence. Some prisoners come to

believe that they deserve the degradation and stigma to which they've been subjected while imprisoned.

>> **Becoming institutionalized:** Prison is a *total* institution, in which every aspect of the inmates' lives is controlled. Prisons withdraw much of the inmates' *independence,* or right to decide for themselves. This situation can be difficult for prisoners to cope with initially, but on release causes problems when trying to readjust. People can become institutionalized and passively accept everything the regime requires them to do. Consequently, they can have difficulty taking any active role themselves in the future.

>> **Anger with specific individuals and with the system:** Prisoners may believe that certain prison officers or other inmates have caused them harm, whether or not that is the case, as well as feeling that the whole legal process and incarceration are unfair and should be challenged.

>> **Hypervigilance, interpersonal distrust, and suspicion:** General distrust becomes natural in prison because, after all, it's full of criminals, many of whom have a history of violence. Some male prisoners learn to project a strongman image, believing that unless they do, they're likely to be dominated and exploited. They don't tolerate anything that they consider an insult, no matter how trivial, which can get them into trouble in prison as well as on release.

>> **Emotional overcontrol, alienation, and psychological distancing:** These are consequences of the potential threats prisoners may see all around them. Prisoners who develop an unrevealing and impenetrable prison mask risk creating an enduring and unbridgeable distance between themselves and other people.

>> **Social withdrawal and isolation:** This is part of the process whereby prisoners protect themselves by hiding behind a cloak of social invisibility and becoming as low-key and discreetly detached from others as possible. In extreme cases, this behavior can make prisoners seem to be clinically depressed.

>> **The exploitative and extreme values of prison life:** Prisoners sometimes agree to the unwritten prisoner code of conduct or risk repercussions. This can include not reporting any assaults they have experienced or witnessed and relying on any gang hierarchy for guidance on what they should do. This can tie them into a criminal subculture that's difficult to shake off once outside prison.

ISOLATING A PRISONER

Today, solitary confinement in prison occurs for one of two main reasons: the prisoner's own protection (for example, for abusers of young children who are likely to be picked on and attacked by other prisoners) or for punishment and control (for example, if a person breaks important prison rules, violently attacks another prisoner or prison officer, or smashes up their cell in anger).

Solitary confinement can be extremely debilitating for some people, especially if the prisoner has no contact with others. In some progressive prisons, it's used as an opportunity to help a prisoner calm down and then open up to one-to-one counseling in a controlled environment. Most jurisdictions have legal limits on how long a person can remain in solitary confinement as a punishment.

Spending 23 hours a day in a cell with nothing to do can be soul-destroying for anyone. For a person who has difficulty reading and who never had awareness of the possibilities broadened by effective education, it can be extremely destructive.

All these aspects cause difficulties when working on psychological issues with prisoners. The central challenge was expressed clearly by an experienced prison psychologist, Kevin Rogers, who told me:

Prison culture looks down on any sign of weakness and susceptibility and discourages the expression of sincere emotions or familiarity. Some prisoners embrace this in a way that encourages a keen investment in one's reputation for toughness and promotes an attitude toward others in which even apparently irrelevant verbal abuse, disrespect, or physical infringements must be responded to speedily and intuitively, often with decisive force. In some cases, the failure to take advantage of weakness is often seen as a symbol of weakness itself and viewed as provocation for manipulation. In male prisons, it may encourage a type of hypermasculinity in which power and control are overestimated as critical parts of one's identity.

These consequences of imprisonment make exploring any psychological problems an inmate may have extremely difficult, especially any aspects of themselves that may indicate weakness or require them to acknowledge and explore their emotional reactions. Prisoners can be particularly reluctant to seek any help with their difficulties or even recognize that they have any problems in dealing with other people.

SPECIALIZING IN WORKING IN PRISONS

Psychologists who spend their careers working in prisons sometimes call themselves *correctional psychologists* and have their own associations, such as the American Association for Correctional Psychologists (AACP), which has hundreds of members.

The bulk of British psychologists working in prisons and secure units would look to the Division of Forensic Psychology of the British Psychological Society. They're regulated, like all professional psychologists, by the Health Professions Council. Typically, they refer to themselves as *prison psychologists* or even just *applied psychologists.*

Some psychologists provide guidance to the institution rather than individual prisoners, to help prisons work as organizations that contribute to reforming their inmates. This work can include helping to select or train staff or to set in motion various programs of working with offenders. Sometimes this type of work is quite challenging because the institutions have an ingrained set of attitudes and a culture that's fundamentally punitive, not informed by any understanding of the causes and processes that underpin criminality.

In certain crisis situations, such as a prisoner taking someone hostage, psychologists may help negotiate and deal with the situation, as I discuss in Chapter 12.

REMEMBER

A further aspect that makes psychological help difficult within a total institution is that a high percentage of prisoners have experienced some form of childhood abuse, which featured similar qualities of coercive strictness and psychological and possibly physical insult. The callous nature of prison existence may seem to some prisoners as just business as usual — that's what their world is like, inside or outside prison. Imprisonment just reminds them of what made them feel unworthy initially, which may have been part of the reason for the criminality that brought them to prison in the first place.

The uses of imprisonment

Education is a positive possibility for prisoners, if it's available. Many offenders failed in school and can barely read or write or do elementary arithmetic. Crime may have been the only way they could survive with these disadvantages. When prison provides the opportunities that school never did, it can make a difference in their lives — although it can, of course, also enable them to commit more sophisticated crimes.

Training in prison is also useful, especially with younger offenders. Giving a person a trade qualification can open up job opportunities that were never available to them, although setting up training facilities is demanding for prisons. Where it's done, it can be quite effective.

Investigating Certain Approaches to Treatment

Although all offenders are subject to the pressures of institutionalization that I describe in the preceding section, and respond in various psychological ways and to varying degrees, some prisoners are much more vulnerable to these pressures and the overall pains of imprisonment than others. These inmates include the mentally ill and those who aren't very bright — they're often learning disabled and have been passed over in their schooling — as well as those held in solitary confinement because of their inability to cope with prison. (Flip to the earlier sidebar "Isolating a prisoner" for more on this issue.)

Psychologists often treat these specific difficulties individually — usually, in a one-to-one format using cognitive behavioral therapy (see the later sections "Getting people together" and "Using cognitive behavioral methods") over an agreed-on time span and number of sessions. Ideally, prison staff monitor changes in mood or behavior that the vulnerable inmate suffers and reports these to psychologists on a regular timescale with interventions amended accordingly.

In this section, I focus on the opportunity that incarceration provides for psychologists to work directly with inmates, providing various programs that may be thought of as forms of treatment. These programs are also provided for people on probation and outside prison in therapeutic communities and various forms of secure units and other settings. Except in a small subset of offenders, I'm not implying that people commit crimes because they're ill. I use the word *treatment* to describe many different forms of intervention with convicted criminals.

Working with offenders

Psychologists work with convicted offenders in relation to the following broad tasks that connect to three different stages of the offender's life:

REMEMBER

>> **Past:** Helping offenders deal with problems that may have been a direct cause of the actions that produced the offense, such as the inability to manage their own aggression, drug or alcohol addiction, or longer-term problems such as mental illness or personality disorder.

>> **Present:** Counseling to assist offenders to cope with their current circumstances — for example, reducing the risk of suicide in prison or helping people who've recently been given a life sentence.

>> **Future:** Trying to determine what risks individuals pose to themselves and others and the most appropriate way of managing those risks. (I discuss risk assessment in Chapter 5.) These assessments may relate to managing these individuals within a specific institution or determining the risks of releasing them into the wider community.

Assessing effectively: Horses for courses

For any work with offenders to be effective, it needs to start with some form of assessment (just as a doctor diagnoses a patient's problem to determine the most appropriate form of treatment). Many reasons for criminal behavior exist. Careful analysis of each individual's circumstances can help guide the process of intervention.

REMEMBER

Assessment takes into consideration the fact that plenty of people suffer particular traumas yet don't commit crimes. It's important to understand the full context from which a person's offending grows. In a psychological context, one specific cause — such as a mental abnormality or a particular experience (such as sexual abuse as a child) — is unlikely to explain criminal behavior, although these aspects can be important contributing factors. Instead, assessment includes forming a broader understanding of individuals, their lives, and all relevant aspects.

Most of the psychological measurement procedures I mention in Chapters 5 and 6 also play a part in getting a handle on an offender's particular problems. In some cases, the assessment may be just an induction interview, explaining how the prison works and specifying what's expected of the prisoner. But in more forward-thinking prisons, an assessment of two distinct aspects of the inmate takes place:

>> **Issues directly relevant to the person's criminality,** such as substance abuse, attitude to employment, and their background in crime.

>> **Broader issues that the person may need help with,** such as depression, low self-esteem, or any other mental health problems. Even day-to-day problems, such as the difficulty of finding a place to live, may be important to note so that they can be dealt with before release.

One standard measurement procedure, developed by psychologists and gaining in popularity and used for assessing offenders when they first arrive in prison, is the *Level of Service Inventory*. This procedure consists of 54 questions that explore ten aspects relevant to determining how a person should be dealt with in prison and the forms of intervention that are likely to be most relevant. The inventory covers these aspects of a person's life:

>> Criminal history and experiences

>> Educational and any employment history

>> Financial aspects

>> Family or marital issues, including upbringing and family background

>> Accommodation history and experiences

>> Leisure and recreation preferences

>> Companions, such as friends and criminal associates

>> Alcohol or drug problems

>> Emotional or personal issues, including personality characteristics

>> Attitudes or orientation, especially toward criminality

MODIFYING BEHAVIOR

Some approaches — known as *behavior modification* — sought to change prisoners' actions directly. They were quite fashionable in the 1960s and derived from the idea that human and animal behavior is directly shaped by the associated pattern of rewards and punishments.

The idea involved providing or withdrawing rewards for acceptable behavior. For example, prisoners were given access to the prison store or gym only if they had no disciplinary violations over a given period.

Although some such programs produced initial successes, they eventually lost favor, mainly because they produced no long-term benefit. People behaved well for the rewards, but after those were withdrawn, their actions reverted to earlier patterns.

The great mistake of the behavior modification approach was to forget that human beings, unlike animals, can think about their actions and their implications. They make sense of what's happening and use that sense to guide how they behave. Although most people are aware of this concept every day, sadly, it took psychological experiments to convince psychologists. One benefit, however, was that this awareness gave rise to a therapy that combines actions with thoughts — cognitive behavioral therapy.

Getting people together

Much of the therapeutic work in prisons is carried out in groups — typically, of 6 to 12 individuals. The purpose of such group work is to enhance the power of therapy by enabling people to share experiences and to learn from each other's attempts to deal with their problems.

For people who have difficulty relating to and trusting others, which is a common problem for inmates (as I describe in the earlier section "Can prison make offenders worse?"), such group sessions can be demanding and, if managed properly, have a powerful effect. They're also much more cost-effective to run than one-on-one therapeutic sessions.

Using cognitive behavioral methods

In the late 1970s, in many countries, there was a growing dissatisfaction with the ineffective, punitive emphasis of incarceration. In response, the growing evidence on the cognitive distortions and criminal patterns of thinking that underlie offending (explored in Chapter 4) was drawn on by introducing *cognitive behavioral therapy* (CBT) into prisons. This concept focuses on challenging unwanted thinking patterns and emotional and behavioral reactions that are learned over a long period. The aim is to identify the thinking that causes unhelpful or unproductive feelings and behaviors and discover how to replace them with more positive ones. CBT helps prisoners make sense of potentially destructive experiences by breaking them down into these smaller parts:

>> A situation (problem, event, or difficult circumstance) gives rise to:

- Thoughts

- Emotions

- Physical feelings

>> With consequence:

- Actions

- Each area affects the others

    (How an offender thinks about a problem can influence feelings and also alter what's done about it.)

Figure 14-1 shows how different thoughts, feelings, and actions feed on each other, producing a positive, productive circle or a negative, destructive one.

FIGURE 14-1:
The cycle of
thoughts,
feelings, and
actions that is
dealt with in
cognitive
behavioral
therapy.

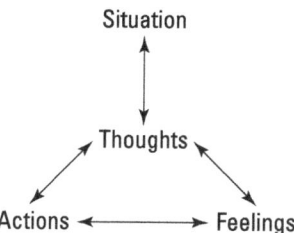

This vicious cycle can make someone feel worse and is likely to give rise to other situations that produce even worse feelings. The person's beliefs can also be distorted during this process, leading to unrealistic and uncomfortable thoughts about themselves. The added distress can make a person more jumpy and ready to interpret things in extreme and unhelpful ways.

Here's an example of how this process works in practice. A prisoner is expecting a visit from his partner, who promised to arrive by 2 p.m. At 2:15 p.m., he's escorted to the visitation room and she's not there. Table 14-1 contains some helpful and unhelpful responses that he may feel.

TABLE 14-1   **An Example of CBT Being Used with a Prisoner**

	Helpful	Unhelpful
Thoughts	Perhaps she has missed the bus; she won't be long.	She's left me and doesn't want to tell me.
Feelings	Happy, positive, in high spirits.	Angry, upset, jealous.
Physical	None; feeling comfortable.	Stomach cramps, low energy, feeling sick.
Action	Wait quietly, get a coffee, and chat with prison staff.	Go back to the wing, telephone, accuse her of being unfaithful.

The prisoner is told that if he returns to his cell feeling depressed, he may become moody and brood over what has happened. This reaction would make him feel worse. If he doesn't do this, he has the chance to correct any misunderstandings about what his partner thinks of him and what he thinks of her.

A great deal of skill is involved in providing CBT and setting up effective programs. In general, these programs only work if they do the following:

REMEMBER

>> **Use methods that take account of how participants come to understand what they're told:** For example, some people learn by active involvement, and others from reflecting on what they have to learn. Some want to see immediately the practical implications of what they're learning, whereas some may want to fully understand the ideas behind what they're being taught.

>> **Address in a clearly planned way the specific factors associated with offending:** This happens instead of the program being a general exploration of unacceptable behavior.

>> **Are delivered as designed:** This requirement may be more difficult than it seems, because staff and inmates get moved around, and pressures from other areas — such as attendance at court — can interfere with participation. The staff in a prison may offer the program without adequate training.

PROGRAMS BASED ON CBT

Over the past half-century, various developments have been initiated that emphasize various features of CBT. Here's a summary:

US programs:

- **Modified therapeutic communities (MTC):** Often CBT-informed, these are used for substance abuse and behavioral rehabilitation in prisons. They integrate peer-led accountability with structured CBT modules.

- **Reasoning and rehabilitation (R&R):** This CBT program is used in various US states, focusing on cognitive restructuring, impulse control, and prosocial skills.

- **Moral reconation therapy (MRT):** This program emphasizes moral development and decision-making, widely used in correctional settings.

UK programs:

- **Thinking Skills Programme (TSP):** Develops problem-solving, perspective-taking, and emotional regulation to reduce reoffending

- **Building Choices:** A CBT-based program designed for both men and women, including those with learning disabilities, that uses a strengths-based, person-centered approach to address versatile offending patterns

- **Kaizen:** A high-intensity CBT program for high-risk violent and sexual offenders, focusing on dynamic risk factors and long-term behavioral change

- **Resolve:** Targets violent behavior through CBT techniques, including anger management and moral reasoning

The CBT course explores these categories:

- Impulse control
- Flexible thinking
- Social perspective taking
- Values and moral reasoning
- Logical reasoning
- Interpersonal problem-solving

The Good Lives Model

Complementary approaches that deal directly with thoughts and actions, evolving out of CBT interventions that emphasize how offenders live their lives are gaining ground. This is known as The *Good Lives Model* (GLM), a rehabilitation framework that focuses on helping individuals build meaningful, fulfilling lives.

Rooted in principles of human dignity and agency, the GLM emphasizes that everyone has the right to pursue a good life and should be supported in doing so. Central to the model is the recognition of the human need for relationships, autonomy, knowledge, inner peace, and creativity. The rehabilitation programs aim to satisfy these needs via prosocial, nonharmful means by tailoring interventions to each individual's aspirations and addressing deficits like poor emotional regulation and lack of education.

In prison settings, participants are encouraged to reflect on their values, aspirations, and strengths — not just their risks. This is aided by focusing on enhancing capabilities (for example, emotional literacy or vocational skills) that support good lives. Such processes help prisoners reconstruct their life stories to include hope, growth, and responsibility.

ANECDOTE

Where I used to live, a family was known for committing petty crime. Unaware of that, I employed them to build a complex set of stairs, out of bricks, in my garden. Observing the team at work, I noticed that only one young man was doing the actual bricklaying. All the others were heaving the bricks and organizing supplies so that he could do his job. I asked him where he had learned to lay bricks so efficiently, and he mentioned a place that happened to be a prison for young offenders — and that I had recently visited. In the prison, the man supervising the bricklaying course had mentioned the benefits of providing young men with a proper skill. The evidence I had seen showed that having even one person in the family who could do an honest job had the potential to prevent the others from serious offending.

Treating in therapeutic communities

As I note in the earlier section "Can prison make offenders worse?", prisons aren't effective environments in which to carry out therapeutic interventions with inmates. Therefore, a number of communities have been created in the US, UK and other countries for offenders which counteract the prison culture, that can maintain criminal behavior.

A central part of this approach is to remove the strongly hierarchical, coercive nature of prisons and open up decision-making to all those involved. For that reason, these communities are often referred to as *democratic therapeutic communities.* Their residents are usually selected by those already there, or at least by a subset elected by the community. (Yes, the prisoners are often involved in deciding which new inmates should be allowed to join their community.) The community also decides when a person can be discharged. Any new member also has to be clear about what they're signing up for, which includes an acceptance of a range of aspects that are alien to a prison environment and are often psychologically demanding to deal with — for example:

>> **Democratization** is embraced with gusto. All major decisions relating to the community are made jointly by all its members, including staff and residents. Residents are expected to take an active role in this process.

>> **Communalism** takes the democratic process a stage further. Open and free communication between everyone is encouraged, with no secrets between people.

>> **Permissiveness** means that although people must obey the rules of the community, low-level misbehavior is considered for its reasons and for ways to ensure that it doesn't reoccur, instead of being a reason for punishment or ejection from the community.

>> **Reality confrontation** requires that residents face up to their true colors. They can't hide behind denial, withdrawal from contact with others, or distortion of the facts to suit themselves (see the later section "Dealing with denial").

>> **Group therapy and group sessions** are used to deal with the problems that originally led people to be sentenced; these sessions can follow various therapeutic principles.

>> **Community meetings** are how the community makes decisions and manages its affairs.

WHEN TREATMENT GOES WRONG

ANECDOTE

In the late 1980s, a novel form of therapeutic community, the *Oak Ridge Therapeutic Community* (named after the original program in Ontario, Canada) was set up in the US especially for people diagnosed as psychopathic. Its activities were built around 80 hours of therapy each week. As a result, virtually no time was left for leisure, opportunities for training, or the development of useful skills. The program also included two weeks in a self-contained chamber where food and drink were provided from pipes in the walls. Along the way, the inmates were made to use a variety of psychotropic drugs, such as LSD. People were expected to participate for two whole years and weren't allowed out until they showed that they had complied with what the treatment was expected to achieve.

Perhaps not surprisingly, many of the people who were identified as psychopaths before they joined this community were more dangerous and disturbed when they left than before they entered.

The environment of a therapeutic community is an intensely social one in which every aspect of every day is regarded as some form of therapeutic intervention. Unsurprisingly, many offenders can't tolerate these conditions and prefer to spend their time quietly in prison. The communication demands of these communities also mean that they tend to attract and select the more capable and articulate offenders.

REMEMBER

The success of therapeutic communities usually relies on a charismatic leader who can keep the highly charged atmosphere in a positively supportive state rather than let it implode. Any success they have seems to depend on offenders spending at least a year or longer as members. This length of time allows people to move through various reactions to the therapeutic community experience, such as hostility and depression, before they can benefit from the new perspectives on themselves and others.

Therapeutic communities, however, are expensive to run (which is why they work well for the addicted rich-and-famous). They require special buildings and many dedicated staff. Impoverished prison systems rarely have the resources to maintain such institutions despite any benefits they may have.

Determining which interventions work

A concerted effort has been made in various countries to evaluate interventions with offenders that are effective. That is much more difficult than you may think.

One crucial question is which criterion of success to use. Some experts prefer to look at whether a person's attitudes or behavior in prison have changed subsequent to participation in an intervention. The problem with this approach, however, is that offenders may just discover how to adopt a therapeutic vocabulary to describe their actions and get to know what sort of opinions they're supposed to express, without ever fully embracing the attitudes involved. This problem leads to the possibility that their behavior changes back to their criminal ways when they leave the institution.

Other evaluations focus on offending activity after the intervention. But again, the question arises of what exactly should be monitored — reduction in criminal activity or total cessation? And over what period? Should it cover serious crimes or arrests or all illegal activity?

The possibility also exists that interventions make offenders more aware of the risks of getting caught. They don't reduce their criminality, but merely their coming to the attention of the police. They learn how to talk their way out of situations where they're challenged about their crimes, or even just learn more in the group sessions about how others got away with their offending.

A somewhat different approach to considering these interventions with offenders is to make sure that they're at least professionally conducted and follow appropriate guidelines so that programs are as effective as possible. This approach led to the accreditation of programs in the UK to ensure that the required standards are maintained, as described in this list:

>> **A clear model of change:** An explicit model is necessary to explain how the program intends to bring about relevant change in offenders, by specifying how it will do this and what's achieved at each stage of the program. The model must describe why this combination of targets and methods is likely to work with the selected offenders.

>> **Selection of offenders:** Clear specification is required of the types of offenders for whom the program is intended and the methods used to select them. The program has to identify the characteristics of the selected offenders, such as the nature of the offenses that the program tackles, risk, motivation, learning style, gender, and race. The program must have ways for dealing with offenders who have started and are then found to be unsuitable.

>> **Targeting a range of dynamic risk factors:** A range of risk factors known to be associated with reoffending must be addressed in an integrated manner within the program. The program needs to focus overtly on the factors that are open to change — the dynamic risk factors I consider in Chapter 5.

>> **Effective methods:** Evidence needs to show that the methods used are likely to have an impact on the targeted dynamic risk factors. For example, CBT methods work well with most types of offenders, including sex offenders. (Check out the earlier section "Using cognitive behavioral methods.") Structured therapeutic communities are helpful in changing the lifestyle of people with drug or alcohol addictions or other patterns of antisocial behavior. (See the earlier section "Treating in therapeutic communities.")

>> **Skills-oriented:** The program needs to facilitate the learning of skills that support involvement in legitimate pursuits, including literacy, numeracy, and general problem-solving, as well as how to find work and form and sustain relationships.

>> **Sequencing, intensity, and duration:** The length of programs needs to match the risk. The amount of treatment provided must be linked to the needs of program participants, with the introduction of various treatment components, timed so that they complement each other. Offenders with a high-fixed risk (for example, they have a history of antisocial behavior) need programs long enough to change established attitudes and habits. For lower-risk offenders, a shorter program may be sufficient.

>> **Engagement and motivation:** The program must be structured to maximize the engagement of participants and to sustain their motivation throughout. Staff need to be positively committed to the program.

>> **Continuity of programs and services:** Clear links are necessary between the program and the overall management of the offender, both during a prison sentence and in the context of community supervision. Relevant information needs to be shared. Key agencies concerned with protection of the public are to be kept informed, to aid work with victims and to monitor offenders.

>> **Maintaining integrity:** Provision is needed to monitor how well the program functions, as well as a system to modify aspects of it that don't perform as expected.

>> **Ongoing evaluation:** Provision needs to be built into the program to evaluate its efficacy. Checks must be done to ensure that staff are properly selected, trained, and supervised and that the program is run as intended. Given the challenges of carrying out therapeutic treatment in prisons, this list of requirements for effective interventions is a tall order indeed. They're unlikely all to be achieved all the time. These points give targets to aim for. If they aren't achieved, people shouldn't be surprised that the interventions fail to reach their goal of reducing reoffending.

Acknowledging the Challenges to Treatment

When a person walks into a doctor's consulting room and asks for treatment, the only limits are those that stem from the doctor's professional situation and what the patient needs. Psychological interventions with convicted criminals, in contrast, are constrained by legal, security, confidentiality, and institutional factors.

Facing up to legal constraints

In democracies and other open societies, persons convicted of a crime still have the same human rights as anyone else. Their liberty may be restricted, or they may be required to fulfil community service, but in theory, beyond that, they have access to the full assistance of the law. As a result, they can claim legal support for certain aspects of their activities that aren't compatible with obtaining appropriate treatment to help reduce the likelihood of their reoffending.

Like everyone else, prisoners have the right to refuse medical intervention as long as this refusal doesn't cause harm to anyone else. For example, inmates with an infectious disease, such as tuberculosis, may not be allowed to continue to associate with others in prison unless they accept treatment to cure the disease. But the situation becomes more complicated in relation to psychological interventions. These interventions may open up legal implications that confound the possibility of treatment.

ANECDOTE

THE LEGAL COMPLEXITIES OF TREATMENT FOR INMATES

A convicted rapist was reaching the end of his sentence, and the authorities, understandably, feared he might offend again on his release. Therefore, they required him to undergo a program that they hoped would reduce that risk. This program required him to talk about all the crimes he had committed, to gain a full understanding of his actions and their causes. He challenged this request, saying that this requirement may mean that he would mention crimes he hadn't been convicted of, and thus was against his human right not to incriminate himself. This challenge underwent various legal considerations, but in the end, the courts decided that he had no such right to refuse treatment in this case.

The prison environment may compromise the professional requirement known as *informed consent,* which demands that any interaction with a professional, especially in therapy, is based on the patient willingly accepting the treatment and knowing the implications of that treatment. But in a prison, coercion often takes place (as I note in the earlier sidebar "The legal complexities of treatment for inmates"). The requirement to attend treatment may be implicitly or explicitly associated with how the person is dealt with in prison, such as the privileges they're allowed or their opportunities for parole. As a consequence, in some US states, possible interventions with prisoners are extremely limited, and it is assumed that the prisoners cannot give informed consent.

Handling constraints of confidentiality

A sacrosanct necessity of privacy and confidentiality exists in conversations between therapist and client, which can be compromised by legal necessities. For instance, when the client is an offender, the person may reveal incriminating information relating to past or intended criminal activity, yet this sort of information is precisely what a therapist needs to work with. If a prisoner indicates in therapy that they intend to commit a crime — for example, to kill someone — it's the therapist's duty to report it to the authorities.

Dealing with denial

STRANGE BUT TRUE

You may be surprised by how many people in prison claim to be innocent! I regularly receive letters from prisoners who claim that they were wrongly convicted, asking my help to reveal the truth. Whether they are innocent or not, a problem clearly exists when setting up any treatment scheme to help them if they deny any wrongdoing. Of course, many people who claim to be innocent simply refuse to enroll in any sort of therapeutic program; but where individuals are required to attend a program, and strong evidence exists that they were involved in the crime they were convicted of, dealing with their denial can be an important part of a therapeutic intervention.

This problem can be dealt with by exploring the reasons that the inmate believes they were convicted and then considering various interpretations of the actions that may have convinced others of guilt. This process can be harrowing for all concerned, but at least it may enable offenders to see their actions from other people's points of view and consider the circumstances that need to be avoided.

Needing to work around institutional constraints

Providing treatment programs in prison can be problematic because of conflicting demands from the institution, including these:

» A prisoner's sentence is too short to complete any designated program, so they refuse to start it.

» Disciplinary activity, for the individual or an area of the prison, may not allow them out of their cell to attend a session.

» Staffing levels or other management issues can mean that no one is available to supervise the prisoner's movements or the area where the program is being carried out.

» Other commitments, such as court attendance, visits, or demands of a job within the prison can prevent them from attending.

The great majority of prisoners, especially those serving short (six months or fewer) prison terms, may never be assessed or seen by psychologists (unless they do something bizarre or horrific), because the system can't cope with the logistics, and staff members aren't available to carry out the work.

Chapter **15**

Dealing with Violence

A lthough not the most common of offenses (fortunately!), crimes involving violence are the ones that cause people the most anguish. As a result, psychologists have devoted a great deal of attention to trying to work out why people are violent toward each other and what processes may help offenders reduce their violent aggression.

One central area of research is risk assessment: the challenge of predicting whether a person is likely to be violent again in the future. Psychologists have developed ways of making these predictions. They are quite effective if used carefully.

As well as examining risk assessment for violent offenders, in this chapter I distinguish two basic types of violence, describe treatment programs for anger management, and take a closer look at one particular, often violent, offense: stalking.

Investigating Two Different Sorts of Violence

Many different types of violence exist, as well as many different circumstances in which it can occur. In this section, I describe how psychologists distinguish between two general forms that differ in one crucial aspect:

>> **Instrumental violence** is physical aggression to achieve a particular purpose. This type is the calculated violence (or threat of it) that's used to control other people and make them do what the offender wants — perhaps to obtain money or to make them carry out acts they wouldn't otherwise do.

   Organized crime often keeps people within its networks with the use of this sort of violence.

   People who use violence in a calculated way are less likely to be responsive to treatment programs that focus on anger management and alternative ways of expressing fierce emotions.

>> **Expressive, emotional, or anger-promoted violence** is the explosive aggression that comes from a lack of impulse control, in which someone feels the need to lash out when challenged or frustrated. These hostile individuals are likely to act on their urges in other ways — for instance, by substance abuse, volatile casual relationships, or other aspects of personality disorder.

   These expressively violent people are the ones most open to receiving some sort of psychological help with their impulsive aggression, although their openness to treatment is by no means certain.

Programs to treat violent individuals need to explore which type of violence a person has exhibited in the past in order to ensure that any treatment offered is appropriate. Working out which type of violence someone indulges in isn't always easy, however, because in some subgroups, wearing your emotions (especially your anger) openly is a way of exerting control. In such cases, what may seem to be expressive violence may in fact be instrumental — the person develops a reputation for having a short fuse, which gives a power that wouldn't otherwise be possessed.

Considering the reasons for violent behavior

When thinking about violent behavior (and, particularly, ways to reduce or manage it), keep in mind these features of violent events:

>> Particular situations that may trigger violence, such as confrontations

>> Beliefs, such as the need to defend oneself against any insult

>> Emotional states, such as anger or depression

>> Personal goals that are seen to be assisted by violence

>> Inability to cope with threats or frustration in a nonaggressive way

>> Possibility of brain damage

>> Impulsivity and emotional extremes

>> Substances that reduce inhibitions, notably alcohol

>> Availability of weapons

Examining the situations in which violence occurs

Violence occurs in a variety of situations. The psychological implications of violence vary depending on the particular situation, which always needs to be closely considered:

>> **Brawls:** These commonly emerge from interpersonal conflicts between people in competition over a person or a resource. They can also be fueled by struggles for power within particular subgroups. The sometimes ritualistic threats between different gangs can spill over into violent gang fights as well.

All the people involved may display a similar degree of aggression. In these cases, who is the victim and who is the aggressor is an accident of timing or the use of a weapon. Things could have easily gone the other way.

>> **Domestic violence:** Sadly, violence takes place between those who share an intimate relationship in many different types of circumstances. This can be the consequence of one partner — typically, but not always, the man — being a violent individual who expresses his anger, jealousy, or frustration only in an aggressive way. His violence can also be coercive, as a way of trying to control aspects of the relationship, such as when the woman indicates she wants to leave him. (Check out the later section "Predicting domestic violence" for more on this subject.)

Situations do occur in which the woman is the violent partner. Most commonly, any violence from the woman is in self-defense, but aggressive women sometimes initiate violence. This event can be so unexpected that male victims of such aggression can have difficulty persuading law enforcement to take it seriously.

>> **Criminal coercion:** The use of violence as part of criminal activity *(instrumental violence)* can include street muggings, bank robberies, aggravated burglaries, and sexual assaults. In such cases, criminals choose to be violent or not. Some bank robbers, for example, insist that they ensure that the people in the bank are so afraid of them that the thieves don't have to assault them physically. (At least, this is their claim for why they carry a gun.)

Predicting domestic violence

The Spousal Assault Risk Assessment Guide (SARA) is a standard set of items that provides a checklist developed specifically to predict the likelihood of violence against family members or others. Tribunals and review boards use SARA when making decisions about individual cases. Its latest version, SARA-V3, is widely respected for assessing and managing the risk of intimate partner violence (IPV) across criminal justice, mental health, and victim services settings.

The guide has been translated into 15 languages now being used internationally. It uses a combination of structured professional judgment that combines information on these areas:

>> **Spousal assault history:** Considering violence that has occurred within the family in the past and the circumstances in which that happened

>> **Criminal history:** The number and nature of previous crimes that individuals have committed

>> **Alleged or most recent offense:** Careful consideration of the activities that brought the person to notice for the review

>> **Psychosocial adjustment:** Examination of how the person has related to others in a variety of situations and any indications of particular personality problems

Assessing the Risk of Future Violence

Legal and therapeutic processes contain many aspects that seek to determine whether a person is dangerous. The concept of dangerousness, however, is rather difficult to define, because it implies an all-or-nothing categorization. Instead, experts consider the *probability* that a person may be violent in the future. As a result, risk assessment has become a common activity for forensic psychologists.

(I mention risk assessment briefly in Chapter 5 as it relates to general reoffending, but such assessments are so fundamental to dealing with violent offenders that I consider the subject in more detail in this chapter.)

Forensic psychologists can be requested to produce predictions of the risk of future violence at many stages in the legal process:

>> **During bail hearings,** to decide whether a person is allowed out on bail or kept imprisoned while awaiting trial

>> **During sentencing,** to influence where an offender may be sent to serve a sentence or whether to be placed on probation or sent to prison

>> **During decisions about which treatment program to offer a person** or whether to insist they take part in one

>> **During decisions about release** or whether a person is eligible for parole from prison or other institutions

Using risk predictors of possible future violence

The risk of violence is higher for people who have one of these characteristics:

>> Are male; the great majority of violent crimes are committed by men

>> Experienced physical abuse as a child

>> Live in an area with high levels of crime and violence

>> Report violent thoughts and imagine violence in the future

>> Are found to have a high degree of anger

>> Have any previous history of violence or serious criminality

>> Have a history of substance abuse and dependence

>> Have a personality or adjustment disorder, such as those I discuss in Chapter 6

>> Have other mental disorders, such as schizophrenia are typically *less* likely to be violent in the community

>> Have hallucinations (as psychiatric patients) of voices commanding violent acts

The risk of future violence can be greatly reduced if any of a number of things happen to a person to change how they see the world and themselves. These *protective factors* include securing a satisfying job, forming a caring relationship, and having children. Certain sorts of mental illness, for example, in which a person suffers from delusions, can make the person so tied up in their own thoughts that they're not a danger to others, but may be a danger to themselves.

The details of a person's previous offenses are vital. If the violence erupted against particular targets or in certain situations, then understanding them and the person's views about them can be helpful in predicting future violence and in setting up any therapeutic treatment.

One particularly important predictor of violence is when an offender has a specific target in mind. If the person is angry or vengeful toward a particular individual and is willing to mention that fact, then the forensic psychologist must take that statement seriously. Plenty of examples exist where released offenders said that they would exact violent revenge and then did exactly that.

The risks of risk assessment

If, as a forensic psychologist, you're asked to say whether a person is dangerous, a great deal of pressure is on you to say, "Well, yes, I suppose so." After all, the individual's name hasn't been pulled from a hat at random, so some background applies to make people suspicious. If you say that the person is dangerous, people accept that statement, and the person is kept under observation, or even under lock and key, which may reduce the risk of them becoming violent. On one hand, if the person is then violent, you can say, "I told you so." On the other hand, if you say, "He's a nice person, and I'm sure we'll have no trouble with him" and later he acts violently, you look ridiculous, and someone else suffers.

The risk of the risk assessment being wrong is therefore much greater if you say that no risk exists than if you say risk does exist. Therefore, experts are quite cautious when making risk assessments and tend to err on the side of saying that the person does present a risk. Studies of how often people have been violent when it was predicted that they would be, have shown that far fewer were violent than was predicted. This either supports the notion that experts were overcautious or that a prediction of violence is a good way to reduce the chance of people being violent in the future!

Perhaps not surprisingly, then, many prisoners try to avoid contact with psychologists for fear they will undermine their request for parole.

STANDARDIZED RISK ASSESSMENT PROCEDURES

A number of standard procedures have been developed for assessing risk and are now widely used. Here are brief details of two of them:

The Historical/Clinical/Risk Management Scale (HCR-20) is particularly useful for considering people with psychiatric or personality disorders. It contains 20 questions relating to three main categories:

- **Historical:** The person's background and previous experiences
- **Clinical:** The person's attitudes to others and violence as well as any indication of mental disorder
- **Risk:** External risk factors such as housing situation and family support

The *Violence Risk Appraisal Guide* (VRAG-R) aims to predict whether a person will be violent if released into the community over a number of years. It covers 12 issues, including

- Alcohol abuse
- Elementary school maladjustment
- Present mental condition, especially any indications of psychosis or psychopathy

The appraisal guide assigns a person to one of nine categories, from category 1, indicating a low likelihood of future violence, to category 9, indicating the almost certain probability of violence within the following seven years.

Keeping people locked up to protect the reputation of experts is a serious matter, which is why recent moves have been made toward using objective assessment procedures like those I describe in the earlier sidebar "Standardized risk assessment procedures." Even though the procedures aren't foolproof, at least the basis of the decision can be seen to be honest and independent of the expert's subjective opinion.

Appreciating the difficulties of risk assessment

People with a propensity for violence are some of the most difficult individuals to deal with in regard to providing therapy or treatment. They're likely to refuse to participate in any assessment procedure. However, the procedures listed in the earlier sidebar "Standardized risk assessment procedures" can be completed without the person answering questions, drawing on records of their behavior, or talking to those who've dealt with them. Such an approach, however, isn't ideal. Any lack of cooperation and the consequent necessary degree of speculation involved need to be made clear in any reports.

Considering Various Approaches to Treatment

In this section, I take a look at some treatment programs for violent offenders that address anger issues and help reorient unhelpful personal narratives. As I state in the preceding section, people with violent histories are often reluctant to participate in any assessment process and are well-known for being challenging when trying to carry out treatment with them. Compared with other offenders, they

>> Are less determined or motivated to participate in any treatment program

>> Are less likely to show any effects of treatment

>> Are more resistant to what is being suggested in the program

>> Are more likely to be uncooperative in taking part

>> Have a higher rate of dropping out of treatment

One particularly tricky problem that has arisen in recent years is that some prisoners from certain religious groups consider that talking about their previous offenses is against their religion and so refuse to participate.

Managing anger

Treatment programs aimed at helping people manage their violent, angry outbursts typically work on certain key assumptions. The main one is that, although the person's emotional reactions may be difficult to alter, they can be trained to be in command of those reactions. The idea is that these people shouldn't let these strong emotions get the better of them, which can result in a violent outburst.

The treatment programs deal with aspects of violent anger that are open to change, taking into account the dynamic risk factors I mention in Chapter 5. These changeable factors include attitudes and associated ways of thinking about the individual's interactions with others. More static, unchangeable aspects of the person, such as their criminal history, although predictive of future violence, aren't a suitable focus for treatment.

Such treatment interventions often include

>> Showing the offenders how to relax

>> Getting them used to stress without allowing it to take over their whole feelings

This latter aspect includes getting them to recognize when their physiological arousal is building up, and how they can take account of their emotions and focus their attention in a more productive direction.

In addition to enabling offenders how to deal with stress and anger, psychologists question the beliefs that underlie the anger. This process includes examining how offenders interpret certain situations or people as hostile, looking closely at the consequences of their aggression.

The programs therefore combine both a direct examination of the actions and feelings that give rise to violence as well as challenges to thinking patterns that support their aggressive behavior. The central objective is to persuade the participants in the program that their way of acting and reacting in the past hasn't been productive for themselves or others. The idea is to make them accept that even if they believe they were right to feel and act the way they did, it didn't help them or other people. Other ways of behaving would make them more successful.

The following sections provide details about two specific anger management treatment programs one used in UK prisons the other in the US.

Controlling anger and learning to manage it (CALM)

The British CALM program is aimed at people — usually, men — for whom anger and associated violence are factors in current or previous offending.

CALM consists of 24 two-hour sessions, with groups of two to eight people, in which various stages of emotional response are examined and productive ways of dealing with them explored. The treatment is developed to teach and promote a lasting change of inappropriate and unproductive thought and behavior patterns by the use of these methods:

>> **Personal assignments,** which is homework designed to experience what's covered in the group

>> **Modeling,** in which individuals discover appropriate and inappropriate reactions

>> **Role-play,** to experience within the supportive context of the group how violent reactions can unfold and be calmed

>> **Teamwork,** which involves learning to work with others and accepting and providing support

>> **Self- and peer-evaluation** of progress over the course of sessions

The CALM program is so successful that UK courts may require an offender convicted of repeated assaults to participate in it, if the person is thought safe enough to serve a sentence in the community.

Cognitive Self Change Program (CSCP)

The Cognitive Self Change Program (CSCP) that originated in the US, is used in many correctional institutions across many states. It targets high-risk violent offenders and includes group and individual sessions. It equips prisoners with skills to help them control their violence and avoid reconviction. CSCP is aimed at offenders with a history of violent behavior and is suitable for those whose violence is emotional or calculated.

The program typically runs over six to eight months with two two-and-a-half-hour sessions each week. It consists of acquiring and demonstrating the ability to perform these four skills:

>> Paying attention to what and how offenders think in potentially violent situations

>> Recognizing when thoughts and feelings are leading an offender toward committing a violent or criminal action

>> Cultivating new thinking that leads away from violence and crime, which they feel is an acceptable way to think

>> Practicing using these new ways of thinking in real-life situations

Participants also have to prepare a Thinking Report in which they report objectively the thoughts and feelings they experienced during the commission of past offenses.

After a person finishes the CSCP, in some jurisdictions, they're encouraged to move into the Making Choices Program, which helps them make sense of how they came to offend. It teaches them to recognize points in their life where they could have made a different choice. It gives them skills to gain a better outlook on life and to think about positive aspects of themselves and their activities.

THE DANGERS OF A DESTRUCTIVE NARRATIVE

When 33-year-old Gavin Hall described in court how he fed his 3-year-old daughter antidepressants to make her drowsy before smothering her, he said that the two of them were just like Romeo and Juliet. This statement showed how, in his depressed state (which he said was brought on by his wife's infidelity), he drew on a well-known storyline to explain his actions to himself.

CSCP participants are helped to manage their emotions and situations better and improve their relationships as well as live a life free from crime. At the end of the program, they're asked to prepare a *safety plan* that identifies particular situations in the past in which they may have been prone to violence. They have to prepare details of what they'll do in those situations in the future to ensure that they don't act violently.

Reconstructing personal narratives

One innovative way of helping violent offenders change their way of dealing with others is to help them reconstruct their personal narratives. The idea is that all people see themselves as living out some sort of story built around the roles they lead — for example, being a supportive parent, conscientious shopkeeper, or gifted choirmaster.

These roles and their associated narratives evolve from the individual's experiences and interactions with other people. They're supported by memories, especially of key episodes and points in their history that signified changes to the unfolding plot (that is, their life story).

Many violent offenders see themselves as part of a *destructive narrative* in which their identity is defined by hitting out and other acts of violence. (Check out the earlier sidebar "The dangers of a destructive narrative.") They tend to think about and perhaps focus on past events that validate this view of themselves. This allows psychologists to persuade them to reconsider key episodes in their lives and interpret them in a new way to give them a different way of seeing themselves. The offenders are encouraged to reconstruct a more positive personal narrative, in which the violent character they had thought themselves to be no longer plays a role.

Managing Stalking

Stalking consists of unwanted attention over a period that gives rise to fear in the targeted person. In about half of reported cases, some physical act of aggression occurs. Unlike other crimes of violence, quite a high proportion of stalkers are women, perhaps as high as one in four. Stalking doesn't always include violence, but it certainly generates a fear of violence and can lead, in extreme cases, to murder.

Because of a number of high-profile cases that led to assaults, some countries introduced laws that make stalking a specific crime. The essence of the crime is that the targeted person is fearful because of the attentions of another person. In other words, it is harassment rather than "stalking" that's been made illegal.

In the UK, this was the Protection from Harassment Act 1997, routinely used against stalkers in England and Wales, with slightly different details in Scotland and Northern Island. The general prohibition against harassment doesn't require the law to define the behaviors that constitute stalking. If named actions were made illegal, then stalkers would just find other ways of harassing their victims.

REGIONAL TIP-OFF

In the US, a variety of laws are similar to the UK Harassment Act, which exist at both the federal and state levels. They vary from state to state, but broadly, they outlaw repeated, unwanted behavior causing fear or distress.

Here are some typical stalking behaviors

>> A high degree of inappropriate intimacy

>> Contact via various media, especially over the internet *(cyberstalking)*

>> Attempts at face-to-face contact

>> Overt or covert surveillance

>> Invasion of personal property

>> Intimidation and harassment

>> Threats and attempts at coercion

>> Direct aggression

Stalking can cover a great range of actions and continue over a long period — sometimes, many years. Some cases have lasted for 20, 30, or even 40 years! The act may include sending many different messages (by phone, letter, or email), unwanted presents, or directly watching the person targeted — even entering their house and stealing personal objects. Celebrities aren't the only people who are stalked, although they're particularly vulnerable to this sort of unwanted attention. But most stalking occurs when the victim has had some sort of previous relationship with the stalker, whether it is intimate or not. Some estimates indicate that as many as one in four women have had some form of continuous harassment from another person during their lifetime. Men can also suffer, with more than one in ten experiencing this type of harassment. Companies or other organizations can also become the target of stalkers who bombard their executives and managers with various missives.

The following aspects of stalking relate to the stalker's potential to become violent:

» Threats

» Substance abuse

» An earlier intimate relationship with the victim

» Personality disorder

» History of violent behavior

People who have a severe mental disorder are less likely to be violent stalkers than those who don't suffer from this problem, although those who are psychotic are more likely to stalk people with whom they have had no contact.

REMEMBER

Stalkers are typically men in their 40s known to have some established problem of relating to other people. They can be *serial* stalkers, moving on from one target to the next.

Don't confuse stalking with the sort of adulation that can come from a fan. Even a person as lacking in celebrity as I am receives the odd letter or another type of contact from time to time, out of the blue, from someone with whom I've had no previous contact, who wants to indicate their admiration of my work.

ANECDOTE

This behavior is quite different from the secretary who phoned me at home more than 100 times a day, demanding that I continue her employment after her contract ended. Only after I secured a court order to have her desist (under the Protection from Harassment Act mentioned earlier) was I able to hear the phone ring without experiencing immediate anxiety. The university eventually moved her to the department supporting the vice chancellor (the head of the university). She then started stalking him instead of me!

Trying to explain stalking

Different psychological processes seem to shape various forms of stalking:

>> **Obsessional stalkers,** who are the most common, tend to emerge from the breakdown of an existing relationship. The stalker feels demeaned and helpless and seeks to increase their self-esteem by demoralizing and creating anxiety and fear in the former spouse or partner. This behavior is often a continuation of domestic violence by another means, and wanting to control the victim even though they may no longer be together. A stalker who thinks that their victim is trying to remove themselves even further from their attempts at control may become even more violent. This type of stalking is most likely to lead to murder.

>> **Love-obsession stalking** takes place where the target is a casual acquaintance, such as a co-worker or neighbor, or even a celebrity the stalker has never met, with whom the person desires to establish an intimate relationship. This obsession can also stem from low self-esteem and depression. These stalkers believe that they'll be more significant if they establish a relationship with their desired target. They're likely to reinterpret any response, no matter how negative, as some indication of a desire for a relationship. Or they may resort to violence to gain attention from the victim. The most well-known example of this type of stalker is John Hinckley, who shot President Ronald Reagan in the belief that it would make the actress Jodie Foster love him.

>> **Erotomania** is a delusional state where the stalker believes that an intimate relationship with the victim already exists. These people usually have a serious mental illness, such as schizophrenia, and are unable to discern reality from the confused world in which they live. They're erratic and greatly troubling to their victims, but are typically more dangerous to themselves than anyone else. Margaret Ray is an example: For about ten years, she believed herself to be the wife of David Letterman, the talk show host, even thinking she had given birth to his children. She broke into his property on many occasions, was arrested driving his car, and sent him flowers and sweets. She eventually killed herself.

>> **Vengeance stalkers** don't want to form a relationship with their target — they want to change the behavior of others or just get revenge for what they regard as an insult and damage the person or organization that has caused them hurt. However, what turns their behavior into stalking is its obsessional quality, with a great deal of activity over a long period. A stalker who has some intellectual capability can become an expert on the target and ferret out many details that can be used against them, which can be enormously intrusive and disturbing. The stalker gains a feeling of significance and self-worth in the reactions that the stalking generates in the victim.

>> **Political stalkers** may consider themselves heroes who are taking on the might of an organization. Their constant challenge to individuals or groups whose activities or opinions they dislike gives them a sense of achievement and supports their view of themselves as involved in a just cause. They'd never consider themselves as being in the same class as the other types of stalkers listed here, but their incessant activity beyond the bounds of acceptable political debate and action brands them as disturbed individuals whose behavior owes more to their particular psychology than to the opinions they espouse.

Asking the question "Do stalkers ever stop?"

The great challenge of dealing with stalkers is that often they refuse to accept that they're doing anything wrong. They may see themselves as any other infatuated fan, or a lover whose target really wants to reciprocate, or a person on a mission to avenge wrongdoing or stop unacceptable activity. Almost invariably, stalkers have some background of relationship problems and in some cases are clearly mentally ill. These factors all come together to make stopping their stalking behavior quite difficult without addressing the more fundamental aspects of their personality that lead them to use stalking as a way of dealing with their challenges and frustrations.

REMEMBER

The key to stopping the stalking is the victim's refusal to give any indication that the stalker exists or that their actions have any significance. The overt and psychological objective of stalking is to obtain some reaction from the victim — perhaps an indication of the desire for a relationship, new or continued, or to show that the victim is suffering. If the stalkers can't have that effect, then they are more likely to move on to other targets.

STRANGE BUT TRUE

Of course, ignoring constant pressure from stalkers is extremely difficult, and victims may be tempted to try to reason with them. This attempt is almost universally pointless: Stalkers simply reinterpret the contact the way they want. It usually *fuels* their actions.

Unfortunately, a nil response can also lead to more aggressive or intrusive actions. In that case, the use of harassment laws to secure a court order may be the only way forward. In some cases, they succeed in persuading the stalker to desist. The stalker may find another love object to attend to.

Police intervention, such as arrest and conviction, has to be handled sensitively because it can make matters considerably worse, antagonizing the stalker and causing even more violent actions. If combined with some removal of access to the victim, then this type of intervention may be of help.

Sadly, removing the possibility of contact with the victim may require the target to physically move away from any area to which the stalker has access. This requires hiding the new location from anyone who may have contact with the stalker. That can be enormously disturbing and still leave the victim with the fear that the stalker may discover their new whereabouts.

Chapter **16**

Treating Sexual Offenders

S exual assault is particularly disturbing because it violates the most intimate aspects of the victim. Sexual crimes also raise fundamental challenges around attitudes held by various subgroups or within different cultures. Such problems are illustrated by the stark fact that in Western developed countries, until quite recently, the law didn't recognize rape in marriage. Even today, many countries in the world fail to accept that a husband's sexual assault of his wife is against the law.

In addition, male victims of rape in many countries still have difficulty getting the crime against them taken seriously. Also, as has recently been widely publicized, certain institutions, such as the Catholic Church and children's hostels, have hidden from public view — or even implicitly condoned — the sexual abuse of children.

These examples show that sexual assault is, probably more than any other crime, embedded in a set of norms and accepted values that are part of local customs and ways of life.

ME TOO MOVEMENT

Throughout history, in many places, sexual and related intimate violence against women has been tolerated or even encouraged. Sadly, that is still sometimes the case. However, in 2006 Tarana Burke coined the phrase *Me Too* to support survivors of sexual violence, especially women of color from underprivileged communities. This gave rise to a global social campaign against sexual harassment, abuse, and assault, particularly in the workplace. There followed an unprecedented widespread acknowledgment of the nature of sexual misconduct across industries — from entertainment and politics to academia and corporate sectors.

Me Too has reshaped public discourse on gender, power, and justice, encouraging a broader reckoning with inequality and the structures that enable abuse. As a consequence, awareness is growing:

- That these crimes have to be dealt with.
- That sexual offenders may benefit from special forms of treatment.

As with all such interventions, the starting point is a careful assessment to diagnose the individual's particular problems as well as the need for a prognosis, which amounts to a prediction of the likelihood of them offending again (in other words, risk assessment).

In this chapter, I give a brief introduction to the various types of sexual assault and their associated psychological aspects, and I examine ways of assessing the perpetrators. I also discuss several treatment programs and focus more closely on a particularly widespread yet problematic area: child sexual abuse within the family.

Defining Sexual Offenses and Offenders

Sexual offending integrates many psychological issues. It involves behavior and attitudes, aspects of the offender's personality, and ways of relating to other people. Unsurprisingly, therefore, sexual crimes are the ones that forensic psychologists have studied the most.

Many different types of sexual offenses and offenders exist. Being aware of this large variation is important because different types of offense require different forms of treatment (check out Table 16-1).

TABLE 16-1 **Varieties of Sexual Offense**

Type	Activity	Psychological Features
Child abuse	Can take many forms, within the family or with strangers; can be violent or seductive	Main sexual interest: children (pedophilia) Absence of a preferred partner
Rape	Adult male or female	Believes they have the right to sex (denies lack of consent) Angry wish to demean the victim Extreme desire for sexual gratification Sadism
Sexual murder	Usually, a female victim and often part of a series of crimes	Kills the victim so that she cannot testify Sexually aroused by violence Wishes for sex with a corpse (necrophilia)
Child pornography	This activity usually involves downloading (or creating) images of children involved in sexual activity. Ownership of sexual images of children, but not of adults, is illegal in most countries. The fundamental crime is creating the images; without their uptake by "customers" who acquire the images, they would never be created.	Sexual preference for children; often, does not want to have direct contact, sometimes is preparation for direct contact

In addition to the criminal sexual offenses listed in Table 16-1, a variety of sexual activities *(paraphilias)* are generally regarded as sexually deviant. Some of these are clearly illegal, and others, less so (see Table 16-2). Many paraphilias can be part of fantasy explorations between consenting adults. In some cases, they shape or cause a person to become involved in the illegal activities listed in Table 16-2 or other crimes that these desires engender.

TABLE 16-2   **Selection of Paraphilias**

Label	Description
Exhibitionism	Exposing genitals to a stranger, sometimes while masturbating, but with no attempt at direct physical contact
Fetishism	Can involve a wide range of nonliving items, such as boots or female underwear, to provide sexual arousal while holding or smelling the item or while the partner is wearing it
Frotteurism	Feeling sexual excitement from rubbing against a non-willing, or even unaware, person — usually, in a crowd
Sexual masochism	Sexual arousal from being humiliated, beaten, or bound, or being made to suffer, either self-inflicted or by a partner
Sexual sadism	Sexual excitement created by the physical or psychological suffering of a victim by domination or torture
Transvestite fetishism	For heterosexuals, arousal from cross-dressing as a woman (or, if not, possibly considered to be a transvestite but not fetishistic); not to be confused with transsexualism, in which the person wants to acquire the anatomical characteristics of a person of the opposite sex
Voyeurism	Gaining sexual excitement by watching people — usually, without their knowing — who are naked or undressing or having sex
Picquerism	Obtaining sexual pleasure from inserting sharp objects, such as pins or knives, into a victim

Assessing Sexual Offenders

To provide the most effective treatment *(intervention)* for offenders, psychologists explore their characteristics and aspects of their background relevant to their crimes. As with the assessment of violent offenders (which I discuss in Chapter 15), such assessments deal with static and dynamic factors:

>> *Static* factors relate to the fixed aspects of a person, who they are, and their offending history. These factors are most useful in estimating the probability that a person may reoffend in the future.

>> *Dynamic* factors relate to the person's interests, attitudes, and personality. These factors are particularly useful in determining appropriate treatment programs, as I describe in the later section "Managing and Helping the Sex Offender."

In this section, I examine the assessment of sexual offenders, including risk assessment, and take a closer look at particular issues surrounding rape.

Considering the risk of future offending

A number of standard procedures have been developed for assessing the risk of future sexual offending, almost invariably used with male offenders (even though women do commit sexual assaults), which is a crucial aspect of any consideration of what to do with a convicted offender. In this section, I summarize two widely used procedures.

Static-2002R

This procedure deals with those aspects of a person not likely to change their offending history:

>> Age at which to be released

>> Number of times previously sentenced for sexual offenses

>> High rate of sexual offending

>> Two or more victims under the age of 12

>> Any arrests as a juvenile for a sexual offense

>> Any convictions for noncontact sexual offenses

>> Any male victims

>> Any strangers as victims

>> Any breach of conditional release

>> Any convictions for nonsexual offenses

Sex Offender Risk Appraisal Guide (SORAG)

This procedure pays more attention to offenders' characteristics and the violence in their background:

>> Indications of psychopathy

>> Behavioral problems at school

>> Diagnosis of personality disorder

>> Age at time of most recent offense

>> Evidence of mental disorder

>> Alcohol problems

- >> Long-term intimate relationships (especially lack of them)
- >> Violent criminal history
- >> Deviant sexual preferences

REMEMBER

Risk assessments, of course, aren't foolproof. They give only general probability estimates that are based on samples drawn from the past of people who have been assessed and then followed up. Broadly speaking, these assessments predict correctly whether the offender will offend in the future in 60 to 70 per cent of cases. They don't get it right in all cases because they can't consider individual circumstances, such as a person losing a job, which may increase the risk, or finding a caring partner, which can reduce the risk.

Looking into the role of fantasies

Assessing offenders' fantasies is crucial to being able to assess these people effectively. Some sex offenders do seem to have particularly deviant fantasies and a strong desire to act on them. It has also been claimed that some sexual crimes are carried out in order to feed a fantasy. The proposal is that the person commits the offense in order to be able to draw on the experience for later private sexual gratification.

Although attempts to control offenders' fantasies haven't been successful in reducing the likelihood of their reoffending, identifying and assessing what the fantasies are can be useful in setting up other forms of intervention. The plethysmograph that I describe in the nearby sidebar "The penile plethysmograph" has been found to be helpful in this regard.

REMEMBER

Lots of normal, acceptable sexual contact between caring partners involves some sort of fantasy about the context of the activity or the person involved or the activities associated with it. In a high proportion of cases, these fantasies can include thinking about activities that may be considered paraphilias (refer to Table 16-2) or even violently deviant. Consequently, sexual fantasies in and of themselves can't be regarded as the reason for sexual assaults.

Reviewing the dynamic aspects of sexual offending

When assessing sex offenders, psychologists carry out a careful examination of their ways of relating to other people and their ways of making sense of the world that may be open to change. Many systematic assessment procedures are in use (see Table 16-3).

TABLE 16-3 Assessment Procedures Examining Dynamic Aspects of Sex Offending

Instrument	Purpose	Process	Context
Risk Matrix 2000	Actuarial tool to estimate the static risk of sexual and violent recidivism	Uses criminal history, age, and victim characteristics to classify offenders into risk categories	Probation, prison psychologists
RM2000/S	Sexual offending-specific variant of Risk Matrix 2000	Focuses on sexual offense history and victim profile to assess the likelihood of sexual reoffending	Probation officers, treatment teams
OASys (with sexual modules)	Structured assessment of likely causes of crime and risk factors	Combines static and dynamic factors; includes modules on sexual offending, motivation, and responsivity	Probation services, prison staff
RMS	Dynamic risk management tool for community supervision	Tracks changes in risk over time using protective and risk factors; supports active case management	Community probation officers

Inquiring into the motives for rape

Psychological assessments of sexual offenders and rapists focus on the aspects of the person that contribute to carrying out sexual assaults. They indicate enduring features of lifestyle as well as attitudes and beliefs.

REMEMBER

Many of the dynamic (changeable) components exist in people who don't rape and would never consider doing so. Psychologists have to explore a little more deeply the explanations that rapists give for carrying out sexual assaults.

The various reasons that offenders offer for raping tend to overlap and usually have their roots in rape myths (as I describe in the later "Rape myths" section), as well as limited empathy for the victims. These allow rape to be used as a weapon in many wars, harnessing propensities in some men to try to destroy a population regarded as the enemy. Some people even suggest that rape is an inevitable product of male dominance in society, a requirement for men to demonstrate their masculinity. This feminist view of rape sees such crimes as part of a general picture in which men attempt to keep women in fear as a means of maintaining control over them. This accords with the fact that the most rapes happen between acquaintances.

STRANGE BUT TRUE

The idea that all men are potential rapists is taken a stage further by *sociobiologists.* They claim that rape offers an evolutionary advantage for men, who can't have sex any other way, to pass on their genes. This bizarre notion doesn't explain why homosexual rape happens or why women may be involved in rape. Nor does it explain why some men in established sexual relationships still sexually assault other women.

Rape myths

One argument is that many people, mainly men, in Western societies hold views about rape that are conducive to sexual assault. Psychologists have even developed a Rape-Myth Acceptance Scale that asks people whether they agree or disagree with such statements as these:

>> If a drunken woman has sex with a stranger, then she's asking for other men to have sex with her, too.

>> It is a woman's own fault if she is involved in some mild sexual activity and she lets it get out of hand.

>> A woman who snubs men deserves to be taught a lesson.

>> Women subconsciously want to be raped.

Men who agree with many such statements would be expected to be more willing to participate in sexual assaults. Their attitudes are seen as drawing on a set of views prevalent in their subculture. Men who share these attitudes and who end up in treatment programs sometimes have great difficulty recognizing that what they did was rape. I remember one such man in a treatment program saying this: "Oh. If that's rape, I've done it quite often."

Sadism as an explanation of rape

Although sadism is regarded as a paraphilia (see Table 16-2), it's sometimes given as an explanation of rape when the person wants to be coercive in their sadistic activity. Those men (and some women) gain sexual gratification from hurting others and obtaining sex violently. They force their victims to have sex because of the pleasure they get from doing so.

These people are, fortunately, extremely rare, but they do make the headlines when they act on their disturbing impulses. They're likely to attack strangers and become serial offenders. They prepare for and plan their attacks, possibly gaining some gratification from anticipating what they're going to do.

Anger in rape

Some men develop a feeling for revenge against women — sometimes particular women or a type of woman. Their victims become substitutes for the people the rapist is angry with. Their anger may be fueled by alcohol or drugs and explode when a particular possibility occurs. The sex is a way of insulting the victim and so is likely to be violently aggressive.

Opportunity

Men who lack any sort of empathy or concern for the feelings of others may select victims simply because they spot the opportunity for forcing them to have sex. These men are often referred to as sexual predators, accosting a woman in a bar and then assaulting her if she refuses to have sex. Their violence is used to control the women, as opposed to playing any role in deviant fantasies or desires. They just want sex and then to get away. They may even mistakenly think that after they start carrying out their sexual activity, the woman enjoys the act and wants to participate.

REMEMBER

As with so many violent crimes, alcohol or drugs can reduce a person's inhibitions and their ability to control themselves. Even if that isn't the case, then perpetrators may use alcohol as an excuse, as in: "It was the drink that made me do it."

Power

Some men see rape as a way of demonstrating their power over women, usually a result of their own feelings of inadequacy and insecurity. They think of sexual conquest as an important way of demonstrating their control and significance. These views may be magnified by constant brooding on sex and developing fantasies of control and sexual prowess.

Managing and Helping the Sex Offender

The preceding section contains several possible explanations for rape, some more convincing than others. But the fact is that the great majority of men don't carry out sexual assaults and indeed find the whole idea abhorrent. Therefore, explanations that relate directly to an offender's particular background, upbringing, and related attitudes and personality characteristics are the most useful areas to investigate. These form the basis of most treatment programs.

The question of whether and how to treat (or, indeed, simply manage) sex offenders is a difficult issue. In this section, I examine some of the difficulties involved and describe some approaches to treatment now in use around the world.

Investigating the complexities of treating psychopaths

Unfortunately, little evidence exists that any of the therapeutic interventions I describe in the later section "Appraising some sex offender treatment programs" are particularly effective. They may help in some cases, but for many sex offenders, they are irrelevant or have little impact. As an extreme example of the difficulties involved, in this section, I illustrate the complexity of the processes that need to be explored when dealing with serial rapists and sexual murderers.

One notable case was that of Fred West. He killed at least ten young women and probably many more over a 20-year period without ever being caught. He and his wife, Rose, sexually and physically abused these young women before killing them and burying them in the garden of their house in Gloucester, UK. What would a forensic psychology assessment have revealed of Fred West if one had been carried out before he killed himself in prison?

An interview and study of West's actions would reveal he was almost illiterate and likely had learning disabilities. His behavior suggested he did not grasp the seriousness of his situation: when told a body was found under his patio, he worried only about replacing the paving. After admitting involvement in a murder, he asked to go home. A psychologist exploring his background would have found a highly sexualized upbringing. In a memoir written before his suicide, West described family sexual activity — including his father's abuse of West's daughter — without recognising it as wrong, presenting it as normal family life.

The crucial point is that West didn't seem to recognize the destructive quality of all the sexual activity within the family, taking it much more for granted than the great majority of people would.

Appraising some sex offender treatment programs

Treating sex offenders needs to deal with the many different aspects of their thoughts, feelings, and actions that contribute to their offending. This involves intensive and frequent contact with offenders in a supportive and open context, which can be quite difficult to achieve in a prison. Also, many sex offenders don't want to participate in such activities.

REMEMBER

Those offenders willing to participate in treatment programs may discover how to "fake being good." They master the vocabulary of therapy and know what to say without ever totally accepting the new attitudes and behaviors that society requires of them. But providing some form of treatment is better than leaving these people to rot in prison or letting them back into the community with no hope of rehabilitation.

The Good Lives Model (GLM) approach

Many sexual offenders come from dysfunctional families and have themselves experienced abuse. They've often been told that they're worthless. Their criminal offending may well emerge from a mixture of doing to others what's been done to them, as well as attempts to gain some feeling of significance.

In recognition of the extent to which offending can grow out of habits, and beliefs embedded in destructive, personal processes, one approach to therapy emphasizes enabling offenders to develop the skills to achieve a good life in an acceptable way, as also considered for violent offenders in Chapter 15. Rather than focus on the reduction of the risks of reoffending, this more humanitarian approach deals directly with helping to achieve positive aspects of life.

Central to this approach is the proposal that everyone, offender or not, seeks a number of primary features in their lives:

>> Autonomy

>> Community

>> Creativity

>> Freedom from stress

>> Friendship

>> Happiness

>> Health

>> Knowledge

>> Mastery of experiences

>> Meaning in life

REMEMBER

The good-lives treatment approach works with offenders to determine how they can achieve this range of positive outcomes in an acceptable and productive way. Achieving this aim is a tall order for people imprisoned because of despicable actions, which they themselves may abhor. With appropriate guidance, the approach offers an optimistic way of helping offenders.

The Risk-Need-Responsivity (RNR) Model approach

The RNR Model is a down-to-earth approach to intervention with offenders and deals directly with the issues that their offenses reveal:

>> **The more at risk of reoffending a person is (as indicated by the assessments I mention in the earlier section "Assessing Sexual Offenders"), the more intensive the treatment needs to be.** This process includes longer sessions over a longer period that deal more exhaustively with the cognitive and emotional aspects of the person's offending.

>> **Treatment focuses as directly as possible on the needs revealed in the assessment of the individual.** This approach deals with the dynamic risk factors that may be open to change, including attitudes and beliefs as well as sexual preferences.

>> **No aspects of the treatment program can work without a degree of responsiveness from the offender and the therapist.** The program requires the offender to be willing to participate and the therapist to be able to adjust the way the program is delivered to suit the individual. This will include adjustments that take into account the subculture and belief systems of the offender.

Sex offender treatment program (SOTP)

A detailed program for treating sex offenders is in use across prisons in the US and UK. SOTP emphasizes teaching offenders how to understand and control their thinking, feelings, and behavior. A range of versions of the program is available to teach a person how to adjust the activities in which he participates to suit his particular risks, needs, and priorities:

>> **Core program:** The treatment goals of this program include

- Helping offenders develop an understanding of how and why sexual offenses are committed

- Increasing awareness of the harm to victims of the offenses

- Developing meaningful life goals as part of a plan to prevent relapse

>> **Extended program:** This one is for high-risk offenders and covers

- Dysfunctional thinking styles

- Emotion management

- Offense-related sexual fantasies

- Intimacy skills

- Detailed consideration of how to develop adequate plans for relapse prevention

» **Adapted program:** Although the goals of this program are similar to the core program, the methods are adjusted to suit learning-disabled sex offenders across all risk levels. An adapted program is designed to:

- Increase sexual knowledge

- Modify offense-justifying thinking

- Develop the ability to recognize feelings in themselves and others

- Gain an understanding of victim harm

- Develop relapse prevention skills

» **Rolling program:** This program covers the same topics as the core program but with more emphasis on relationship skills and dealing with feelings of loneliness and abandonment.

» **Booster program:** This option is designed to provide an opportunity for offenders to refresh their learning in treatment and to prepare for additional relapse prevention and release work.

» **Healthy relationships program:** Especially aimed at offenders who are at risk of being violent to intimate female partners, it targets:

- Attitudes and beliefs that condone domestic violence

- Poor emotional control

- Deficits in social skills

- Anger or other reasons for offending

Taking a more direct approach: Chemical castration

On the assumption that sex offending is a product of heightened sexual proclivity and uncontrollable libido, from time to time, special medication has been administered to persistent sex offenders in order to reduce their sexual desires and greatly reduce their libido. In the US, it's voluntary in some states (for example, California, Florida, and Texas) and mandatory in others under specific conditions (for example, repeat offenses involving minors). This procedure has had some success in very specific cases.

MYTH BUSTER

If the sexual assault arises from anger, power, or feelings of revenge (issues I discuss in the earlier section "Inquiring into the motives for rape"), then this sort of "castration" can lead to the offender becoming violent and much more dangerous.

Dealing with Child Sexual Abuse in the Family

Around one out of ten adults report that they experienced some sort of abusive sexual contact as a child. The prevalence for women is somewhat higher than for men. The sexual abuse of children most commonly occurs within the family, although the perpetrators are also likely to carry out sexual assaults on people who aren't family members. The great majority of abusers are men, but as many as 1 in 20 is female.

Examining child abuse in the family

The disturbing fact is that many children are abused within the home and family. They suffer sexual or physical assaults a number of times, often by different people and over many years. This abuse typically occurs within an abusive family that is able to hide what they're doing from the authorities. Consequently, any disclosure of the abuse by the child to teachers, social services, or others is ignored. In contrast, a one-off assault by someone the child has little or no prior relationship with is more likely to be acknowledged by the child's caregivers and dealt with quickly, reducing its impact and ensuring that it doesn't happen again.

All types of abuse and neglect of children can leave their mark on them in many different ways:

>> Aggressive behavior

>> Antisocial activity

>> Emotional instability

>> Mental illness

>> Self-harm

>> Sexual assaults on others

>> Sexual dysfunctions

>> Substance abuse

>> Symptoms of post-traumatic stress

Unsurprisingly, given the far-reaching effects on the individual that such childhood abuse can cause, as many as three out of every four young people in prison have been abused or neglected when they were children. However, the resilience of young children is shown by the fact that as few as one in ten sexually abused boys goes on to commit sexual assaults later. The ones who do are usually the children who suffered multiple and varied assaults and neglect. Girls who are sexually abused are quite likely to become violent in later life.

Sexual child abuse is frequently associated with violence within the family, especially toward the child's mother. Therefore, any consideration of sexual abuse needs to take into account the possibility of many other forms of dysfunctional activity within the home. Abuse of alcohol and drugs is to be expected as part of this pattern, as well as a generally coercive and violent atmosphere. Relatives such as uncles, brothers, or cousins may also be party to extended sexual abuse.

Some good news is that many children survive physical and sexual abuse remarkably well, although others are psychologically and often physically scarred for life. Many factors influence how severe the effect is on the child:

» Whether the abuse involves direct contact or verbal abuse and a climate of acceptance of sex and violence

» The particular developmental stage of the child when maltreated

» The duration and frequency of the abuse

» How violently any victim resistance was dealt with

» Whether an abuse of trust is involved because of the close relationship between the child and the perpetrator

» If the child was listened to when telling about the abuse

» How helpful the support was from teachers, social services, police, or psychologists

Preventing child abuse in the family

Attempts to deal with sexual abuse within the family operate at these three levels:

» *Primary prevention* is aimed at the whole population and includes public awareness campaigns that emphasize zero tolerance. Useful programs within schools also deal with bullying and explain the difference between good and bad secrets to encourage children to report abuse. However, these aren't as effective as dealing directly with women and children to increase their self-esteem and empower them to disclose their concerns.

>> *Secondary preventions* are services targeted at families who are deemed to be at risk or in need of further support. This approach is most effective when it consists of a number of various agencies working together, including special child-protection units within the police, social services, probation services, and education and health authorities. Coordinating these various agencies in the interest of children at risk can be a complex and daunting task, though.

>> *Tertiary prevention* is the most common strategy and has some of the qualities of closing the stable door after the horse has bolted. It's a reaction to the discovery of abuse within a family, setting in motion procedures to prevent it from happening again and to punish or treat the perpetrator, or both.

This strategy has to deal with the possibilities of false allegations and the need to gain a clear and full account of what has been going on. It also has to manage the problems that arise from removing the perpetrator from a family, who may be the only breadwinner, and protecting the victims from reprisals by the perpetrator. The offender is likely to eventually be released from custody, so the challenge arises of how to manage his return into the community.

The treatment of offenders, as I describe in the earlier section "Appraising some sex offender treatment programs," is perhaps the most effective way of protecting children. If the risks of a person reoffending are low enough for that person to be managed within the community, a greater chance exists of his eventual rehabilitation. Without treatment, he's more likely to reoffend.

ANECDOTE

AUTOBIOGRAPHY OF AN ABUSED PERSON

Gypsy Boy is a remarkably candid and detailed account, written by Mikey Walsh, about the violence and sexual abuse he experienced as a child over many years. This abuse included regular beatings by his father and frequent sexual assaults by his uncle. When he tried to tell his father about these, he was beaten again.

A number of similar autobiographies exist. What's remarkable about all these books is that the authors invariably manage to survive their appalling childhood and seem to be able to lead healthy, well-balanced adult lives. This process is often a consequence of finding one or two caring people who believe their stories and support them. Publishing their stories undoubtedly helps their therapeutic process as well.

Chapter **17**

Working with Juvenile Offenders

The truth is that young people commit a majority of crimes (as I note in Chapter 4). Youngsters who commit a series of crimes are likely to develop into adult offenders if they aren't helped in some way. Understanding and dealing with young offenders is therefore a crucial basis for reducing crime now and in the future. In the great majority of cases, children and young adults become involved in crime because of their family circumstances, so the most effective procedures aimed at reducing juvenile offending are the ones based on working with families.

The various treatment interventions that I review throughout this chapter have been shown time and again to be more effective than institutionalization. But early intervention to reduce the chance of serious offending occurring is even better. Positive parenting programs and targeted interventions of children at risk are more powerful and, in the end, much more cost-effective than prison. The earlier a child reveals serious problematic behavior, the worse the risk is for future criminality unless interventions are carried out to help the child.

Most offending behavior occurs in adolescence, when people's identity begins to settle down as they explore what they can do and who they are. This crucial period is when minor legal infringements can be a passing phase or, more seriously, the start of a criminal career. What subsequently happens often depends on how minor crimes are dealt with. Stopping adolescent misdemeanors from becoming a habit of offending is therefore a major focus of many interventions with children and their families.

In this chapter, I investigate the main elements that can cause youth crime as well as some protective factors that reduce the risk of youngsters becoming offenders. I also examine the central role of parenting and the family, and for an extreme case of youth crime, I take a look at school shootings, particularly in the US.

Understanding the Cycle of Youth Crime

Half or more of prisoners reveal that they committed antisocial behavior as youngsters — typically, in their midteens. Their early delinquency set in motion a pattern of behavior that became a criminal lifestyle because it wasn't stopped. How this process can happen is the topic of this section. Crucially, these antisocial activities tend to be learned, condoned, or in some way influenced by the family or institution in which the youngster grows up.

Children who become habitual criminals are likely to have children who also become offenders, so the cycle continues (check out Figure 17-1). Anything that can be done to break this cycle is consequently of value for not only the individuals concerned but also future generations and their victims.

Despite all the evidence showing that a great deal of youth offending is rooted in the domestic circumstances of the child, and considering the ways in which the school and community can help to reduce any debilitating impact that results from those circumstances, a surprisingly large number of youngsters in many countries are still incarcerated. Taking them away from their criminal backgrounds may have some simple-minded appeal, but two-thirds of incarcerated young offenders reoffend within a year of their release. And they're the ones who are caught! Surely many others, when separated from nondeviant friends and people who could care for them, find out how to avoid detection while in prison.

REMEMBER

Locking youngsters up does nothing to deal with their difficulties in relating to other people, their low self-esteem, and all the criminal habits they've developed to help them cope with their often-difficult lives.

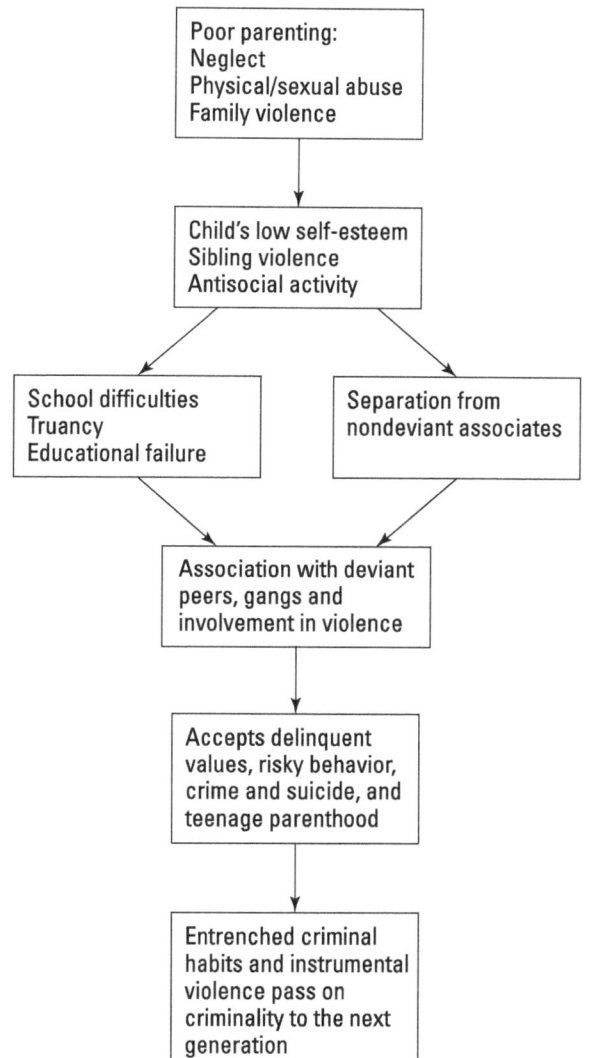

FIGURE 17-1:
The process that underpins the development of criminality.

Committing antisocial behavior that can lead to adult criminality

A child who exhibits three or more of the following attributes is at risk of becoming seriously antisocial as an adult:

» Breaking into buildings or cars

» Cruelty to animals

>> Cruelty to people, especially vulnerable people

>> Deliberate fire-setting

>> Destroying property — their own or others

>> Frequent truancy

>> Habitual lying

>> Running away from home overnight more than once

>> Stealing more than once

Although a family's attitudes and behavior are crucial for the development (or otherwise) of criminality in young people, the social and economic circumstances a child experiences can make matters better or worse. Children from large families with a low income or with unemployed parents or who live in poor housing are more at risk of becoming criminals. If the family unit has been broken in a distressing way through a messy divorce and a stepparent who doesn't relate well to the child, then this situation can also increase the prevalence of antisocial behavior in the child.

REMEMBER

When one or more members of a child's family have been convicted of a crime, the probability increases of the child also drifting into criminality. This probability increases further if the child isn't particularly bright and if schooling fails to deal with the problem and ignores the child. This situation can also result in the youngster leaving school early and so being even less equipped to gain an honest living. Some children don't engage with school but are shrewd enough to become effective criminals.

Examining causes of antisocial behavior within the family

Research has established a number of aspects of family life as being at the root of delinquent behavior:

>> Little involvement by the parents in the lives of their children

>> Poor communication within the family

>> Little feelings of attachment to each other and the related lack of family cohesion

>> Erratic discipline, which can be too harsh or too permissive, and which often varies from one parent to the other

>> High levels of conflict at home framed in anger

MYTH BUSTER

Sometimes, people (perhaps the parents) claim that a child "got in with the wrong crowd" — in other words, the child's friends and associates led them astray and are to blame. But a dysfunctional family life aggravates this process. When the relationship between the parents and child is poor — for example, with little interaction between them and when the interaction that does exist doesn't support the child and is full of conflict — it increases the child's search for significance among other children. In addition, the aggressive style of interaction characteristic of such families is mirrored in the child's interaction with peers, so that other children who aren't comfortable with that behavior reject the child. They then drift into contact with deviant children and, by this route, can find their way into drug and alcohol abuse, theft, and violent offending.

Dealing with delinquency

REMEMBER

As I describe in Chapter 4, males are more likely to commit crimes. Research reveals that boys who get involved in crime do so at a younger age than girls and that their crimes include violence much more often than they do for girls.

REGIONAL TIP-OFF

The high number of youngsters who carry out some sort of criminal activity is surprising. For example, Sweden isn't known for its high crime rate, but in one recent survey, over half the boys questioned, and only slightly fewer girls, admitted theft. Also, about one in five boys reported committing a violent offense, but fewer than one in ten girls.

In the US, gang culture is an important aspect of youth offending. Among 17-year-olds, about 1 of every 12 declares that they're in a gang; and of these, almost one in five reports having sold drugs and carried a gun. These young gang members appear to be responsible for a high proportion of violent and nonviolent offenses in the US. Gangs are active in all 50 states, with more than 33,000 gangs and more than 1 million members nationwide. Urban areas like Chicago, Los Angeles, and New York remain hotspots, but gang activity is found in suburban and rural regions as well.

Youthful offending appears to be rather common, but only a small minority of people who commit some sort of offense as youngsters go on to be criminals as adults. It is those who commit a number of offenses who are most likely to drift into a criminal career. The task for the authorities is to distinguish between those juvenile delinquents who are on a path to serious crime and those who are exhibiting youthful exuberance and impulsivity. Often, the difference lies in the family's reactions to the youngster's misdemeanors, as I emphasize throughout this chapter.

When thinking of children as criminals, the legal requirement of *mens rea* (the person knew what they were doing and that it was wrong; see Chapter 1 for more) has to be considered. This may mean the child can't be tried at all or that, in serious crimes, they have to undergo a process quite similar to the one adults experience. Then *mens rea* becomes a crucial part of the trial and can be difficult to establish with a young person. The individual may be unable to express thoughts or feelings clearly or even to have an effective understanding of what has gone on, and may be confused by the questioning process.

Many jurisdictions therefore have a blanket assumption that children below a specific age can't be regarded as being responsible for their actions. The curious fact is that this age of criminal responsibility varies considerably from place to place (and some countries don't bother to even specify an age). Some countries have ages that vary (the US age ranges from 6 to 12 years old across different states, and Iran shows a sexist attitude by using 9 years old for girls and 15 years old for boys).

REGIONAL TIP-OFF

Here are some ages of criminal responsibility in a few countries, from lowest to highest:

>> 7 years old: India

>> 8 years old: Kenya

>> 10 years old: England and Wales

>> 11 years old: Turkey

>> 12 years old: Scotland, Israel, and Japan

>> 13 years old: France

>> 14 years old: Austria and China

>> 15 years old: Sweden

>> 16 years old: Portugal

>> 17 years old: Poland

>> 18 years old: Belgium and Brazil

Focusing on a distinct group: Child sex offenders

Child offenders who commit sexual offenses — such as sexual harassment, child molestation, and rape — are a separate group of young criminals. Youngsters in their mid- to late teens or younger commit perhaps as many as one in four of these sorts of crimes.

A YOUNG PERSON RECEIVES A LIFE SENTENCE

STRANGE BUT TRUE

In 1999, Kathleen Grossett-Tate was babysitting 6-year-old Tiffany Eunick along with her 12-year-old son, Lionel Tate. Not long after Kathleen went upstairs to rest, leaving the two children alone together, Lionel disturbed her to say that Tiffany had stopped breathing. She was indeed dead. He said that he had been showing her "professional wrestling moves" — he was about four times larger than Tiffany.

The prosecution claimed that Tiffany's injuries were so brutal that they couldn't have occurred as Lionel claimed. He was convicted and became the youngest person in the US to be sentenced to death. He won an appeal against the conviction on the grounds that his competency to stand trial hadn't been assessed for his initial trial. However, his subsequent criminal activity, including holding up a pizza delivery man with a gun, led to him being sentenced to 30 years in prison in May 2006.

BOOT CAMP FAILURE

One approach to trying to rehabilitate juvenile offenders, favored by many conservative politicians, is known as the *boot camp*. This idea follows the model of basic training in the military. The youngsters assigned to these places are forced to live a highly regimented life. They arise early each morning and have plenty of drills and exercise with harsh discipline, rigid codes of dress, and frequent admonishments to ensure that they follow camp rules.

The idea is that these children simply need some firm authority and a healthy lifestyle to refrain from antisocial behavior and criminality. However, studies of the effects of these regimes show that, although most inmates obey the rules while in the boot camp, these institutions have no lasting effect. They don't deal with the underlying psychological problems that lead to delinquency in the first place. All society ends up with is fitter, more athletic criminals!

Male and female juvenile sex offenders tend to be rather different from other sorts of young offenders. They often exhibit sexually abusive behavior at a young age; some of their victims are male, and they often have had a number of different victims. Lack of social skills can be an important aspect of their offending, as well as low intelligence, but a family history of sexual abuse is also often present.

Don't confuse sexually abusive children with youngsters taking part in natural childhood explorations of sexuality. The "I'll show you mine if you show me yours" games of early childhood can be healthy if limited and under control, and not turned into some desperate secret that then produces tremendous adult disapproval. Discovering what's private and what's for public display is a natural part of child development that needs to be handled sensitively.

Looking into the criminal careers of young offenders

Not all young offenders set out on a criminal career in the same way. This has been demonstrated by a major study carried out over many years by (the late) David Farrington and his colleagues at Cambridge University, UK. They followed youngsters from their early years to see which of them became involved in crime, how they did, and why. Their different journeys to becoming adult criminals help to clarify the nature of their criminal behavior and the likely progress it may follow:

>> **Early-starter persistent offenders:** The teachers of these youngsters often recognize when they are 8, 9, or 10 years old that the child is already on a path to criminality. By the age of 10, a few children already show serious signs of deviance (as I describe in the earlier section "Committing antisocial behavior that can lead to adult criminality"). If these children aren't helped, then they go on to extensive criminal careers and may spend a large portion of their lives in prison.

>> **Offenses limited to adolescence:** Some youngsters drift into deviant peer groups in their midteens, and their criminal activity fades as they move into their mid-20s, being limited to trivial crimes (mainly drug-related). They become isolated from their criminal friends, finding a noncriminal lifestyle through work and entering into a caring relationship and starting a family.

>> **Serious offenders of limited duration:** A crucial period exists in people's mid-20s when some can become involved in serious crime. This period can even include murder, despite them having no previous history of significant violence. This behavior seems to be part of what may be called late adolescence, in which a person is trying to make sense of who they are. Often, these people are capable but for some reason failed at school. By their early 30s, they may have found themselves and dropped out of criminality or ended up in prison or committed suicide.

Recognizing Protective Factors: The Good News

The great majority of children from vulnerable backgrounds don't become criminals. Many factors can protect youngsters from the potential impact of debilitating circumstances. For example, they may be poor but well cared for by their parents, or a stepparent may be delighted to take on a supportive parenting role. Even if these cases don't apply, children may find someone who cares for them outside their immediate family, such as a grandparent or teacher. They may discover success in some areas, such as sport or music, which gives them a feeling of healthy self-esteem and provides opportunities that take them away from delinquency and deviant friends. Inherent personality aspects that include lower impulsivity and more self-reliance can also reduce the impact of negative environmental factors.

REMEMBER

Protective factors can be enhanced by various activities set up specifically to generate contact with people whom the child senses care about them, and who engender feelings of self-confidence and achievement. Examples include after-school programs of positive activities. Scouting is an obvious example, but other activities such as youth clubs, sports organizations, and orchestras or bands, or mentoring projects in which an adult gets to know and support the child on a one-to-one basis, have all been found to help children who may be vulnerable avoid drifting into criminality. Trained foster caregivers are a more intensive and highly effective way of taking mentoring a step further.

Working with parents and families on such concepts as literacy skills or with reading schemes also helps give the child some feelings of achievement. Tackling school truancy directly and tackling why a school is excluding pupils also provides positive support that can counteract youngsters' potentially destructive experiences.

Keeping Things in the Family: The Central Importance of the Home

The most effective treatments to reduce delinquency and later criminality are those that work with the whole family (as I describe in this section). Importantly, these approaches keep the child in question at home and in the community so that any interventions are integrated into their daily life. As a result, they avoid the many problems associated with institutionalizing the child, including any deviant changes in behavior that have occurred in the institution being transferred to the world outside.

Family-oriented approaches see the child as being part of a system of activities, feelings, and attitudes. For this reason, they're often called *systemic* therapies. They explore not only the troubled individual's characteristics and problems but also the dynamics within the family and any problems that parents and siblings may be facing.

Parenting wisely

In this section, I take a look at two approaches to improving the parenting of problem children. One is often referred to as *wise parenting.* Many child developmental psychologists have provided guidelines that advocate sensitive, evidence-based approaches to being a parent.

REMEMBER

A central idea behind wise parenting is that many of the problems the family faces can be reinterpreted to form the basis of positive, productive activity rather than negative, disturbing concerns. For example, if fights between children are seen as a problem, then parents can instead think of them as being a product of jealousy, boredom, or a desire for attention. Dealing with conflicts as signs of such issues allows parents to deal with the issues effectively, as opposed to just shouting at the children and making matters worse. The other central principle of wise parenting comes from the significant work of the psychologist B. F. Skinner, which was mainly conducted on pigeons but nonetheless provides a simple and direct piece of guidance for many aspects of human behavior.

Skinner's central notion is that punishment doesn't make people behave better — it just suppresses the actions that are punished. To encourage people to do the right thing, they need positive support and encouragement for any steps they take along the way toward doing what's required. An illustration is that if a child is regularly late for school, shouting at the child is less likely to have an impact than finding out the stages that lead to lateness, such as going to sleep so late that there's difficulty rousing them in the morning. Encouraging the child to go to bed earlier, and being rewarded for that, even if initially this approach doesn't lead to being on time at school, is a step in the right direction.

Here's a brief summary of the stages in a wise parenting process to show how these principles can be put into practice. Essentially, four stages take place in each meeting with the family:

1. Building rapport and trust with the family by relating to their daily concerns and experiences

2. Establishing goals of what the family wants to achieve

3. Reviewing any successes in achieving initial changes, however small, so that the family begins to feel that the process is having some effect

4. Identifying parenting skills that can be developed and tried out between the sessions with the therapist

These stages are repeated at every meeting with ever more intensive consideration of the goals and problems the family is facing, as well as developing the skills needed to achieve the goals. These skills include both the ability to make sense of the behavior of the children and the parents, and the social skills of managing conflict and dealing with heightened emotions.

Of particular importance in wise parenting is helping the family as well as their children make effective use of schooling, including

>> Minimizing criticism of schoolwork and increasing the children's confidence in what they're doing at school

>> Setting in motion good homework habits around a regular, cooperative routine

>> Setting clear limits on what's acceptable, which are agreed on within the family

>> Communicating effectively with teachers

Family therapy

To illustrate, here's an example that demonstrates the value of family therapy in practice in the case of delinquent behavior.

Sixteen-year-old Laurence was referred to for family therapy by the juvenile court after being convicted of theft for the third time. He was known to be active in a gang and involved in fights after school. But the court thought that a greater chance of his rehabilitation existed outside of an institution. His stepfather was disabled and looked after the house, and his mother had a full-time job in a nearby factory. His sister, Louise, was 14 years old and seemed to avoid getting into any trouble.

Over three weekly meetings, family therapists established that little listening was taking place within the family, and a readiness existed to blame each other. Small problems weren't resolved, so they blew up into major rows. Laurence dealt with this situation by running out of the house. Louise stayed in her stepfather's good graces (and was obviously his favorite) by reporting on Laurence's misdemeanors. No effective monitoring was undertaken of either child's behavior, even though the parents complained about this problem.

Over the following five weeks, the therapists dealt with the family's resistance to talking and listening to each other. They pointed out that the parents' lack of consistent support for appropriate behavior in the children reflected their own experiences when they were growing up. The parents were told that Laurence obtained feelings of significance and respect from his friends that he didn't receive at home. Each of these debilitating actions identified within the family was examined to show that a positive opportunities existed if they were used only to encourage good behavior rather than punish bad. For example, Louise's reporting on Laurence was presented as wanting parental approval, but she could also achieve that approval by reporting any good things Laurence did.

After the family began to accept the reexamination of what was going on, they were trained in various skills to help them communicate and deal with anger and conflict. They were encouraged to rehearse these skills in the presence of the therapist and then to try them out as "homework" before the next therapy session. Follow-up sessions a couple of months later showed that far less conflict was occurring in the family and that they had the capability to resolve future difficulties.

Bringing all the groups together: Multisystemic therapy

Working with the family is central to any treatment program, but psychologists can't focus on the family in isolation. *Multisystemic* is a technical term for an approach to helping juvenile delinquents that works with all the groups of relevance — friends and associates, family, school, and broader aspects of the society with which the individual has contact. Multisystemic therapy has a number of key principles:

>> **Understanding the context:** This is the need to assess how the identified problems relate to the family, friends, school, and community of which the child is a part. Determining the ways in which any successes with the child interact with these contexts is also important.

>> **Concentrating on strengths and other positive aspects of the people and their circumstances:** Effective and capable aspects of the child along with access to protective factors can set in motion important changes. The strengths in the family provide opportunities that the family already knows how to use — building feelings of hope, identifying protective factors (see the earlier section "Recognizing Protective Factors: The Good News" for more), decreasing frustration by emphasizing problem solving, and enhancing caregivers' confidence.

>> **Taking responsibility by all those involved:** Interventions are designed to promote responsible behavior and decrease irresponsible actions, by not only the child at the core of concerns but also all family members.

>> **Focusing on the here and now and what can be done about it:** Actions are sought that can be taken immediately, targeting specific and well-defined problems. Such interventions enable participants to track the progress of the treatment and provide clear criteria to measure success. Family members are encouraged to work actively toward clearly defined goals. This focus contrasts with traditional approaches that spend lots of time looking into the past and assessing its impact. Examining what can be done now with a view to future implications is a different strategy.

>> **Unpacking the sequence of actions that gives rise to problems:** Unwanted behavior typically emerges out of a sequence of events. This sequence needs to be identified and interventions introduced that target specific aspects within and between the various facets of the adolescent's life — family, teachers, friends, home, school, and community.

>> **Ensuring that interventions are appropriate to the stage in development:** Children of the same age may be at different levels of maturity. Any interventions therefore need to fit the child's developmental needs. This requirement stresses building the adolescent's ability to get along well with peers and acquiring academic and vocational skills that promote a successful transition to adulthood.

>> **Encouraging continuous effort:** Interventions require daily or weekly effort by family members so that the youth and family have frequent opportunities to demonstrate their commitment. Advantages of intensive and multifaceted efforts to change include more rapid problem resolution, earlier identification of when interventions need fine-tuning, continuous evaluation of outcomes, more frequent corrective interventions, more opportunities for family members to experience success, and giving the family power to orchestrate their own changes.

>> **Evaluating and being accountable:** Intervention effectiveness is evaluated continuously from multiple perspectives with support in place to help overcome barriers to successful outcomes. Everything possible is done to avoid blaming the family for any lack of progress. Responsibility for positive treatment outcomes is placed on the team supporting the therapy.

>> **Working toward positive accounts now and in the future:** All interventions are designed to enable the family and those associated with the child to be effective and successful in producing positive outcomes. The family must be able to maintain any gains during therapy after the support team withdraws.

All this is a tall order and quite expensive, especially if many different agencies and well-qualified experts are involved. But it's much cheaper than dealing with the consequences of crime, keeping offenders in prison, and all the fallout effects within society.

Going Back to School: Investigating School Shootings

An especially disturbing example of juvenile violence is when killing occurs in schools. The horrific shooting of many students in one spree captures headlines around the world, such as Columbine High School in Colorado in 1999, where two boys in their midteens killed 12 students and a teacher, and Jokela High School, in Finland, in which an 18-year-old killed 9 people in 2007. Although these events are rare, they do seem to emerge in spates after a particularly bloody incident, particularly in the US. In 2025, there were more than 50 such shootings in the US, most involving youngsters as the shooters.

The destructiveness of these rampages doubtless owes something to the availability of firearms to youngsters, but as in spree killings committed by adults (mentioned in Chapter 6), school shootings almost invariably end in the death of the perpetrator(s). Therefore, they have to be considered as a form of extremely violent suicide, and their roots are likely to be similar to the roots of many suicides: despair, anger with those nearby, and a desire to leave the world in some significant manner that sends a message.

REMEMBER

Any attempts to summarize a complex psychological issue, with many variations between individuals, aren't to be drawn on without careful consideration of particular persons and their context. The vast majority of youngsters who experience insult and isolation from others don't get hold of guns and seek to kill their schoolmates.

Broadly speaking, the following indications are common characteristics of those youngsters who carry out school shootings:

>> **Someone is likely to have been told about the intention to carry out the attack.** In three out of four incidents, the attacker(s) told a friend or sibling of the plans. This shows the sorts of thought processes growing out of personal narratives, which I discuss for other violent offenders in Chapters 4 and 6.

- **A plan of attack nearly always exists.** They're rarely impulsive acts, which means that careful surveillance can reveal aspects of this preparation.

- **These spree killers have access to often high-powered weapons.** In most cases, they obtain guns from their own home or a relative. This shows that the family context, as with all young offenders, is relevant.

- **Some explicit or implicit support from friends or schoolmates is often present for the idea of the attack, if not for the actual shootings.** The power of the peer group in influencing youngsters is present here as in other delinquent behavior I discuss earlier in this section.

- **Many perpetrators have experienced bullying and harassment.** This is true although no characteristic profile for the typical school shooter exists, because they differ from each other in many ways.

- **Early warning signs often indicate that the individual needs help, if the signs can be spotted and interpreted.** This can be talk of suicide or general anger, as described for violent offenders in Chapter 15.

REMEMBER

Two issues emerge as central to juvenile offending. One is the significance of the family. It's rare to find prolifically criminal young offenders who have not experienced various forms of dysfunctional family life. The other is the power of schooling. Ineffective, unsupportive educational establishments fail to provide the protective factors that can overcome family and peer group influences. They may even aggravate the impact of the circumstances that support a child's criminality.

6

The Part of Tens

Forensic psychology is a professional activity, constrained by legal and ethical and practical boundaries. The activity itself is carried out by people who undergo many years of training. This part gives some examples of the stages in becoming a forensic psychologist and the principles by which its practitioners are bound. I give examples of cases that illustrate some of the matters I discuss earlier in this book. This part draws heavily on my own experiences over the past quarter of a century in training forensic psychologists and providing consultancy in many different legal situations.

Chapter **18**

Ten Professional Requirements for Forensic Psychologists

Forensic psychologists in fiction are often portrayed as gung ho characters who totally ignore the ethical and legal constraints of the profession — no doubt, the everyday realities are likely to slow the story down. But if you employ or have to challenge a forensic psychologist, you need to make sure that they're following the rules and not stepping outside their professional remit. Or, if you're an aspiring forensic psychologist, you need to be aware of the scope and boundaries of professional practice. In this chapter, I look at some central rules and principles guiding the work of forensic psychologists.

Providing Evidence for the Court, Not the Client

You may think that he who pays the piper calls the tune, and that if you're hiring a forensic psychologist as an expert, that person is accountable to you. But as with many aspects of the legal world, the one who foots the bill doesn't necessarily control the proceedings.

In the UK, a defendant can pay for an expert out of their own pocket or from legal aid; the expert can also be employed by The Crown (the State) or in civil cases, by the plaintiff.

MYTH BUSTER

When an expert gives evidence, the legal requirement is that the expert is a neutral advisor to the court and not a servant of whoever's paying the bill.

Contrary to what you see in TV and films of courtroom dramas, and from reports of legal cases, the expert is there to serve the court, even though attorneys may try their utmost to make sure the expert gives the necessary evidence to support their case.

One consequence of the attorney only presenting evidence to the court that supports their case I have experienced in a number of cases I have advised on, and colleagues have reported similar events: The attorneys ask for a report for which (eventually) I will get paid, but then the report isn't presented in court, because the attorney doesn't think it will help the client. I am doing my job of producing a report for the court. But the attorney doesn't want the judge or the jury to see my report. I am thanked for my services, but what I have written is quietly filed away.

Securing Ethical Approval for Research

Before starting on a piece of research, the forensic psychologist writes a research proposal. Most Western countries require any research proposals for any discipline to be vetted by *ethical committees* (particularly if the research deals with people or animals), made up of those experienced in the type of research but who are often also members of the public or representatives of client groups.

Ethical committees have many areas of concern, including the need to obtain:

>> **Informed consent:** Making sure that anyone taking part in the research knows the purpose of the research and how it affects them. Whenever you

take part in a study, you're asked to sign a consent form to show that you fully understand and agree with the objectives of the research.

>> **Privacy:** Making sure that the results of the study and the records kept of what people say or do maintain suitable levels of confidentiality and anonymity. Ensuring privacy means that people's responses can never be used for purposes other than the research, and that people can't be embarrassed or otherwise discomforted by what they said or did in the research process. Maintaining privacy includes destroying the records of the raw information collected when the research is over.

>> **Safety:** Making sure that no one is physically or psychologically hurt or abused during the research.

Following Codes of Practice

Members of a professional body usually work within a well-established code of practice (the rules) of the organization. The American Psychological Association refers to this as *Ethical Principles of Psychologists and Code of Conduct.* It is comprehensive and detailed, forming a substantial tome. Other professional bodies around the world have similar, though less extensive, lists of do's and don'ts (usually, more don'ts than do's).

Such Code of Conduct relates to a wide range of matters, from the need to declare conflicts of interest — for example, a commercial interest in the results of an experiment — to avoiding compromising relationships with clients (even though fictional forensic psychologists can't seem to help falling in love with suspects). Staying up-to-date with developments in the relevant subject areas, called *continuing professional development* (CPD), is a requirement that's usually included.

Avoiding the Ultimate Question

I talk about what the court expects of the experts in the earlier section "Providing Evidence for the Court, Not the Client." But experts also have to bear in mind a crucial issue that may be a little surprising: being careful not to steal the court's thunder. Stating an opinion can be particularly problematic for forensic psychologists because their evidence isn't usually the hard evidence that, for example, forensic scientists may offer.

Forensic psychologists are commenting directly on the character of the accused, the mental state of the defendant, the reliability of testimony, or other aspects of the person involved. Therefore, they're dealing directly with the opinions that the judge or jury form of the defendant.

Experts can all too easily slip into offering an opinion that implies guilt or innocence. The expert's statement can appear as an indirect, corroborative opinion, such as stating that a key witness couldn't possibly have remembered what they claim to remember, or the statement can be more direct, such as whether the defendant has the intellect or skills to carry out the crime. If the jury accepts the expert's opinion, that amounts to the expert making the crucial decision about guilt. Judges don't like that subversion of the court's role and therefore try to avoid letting the expert be so direct.

Consequently, experts in court have to be cautious about how their opinions are expressed. This situation is well understood in forensic science, when experts say, for example, that the blow to the head is "consistent with that produced by a blunt instrument," even though everyone knows that a piece of lead pipe lies at the heart of the case. For forensic psychologists, however, avoiding the direct implication of their opinions may be more difficult. But if forensic psychologists sail close to the ultimate question of innocence or guilt, such as saying that what is known about memory is incompatible with the claims of the witness, the judge is likely to keep such opinions away from the jury in order that the trial is truly a trial by jury and not a trial by expert.

The judge reviews the evidence to be presented to the jury and other legal aspects of the case in what's known as the *voir dire* (an investigation, in the course of the trial, into the truth or admissibility of evidence about to be given without the jury present). If the judge considers that the forensic psychologist's opinion is one on which the jury may be able to form a view without expert advice, or that the expert advice may be too close to the ultimate question, the forensic psychologist's statement isn't allowed. As I mention earlier (in the earlier section "Providing Evidence for the Court, Not the Client"), the judge is also careful to ensure that the expert is offering an objective opinion supported by professional expertise and is not just a someone who has been hired to give the opinion the attorney require.

Working within Your Area of Competence

Despite what crime-drama psychologists get up to on TV — interrogating suspects in dark alleys and impatiently charging into dangerous locations in front of armed police — in real life, codes of practice emphasize the importance of the professionals having the necessary skills, training, and qualifications to practice particular aspects of their profession. Professionals need to know what areas are outside of their competency level, even though many people may assume they have the knowledge, skills, and training to operate in those areas.

Competency in carrying out the job may seem obvious — the thought of having a leg amputated by a furniture restorer is scary — but within forensic psychology, the precise boundaries of someone's competence for a particular case can be subtle. Even if forensic psychologists themselves are clear regarding where their competence lies, the people who employ them may not be, introducing pressures that aren't always easy to avoid. Lawyers in particular often have a limited understanding of the precise nature of forensic psychology, and the various skills that different aspects of forensic psychology require, how it differs from psychiatry, or even criminology, and what the various specialisms are within the different professions.

ANECDOTE

Once, despite being clearly listed as a forensic psychologist, I was asked by an attorney to carry out an examination of a rape victim to determine whether an assault had taken place. I have no medical qualifications and therefore have never been trained in how to carry out a medical examination.

This extreme example serves to illustrate how readily experts can be drawn into areas in which, well, they're just not expert. In such situations, I take the opportunity to point out to the legal profession the difference between the disciplines and the various qualifications needed to be competent to carry out the job.

A subtle example is when a forensic psychologist is giving advice to a family court on the likelihood of abuse occurring if a child is returned to their parents. The advice may be based on talking to the child and careful examination of the parents, their background, and any offence history. During the course of the proceedings, the forensic psychologist may be asked whether the information from certain witnesses is likely to be accurate. However tempted the forensic psychologist is in wanting to assist the court, if that person hasn't studied the research on witness testimony or had the opportunity to examine carefully the claims of the witness, there has to be an acknowledgment that offering an opinion on the matter is beyond their competence.

Submitting Peer Review

How can busy professionals be sure that they're conforming to their code of practice (check out the earlier section "Following Codes of Practice") and staying within the bounds of appropriate competence? The answer is to do as the contestants do on the quiz show "Who Wants to Be a Millionaire?" and phone a friend — consulting with colleagues is a practice called *peer review*.

Peer review involves a set of experts in the same field, but not directly involved in your work, considering what you're proposing or writing and then evaluating your work in the light of what they know and understand.

Peer review is standard practice for evaluating research grant applications and is at the heart of the work of ethical committees (discussed in the earlier section "Securing Ethical Approval for Research"). The process is also used for assessing research work being submitted for publication in academic and professional journals.

Of course, peer review isn't a foolproof system and is open to misuse. Most notably, peer review can stifle innovation, for example, when established experts believe that the proposal threatens their own livelihood or simply feel uncomfortable with the proposal's implications.

Nonetheless, peer review greatly reduces the possibility of professional abuse by making sure that individuals in the profession avoid drifting into areas of activity in which they risk being incompetent — or worse. The process limits the impact of arrogance and egotism and can save experts from being inappropriately self-confident.

Also, the peer review process needs to consider the confidentiality central to any reports prepared (see the later section "Respecting Confidentiality"). Reports for the court are confidential until the judge agrees that they can be made public.

Having a Duty of Care

Forensic psychologists deal with people and how a person is thinking and behaving. Unlike the forensic scientist examining fibers or carrying out autopsies on dead bodies, the forensic psychologist is talking to people and making use of what the person is saying. Thus, codes of practice draw attention to the special duty of psychologists to take care in avoiding harming people with whom they're interacting.

Determining the boundaries of the duty of care can be challenging for forensic psychologists because their paymaster or client may not be the person they're dealing with directly or whose life they're influencing. (I describe the complex relationship between the professional and the hirer in the earlier section "Providing Evidence for the Court, Not the Client".) For example, while talking to a defendant to determine their sexual fantasies, the forensic psychologist has to avoid doing so in a way that may be disturbing or upsetting.

ANECDOTE

An illustration of the duty of determining the boundaries of care is the case in which a forensic psychologist was guiding an undercover police operation. A police officer was directed to elicit a confession from a suspect she was deliberately befriending. The suspect turned out to be completely innocent, but was greatly disturbed by the whole experience, which included spending 11 months in prison. Also, the police officer suffered mental distress as a result of the event. The forensic psychologist appears to have failed in carrying out his duty of care in guiding the police operation. In this particular case, no inquiry ever established failure, but the suspect and the police officer were awarded substantial sums of money in recompense for the harm they were suffering, a tacit acknowledgment that something had gone badly wrong.

Respecting Confidentiality

In some informal professional discussions between colleagues, one may mention to the other the sorts of problems their clients have in very general terms, perhaps because these problems are particularly interesting. But professionals are always careful to never, ever, mention a client's name. Nor do they mention any details that would allow a colleague to guess who the client is, where they worked, or any other information related to the client's identity. You could meet their clients in many social or professional situations and not have the slightest idea that they had ever had psychological advice or had any private concerns. That is the essence of confidentiality: The identity of people with whom the psychologist has professional interaction is protected, as are the details of their condition.

REMEMBER

Maintaining confidentiality is hugely important. Forensic psychologists have to protect the identity of persons with whom they interact professionally, together with the details of the person's situation, condition or problem.

In the legal context, confidentiality is vital because of the adversarial nature of the procedure; the prosecution and defense prepare their arguments in secret until they can present their cases in court. Any knowledge that one side is using a forensic psychologist, with some prospect of their opponents guessing why, can weaken the whole process. Even the fact that a forensic psychologist was employed but their report not used can provide ammunition.

The information that comes out during the course of forming an expert opinion also has to be kept confidential. Such information may be of use to criminals or others who have an axe to grind with a client. People can take advantage of the fact that a forensic psychologist is involved in the case.

This situation is especially true in cases where psychologists give advice to criminal investigations Usually there is no public indication that a psychologist is involved, particularly in cases that attract lots of public interest. Psychologists can come under a great deal of unwanted pressure (for example, from the media) to reveal their opinions if people discover that the police have consulted them. The identities of psychologists who advise police investigations are therefore usually kept secret.

Professional Humility

Some years ago, I coined the term *professional humility* to draw attention to the fact that no single professional discipline has all the answers. The need always exists to work with others and learn from their insights.

Forensic psychologists may sometimes think they hold the answers to a case just because they're dealing directly with the key people involved. Their exploration and finding out what the criminal felt or thought, and why they're behaving a certain way, isn't the whole answer. Not realizing that can lead to misleading arrogance.

REMEMBER

Everyone involved in the case has a useful perspective. Everyone needs to recognize that they see only a part of the picture.

Telling the Truth

You may think that the need to tell the truth in a court of law is stating the obvious, but forensic psychology is such a complex and growing area, having many challenges and demands, that I believe stressing the need for honesty is vital.

Unfortunately, forensic psychologists may sometimes be tempted to take short-cuts or give in to the pressures from clients, lawyers, the press, or the police to provide the answers or opinions most wanted. Material can even be presented to the forensic psychologist in ways that are subtly biased to suggest the desired answer. In some cases, the people commissioning psychologists may omit crucial information to try to influence the opinion they form. Psychologists, like all the other advisors to the courts or investigations, have to be alert to what background information they are given and whether it may be biased in any way.

ANECDOTE

On one occasion, I was asked to comment on a suspicious death, after being told, "We found the wife dead on the bed, and the husband says he was away in Aberdeen at the time." Clearly, by phrasing the information in this way, the police officer wanted an opinion that incriminated the husband. I had to step back from this nudge by trying to build up a picture of the circumstances of the death that made no assumptions about guilt. In other words, I had to tell the truth as I saw it.

Chapter **19**

Ten Stages in Becoming a Professional Forensic Psychologist

O ne thing that makes forensic psychology fascinating is the overlap of the austere academic discipline of psychology with the law in its many manifestations, and the range of contexts in which the profession is carried out.

Although the professional position of the forensic psychologist is just gaining a foothold in the US, it's well established and the label is protected in the UK and Australia. In these countries, controls exist on who can call themselves a forensic psychologist and the qualifications a person needs in order to practice.

The profession attracts many capable people who work in a wide range of settings, not just prisons and mental hospitals. The various techniques, approaches, and applications I describe throughout this book provide plenty of work for the forensic psychologist, but getting into the profession is highly competitive, although this chapter can help. In this chapter, I describe ten stages a forensic psychologist undergoes before they can practice as a professional.

REMEMBER

Although you can read the following sections in logical sequence, please don't see the process as an inevitable route. For example, I became involved in forensic psychology after 25 years as an applied psychologist, and a number of my students moved into the profession from the police. People from backgrounds not directly related to psychology or the law have also become professionals in this area after gaining academic qualifications and experience in other contexts. When such people qualify, they often bring fresh perspectives and new insights not immediately available to people who follow more traditional routes.

Thinking about the Profession while at School

If you're attending school and you have a definite long-term goal of becoming a professional forensic psychologist, remember that it is highly competitive to enter the field. The most important starting point is to do well in whatever subjects you're studying. But of course, studying subjects relevant to psychology is a good idea: for example, biology, mathematics, philosophy, and geography.

MYTH BUSTER

Personally, I don't think that studying psychology at school is a useful idea if you want to go on to be a psychologist professionally. Many of my colleagues may howl in disagreement, but my view is that in order to convert psychology into a subject that can be digested by teenagers, it needs to be made less problematic than it really is, so it's dumbed down. As a consequence, a great deal of material presented in school as reasonably clear-cut has to be questioned later at university and then needs to be unlearned, so to speak. A better idea, therefore, is to get a good grounding in other subjects that psychology relies on than to start on a subject that can become your life's obsession. I don't mean to suggest, however, that you don't read any psychology books before attending university. You're reading this one, and I certainly approve of that!

REMEMBER

School students' ideas about their future topics or professions are likely to change as they mature and gain a wider experience of the world. In addition, forensic psychology is evolving and changing and takes on many different forms in different situations. For these reasons, having in mind only one fixed career choice from very early on can be a mistake. Many other possibilities may become attractive, and a wider education allows you to take advantage of new opportunities as they arise.

Studying at University

Forensic psychology isn't usually a first (undergraduate) degree in any country. Though a growing number of universities in the UK have recently begun to offer such degree courses. Your choice of university and degree may be best based on opportunity, location, and other interests rather than on any particular focus on this area of psychology.

A degree in psychology is the most direct route toward becoming a forensic psychologist. Generally, any good university qualification in psychology is a sound basis for further professional development. It doesn't have to be a psychology degree that emphasizes criminal areas of psychology. Many other university qualifications may be acceptable for the next step. Sometimes, some form of additional study beyond a first degree as preparation for subsequent higher-level study is advisable if psychology wasn't the dominant part of the first qualification.

Universities in the US often have opportunities for mixing a much wider range of courses. Consequently, as well as psychology, a course in criminal justice or aspects of law could prove useful.

I counsel against focusing on forensic psychology as a major part of a first degree. Again, achieving a high standard at bachelor's or master's level in a highly regarded university is much more important than the specific topics you study. However, as the big, wide world beckons, you should get a taste for a range of future professional prospects.

REMEMBER

When choosing a university, many try to attract students by indicating that they offer courses that have plenty of bits and pieces of popular subjects (such as forensic psychology or, heaven forbid, offender profiling). In fact, the people teaching those subjects are often only a chapter ahead of the students who use the book for the course — they may have no direct knowledge of the topics. Carry out a quick search on the internet to see who the lecturers are on any particular course. Find out what they've published to see an indication of what they're likely to be experts in and able to offer.

For most serious university degrees, you need to complete some sort of research project toward the end of the course. This point is where you need to focus on subjects relevant to your later career. Such projects not only help you explore in some depth a topic that's relevant to you later but also provide a topic for future job or higher degree course applications and interviews, showing both some expertise in, and commitment to, the chosen profession.

Gaining Direct Work Experience

Although forensic psychology work experience after graduating with a bachelor's degree is a definite benefit, it isn't essential to being accepted into postgraduate courses that provide the thorough training necessary to become a professional. (See the later section "Securing a Master's Qualification.")

Perhaps this is fortunate because getting relevant work experience is difficult. The number of people looking for such opportunities is so large that finding somewhere to provide you with practical activity is challenging. Part of the problem is that, at this stage, people looking for professional experience have little in the way of skills to offer beyond what they've learned as an undergraduate.

Here are some of the many values, however, that derive from practical involvement in real work of relevance to forensic psychology:

>> Seeing what the real working day is like, with its challenges and demands

>> Getting to understand how the law works in practice, with its tedium, delays, confusions, and frustrations

>> Appreciating the various areas of activity, including those for which further qualifications are unnecessary and those for which they're essential

>> Finding out about the sorts of people involved in this area, clients and staff, and whether you want to spend your professional career with them

>> Opening up possible job opportunities for the future

You can achieve this type of practical experience in many different settings; you don't need to shadow an established professional psychologist. As long as the placement has contact with the legal process and a link with psychologists, your experience will be worthwhile. Therefore, consider these possibilities:

>> Assisting a lawyer who deals with criminal cases

>> Being part of rehabilitation projects for former prisoners

- >> Working as a volunteer for a victim-support service

- >> Joining a prison's prison-visitor scheme that involves meeting with prisoners and hearing their accounts of their experiences

- >> Taking advantage of what some police forces offer to be a community officer, where you lack the powers or responsibilities of a full-fledged officer, but the role provides experience in many law enforcement activities and the people they deal with

- >> Helping out with a forensic psychology research project that helps you discover the feel of the area and perhaps get a foot in the door for future training or employment

- >> Supporting the work of a forensic psychologist, though such opportunities are few and far between

- >> If this type of opportunity does arise, seize it; even simply photocopying, filing, printing out reports, or sorting out websites is useful. Any contact provides insights into the work and organization.

REMEMBER

In all these areas, bear in mind the legal, professional, and ethical considerations I discuss in Chapter 18.

Securing a Master's Qualification

A first serious step that commits you to developing a career as a forensic psychologist is obtaining a postgraduate qualification. The nature of this qualification varies considerably around the world; however, in some countries, it's a 2-year period of study, whereas in others, a master's is more of a doctorate qualification, spread over at least three years. (See the later section "Striving for a Doctorate.") It varies a little from state to state in the US, but is typically part of doctoral-level training. This is followed by supervised practice and gaining the appropriate license from the State in which you will be working.

Master's qualifications are demanding courses, often including some practical experience. They open up the range of topics that forensic psychology covers and allow in-depth study of many of them. A project is usually required that allows the development of research skills and the opportunity to contribute to the development of the discipline.

Master's and doctorate courses are usually accredited by a national or state organization as a crucial step to achieving a recognized professional qualification. These organizations typically provide a framework of the minimum requirements of topics that the course needs to cover. This book covers the range of issues I would expect to be included in any master's course in forensic psychology (various universities may have different emphases that are worth exploring, such as ones that relate broadly to the contexts in which forensic psychologists operate):

» Giving evidence, as an expert in court, on fitness to plead or *mens rea*, for example (the sort of topics I discuss in Chapter 12).

» Working with offenders in prison, as I describe especially in Part 5.

» Contributing to the investigative process, which I introduce in Part 3. But only a handful of places around the world emphasize it.

» Providing an emphasis on the psychology of the court process, which I outline in Chapter 12 (a few places in the US do this).

» Working with extremely disturbed individuals who've committed serious crimes, in secure treatment centers or special hospitals, or in correctional establishments in the US.

Becoming an Intern

Opportunities for working as an intern within a forensic psychology setting usually open up during a master's course or immediately afterward because people have developed the crucial skills, internalized the professional ethics, and established stronger contacts. These internships have all the benefits of gaining experience that I mention earlier in this chapter (in "Gaining Direct Work Experience"), but now the person is much more part of the team than a lowly assistant. Many organizations survive because of the help given by people at this stage in their careers.

These internships are supervised by an experienced, qualified professional, and the supervised professional practice may cover a defined set of professional activities. The intern gets some contact with the major aspects of the discipline. Logbooks and other forms of assessment and recording of the experience are also a normal aspect of this professional training.

An internship can be just another way of gaining experience (and, possibly, earning some money) while more direct opportunities for developing professional skills emerge. But, for this experience to count as a formal step toward becoming a qualified forensic psychologist, it needs to be properly supervised.

Being Supervised

Usually, you need to undertake a 2-year period of supervised professional practice after your master's or doctorate course before being regarded as a qualified forensic psychologist. So, after 3 or 4 years of an undergraduate degree, typically 2 years in a master's course, and 3 or more years of studying for a doctorate, and then these 2 additional years, a total of 7 to 10 or even 11 years are needed for you to be able to stand up in court as a qualified forensic psychologist, or to lock down many of the jobs that advertise for a qualified forensic psychologist. This length of time may be extended if any of these courses are studied part-time.

REMEMBER

All established forensic psychologists see part of their role as lending guidance and support to those who aspire to emulate them. Such support can include supervising, lecturing as part of university courses, and participating in research projects. Any well-established forensic psychology department in a university has a network of contacts for gaining supervision.

Striving for a Doctorate

A doctorate (PhD, PsyD, DPhil, or DClinPsy, for example) is nearly always awarded for making what most universities call a "contribution to knowledge." This contribution is based on a major research project that takes about three years to complete, full time (or at least double that part-time), and write up as a significant document. The topic of research is agreed on between a supervisor (or supervisory team) and the student. These topics vary enormously and delve into the chosen area in great depth. People who complete a doctorate often become world experts in the topic of their thesis.

In forensic psychology, these projects will often be carried out while employed in professional practice. They can deal with any topic covered in other parts of this book, but usually relate to the particular area of forensic psychology in which the person is engaged.

REMEMBER

Various academic institutions are emerging that offer professional doctorates that have a little less emphasis on the conducting of research contributing to knowledge. They have more concern with developing professional skills and understanding. In the future, these 3-year (or longer, if part-time) qualifications are likely to replace the master's degree.

To become a licensed psychologist in any professional area of psychology in the US, you need state licensure, which usually requires passing special exams.

Deciding to Specialize

As your professional experience develops and particular opportunities emerge, you may well begin to specialize in some particular area of activity: perhaps a special set of patients, such as those with severe mental disorders or alcohol problems, or specific areas, such as giving evidence of malingering or suggestibility.

These special areas often emerge from research activity — notably, at the PhD level — but can also be a consequence of particular earlier experiences. For example, I became involved in human rights cases about prison conditions because of my earlier work as a psychologist working in a school of architecture. People become known for their special expertise and therefore are asked to work on cases that involve this activity. In turn, their experience and understanding increase, which strengthens the contribution they can make.

Flying Solo

After a few years within a professional framework, people gain the experience and confidence to work independently, which isn't necessarily an entirely good thing to do. Many of the ethical and professional issues I discuss in Chapter 18 imply the need to keep in contact with other experts.

Indeed, many professional bodies require continuing professional development (CPD) to maintain registration as a professional, in order to ensure that individuals stay up-to-date with developments in their field, particularly their own specialisms. People can also enhance their skills by attending various courses, for example, on some new method of assessment.

Attaining Guru-Like Status

Many doors open after a person becomes established in the energetic, rapidly developing discipline of forensic psychology. Senior members of the forensic psychology profession move into important administrative posts. They may continue to contribute to popular understanding and the development of the science and profession, or they may engage in equally important administrative duties in offices. Such people can become deans in universities, advisors to prison administrators, or even significant personnel in government departments, helping to shape policy and inform professional practice at national and international levels.

A few forensic psychologists make such significant contributions to the profession that they become like gurus. These people are regarded as having special wisdom and deep experience that they can pass on to others. In the modern world, such people can be bombarded with emails asking for assistance or even (amazingly and amusingly) asked to sign photographs of themselves to be made into wedding presents. Forensic psychologists can also be asked for help in apparent miscarriages of justice (or even receive weird requests that have no obvious rhyme or reason).

Sadly, such fame often owes more to the person being drawn on by the broadcast, online, and printed media for comments than through any substantial contribution to the development of the science or the profession. That, however, is changing as more people with professional and scientific qualifications become the gatekeepers for the mass media. Any person with some degree of popular recognition for their contributions to the profession has to steer a course between overexposure and the inevitable trivialization of the discipline. This includes ensuring that some sensible, well-informed account of the established science is used in popular accounts, such as writing *Forensic Psychology For Dummies!*

Chapter **20**

Ten Cases in Which Forensic Psychology Proved Crucial

orensic psychologists make most of their contributions outside of any public gaze, through assessments of individuals, and running therapeutic programs. That work is, typically as part of a multidisciplinary team. Yet, from time to time, individuals do make notable contributions to particular legal proceedings.

Forensic psychologists do much more than just give evidence in court. However, the cases I describe in this chapter reveal various ways in which psychologists contribute to court decisions affecting the lives of individuals. In many cases, evidence from a forensic psychologist may be ignored by the courts. Furthermore, not all psychologists advising the courts or police investigators do so validly, within their realm of competence (see Chapter 19).

I was personally involved in a couple of these cases. I include them in this chapter because it is not always easy to sort out the complexity of a legal case — and summarizing key aspects of it in a few paragraphs. My own involvement makes it easier to recognize the forensic psychology contribution.

Considering the Effects of Media Accounts

One of the earliest uses of modern psychology in court is still relevant today. It concerns the influence of accounts in the press of matters relating to an ongoing trial. This event happened in 1896, so nothing much has changed.

Albert von Schrenck-Notzing was a German physician who devoted much of his time to examining psychics and related paranormal phenomena. As part of these studies, he became aware of the ways in which memory can be distorted by subsequent events that intervene between those that are being remembered and the occasion of the recall of those events. This subject would remain an active area of psychological research well over a century later (as I discuss in Chapter 7), but at the time, such a claim was a challenge to conventional views of how memory operated. The baron pointed out that his finding was particularly important when evaluating the reports of witnesses.

In a case of great public interest, a man from Munich was accused of murdering three women. Then, as now, press coverage of the case was widespread, and speculation abounded about what had happened and who was involved.

The baron argued in court that witnesses were likely to have confused their actual memory of what had happened and what they had seen with ideas they may have gleaned from the newspaper accounts. He even coined a rather grand term for this effect, calling it *retroactive memory falsification.* However, the court disregarded the baron's evidence. The defendant was found guilty.

The legal system in the UK acknowledges that reports and comments about events, and especially about suspects, can influence juries. Therefore, the law forbids comments to be broadcast or published that may influence the jury. These *sub judice* laws make it illegal to comment on a court case before it's completed. Straightforward reports of what happens in court are allowed, but, for example, speculation on the character of the accused would be regarded as contempt of court.

REGIONAL TIP-OFF

Sub judice laws apply only after a person has been charged with a crime and the court proceedings have started. In the US, the freedom of the press is regarded more highly than the possibility of distorting a jury's memory, and so the *sub judice* rules are much more lenient there. Consequently, in many cases in the US, the baron's opinion would be relevant. Prosecuting attorneys are aware of this and, in high-profile cases, may actually encourage trial by the press or media.

Determining whether a Convicted Murderer Is Telling the Truth

Hugo Münsterberg was a highly regarded psychologist in the US at the turn of the 20th century. He was aware of the many contributions that scientific, experimentally based psychology could make to legal processes and wrote popular articles and academic accounts of his work for the courts. He introduced many of the topics that forensic psychologists still deal with today, including false confessions, distortions in eyewitness testimony, and determination of lying. At the time, however, he wasn't taken seriously.

In 1908, Münsterberg published the controversial book *On the Witness Stand*, in which he describes his experiences of providing evidence in court cases. The book advocates much more use of psychological scientific findings in legal proceedings, but many years passed before evidence from psychologists became accepted in court. Indeed, many of his recommendations have still to be taken up.

One example of his account, in his own words, illustrates how innovative his thinking was. In this case, one convicted murderer was giving evidence against another, and Münsterberg was seeking to determine whether this man, who claimed that he'd become religious and was now telling the truth, was lying.

Münsterberg first made sure the witness believed in the powers of the psychologist:

I told the witness directly that I had come to examine his mind and find out what was really at the bottom of his heart . . . I began with some simple psychological tricks . . . which were naturally unknown and somewhat uncanny to the witness . . . and soon he was entirely under the spell of the belief that I had some special scientific powers.

Then I began with a real experiment. I told him that I should call at first fifty words, and each time, when he heard a word, he was to name to me as quickly as possible the first thing which came to his mind on the hearing of the word . . . My first word was "river," he associated "water"; then "ox," he said "yoke"; "mountain," he said "hill"; "tobacco," he said "pipe." All the interest thus seemed to belong to the choice of the words, and he saw that I wrote his answers down. But the fact is that I did something else also; I measured in fractions of a second the time between my calling the word and his giving a reply. Between his hearing of the word "river" and his speaking the word "water," eight-tenths of a second passed; between "ox" — "yoke," six-tenths; between "tobacco" — "pipe," eight-tenths. On the whole, seven to eight-tenths of a second was the very short standard time for those associations which represented familiar ideas.

Now, there were mixed in among the fifty words many which had direct relation to his criminal career and to his professed religious conversion — for instance, the words confession, revolver, religion, heaven, jury, death, Bible, pardon, railroad, blood, jail, prayer, and some names of his victims and of his alleged accomplices. Let us not forget that he was fully under the belief that I had a special power to discover from his spoken words the real tendencies of his mind. If he had had anything to hide, he would have been constantly on the lookout that no treacherous word should slip in . . . and yet, however quickly he might have done it, it would have taken at least one or two seconds more; and he would have used the longer time the more freely, as he had no reason to suspect that time played any part in the experiment.

But the results show the very remarkable fact that the dangerous words brought, on the whole, no retardation of the associative process . . . Even the names of his accomplices and of his victims awoke associations in less than nine-tenths of a second. The fact that these associations were produced by the witness in the minimum time, which made deliberation impossible, while he was convinced that the words would unveil his real mind, is strong evidence indeed that this man did not want consciously to hide anything, and that he himself really believed his confession.

This quote shows Münsterberg using the psychological procedure of measuring reaction time to determine how much the witness needed to think about the answers before uttering them. Münsterberg thought that the longer the reaction time, the more the person was trying to develop in their mind an appropriate answer. If the person gave an instant answer, then they weren't trying to invent anything — so their answers could be trusted. Like any good scientist, Münsterberg also made sure he had some comparison figures for the individual in question under neutral conditions. Psychologists still use similar explorations, but with much more sophisticated equipment. However, I've not heard of this being used as an assessment of the trustworthiness of a witness in court.

Re-Creating Events to Test a Claim's Validity

Professor Lionel Haward is primarily responsible for establishing the use of psychological evidence in UK courts. In the first major book published in the UK, *Forensic Psychology* (1981), on the work of forensic psychologists, he describes many of the cases for which he appeared in court.

One case in particular illustrates Haward's approach of setting up studies specifically to test the validity of claims in a case. It relates to a road accident in which a 14-year-old boy was hit by a car as he turned from a farm track onto a country road on his bicycle.

The defense of the driver related in part to the suggestion that the boy was of low intelligence and, as a consequence, had been guilty of contributory negligence. In other words, the accident was to a certain extent the boy's own fault because he hadn't been cycling sensibly. Professor Haward therefore tackled this claim directly:

» **He established the boy's intellectual ability before the accident.** This process wasn't simple, because the boy had suffered severe head injuries from the accident, so Haward had to consult the boy's school records and other information.

» **He selected two groups of cyclists — one with the measured intelligence of the boy before the accident and the other of average intelligence.** The boys rode their cycles through a puddle containing fluorescent dye so that their precise wheel tracks showed up on the road. Each set of cyclists then rode, one at a time, into a road from a junction similar to the one where the accident took place.

» **He carefully measured the tire tracks and evaluated the route taken to determine how dangerous the taking of the curve had been.** The crucial issue was how close the cycles kept to the side of the road or how likely they were to swerve into the middle, which was much more risky.

The results showed that cyclists of low intelligence were no more likely to take the corner in a risky curve than riders of normal intelligence. In addition, the average curve followed by the cyclists was compared with the line the victim had taken to show that his behavior was normal. This allowed the court to dismiss the claim of contributory negligence.

Haward used the process of setting up specific experiments to test aspects of claims in many cases. In doing this, he was following directly in the footsteps of Münsterberg and the baron I mention earlier. The same sort of action is still taken today in some cases, as I did in relation to the case I describe later in this chapter, "Examining the Possible Role of Implicit Influence in the Lockerbie Bomber Case."

Forcing Drugs to Make a Defendant Fit to Stand Trial

Charles Thomas Sell was a St. Louis dentist, long known to suffer from delusions. Although he hadn't been convicted of any crimes, in 1997 he was charged with more than 60 cases of fraud. Psychiatric examination determined that his mental state was such that he wasn't fit to stand trial. The courts sent him to a mental institution with the plan that he'd receive sufficient treatment to become competent enough to face the charges. However, while hospitalized, Sell refused to accept any medication that would influence his mental state. Prosecutors requested that the law require him to be forced to take the medication so that he'd become fit to stand trial.

This case was a *cause célèbres*, and a number of professional organizations submitted reports offering opinions on what should happen, including the American Psychological Association. These reports provided detailed guidance on the conditions under which various medical interventions are ethically acceptable.

The resulting guidelines have since found their way into various statutes. They include the recognition that any administered medications that influence a person's thought processes are matters over which the individual should have an influence. Furthermore, the courts need to be aware that such drugs are liable to influence other aspects of a person's behavior that can modify how that person seems in court. Therefore, courts need to be extremely careful before requiring coercive treatment with drugs to make a person competent to appear before a judge and jury. All other, less-invasive methods should be considered first.

In a protracted set of legal judgments, the parties eventually agreed that it was probably appropriate for Charles Sell to be given medication involuntarily.

By then, however, he'd spent longer incarcerated than he would have if he'd been found guilty of the original charges, and the case was dropped!

STRANGE
BUT TRUE

A Honey Trap Gone Wrong

The young model Rachel Nickell was murdered while walking her dog with her 2-year-old son on Wimbledon Common in South London in July 1992. A couple of months later, the police decided that Colin Stagg was the likely culprit. He had come to their notice by way of some lonely hearts correspondence he had carried out with a woman, who thought it was rather odd.

The police set about trying to get Stagg to admit to the murder using what's often called a *honey trap*. A woman police officer, Lizzie, pretended to be part of the lonely hearts circle and opened up correspondence with Stagg. Her activities were guided by a person with some forensic psychology background who'd generated a profile of the killer that he thought fit Colin Stagg.

Over six months, Lizzie corresponded with Stagg and met him a few times. Using pointers provided by the psychologist, she got as close as she could to offering Colin sex if he admitted to the murder of Rachel Nickell. He never did admit that (nor did he take advantage of the offer of sex), but seemed to mention some aspects of the case that the police thought indicated knowledge only the culprit would know. Armed with this and the willingness of the psychologist to give evidence that Stagg fit the profile of the killer, the police charged Colin and took him to court.

ANECDOTE

As part of Colin's defense, I and a number of colleagues examined closely the transcripts of all the interactions between Lizzie and Colin. We saw quite clearly that a concerted effort had been made to use various well-known psychological persuasion techniques to elicit a confession from Stagg, and that any claim that he fit some sort of profile of the killer was speculative in the extreme.

When the case eventually came to court, after Stagg had been in prison for 11 months, at the earliest stage of the trial, the judge, Mr. Justice Ognall, commented on the honey trap activity: "I am afraid this behavior betrays not merely an excess of zeal but a substantial attempt to incriminate a suspect by positive and deceptive conduct of the grossest kind."

He threw out the case, and Colin Stagg walked free.

Some years later, a quite different man was convicted of the murder. While the police were focusing on Colin Stagg, the man carried out a similar murder. In other words, the obsession with honey-trapping Stagg enabled the real killer to go free and kill another young woman. Many people criticized the psychologist for his abusive role and for the police taking notice of his advice.

In January 2007, Colin Stagg was awarded £250,000 (around $330,000) in damages. Lizzie also received a substantial sum in payment for the trauma she endured from her participation in the fiasco.

Profiling Howard Hughes

When the eccentric billionaire Howard Hughes died in 1976, people expressed the concern that he'd been so reclusive and generally odd in his later years that he hadn't been competent to make an appropriate will. The then-president of the American Psychological Association, Raymond Fowler, was called in to review what was known about Howard Hughes and offer an opinion on his mental state and competence toward the end of his life. Dr. Fowler was thus asked to perform a *psychological autopsy* (a topic I describe in Chapter 12).

Fowler obtained a vast amount of material about Hughes, which he studied over a number of years. The material included Hughes' diary and those of people close to him; business memoranda; articles in newspapers; interviews with Hughes; and letters he'd written or others had written to him or about him.

Dr. Fowler's conclusion was that Howard Hughes was a deeply disturbed man when he died. This mental disturbance had been evident from his earliest days, but developed into a serious obsessive-compulsive disorder. At no time, however, had he been psychotic and totally out of touch with reality. He always knew what he was doing and had logical, if rather misinformed, reasons for doing what he did.

After extensive legal battles, the will was generally accepted, and many relatives of Hughes — as well as a number of good causes — received payouts.

Evaluating a Suicide Note

On June 4, 1992, Paula Gilfoyle, who was eight and a half months pregnant, was found hanging in her garage in the northwest of England. Her husband, Eddie Gilfoyle, found a suicide note in Paula's handwriting, which he showed to the police. Initially, the event was assumed to be a suicide, although Paula had told her friends how she was looking forward to having the baby and had made many arrangements in preparation.

A few days later, friends of Paula told the police that she had told them Eddie persuaded her to write the suicide note because, they said, she had told them her husband claimed to be studying on a course for which he was required to provide a simulated suicide note!

If you think this story is all rather odd, I agree with you. Certainly, what one person says another person said (called *hearsay evidence*) isn't usually allowed into court. It wasn't allowed as evidence in this case, but it did form the background gossip that informed how the police went about the investigation.

Eddie denied any wrongdoing, but was convicted of the murder and, after serving many years in prison, was released on parole. Along the way, he appealed against the verdict. I was asked to consider the possibility that the crucial suicide note, which Paula had written, had been dictated by Eddie.

ANECDOTE

I discovered that Eddie and Paula were working different shifts and so had been leaving notes for each other. In addition, two other notes came to light that appeared to be precursors to the suicide note. In total, 11 communications existed from Paula to Eddie in the months leading up to the suicide. By examining the narrative that these notes implied, it was plausible that Paula had been contemplating leaving Eddie and then thinking over a long period about ending her life, but hiding this information from others. Other studies I subsequently completed on genuine and simulated suicide notes also supported the idea that Paula had written the suicide note herself.

Although the attorneys commented on the thoroughness of my report, the appeal judges refused to accept it as evidence. They claimed that my report provided no indication that Paula had been mentally disturbed and amounted to a form of profiling, which was unacceptable. (This unacceptability of profiling was partly a consequence of the disastrous honey trap case I describe in the earlier section "A Honey Trap Gone Wrong.") The judges made this decision, even though the analysis I carried out hadn't been done for the original court proceedings when Eddie was tried and convicted. This was legally new evidence, which, had it been available at the original trial, may have swayed the jury. Later, a box was found in which Paula had locked away her private papers. These show that she sometimes hid important feelings from those close to her, supporting the view that the happy disposition she presented to others before her death may not have been an indication of her true state of mind. That was never presented to any jury.

Researching False Confessions

A few hours after two weak, elderly women were found battered to death in 1987 in their home in the South of England, a local 17-year-old was arrested and questioned intensively for over 14 hours. Eventually, he made statements that the police believed incriminated him in the murders and associated sexual assaults and theft. This case is one of hundreds that Professor Ghisli Gudjonsson (see Chapter 8), a British forensic psychologist, studied that provide a clear example of a false confession. He examined cases, like this one, in which it was clear from later evidence that the suspect had confessed even though he didn't commit the crime. Professor Gudjonsson tried to establish what prompted the confession.

In this case, the youth initially repeatedly denied any involvement in the murder or even being in the house. Yet after five different officers took turns questioning him, telling him that witnesses had seen him near the victims' house around the time of the murder, and repeatedly challenging his account of what he'd done and where he'd been, the teenager became distressed, shaking, and sobbing. Eventually, he admitted being near the house and agreed with the incriminating claims made by the police.

The next day, however, after he'd rested, he again denied any guilt. For a year, he was kept in custody, but throughout all that time, he maintained his innocence. He said he'd offered self-incriminating agreement to the claims put to him because the police kept questioning in such a way that he felt they'd never stop. He felt exhausted and just wanted the interrogation to end. He became frightened of what they may have done to him, so eventually he gave in and told them what he thought they wanted to hear.

A year later, another man was charged with the murders and pleaded guilty. He had his guilt corroborated with other evidence and was convicted.

Because of these cases and the intensive research that Professor Gudjonsson and his colleagues carried out over many years, courts around the world are much more cautious about accepting confessions as indications of guilt. The most extreme example of this situation is in India, where a confession isn't accepted by the courts unless it's given in court to a judge with no police officers present.

Examining the Possible Role of Implicit Influence in the Lockerbie Bomber Case

On December 21, 1988, Pan Am flight 103 blew up over Lockerbie in Scotland, killing all 243 passengers and 16 crew members. The police investigation identified clothing that had been close to where the bomb had been placed and believed that the clothing may have come from a shop in Malta, where the shopkeeper at the time was Anthony Gauci.

Police approached Gauci about a year after the bomb exploded to see whether he was able to remember selling the clothing and who had bought it. They therefore presented Gauci with various sets of photographs, some of which included a picture of al-Megrahi, known to work for the Libyan secret service. They wanted to see whether Gauci was able to identify the customer from a year earlier. When Gauci selected al-Megrahi from the set of photographs, apparently the police threw a party to celebrate.

The investigation and the identification of al-Megrahi were much more involved and complicated than I can indicate in a couple of paragraphs. But even this brief summary reveals reasonable doubts that a shopkeeper could remember who'd bought certain clothing many months earlier. The possibility has to be considered that the police, even inadvertently, influenced Gauci's judgments because they were so keen to secure identification in this internationally significant case.

ANECDOTE

As part of a detailed examination of all the evidence provided by Gauci, that I was asked to carry out in preparation for an appeal al-Megrahi wanted to make against his conviction, I set up an experiment to see whether people can be indirectly influenced to select a certain photo without being aware of that influence. In this experiment, two different sets of administrators were each given similar instructions. They were asked to show the set of photos, which Gauci had been shown, to a number of different people and ask them to guess which one in the set was involved with the Lockerbie bomb plot.

One crucial difference existed in the instructions given to the administrators. One set was told which picture was al-Megrahi, but they were instructed not to tell anyone else. The other set of administrators wasn't given this simple piece of information.

The results showed that the administrators who didn't know who was in the target photo never had the photograph selected, whereas those who knew had the target selected in about a third of cases, much more than would happen by chance. This result showed that implicit influence (known as an *experimenter effect*) could possibly have been relevant in this case.

Al-Megrahi was diagnosed with terminal cancer and released from prison on compassionate grounds, and his appeal was dropped.

Identifying Ritual Murders in South Africa

Brigadier Gerard Labuschange (now retired) was unusual as a forensic psychologist within a police force. He's a qualified clinical psychologist but led an investigative psychology unit within the South African Police Service. Therefore, uniquely, he carried out investigations as well as provided psychological evidence in court. He thus brought a rarely found systematic, scientific approach to his detective work as well as psychological insights.

Labuschange was particularly interested in distinguishing a particular type of murder, which is usually found only in Africa, from other forms of murder. These murders are ones that happen because body parts of the victim are used in traditional African medicine. People outside of the culture that supports this type of murder have difficulty understanding just how powerful such long-established belief systems can be.

The brigadier's gruesome task was to distinguish mutilations found on a murdered victim from those that may be the result of some psychotic, bizarre sexual or other mentally disturbed feature. This job required understanding the belief systems involved that sustain this sort of murder and the sorts of victims (often children) that are considered appropriate for providing the necessary anatomical component. This understanding goes beyond the knowledge that a physician who carries out an autopsy would have. It requires psychological awareness that can help to recognize that the killer isn't mentally disturbed, but totally accepts the attitudes and beliefs that support these horrible crimes.

Index

A

Abagnale, Frank, 182
academic strand, 15
accuracy, 138
acquisitive crime, 33, 182
act of remembering situation, 124
actus reus, 14
acute stress disorder, 244
adult criminality, juvenile committing antisocial
    behavior leading to, 335–336
adults
  with learning or mental disability, 144
  vulnerable to effects of brain injury, 204
adversarial system, 44–45, 46
advocate, 262
ADVOKATE, 139
age
  and crime prevention, 83–84
  for juveniles being considered responsible for their
    actions, 338
aggravation, 267
alcohol abuse
  and alcohol dependency, 197
  treating alcohol abuse as method for crime
    prevention, 222
alcoholism, 71
alienation, 284
alleygating, 221
al-Megrahi, 381
American Association for Correctional Psychologists
    (AACP), 286
American Psychological Association (APA), 140
amnesia, diminished responsibility due to, 238
Anatomy of a Fall (Anatomie d'une chute), 262
anchoring, 37
anger
  management, 308–309
  at prison, 284
  promoted violence, 302
  in rape, 324–325

answers, giving cross-examination, 271
antisocial activity, 111, 117
aptitude tests, 94
arousal, 147
arson, 183–184
assessment
  criminal mind, 103
  of victims of crimes, 206–208
Atkins, Daryl, 93
Atlas of Criminal Types, 66
attention, 94
attitudes, 95
attorneys, 262
attractiveness of object increasing likelihood of
    crime, 194
automatism, 80, 239
autopsy, psychological, 89
availability bias, 38

B

bad company, keeping, 70
barristers, 262
battered woman syndrome, 245–246
behavioral approach, for deception and lying,
    146, 147, 152
behavioral scientists, 169
behavioral syndromes
  battered woman syndrome, 245–246
  court, examining syndromes in, 243–250
  Munchausen syndrome, 249
  parental alienation syndrome, 247
  post-traumatic stress disorder (PTSD), 244–245
  premenstrual stress syndrome, 248
  rape trauma syndrome (RTS), 248
behavior modification, 289
Bianchi, Kenneth, 106, 239, 241
bias in police lineup identifications, 140–141
Big Five, 95
biological characteristics as cause for committing a
    crime, 122

bipolar disorder, 239
Bitcoin fraudster, 32
black sheep effect, 276
body language, 152, 153
Bond, Thomas, 169
boot camp, 339
borderline personality disorder (BPD), 78, 111
brain fingerprinting, 151
brain injury, children vulnerable to effects of, 204
brain-mapping research, 151
brawls, 303
breach of contract, claims of, 256
Briggs, Steven, 69, 82
Brussel, James, 171
Bull, Ray, 123
burden of proof, 267
burglary
  crime rate, 217
  criminal characteristics, 65
  offender profiling, 183
  psychological effects of crimes on victims, 200
  versus robbery, 267
  as violation, 200

C

CALM (controlling anger and learning to manage
    it), 309–310
Canter, David, 189, 273
career criminals, 68
cases involving forensic psychology
  convicted murderer, determining if truth is told
      by, 373–374
  false confessions, researching, 379–380
  honey-trap, investigation of, 377–378
  Lockerbie Bomber case, examining role of implicit
      influence in, 380–381
  media affecting witness accounts, 372
  suicide note, evaluation of, 378–379
  validity, recreating events to test a claim's, 375–376
casting doubt, 272
castration, chemical, 329–330
Cattell, J. McKeen, 13
causes of crime, reducing, 218–219
chemical castration, 329–330
child abuse, 319
  consequences of, 203

child custody cases, 256
child pornography, 319
children
  interviewing, 135–136
  physical abuse of, 202–203
  vulnerable to effects of brain injury, 204
child sexual abuse
  in family
    dealing with, 330
    examining, 330
    preventing, 331–332
    primary prevention, 331–332
    secondary prevention, 332
    tertiary prevention, 332
  long-term consequences, 203
  types of, 330
civil proceedings, 12, 256–257
  expert in, 53–54
civil rights claims, 256
Clark, Sally, 56
clinical psychologists, 20
coaching witnesses, 276–277
codes of practice, following, 353
coercion, 133
cognition, 73
cognitive behavioral therapy (CBT), 290–292
cognitive distortions, 108
cognitive interview, 131–132
Cognitive Self Change Program (CSCP), 310–311
cognitive style, 73
cognitive tests, 94
communalism, 294
communication links, 230
community meetings, 294
compensation, assessing civil proceedings for, 257
competence, working within your area of, 354–355
competency, 241–243
confessions, 161
  false, 133
  written, 163
confidence, 138
confidentiality, 299
  respecting, 357–358
confirmation bias, 37
confrontational homicide, 187
construct validity, psychological tests, 99

criminals *(continued)*
  networks, 227–228
  versus non-criminals, 66
  opportunities for, 216
  social changes, 216
  specialists or versatile, 68
  varieties of, 34
  as victims, 194
  victims of crimes becoming, 196–197
Criminal Shadows: Inside the Mind of the Serial Killer (Canter), 189
Criminology For Dummies (Briggs), 69, 82
cross-examination, psychological aspects, 45
  answers, giving, 271
  leading questions, avoiding, 270–273
  questions, setting, 271
Crown Courts, 261
Crown Prosecution Service (CPS), 46
cruel punishment, banning of, 283
CSCP (Cognitive Self Change Program), 310–311
cultural differences, 133
Cybersecurity for Dummies (Steinberg), 183

D

dampening, 221
Daubert, Jason, 52
Daubert v. Merrill Dow Pharmaceuticals Inc., 52
decay over time, memory, 128
deception and lying
  in crime
    extortion, 158–159
    false allegations, 157–158
  detecting
    behavioral approach for, 146, 152
    difficulty in, 145–146
    legal approach for, 147, 156–157
    physiological approach for, 146–148
    by police officers, 152
    by secret service, 152
    semantic assessment approach for, 147
  interviewing suspects
    false confessions, 159–160
    IEE approach to help determine truthfulness, 161
    interrogating suspects, 162–163
  successful deception, difficulties in, 145

decision-makers, detectives as, 37
delinquency, dealing with, 337–338
delusions, 79
democratic therapeutic communities, 294
democratization, 294
denial of criminality, 75
depression, 80
  in prison, 283
destructive narrative, 311
detectives
  as decision-makers, 37
  versus forensic psychology, 19
deviant psychopathy, 113
Diagnostic and Statistical Manual of Mental Disorders, 96, 97, 110
dimensions, 95
diminished responsibility, 237–239
directed choices, 272
directed questions, 272
displacement, 219–220
dissociative identity disorder, 239
distancing, psychological, 284
distorted attitudes, 115
distraction, 207
doctorate, 367
domestic violence, 186, 303, 304
door-pushers, 217
double-blind testing, 140
Dow, Merrell, 52
drug abuse, 71
  law, changing, 223
  treating as method of crime prevention, 222
drug dependency, 197
Drummond, Edward, 14
Duffy, John Frances, 172, 180
duty of care, 356–357
dynamic factors in risk assessment, 114, 320

E

education
  crime prevention with, 218–219
  for prisoners, 286
effort, lack of, 207
Ekman, Paul, 153
Ellis, Havelock, 215

H

hallucinations, 79

Hare's Psychopathy Checklist, 115, 116

Harris, Thomas, 167

Haward, Lionel, 21, 375–376

hearsay evidence, 379

Historical/Clinical/Risk Management Scale
  (HCR-20), 307

histrionic, 111

Hollywood psychopath, 113

Holmes, Sherlock, 40

homicide, 186

  confrontational, 187

  crime-related, 187

homosexual encounter, male victims, 202

honey-trap, investigation of, 377–378

hostage situations, 224–225

hostile attribution bias, 74

Hughes, Howard, 255, 378

humility, professional, 358

hypervigilance, 284

hypnosis, 134–135

I

identifying potential victims of crimes, 193–196

IEE approach to help determine truthfulness, 161

impartiality, 141

impressions, 122

imprisonment, uses of, 286

impulsivity, 75

inadmissible evidence, 269–270

Inbau, Fred, 162–163

inclusion, restorative justice process, 211

independent work, 368

inference, 175

informed consent, 299, 352–353

Ingram, Paul, 131

inheritance and criminality, 73

innocence project, 138

inquisitorial system, 46–47

insanity, legal definition of, 238

insanity pleas, 236–237

instrumental violence, 302, 304

intelligence, psychological tests, 91

intelligence quotient (IQ), 86

  tests, 92

intense paranoia, 79

intent, 267

International Statistical Classification of Diseases and
  Related Health Problems, 96

internship, 366

interpersonal distrust, 284

interrogation, 162–163

interviewer, 123

interviewing suspects

  false confessions, 159–160

  IEE approach to help determine truthfulness, 161

  interrogating suspects, 162–163

intimate partner violence (IPV), 304

intoxication, diminished responsibility due to, 239

investigative hypnosis, 134–135

investigative psychology

  actions, 177

  arson, 183–184

  burglary, 183

  characteristics, 177

  contingencies, 178

  criminal narratives, 179

  cycle of activity, 176

  delving into, 175

  locating offenders geographically, 180, 181

  property crimes, dealing with, 182

  questions that detectives need answered, 177

  type of criminal acts, 181

isolation, 284

J

Jack the Ripper, 169–170

job satisfaction, 82

judge, 262

jury psychology

  decisions, how juries make, 265–266

  evidence, 270

  inadmissible evidence, 269–270

  legal terms, understanding of, 267–268

  overview, 264

  scientific or technical evidence, 270

jury selection, 275–276

justification, 74, 108

penile plethysmograph, 322

permissiveness, 294

personal characteristics and vulnerabilities increasing likelihood of becoming victim of crime, 193

Personality Assessment Inventory (PAI), 88

personality, criminals, 74–75, 94

personality disorder, 76
  diminished responsibility due to, 239
  DSM listed, 111
  type of, 110

personal narratives, 74

personal narratives, reconstructing, 311

personal records, 122

photographic memory, 126

physiological approach, 147
  for deception and lying, 146–148
  detecting deception
    behavioral approach for, 146, 152
    difficulty in, 145–146
    legal approach for, 147, 156–157
    physiological approach for, 146–148
    by police officers, 152
    by secret service, 152
    semantic assessment approach for, 147

picquerism, 320

plausibility, 157

police officers
  in criminal investigations, 29
  deception and lying by, 152

political hostage situations, 225

political stalkers, 315

polygraph, 51, 148

post-traumatic amnesia, 205

post-traumatic stress disorder (PTSD), 208–210, 244–245

power and rape, 325

prejudice, 57

premenstrual stress syndrome, 248

Pretty Woman (movie), 197

prison
  cognitive behavioral methods into, 290–292
  crime prevention and, 217–218
  exploitative and extreme values of prison life, 284
  forensic psychologists task, 28
  isolating prisoners, 285
  overview, 282–287

specializing in working in, 286
therapeutic work in, 290
as total institution, 284
treatment for prisoners, 287–300

privacy, ethical approval for research, 353

probity profiling, 29

professional ethics, 26

professional humility, 358

professional requirements for forensic psychologists
  codes of practice, following, 353
  competence, working within your area of, 354–355
  confidentiality, respecting, 357–358
  court not client, providing evidence for, 352
  duty of care, 356–357
  ethical approval needed for research, 352–353
  humility, professional, 358
  opinions, care in expressing, 353–354
  peer review, submitting to, 355–356
  truth, telling the, 358–359
  ultimate question, avoiding, 353–354

projective techniques, 89

property crimes
  arson, 183–184
  burglary, 183
  dealing with, 182
  fraud, 182–183

prosecution, 45

protective factors, 82

protective factors in risk assessment, 115

proximity increasing likelihood of becoming victim of crime, 194

psychiatrists, 20

psychoanalysis, 20

psychological aspects
  of court procedures
    cross-examination, 270–273
    delving into jury psychology, 264–270
    overview, 259
    seating desired jury, 274–277
    uncovering, 260–264
  cross-examination
    answers, giving, 271
    leading questions, avoiding, 270–273
    questions, setting, 271

R

railway murderer, 172–174
rape, 184–185, 319
  anger in, 324–325
  male victims, 202, 317
  motives for, 323
  myths, 324
  opportunity and, 325
  power and, 325
  psychological effects of crimes on victims, 201–202
  sadism as explanation of, 324
  suffering from trauma of, 201
rape trauma syndrome (RTS), 248
rationalization, 74
Raymond Fowler, 255
reality confrontation, 294
reality in investigations, 41
real-life situation study, 24
reasoning, 94
reasoning and rehabilitation (R&R), 292
recalling, 137
recidivist, 214
recognition, 137
recompense, restorative justice process, 211
reconstructive psychological evaluation, 252
records, 122
recovered memories, 130, 131
Reid interrogation technique, 162–163
Reid, John, 162–163
reintegration, restorative justice process, 211
relationships with non-criminals, 82
reliability, psychological tests, 25, 98
repeat victimization, 198
representativeness heuristic, 38
resource bias, 38
response style of victim, 207
restorative justice process, 210–212
retroactive memory falsification, 372
risk assessment
  for domestic violence, 304
  dynamic factors, 320
  legal proceedings, 250–251
  sexual offenders, 320–325
  static factors, 320
  for violence, 304–307

Risk Matrix 2000, 323
Risk-Need-Responsivity (RNR) Model approach, 328
ritual murders in South Africa, identification of, 382
RM2000/S, 323
RMS, 323
robbery versus burglary, 267
Rogers, Kevin, 285
Rorschach Inkblot Test, 87, 89
routine activity theory, 174
RTS (rape trauma syndrome), 248
The Runaway Jury (movie), 17, 277

S

sadism
  overview, 77
  rape, as explanation of, 324
safety, ethical approval for research, 353
salience, 177
SARA (Spousal Assault Risk Assessment Guide), 304
SARN (Structured Assessment of Risk and Need), 115
schizoid, 111
schizophrenia, 79
school shootings, 346–347
Schrenk-Nortzing, Baron Albert von, 372
scientific or technical evidence at jury trial, 270
secondary victims, 196
secret service, deception and lying by, 152
seductions of crime, 117
self-control, lack of, 75
self-esteem and child physical abuse, 202–204, 206
selfish, callous psychopathy, 113
self-management, 115
Sell, Charles Thomas, 376
semantic approaches, 147
semantic assessment, 154–155
  approach, for deception and lying, 147
serial killers, 186
Sex Offender Risk Appraisal Guide (SORAG), 321–322
sex offender treatment program (SOTP), 328–329
  adapted program, 329
  booster program, 329
  core program, 328
  extended program, 328
  healthy relationships program, 329
  rolling program, 329

suicide notes, 378–379
suicides
   examining possible, 253–255
   exposure to, 253–254
   lethal agents, availability of, 253
   psychopathology, assessing, 254–255
   stressors preceding, 253
supervised professional practice, 367
suspects, 122, 132
suspicion, 284
systemic therapies, juvenile offenders, 342
Szondi test, 87

T

target-hardening, 199, 220
Tate, Lionel, 339
testamentary capacity, 255
Test of Memory Malingering (TOMM), 107
Thematic Apperception Test (TAT), 87, 90
theory, psychological, 26
Thinking Skills Programme (TSP), 292
Thomson, Joe, 198
traces, 122
Trail Making Tests A and B, 88
transvestite fetishism, 320
traumatic brain injury from violent assault, 203–205
treatment programmes
   juvenile offenders for reducing
      delinquency, 341–346
   for prisoners, 287–300
   for reducing delinquency
      multisystemic therapy, 344–345
      overview, 341–342
      parenting, improving, 342–343
      wise parenting, 342–343
   for sexual offenders, 326–329
      chemical castration, 329–330
      Good Lives Model (GLM) approach, 327
      Risk-Need-Responsivity (RNR) Model
         approach, 328
      sex offender treatment program (SOTP), 328–329
   for violence
      anger management, 308–309
      overview, 308
      personal narratives, reconstructing, 311

trial, psychological assessments after, 57–58
truth drugs, 150–151
truth, telling the, 358–359
12 Angry Men (movie), 260
Twinkie defense, 239

U

ultimate question, avoiding, 56, 353–354
uncertainty, victims experiencing, 200
unconscious bias, 38
unconscious transference, 140
UN guidance on ethical interviewing, 164
United States
   legal profession, 51
   legal systems, 47–48
university, studying at, 363–364

V

validity, 25
   psychological tests, 98
   recreating events to test a claim's, 375–376
vengeance stalkers, 314
victim, 33
   memories, 124
victimless crime, 33
victimology, 191
victims of crimes, 28
   assessment of, 206–208
   attractiveness of object increasing likelihood of
      crime, 194
   becoming criminals, 196–197
   criminals as victims, 196–197
   helping victims deal with trauma, 205–206
   identifying potential, 193–196
   interviews with, 122
   male, 202
   nation as victim of crime, 211–212
   as object, 185
   overview, 191–192
   as person, 185
   personal characteristics and vulnerabilities
      increasing likelihood of becoming, 193
   proximity increasing likelihood of becoming, 194
   relative incidence of crimes, 195

victims of crimes *(continued)*
   secondary victims, 196
   target hardening, 199
   as vehicle, 185
   vulnerability increasing likelihood of becoming, 194
   women, 202
video identification parade electronic recording, 136
violence
   anger management, 308–309
   during bail hearings, 305
   brawls, 303
   criminal coercion, 304
   criminal history, 304
   during decisions about release, 305
   domestic, 303, 304
   expressive, emotional or anger-promoted, 302
   features of, 302
   instrumental, 302, 304
   modeling, 309
   personal assignments, 309
   predictors of future, 305–306
   protective factors, 306
   psychosocial adjustment, 304
   reasons for, 302–303
   risk assessment, 304–307
   role-play, 310
   self- and peer-evaluation, 310
   during sentencing, 305
   situations where violence occurs, 303–304
   spousal assault history, 304
   stalking, 312–316
   standard procedures, 307, 308
   teamwork, 310
   treatment programmes
      anger management, 308–309
      overview, 308
      personal narratives, reconstructing, 311
   types of, 302
   working on violent crimes, 184–185

Violence Risk Appraisal Guide (VRAG-R), 307
VIPER procedure, 136
voice stress analysis, 150
voyeurism, 320
Vrij, Aldert, 156
vulnerability
   increasing likelihood of becoming victims of crimes, 194
   psychological effects of crimes on victims, 200

W

Walsh, Mikey, 332
Wechsler Adult Intelligence Scale (WAIS), 88
West, Fred (serial killer), 326
White, Dan, 239
wills, psychological autopsy used for contesting, 255
wise parenting, 342–343
witness, 27, 121
   cognitive interview, 131–132
   experience, 137
   interviews with, 122
   memories, 124
   preparation, 276–277
   pressure on, 124
   recalling past events, 125–127
women offenders
   gangs, 228
work experience, 364–365
worthlessness, in prison, 283
written confessions, 163

Z

zero-tolerance, 221

About the Author

David Canter became involved with Forensic Psychology in 1986 when he was asked by Scotland Yard to give guidance to a major police investigation into a series of murders and rapes. The value of this guidance opened doors to many other police investigations and brought him into the work of psychologists in many other areas of legal activity. This facilitated his many publications on criminal behavior and his creation of the new discipline of Investigative Psychology. His popular books on crime psychology have been translated into many other languages, his book *Criminal Shadows* winning a Golden Dagger Award for crime nonfiction in the UK, and an Athony Award in the US. As a Chartered Forensic Psychologist, he developed graduate Master's and Doctorate programs recognized by the British Psychological Society as a step toward chartered status. Hundreds of those who were his students now have senior jobs in universities, police forces and many other organizations around the world. His research and publications have led to him giving evidence in court cases and to government enquiries. He was a Professor of Psychology at the University of Surrey in the South of England, where he was also Head of the Department, and a Professor at The University of Liverpool, where, since his retirement, he now is an Emeritus Professor. He has written for major newspapers, notably The Times, and often contributes to radio and television news and documentary programs in the UK and overseas. He wrote and presented a six-part TV documentary series Mapping Murder that was broadcast around the world. He is an Honorary Fellow of the British Psychological Society, the American Psychological Association and the Royal Society of Medicine.

Dedication

For Rosie, Robin, Felix, Byron and Ivor.

Author's Acknowledgments

The work of many colleagues has been drawn on unashamedly in this book. It is not the *For Dummies* format to cite these directly. However, I would like to mention that I have found the work of my colleagues Kevin Browne and Donna Youngs, as well as more distant associates Curt and Anne Bartol to be of particular value. Ray Bull reviewed the draft thoroughly and I have incorporated his suggestions, although of course any errors are mine. The compendium put together by Jennifer

Brown and the late Elizabeth Campbell, is also a masterwork that I found very useful. Lionel Haward, sadly missed, encouraged me in the early days of my involvement with the law, so his influence is never very far from this book. My obsession with getting this book written has been endured by Sandra Canter with her love, support and good humor that is taxed every time I take up one of my writing commitments.

Publisher's Acknowledgments

Acquisitions Editor: Alicia Sparrow

Project Manager: Gus A. Miklos

Copy Editor: Becky Whitney

Technical Editor: Professor Ray Bull

Senior Managing Editor: Kristie Pyles

Production Editor: Bharaneedharan Murthy

Cover Image: © Bushko Oleksandr/Shutterstock